ENVIRON/MENTAL

Essays on the
Planet as a
Home

Editorial Advisor:
A. Starker Leopold
University of California,
Berkeley

HOUGHTON MIFFLIN COMPANY

BOSTON

New York

Atlanta

Geneva, Illinois

Dallas

Palo Alto

ENVIRON/MENTAL

Essays on the
Planet as a
Home

Edited by

PAUL SHEPARD

Visiting Professor of Environmental Perception
Pitzer College

and

DANIEL McKINLEY

Department of Biological Sciences
State University of New York
at Albany

Quote on page v from John Collier, On the Gleaming Way: Navajos, Eastern Pueblos, Zunis, Hopis, Apaches and Their Land, and Their Meaning to the World. *Denver: Alan Swallow, 1962.*

Quote on page vii from Ellis L. Yochelson, letter to the editor of Science, *166 (December 26, 1969), 1576.*

Quote on page ix from the Whole Earth Catalog, *1969.*

Quote on page xi from Charles E. Raven, Natural Religion and Christian Theology, I. *Cambridge, England: Cambridge University Press, 1953.*

Printed in the U.S.A.

Library of Congress Catalog Card Number: 76-146453

ISBN: 0-395-11246-X

The issue here is nothing less than that of lasting world peace, of the new epoch of peace within the heart, of society–nature morality, of reasserted ecological intent, and of creative living on the part of all men, which must dawn if man and men and earth are to go on existing together.

John Collier

EDITOR'S FOREWORD

It is generally conceded that America is ailing. The nation is mired in the unanticipated wastes of its industrial juggernaut. In some areas the air is scarcely fit to breathe. Waterways are so polluted that swimming is prohibited and fish are dying. Agricultural pesticides have so permeated the ecosystem that many birds no longer reproduce. Urban sprawl is engulfing once-rich farmland. The American public is becoming justifiably alarmed about these manifestations of ecological ill-health.

In 1969 Paul Shepard and Daniel McKinley edited a volume of essays entitled *The Subversive Science: Essays Toward an Ecology of Man*, which presented the thinking of leading ecologists, sociologists, and economists about the current state of the world around us. Its enthusiastic reception, both as a college text and as an environmental primer for interested laymen, testifies to a substantial demand for information about the problems of man's relationship to his habitat.

ENVIRON/MENTAL: Essays on the Planet as a Home resembles its editors' earlier book in the breadth and quality of its content. Its emphasis, however, is on man himself. The social and psychological consequences of overpopulation and community crowding are given particular attention in Part Two. Emotional and esthetic issues are stressed in many of the essays, particularly in Parts One and Two. *ENVIRON/MENTAL* aspires to widen the reader's understanding of the human dilemma which has arisen from our past faith in a mechanistic culture and from the belief that expansion and development are synonymous with progress. This book should contribute substantially to the emerging reappraisal of human values.

A. Starker Leopold

*. . . no organism can survive on its own waste prod-
ucts. Every movement toward changing the world
to a place for man to the exclusion of other living
organisms leads to this end. A world aimed at being
exclusively ours will be a world in which man cannot survive. . . .*

Ellis L. Yochelson

PREFACE ONE

When the epitaph of the last decade has finally become a paragraph in history
books, the sickness of society may receive less attention than the sickness of the
biosphere. By 1970 the long-standing but obscure crusade for conservation, once
dominated by "nature lovers" and modestly aimed at a mixture of amenities and
improved land use, had abruptly graduated to the first rank of national concerns.

Why this occurred so suddenly and dramatically after a century of general
neglect, punctuated by the struggles of a few eccentrics, remains for historians to
explain. But this much seems clear: concern for the environment would not again
be dismissed as mere preoccupation with dust storms or whooping cranes; perceptive leaders in many areas of public life acknowledged that environmental
quality is inseparable not only from the protection of wildlife but also from war,
poverty, and social justice; large numbers of people recognized the dimensions of
the problem for the first time, and the nation had begun a long, hard process of
self-education toward understanding the mix of population, waste, affluence,
ecology, and their own lives and aspirations.

The change in public sensitivity and political priorities was nearly revolutionary.
Almost overnight scores of new publications and organizations sprung up. Books
on environment filled the shelves. Business, government, and news media under-
took crash information programs. Literally thousands of new courses were introduced into university curricula. Even conservative politicians, pressured by their
constituencies, set their staffs to work. The rising tide crested on Earth Day—
April 22, 1970. The popularity of the environment as a political and social issue
was sure to ebb somewhat as its complexities became evident and as it was forced
to compete with other issues for public attention. Nonetheless, it had climbed
forever from the limbo of minor issues, where do-gooders formed uneasy alliances
with foresters and friends-of-the-land for attention and a modicum of power.

With the decade of the 70's a new phase began. For the public it meant that
the environment would get high social priority and constant attention by the
media. In the professions, industry, labor, and education, major programs and

objectives would be adjusted to allow for ecological effects. It would be necessary for private enterprise, government, and religion to make accommodations. A new factor was introduced into the accounting systems of all segments of the culture. This was sure to create conflict, social trauma, and angry confrontation. Nevertheless, the 1970's would witness a slow, grinding end to profiteering in the form of corporate exploitation and private affluence gotten at inordinate expense to the biosphere. It could easily be the bitterest pill Americans ever have to swallow.

I believe that the threat to the biosphere is real, and that life on the planet is endangered by our numbers and our technology, though I am not qualified to prophesy catastrophe or to mark Doomsday on the calendar. I think that the issue is not artificial, however deviously-motivated or poorly informed some "alarmists" may be. If, as some claim, environmental salvage contains a threat of repression, it will be repressive mainly against profligacy and heedlessness, and against the worthless goal of perpetual economic and population expansion.

In our earlier anthology, *The Subversive Science: Essays Toward an Ecology of Man* (Boston: Houghton Mifflin Company, 1969), we attempted to show that current problems are but a temporary configuration in an enduring and far broader set of ecological interrelationships. The articles in this new collection are intended to illustrate the scope of current environmental disorder and the variety of possible perspectives on it. In writing the headnotes to each article in this volume, I have tried to remember that no one can fully grasp the impact of this environmental revolution on our society, and that probably no one science or art holds the key to the future.

Paul Shepard

PREFACE TWO

In the beginning, cause-and-effect must have been a simple equation. There existed only the physical universe, whose parts collided with one another in a dead
pattern of endless reverberation. The effect of the advent of life, whatever its
cause, was to introduce continuity to the universe as a progression of similar but
variable events. The genetic heritage of species, in its unique combination of persistence and mutability, mitigated both determinism and the chaos of chance. In
countless ways that man is too remote from to understand fully, the existence of
even the most primitive forms of life meliorates the devastative power of the
elements. But human intelligence has long since outstripped natural phenomena
in devastative capacity. All animals create waste, but only man makes products
that nature cannot reclaim, and at such a rate that he can spoil the world before
it purifies itself. The ecological implications and consequences of human intelligence are the subject of this book.

While I do not agree with every opinion set forth in this book, I am convinced
the contributors are all looking at the man/nature interaction in a fruitful way.
They offer some hope that there is a way out of our overwhelming difficulties; a
way out which will not make of would-be saviors counteragents as burdensome
to Earth as the despoilers themselves. The Second Law of Thermodynamics applies to good guys as well as to bad: the technology we use to "clean up" the effects of technology also adds to pollution!

Human beings cannot stop creating and inventing, but this does not imply that
more sophisticated technology alone is the answer. Outdated values have forced
us into binds which are difficult to escape: we have come to believe that we must
have supersonic transports, hydrogen bombs, antiballistic missiles—and more and
more people. We predict the fulfillment of these expectations as if we had no
control over their realization; this confirms their inevitability. We are, of course,
capable of preventing them. It will not be easily done, and may not be done at
all unless we can learn that such empty striving is not necessarily part of our biological nature, and thus not immutable.

We need to abandon our assumptions that anything which can be done ought
to be done; that feelings have no value in the proceedings of the world; and that,

for example, a unilateral desire on the part of the United States for a sea-level canal in Central America ought not to go unchallenged by those it would affect but not benefit. And such a challenge need not be of the same order of political opportunism it opposes: it is an opportunity for debate, and for the use of science and technology, both on an international scale, for ecologically wise ends.

This book cannot do more than skim the surface. It tries to show that ecologically informed thought is part of our heritage. We are not limited to a choice between empty political activism and pathologically disinterested ivory-tower intellectualism. Both alternatives are part of what ails us. They are ecologically damaging if they dissociate our minds and bodies from experience of the world our activities create.

Daniel McKinley

> *The study of nature is indeed a perennial obligation for all mankind: we live with it and by it; and our general valuation of it, a valuation so deep-seated as to be largely unconscious, has a profound influence upon our whole life and thought.*
>
> *Charles E. Raven*

CONTENTS

PART ONE

ONE

GENESIS

AND

PERCEPTION

THE STRATEGY OF
ECOSYSTEM DEVELOPMENT

Eugene P. Odum

While it is unlikely that our lifetime will see a true "Age of Ecology," a powerful and growing awareness of environmental destruction surfaced abruptly in the middle of the last decade. It did so not because of the increased availability of scientific information but because environmental damage could be more easily seen, tasted, and smelled. Pollution encroached more shockingly on the landscape, that part of nature about which we have well-developed esthetic feelings. This is not to say that emotion impinges on the thought of ecologists any more than on that of other scientists; it is simply that ecology deals with situations about which people in general have overloaded feelings.

Americans and Europeans have long told themselves that they could have both unlimited technology and scenery, industrial growth and amenities. It is no accident that advocates of exploitation of the environment in the name of progress and civilization are quick to distinguish between utilitarian and esthetic "resources." Ecology repudiates this distinction by treating the whole environment as a complex single system. In doing so it draws public attention to the whole planet. This implies nothing less than the application of our nature esthetic to all of the environment and a radical alteration of the meanings ascribed to "practical" or "economic" values.

The body of data which ecology must generate and interpret before this can happen is painfully slow to appear. Ecologists are being asked to provide solutions to situations which have resulted from semi-catastrophic human population growth and overloads on the planet. What has yet to be understood is the basic question of how ecosystems work.

In view of the characteristic hesitation of scientists to formulate either questions or answers hastily, it is understandable that many ecologists are reluctant to speak out. They still live in peaceful academic isolation from contemporary social circumstances. At the same time we should be enormously grateful for those who are willing to be heard, who are boldly hazarding being wrong about details in order to provide society with the best insight ecology can muster in this time of crisis.

Nor is the possibility of minor errors of conclusion all that they risk. Even preliminary and general ecological constructions reveal that radical changes in

Eugene P. Odum, "The Strategy of Ecosystem Development," Science 164 (April 18, 1969), 262–270. Copyright © 1969 by the American Association for the Advancement of Science.

5

our land-use practices and in the social processes connected to them will be necessary. To say that old distinctions between the beautiful and the useful will be scrapped is to predict far more than a shift in terminology. Carried through, such a change will shake society to its roots. We are prepared to accept the minor promptings of an infant science, but when the full implications of their words become apparent, official culture may turn on ecologists and their naturalist supporters with the wrath it reserves for those who threaten its existence.

The principles of ecological succession bear importantly on the relationships between man and nature. The framework of successional theory needs to be examined as a basis for resolving man's present environmental crisis. Most ideas pertaining to the development of ecological systems are based on descriptive data obtained by observing changes in biotic communities over long periods, or on highly theoretical assumptions; very few of the generally accepted hypotheses have been tested experimentally. Some of the confusion, vagueness, and lack of experimental work in this area stems from the tendency of ecologists to regard "succession" as a single straightforward idea; in actual fact, it entails an interacting complex of processes, some of which counteract one another.

As viewed here, ecological succession involves the development of ecosystems; it has many parallels in the developmental biology of organisms, and also in the development of human society. The ecosystem, or ecological system, is considered to be a unit of biological organization made up of all of the organisms in a given area (that is, "community") interacting with the physical environment so that a flow of energy leads to characteristic trophic structure and material cycles within the system. It is the purpose of this article to summarize, in the form of a tabular model, components and stages of development at the ecosystem level as a means of emphasizing those aspects of ecological succession that can be accepted on the basis of present knowledge, those that require more study, and those that have special relevance to human ecology.

Definition of Succession

Ecological succession may be defined in terms of the following three parameters (*1*). (i) It is an orderly process of community development that is reasonably directional and, therefore, predictable. (ii) It results from modification of the physical environment by the community; that is, succession is community-controlled even though the physical environment determines the pattern, the rate of change, and often sets limits as to how far development can go. (iii) It culminates in a stabilized ecosystem in which maximum biomass (or high information content) and symbiotic function between organisms are maintained per unit of available energy flow. In a word, the "strategy" of succession as a short-term process is basically the same as the "strategy" of long-term evolutionary development of the biosphere—namely, increased control of, or homeostasis with, the physical environment in the sense of achieving maximum protection from its perturbations. As I illustrate below, the strategy of "maximum protection" (that is, trying to achieve maximum support of complex biomass structure) often conflicts with man's goal of "maximum production" (trying to obtain the highest possible yield). Recognition of the ecological basis for this conflict is, I believe, a first step in establishing rational land-use policies.

The earlier descriptive studies of succession on sand dunes, grasslands, forests, marine shores, or other sites, and more recent functional considerations, have led to the basic theory contained in the definition given above. H. T. Odum and Pinkerton (2), building on Lotka's (3) "law of maximum energy in biological systems," were the first to point out that succession involves a fundamental shift in energy flows as increasing energy is relegated to maintenance. Margalef (4) has recently documented this bioenergetic basis for succession and has extended the concept.

Changes that occur in major structural and functional characteristics of a developing ecosystem are listed in Table 1. Twenty-four attributes of ecological systems are grouped, for convenience of discussion, under six headings. Trends are emphasized by contrasting the situation in early and late development. The degree of absolute change, the rate of change, and the time required to reach a steady state may vary not only with different climatic and physiographic situations but also with different ecosystem attributes in the same physical environment. Where good data are available, rate-of-change curves are usually convex, with changes occurring most rapidly at the beginning, but bimodal or cyclic patterns may also occur.

Bioenergetics of Ecosystem Development

Attributes 1 through 5 in Table 1 represent the bioenergetics of the ecosystem. In the early stages of ecological succession, or in "young nature," so to speak, the rate of primary production or total (gross) photosynthesis (P) exceeds the rate of community respiration (R), so that the P/R ratio is greater than 1. In the special case of organic pollution, the P/R ratio is typically less than 1. In both cases, however, the theory is that P/R approaches 1 as succession occurs. In other words, energy fixed tends to be balanced by the energy cost of maintenance (that is, total community respiration) in the mature or "climax" ecosystem. The P/R ratio, therefore, should be an excellent functional index of the relative maturity of the system.

So long as P exceeds R, organic matter and biomass (B) will accumulate in the system (Table 1, item 6), with the result that ratio P/B will tend to decrease or, conversely, the B/P, B/R, or B/E ratios (where $E = P + R$) will increase (Table 1, items 2 and 3). Theoretically, then, the amount of standing-crop biomass supported by the available energy flow (E) increases to a maximum in the mature or

Table 1

*A tabular model of ecological succession: trends to be
expected in the development of ecosystems.*

Ecosystem attributes		Developmental stages	Mature stages
Community energetics	1. Gross production/community respiration (*P/R* ratio)	Greater or less than 1	Approaches 1
	2. Gross production/standing crop biomass (*P/B* ratio)	High	Low
	3. Biomass supported/unit energy flow (*B/E* ratio)	Low	High
	4. Net community production (yield)	High	Low
	5. Food chains	Linear, predominantly grazing	Weblike, predominantly detritus
Community structure	6. Total organic matter	Small	Large
	7. Inorganic nutrients	Extrabiotic	Intrabiotic
	8. Species diversity – variety component	Low	High
	9. Species diversity – equitability component	Low	High
	10. Biochemical diversity	Low	High
	11. Stratification and spatial heterogeneity (pattern diversity)	Poorly organized	Well-organized
Life history	12. Niche specialization	Broad	Narrow
	13. Size of organism	Small	Large
	14. Life cycles	Short, simple	Long, complex
Nutrient cycling	15. Mineral cycles	Open	Closed
	16. Nutrient exchange rate, between organisms and environment	Rapid	Slow
	17. Role of detritus in nutrient regeneration	Unimportant	Important
Selection pressure	18. Growth form	For rapid growth ("*r*-selection")	For feedback control ("*K*-selection")
	19. Production	Quantity	Quality
Overall homeostasis	20. Internal symbiosis	Undeveloped	Developed
	21. Nutrient conservation	Poor	Good
	22. Stability (resistance to external perturbations)	Poor	Good
	23. Entropy	High	Low
	24. Information	Low	High

climax stages (Table 1, item 3). As a consequence, the net community production, or yield, in an annual cycle is large in young nature and small or zero in mature nature (Table 1, item 4).

Comparison of Succession in a Laboratory Microcosm and a Forest

One can readily observe bioenergetic changes by initiating succession in experimental laboratory microecosystems. Aquatic microecosystems, derived from various types of outdoor systems, such as ponds, have been cultured by Beyers (5), and certain of these mixed cultures are easily replicated and maintain themselves in the climax state indefinitely on defined media in a flask with only light input (6). If samples from the climax system are inoculated into fresh media, succession occurs, the mature system developing in less than 100 days. In Fig. 1 the general pattern of a 100-day autotrophic succession in a microcosm based on data of Cooke (7) is compared with a hypothetical model of a 100-year forest succession as presented by Kira and Shidei (8).

Figure 1
Comparison of the energetics of succession in a forest and a laboratory microcosm. P_G, gross production; P_N, net production; R, total community respiration; B, total biomass.

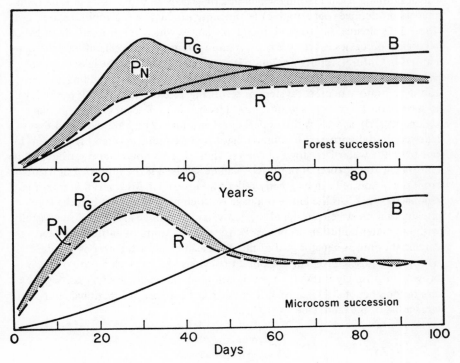

During the first 40 to 60 days in a typical microcosm experiment, daytime net production (P) exceeds nighttime respiration (R), so that biomass (B) accumulates in the system (9). After an early "bloom" at about 30 days, both rates decline, and they become approximately equal at 60 to 80 days. The B/P ratio, in terms of grams of carbon supported per gram of daily carbon production, increases from less than 20 to more than 100 as the steady state is reached. Not only are autotrophic and heterotrophic metabolism balanced in the climax, but a large organic structure is supported by small daily production and respiratory rates.

While direct projection from the small laboratory microecosystem to open nature may not be entirely valid, there is evidence that the same basic trends that are seen in the laboratory are characteristic of succession on land and in large bodies of water. Seasonal successions also often follow the same pattern, an early seasonal bloom characterized by rapid growth of a few dominant species being followed by the development later in the season of high B/P ratios, increased diversity, and a relatively steady, if temporary, state in terms of P and R (4). Open systems may not experience a decline, at maturity, in total or gross productivity, as the space-limited microcosms do, but the general pattern of bioenergetic change in the latter seems to mimic nature quite well.

These trends are not, as might at first seem to be the case, contrary to the classical limnological teaching which describes lakes as progressing in time from the less productive (oligotrophic) to the more productive (eutrophic) state. Table 1, as already emphasized, refers to changes which are brought about by biological processes *within* the ecosystem in question. Eutrophication, whether natural or cultural, results when nutrients are imported into the lake from *outside* the lake—that is, from the watershed. This is equivalent to adding nutrients to the laboratory microecosystem or fertilizing a field; the system is pushed back, in successional terms, to a younger or "bloom" state. Recent studies on lake sediments (10), as well as theoretical considerations (11), have indicated that lakes can and do progress to a more oligotrophic condition when the nutrient input from the watershed slows or ceases. Thus, there is hope that the troublesome cultural eutrophication of our waters can be reversed if the inflow of nutrients from the watershed can be greatly reduced. Most of all, however, this situation emphasizes that it is the entire drainage or catchment basin, not just the lake or stream, that must be considered the ecosystem unit if we are to deal successfully with our water pollution problems. Ecosystematic study of entire landscape catchment units is a major goal of the American plan for the proposed International Biological Program. Despite the obvious logic of such a proposal, it is proving surprisingly difficult to get tradition-bound scientists and granting agencies to look beyond their specialties toward the support of functional studies of large units of the landscape.

Food Chains and Food Webs

As the ecosystem develops, subtle changes in the network pattern of food chains may be expected. The manner in which organisms are linked together through food tends to be relatively simple and linear in the very early stages of succession, as a consequence of low diversity. Furthermore, heterotrophic utilization of net production occurs predominantly by way of grazing food chains—that is, plant-herbivore-carnivore sequences. In contrast, food chains become complex webs in mature stages, with the bulk of biological energy flow following detritus pathways (Table 1, item 5). In a mature forest, for example, less than 10 percent of annual net production is consumed (that is, grazed) in the living state (*12*); most is utilized as dead matter (detritus) through delayed and complex pathways involving as yet little understood animal-microorganism interactions. The time involved in an uninterrupted succession allows for increasingly intimate associations and reciprocal adaptations between plants and animals, which lead to the development of many mechanisms that reduce grazing—such as the development of indigestible supporting tissues (cellulose, lignin, and so on), feedback control between plants and herbivores (*13*), and increasing predatory pressure on herbivores (*14*). Such mechanisms enable the biological community to maintain the large and complex organic structure that mitigates perturbations of the physical environment. Severe stress or rapid changes brought about by outside forces can, of course, rob the system of these protective mechanisms and allow irruptive, cancerous growths of certain species to occur, as man too often finds to his sorrow. An example of a stress-induced pest irruption occurred at Brookhaven National Laboratory, where oaks became vulnerable to aphids when translocation of sugars and amino acids was impaired by continuing gamma irradiation (*15*).

Radionuclide tracers are providing a means of charting food chains in the intact outdoor ecosystem to a degree that will permit analysis within the concepts of network or matrix algebra. For example, we have recently been able to map, by use of a radiophosphorus tracer, the open, relatively linear food linkage between plants and insects in an early old-field successional stage (*16*).

Diversity and Succession

Perhaps the most controversial of the successional trends pertain to the complex and much discussed subject of diversity (*17*). It is important to distinguish between different kinds of diversity indices, since they may not follow parallel trends in the same gradient or developmental series. Four components of diversity are listed in Table 1, items 8 through 11.

The variety of species, expressed as a species-number ratio or a species-area ratio, tends to increase during the early stages of community development. A second component of species diversity is what has been called equitability, or evenness (*18*), in the apportionment of individuals among the species. For example, two systems each containing 10 species and 100 individuals have the same diversity in terms of species-number ratio but could have widely different equitabilities depending on the apportionment of the 100 individuals among the 10 species—for example, 91-1-1-1-1-1-1-1-1-1 at one extreme or 10 individuals per species at the other. The Shannon formula,

$$- \Sigma \frac{ni}{N} \log_2 \frac{ni}{N}$$

where *ni* is the number of individuals in each species and *N* is the total number of individuals, is widely used as a diversity index because it combines the variety and equitability components in one approximation. But, like all such lumping parameters, Shannon's formula may obscure the behavior of these two rather different aspects of diversity. For example, in our most recent field experiments, an acute stress from insecticide reduced the number of species of insects relative to the number of individuals but increased the evenness in the relative abundances of the surviving species (*19*). Thus, in this case the "variety" and "evenness" components would tend to cancel each other in Shannon's formula.

While an increase in the variety of species together with reduced dominance by any one species or small group of species (that is, increased evenness) can be accepted as a general probability during succession (*20*), there are other community changes that may work against these trends. An increase in the size of organisms, an increase in the length and complexity of life histories, and an increase in interspecific competition that may result in competitive exclusion of species (Table 1, items 12–14) are trends that may reduce the number of species that can live in a given area. In the bloom stage of succession organisms tend to be small and to have simple life histories and rapid rates of reproduction. Changes in size appear to be a consequence of, or an adaptation to, a shift in nutrients from inorganic to organic (Table 1, item 7). In a mineral nutrient-rich environment, small size is of selective advantage, especially to autotrophs, because of the greater surface-to-volume ratio. As the ecosystem develops, however, inorganic nutrients tend to become more and more tied up in the biomass (that is, to become intrabiotic), so that the selective advantage shifts to larger organisms (either larger individuals of the same species or larger species, or both) which have greater storage capacities and more complex life histories, thus are adapted to exploiting seasonal or periodic releases of nutrients or other resources. The question of whether the seemingly direct relationship between organism size and stability is the result of positive feedback or is merely fortuitous remains unanswered (*21*).

Thus, whether or not species diversity continues to increase during succession will depend on whether the increase in potential niches resulting from increased biomass, stratification (Table 1, item 9), and other consequences of biological organization exceeds the countereffects of increasing size and competition. No one has yet been able to catalogue all the species in any sizable area, much less follow total species diversity in a successional series. Data are so far available only for segments of the community (trees, birds, and so on). Margalef (*4*) postulates that diversity will tend to peak during the early or middle stages of succession and then decline in the climax. In a study of bird populations along a successional gradient we found a bimodal pattern (*22*); the number of species increased during the early stages of old-field succession, decline during the early forest stages, and then increased again in the mature forest.

Species variety, equitability, and stratification are only three aspects of diversity which change during succession. Perhaps an even more important trend is an increase in the diversity of organic compounds, not only of those within the biomass but also of those excreted and secreted into the media (air, soil, water) as by-products of the increasing community metabolism. An increase in such "biochemical diversity" (Table 1, item 10) is illustrated by the increase in the variety of plant pigments along a successional gradient in aquatic situations, as described by Margalef (*4, 23*). Biochemical diversity within populations, or within systems as a whole, has not yet been systematically studied to the degree the subject of species diversity has been. Consequently, few generalizations can be made, except that it seems safe to say that, as succession progresses, organic extrametabolites probably serve increasingly important functions as regulators which stabilize the growth and composition of the ecosystem. Such metabolites may, in fact, be extremely important in preventing populations from overshooting the equilibrial density, thus in reducing oscillations as the system develops stability.

The cause-and-effect relationship between diversity and stability is not clear and needs to be investigated from many angles. If it can be shown that biotic diversity does indeed enhance physical stability in the ecosystem, or is the result of it, then we would have an important guide for conservation practice. Preservation of hedgerows, woodlots, noneconomic species, noneutrophicated waters, and other biotic variety in man's landscape could then be justified on scientific as well as esthetic grounds, even though such preservation often must result in some reduction in the production of food or other immediate consumer needs. In other words, is variety only the spice of life, or is it a necessity for the long life of the total ecosystem comprising man and nature?

Nutrient Cycling

An important trend in successional development is the closing or "tightening" of the biogeochemical cycling of major nutrients, such as nitrogen, phosphorus, and calcium (Table 1, items 15–17). Mature systems, as compared to developing ones, have a greater capacity to entrap and hold nutrients for cycling within the system. For example, Bormann and Likens (*24*) have estimated that only 8 kilograms per hectare out of a total pool of exchangeable calcium of 365 kilograms per hectare is lost per year in stream outflow from a North Temperate watershed covered with a mature forest. Of this, about 3 kilograms per hectare is replaced by rainfall, leaving only 5 kilograms to be obtained from weathering of the underlying rocks in order for the system to maintain mineral balance. Reducing the volume of the vegetation, or otherwise setting the succession back to a younger state, results in increased water yield by way of stream outflow (25), but this greater outflow is accompanied by greater losses of nutrients, which may also produce downstream eutrophication. Unless there is a compensating increase in the rate of weathering, the exchangeable pool of nutrients suffers gradual depletion (not to mention possible effects on soil structure resulting from erosion). High fertility in "young systems" which have open nutrient cycles cannot be maintained without compensating inputs of new nutrients; examples of such practice are the continuous-flow culture of algae, or intensive agriculture where large amounts of fertilizer are imported into the system each year.

Because rates of leaching increase in a latitudinal gradient from the poles to the equator, the role of the biotic community in nutrient retention is especially important in the high-rainfall areas of the subtropical and tropical latitudes, including not only land areas but also estuaries. Theoretically, as one goes equatorward, a larger percentage of the available nutrient pool is tied up in the biomass and a correspondingly lower percentage is in the soil or sediment. This theory, however, needs testing, since data to show such a geographical trend are incomplete. It is perhaps significant that conventional North Temperate row-type agriculture, which represents a very youthful type of ecosystem, is successful in the humid tropics only if carried out in a system of "shifting agriculture" in which the crops alternate with periods of natural vegetative redevelopment. Tree culture and the semiaquatic culture of rice provide much better nutrient retention and consequently have a longer life expectancy on a given site in these warmer latitudes.

Selection Pressure: Quantity versus Quality

MacArthur and Wilson (26) have reviewed stages of colonization of islands which provide direct parallels with stages in ecological succession on continents. Species with high rates of reproduction and growth, they find, are more likely to survive in the early uncrowded stages of island colonization. In contrast, selection pressure favors species with lower growth potential but better capabilities for competitive survival under the equilibrium density of late stages. Using the terminology of growth equations, where r is the intrinsic rate of increase and K is the upper asymptote or equilibrium population size, we may say that "r selection" predominates in early colonization, with "K selection" prevailing as more and more species and individuals attempt to colonize (Table 1, item 18). The same sort of thing is even seen within the species in certain "cyclic" northern insects in which "active" genetic strains found at low densities are replaced at high densities by "sluggish" strains that are adapted to crowding (27).

Genetic changes involving the whole biota may be presumed to accompany the successional gradient, since, as described above, quantity production characterizes the young ecosystem while quality production and feedback control are the trademarks of the mature system (Table 1, item 19). Selection at the ecosystem level may be primarily interspecific, since species replacement is a characteristic of successional series or seres. However, in most well-studied seres there seem to be a few early successional species that are able to persist through to late stages. Whether genetic changes contribute to adaptation in such species has not been determined, so far as I know, but studies on population genetics of *Drosophila* suggest that changes in genetic composition could be important in population regulation (*28*). Certainly, the human population, if it survives beyond its present rapid growth stage, is destined to be more and more affected by such selection pressures as adaptation to crowding becomes essential.

Overall Homeostasis

This brief review of ecosystem development emphasizes the complex nature of processes that interact. While one may well question whether all the trends described are characteristic of all types of ecosystems, there can be little doubt that the net result of community actions is symbiosis, nutrient conservation, stability, a decrease in entropy, and an increase in information (Table 1, items 20–24). The overall strategy is, as I stated at the beginning of this article, directed toward achieving as large and diverse an organic structure as is possible within the limits set by the available energy input and the prevailing physical conditions of existence (soil, water, climate, and so on). As studies of biotic communities become more functional and sophisticated, one is impressed with the importance of mutualism, parasitism, predation, commensalism, and other forms of symbiosis. Partnership between unrelated species is often noteworthy (for example, that between coral coelenterates and algae, or between mycorrhizae and trees). In many cases, at least, biotic control of grazing, population density, and nutrient cycling provide the chief positive-feedback mechanisms that contribute to stability in the mature system by preventing overshoots and destructive oscillations. The intriguing question is, Do mature ecosystems age, as organisms do? In other words, after a long period of relative stability or "adulthood," do ecosystems again develop unbalanced metabolism and become more vulnerable to diseases and other perturbations?

Relevance of Ecosystem Development Theory to Human Ecology

Figure 1 depicts a basic conflict between the strategies of man and of nature. The "bloom-type" relationships, as exhibited by the 30-day microcosm or the 30-year forest, illustrate man's present idea of how nature should be directed.

For example, the goal of agriculture or intensive forestry, as now generally practiced, is to achieve high rates of production of readily harvestable products with little standing crop left to accumulate on the landscape—in other words, a high P/B efficiency. Nature's strategy, on the other hand, as seen in the outcome of the successional process, is directed toward the reverse efficiency—a high B/P ratio, as is depicted by the relationship at the right in Figure 1. Man has generally been preoccupied with obtaining as much "production" from the landscape as possible, by developing and maintaining early successional types of ecosystems, usually monocultures. But, of course, man does not live by food and fiber alone; he also needs a balanced CO_2-O_2 atmosphere, the climatic buffer provided by oceans and masses of vegetation, and clean (that is, unproductive) water for cultural and industrial uses. Many essential life-cycle resources, not to mention recreational and esthetic needs, are best provided man by the less "productive" landscapes. In other words, the landscape is not just a supply depot but is also the *oikos*—the home—in which we must live. Until recently mankind has more or less taken for granted the gas-exchange, water-purification, nutrient-cycling, and other protective functions of self-maintaining ecosystems, chiefly because neither his numbers nor his environmental manipulations have been great enough to affect regional and global balances. Now, of course, it is painfully evident that such balances are being affected, often detrimentally. The "one problem, one solution approach" is no longer adequate and must be replaced by some form of ecosystem analysis that considers man as a part of, not apart from, the environment.

The most pleasant and certainly the safest landscape to live in is one containing a variety of crops, forests, lakes, streams, roadsides, marshes, seashores, and "waste places"—in other words, a mixture of communities of different ecological ages. As individuals we more or less instinctively surround our houses with protective, nonedible cover (trees, shrubs, grass) at the same time that we strive to coax extra bushels from our cornfield. We all consider the cornfield a "good thing," of course, but most of us would not want to live there, and it would certainly be suicidal to cover the whole land area of the biosphere with cornfields, since the boom and bust oscillation in such a situation would be severe.

The basic problem facing organized society today boils down to determining in some objective manner when we are getting "too much of a good thing." This is a completely new challenge to mankind because, up until now, he has had to be concerned largely with too little rather than too much. Thus, concrete is a "good thing," but not if half the world is covered with it. Insecticides are "good things," but not when used, as they now are, in an indiscriminate and wholesale manner. Likewise, water impoundments have proved to be very useful man-made additions to the landscape, but obviously we don't want the whole country inundated! Vast man-made lakes solve some problems, at least temporarily, but yield comparatively little food or fiber, and, because of high evaporative losses, they may not even be the best device for storing water; it might better be stored in the watershed, or underground in aquifers. Also, the cost of building large dams is a drain on already overtaxed revenues. Although as individuals we readily recognize that we can have too many dams or other large-scale environmental changes, governments are so fragmented and lacking in systems-analysis capabilities that there is no effective mechanism whereby negative feedback signals can

Table 2
*Contrasting characteristics of young and mature-type
ecosystems*

Young	Mature
Production	Protection
Growth	Stability
Quantity	Quality

be received and acted on before there has been a serious overshoot. Thus, today there are governmental agencies, spurred on by popular and political enthusiasm for dams, that are putting on the drawing boards plans for damming every river and stream in North America!

Society needs, and must find as quickly as possible, a way to deal with the landscape as a whole, so that manipulative skills (that is, technology) will not run too far ahead of our understanding of the impact of change. Recently a national ecological center outside of government and a coalition of governmental agencies have been proposed as two possible steps in the establishment of a political control mechanism for dealing with major environmental questions. The soil conservation movement in America is an excellent example of a program dedicated to the consideration of the whole farm or the whole watershed as an ecological unit. Soil conservation is well understood and supported by the public. However, soil conservation organizations have remained too exclusively farm-oriented, and have not yet risen to the challenge of the urban-rural landscape, where lie today's most serious problems. We do, then, have potential mechanisms in American society that could speak for the ecosystem as a whole, but none of them are really operational (*29*).

The general relevance of ecosystem development theory to landscape planning can, perhaps, be emphasized by the "mini-model" of Table 2, which contrasts the characteristics of young and mature-type ecosystems in more general terms than those provided by Table 1. It is mathematically impossible to obtain a maximum for more than one thing at a time, so one cannot have both extremes at the same time and place. Since all six characteristics listed in Table 2 are desirable in the aggregate, two possible solutions to the dilemma immediately suggest themselves. We can compromise so as to provide moderate quality and moderate yield on all the landscape, or we can deliberately plan to compartmentalize the landscape so as to simultaneously maintain highly productive and predominantly protective types as separate units subject to different management strategies (strategies ranging, for example, from intensive cropping on the one hand to wilderness management on the other). If ecosystem development theory is valid and applicable to planning, then the so-called multiple-use strategy, about which we hear so much, will work only through one or both of these approaches, because, in most cases, the projected multiple uses conflict with one another. It is appropriate, then, to examine some examples of the compromise and the compartmental strategies.

Pulse Stability

A more or less regular but acute physical perturbation imposed from without can maintain an ecosystem at some intermediate point in the developmental sequence, resulting in, so to speak, a compromise between youth and maturity. What I would term "fluctuating water level ecosystems" are good examples. Estuaries, and intertidal zones in general, are maintained in an early, relatively fertile stage by the tides, which provide the energy for rapid nutrient cycling. Likewise, fresh-water marshes, such as the Florida Everglades, are held at an early successional stage by the seasonal fluctuations in water levels. The dry-season drawdown speeds up aerobic decomposition of accumulated organic matter, releasing nutrients that, on reflooding, support a wet-season bloom in productivity. The life histories of many organisms are intimately coupled to this periodicity. The wood stork, for example, breeds when the water levels are falling and the small fish on which it feeds become concentrated and easy to catch in the drying pools. If the water level remains high during the usual dry season or fails to rise in the wet season, the stork will not nest (*30*). Stabilizing water levels in the Everglades by means of dikes, locks, and impoundments, as is now advocated by some, would, in my opinion, destroy rather than preserve the Everglades as we now know them just as surely as complete drainage would. Without periodic drawdowns and fires, the shallow basins would fill up with organic matter and succession would proceed from the present pond-and-prairie condition toward a scrub or swamp forest.

It is strange that man does not readily recognize the importance of recurrent changes in water level in a natural situation such as the Everglades when similar pulses are the basis for some of his most enduring food culture systems (*31*). Alternate filling and draining of ponds has been a standard procedure in fish culture for centuries in Europe and the Orient. The flooding, draining, and soil-aeration procedure in rice culture is another example. The rice paddy is thus the cultivated analogue of the natural marsh or the intertidal ecosystem.

Fire is another physical factor whose periodicity has been of vital importance to man and nature over the centuries. Whole biotas, such as those of the African grasslands and the California chaparral, have become adapted to periodic fires producing what ecologists often call "fire climaxes" (*32*). Man uses fire deliberately to maintain such climaxes or to set back succession to some desired point. In the southeastern coastal plain, for example, light fires of moderate frequency can maintain a pine forest against the encroachment of older successional stages which, at the present time at least, are considered economically less desirable. The fire-controlled forest yields less wood than a tree farm does (that is, young trees, all of about the same age, planted in rows and harvested on a short rotation schedule), but it provides a greater protective cover for the landscape, wood of higher quality, and a home for game birds (quail, wild turkey, and so on) which could not survive in a tree farm. The fire climax, then, is an example of a compromise between production simplicity and protection diversity.

It should be emphasized that pulse stability works only if there is a complete community (including not only plants but animals and microorganisms) adapted to the particular intensity and frequency of the perturbation. Adaptation—operation of the selection process—requires times measurable on the evolutionary scale. Most physical stresses introduced by man are too sudden, too violent, or too arrhythmic for adaptation to occur at the ecosystem level, so severe oscillation rather than stability results. In many cases, at least, modification of naturally adapted ecosystems for cultural purposes would seem preferable to complete redesign.

Prospects for a Detritus Agriculture

As indicated above, heterotrophic utilization of primary production in mature ecosystems involves largely a delayed consumption of detritus. There is no reason why man cannot make greater use of detritus and thus obtain food or other products from the more protective type of ecosystem. Again, this would represent a compromise, since the short-term yield could not be as great as the yield obtained by direct exploitation of the grazing food chain. A detritus agriculture, however, would have some compensating advantages. Present agricultural strategy is based on selection for rapid growth and edibility in food plants, which, of course, make them vulnerable to attack by insects and disease. Consequently, the more we select for succulence and growth, the more effort we must invest in the chemical control of pests; this effort, in turn, increases the likelihood of our poisoning useful organisms, not to mention ourselves. Why not also practice the reverse strategy—that is, select plants which are essentially unpalatable, or which produce their own systemic insecticides while they are growing, and then convert the net production into edible products by microbial and chemical enrichment in food factories? We could then devote our biochemical genius to the enrichment process instead of fouling up our living space with chemical poisons! The production of silage by fermentation of low-grade fodder is an example of such a procedure already in widespread use. The cultivation of detritus-eating fishes in the Orient is another example.

By tapping the detritus food chain man can also obtain an appreciable harvest from many natural systems without greatly modifying them or destroying their protective and esthetic value. Oyster culture in estuaries is a good example. In

Japan, raft and long-line culture of oysters has proved to be a very practical way to harvest the natural microbial products of estuaries and shallow bays. Furukawa (*33*) reports that the yield of cultured oysters in the Hiroshima Prefecture has increased tenfold since 1950, and that the yield of oysters (some 240,000 tons of meat) from this one district alone in 1965 was ten times the yield of natural oysters from the entire country. Such oyster culture is feasible along the entire Atlantic and Gulf coasts of the United States. A large investment in the culture of oysters and other seafoods would also provide the best possible deterrent against pollution, since the first threat of damage to the pollution-sensitive oyster industry would be immediately translated into political action!

The Compartment Model

Successful though they often are, compromise systems are not suitable nor desirable for the whole landscape. More emphasis needs to be placed on compartmentalization, so that growth-type, steady-state, and intermediate-type ecosystems can be linked with urban and industrial areas for mutual benefit. Knowing the transfer coefficients that define the flow of energy and the movement of materials and organisms (including man) between compartments, it should be possible to determine, through analog-computer manipulation, rational limits for the size and capacity of each compartment. We might start, for example, with a simplified model, shown in Figure 2, consisting of four compartments of equal area, partitioned according to the basic biotic-function criterion—that is, according to whether the area is (i) productive, (ii) protective, (iii) a compromise between (i) and (ii) or (iv), urban-industrial. By continually refining the transfer coefficients on the basis of real world situations, and by increasing and decreasing the size and capacity of each compartment through computer simulation, it would be possible to determine objectively the limits that must eventually be imposed on each compartment in order to maintain regional and global balances in the exchange of vital energy and of materials. A systems-analysis procedure provides at least one approach to the solution of the basic dilemma posed by the question "How do we determine when we are getting too much of a good thing?" Also it provides a means of evaluating the energy drains imposed on ecosystems by pollution, radiation, harvest, and other stresses (*34*).

Implementing any kind of compartmentalization plan, of course, would require procedures for zoning the landscape and restricting the use of some land and water areas. While the principle of zoning in cities is universally accepted, the procedures now followed do not work very well because zoning restrictions are too easily overturned by short-term economic and population pressures. Zoning the landscape would require a whole new order of thinking. Greater use of legal measures providing for tax relief, restrictions on use, scenic easements, and public ownership will be required if appreciable land and water areas are to be held in the "protective" categories. Several states (for example, New Jersey and California), where pollution and population pressure are beginning to hurt, have made a start in this direction by enacting "open space" legislation designed to get as much unoccupied land as possible into a "protective" status so that future uses can be planned on a rational and scientific basis. The United States as a whole is fortunate in that large areas of the country are in national forests, parks, wildlife refuges, and so on. The fact that such areas, as well as the bordering oceans, are not quickly exploitable gives us time for the accelerated ecological study and programming needed to determine what proportions of different types of landscape provide a safe balance between man and nature. The open oceans, for example, should forever be allowed to remain protective rather than productive territory, if Alfred Redfield's *(35)* assumptions are correct. Redfield views the oceans, the major part of the hydrosphere, as the biosphere's governor, which slows down and controls the rate of decomposition and nutrient regeneration, thereby creating and maintaining the highly aerobic terrestrial environment to which the higher forms of life, such as man, are adapted. Eutrophication of the ocean in a last-ditch effort to feed the populations of the land could well have an adverse effect on the oxygen reservoir in the atmosphere.

Until we can determine more precisely how far we may safely go in expanding intensive agriculture and urban sprawl at the expense of the protective landscape, it will be good insurance to hold inviolate as much of the latter as possible. Thus, the preservation of natural areas is not a peripheral luxury for society but a capital investment from which we expect to draw interest. Also, it may well be that restrictions in the use of land and water are our only practical means of avoiding overpopulation or too great an exploitation of resources, or both. Interestingly enough, restriction of land use is the analogue of a natural behavioral control mechanism known as "territoriality" by which many species of animals avoid crowding and social stress *(36)*.

Since the legal and economic problems pertaining to zoning and compartmentalization are likely to be thorny, I urge law schools to establish departments, or institutes, of "landscape law" and to start training "landscape lawyers" who will be capable not only of clarifying existing procedures but also of drawing up new enabling legislation for consideration by state and national governing bodies. At present, society is concerned—and rightly so—with human rights, but environmental rights are equally vital. The "one man one vote" idea is important, but so also is a "one man one hectare" proposition.

Education, as always, must play a role in increasing man's awareness of his dependence on the natural environment. Perhaps we need to start teaching the principles of ecosystem in the third grade. A grammar school primer on man and his environment could logically consist of four chapters, one for each of the four essential kinds of environment, shown diagrammatically in Figure 2.

Of the many books and articles that are being written these days about man's environmental crisis, I would like to cite two that go beyond "crying out in alarm" to suggestions for bringing about a reorientation of the goals of society. Garrett Hardin, in a recent article in *Science (37)*, points out that, since the

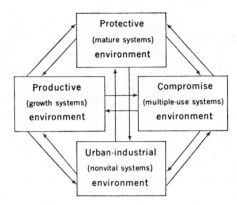

Figure 2
*Compartment model of the basic kinds of environ-
ment required by man, partitioned according to
ecosystem development and life-cycle resource
criteria.*

optimum population density is less than the maximum, there is no strictly technical solution to the problem of pollution caused by overpopulation; a solution,
he suggests, can only be achieved through moral and legal means of "mutual coercion, mutually agreed upon by the majority of people." Earl F. Murphy, in a
book entitled *Governing Nature* (*38*), emphasizes that the regulatory approach
alone is not enough to protect life-cycle resources, such as air and water, that
cannot be allowed to deteriorate. He discusses permit systems, effluent charges,
receptor levies, assessment, and cost-internalizing procedures as economic incen-
tives for achieving Hardin's "mutually agreed upon coercion."

It goes without saying that the tabular model for ecosystem development
which I have presented here has many parallels in the development of human
society itself. In the pioneer society, as in the pioneer ecosystem, high birth rates,
rapid growth, high economic profits, and exploitation of accessible and unused
resources are advantageous, but, as the saturation level is approached, these drives
must be shifted to considerations of symbiosis (that is, "civil rights," "law and
order," "education," and "culture"), birth control, and the recycling of resources.
A balance between youth and maturity in the socio-environmental system is,
therefore, the really basic goal that must be achieved if man as a species is to
successfully pass through the present rapid-growth stage, to which he is clearly
well adapted, to the ultimate equilibrium-density stage, of which he as yet shows
little understanding and to which he now shows little tendency to adapt.

REFERENCES

1. Odum, E.P. *Ecology*. New York: Holt, Rinehart & Winston, 1963, chapter 6.
2. Odum, H.T., and R.C. Pinkerton. *Amer. Scientist*, 43:331 (1955).
3. Lotka, A.J. *Elements of Physical Biology*. Baltimore: Williams and Wilkins, 1925.
4. Margalef, R. *Advan. Frontiers Plant Sci*, 2:137 (1963); *Amer. Naturalist*, 97:357 (1963).
5. Beyers, R.J. *Ecol. Monographs*, 33:281 (1963).
6. The systems so far used to test ecological principles have been derived from sewage and farm ponds and are cultured in half-strength No. 36 Taub and Dollar medium [*Limnol. Oceanog*. 9: 61 (1964)]. They are closed to organic input or output but are open to the atmosphere through the cotton plug in the neck of the flask. Typically, liter-sized microecosystems contain two or three species of nonflagellated algae and one to three species each of flagellated protozoans, ciliated protozoans, rotifers, nematodes, and ostracods; a system derived from a sewage pond contained at least three species of fungi and 13 bacterial isolates [R. Gordon, thesis, University of Georgia (1967)]. These cultures are thus a kind of minimum ecosystem containing those small species originally found in the ancestral pond that are able to function together as a self-contained unit under the restricted conditions of the laboratory flask and the controlled environment of a growth chamber [temperature, 65° to 75°F (18° to 24°C); photoperiod, 12 hours; illumination, 100 to 1000 footcandles].
7. Cooke, G.D. *BioScience*, 17:717 (1967).
8. Kira, T., and T. Shidei. *Japan. J. Ecol.*, 17:70 (1967).
9. The metabolism of the microcosms was monitored by measuring diurnal pH changes, and the biomass (in terms of total organic matter and total carbon) was determined by periodic harvesting of replicate systems.
10. Mackereth, F.J.H., *Proc. Roy. Soc. London Ser. B.*, 161:295 (1965); Cowgill, U.M., and G.E. Hutchinson, *Proc. Intern. Limnol. Ass.*, 15:644 (1964); Harrison. A.D., *Trans. Roy. Soc. S. Africa* 36:213 (1962).
11. Margalef, R. *Proc. Intern. Limnol. Ass.*, 15:169 (1964).
12. Bray, J.R., *Oikos*, 12:70 (1961).
13. Pimentel, D. *Amer. Naturalist*, 95:65 (1961).
14. Paine, R.T. *Amer. Naturalist*, 100:65 (1966).
15. Woodwell, G.M. *Brookhaven Nat. Lab. Pub.*, 924 (T-381) (1965), 1-15.
16. Wiegert, R.G., E.P. Odum, and J.H. Schnell. *Ecology*, 48:75 (1967).
17. For selected general discussions of patterns of species diversity, see Simpson, E.H. *Nature*, 163:688 (1949); Williams, C.B. *J. Animal Ecol.*, 22:14 (1953); Hutchinson, G.E. *Amer. Naturalist*, 93:145 (1959); Margalef, R. *Gen. Systems*, 3:36 (1958); MacArthur, R., and J. MacArthur, *Ecology*, 42:594 (1961); Hairston, N.G. *Ecology*, 40: 404 (1959); Patten, B.C. *J. Marine Res. (Sears Found. Marine Res.)*, 20:57 (1960); Leigh, E.G. *Proc. Nat. Acad. Sci. U.S.*, 55:777 (1965); Pianka, E.R. *Amer. Naturalist*, 100:33 (1966); Pielou, E.C. *J. Theoret. Biol.*, 10:370 (1966).
18. Lloyd, M., and R.J. Ghelardi. *J. Animal Ecol.*, 33:217 (1964); Pielou, E.C. *J. Theoret. Biol.*, 13:131 (1966).
19. Barrett, G.W. *Ecology*, 49:1019 (1969).
20. In our studies of natural succession following grain culture, both the species-to-numbers and the equitability indices increased for all trophic levels but especially for predators and parasites. Only 44 percent of the species in the natural ecosystem were phytophagous, as compared to 77 percent in the grain field.
21. Bonner, J.T. *Size and Cycle*. Princeton: Princeton University Press, 1963; Frank, P. *Ecology*, 49:355 (1968).
22. Johnston, D.W., and E.P. Odum. *Ecology*, 37:50 (1956).
23. Margalef, R. *Oceanog. Marine Biol. Annu. Rev.*, 5:257 (1967).

24. Bormann, F.H., and G.E. Likens. *Science*, 155:424 (1967).
25. Increased water yield following reduction of vegetative cover has been frequently demonstrated in experimental watersheds throughout the world [see A.R. Hibbert, in *International Symposium on Forest Hydrology* (New York: Pergamon Press, 1967), pp. 527–543]. Data on the long-term hydrologic budget (rainfall input relative to stream outflow) are available at many of these sites, but mineral budgets have yet to be systematically studied. Again, this is a prime objective in the "ecosystem analysis" phase of the International Biological Program.
26. MacArthur, R.H., and E.O. Wilson. *Theory of Island Biogeography*. Princeton: Princeton University Press, 1967.
27. Examples are the tent caterpillar [see Wellington, W.G. *Can. J. Zool.*, 35:293 (1957)] and the larch budworm [see Baltensweiler, W. *Can. Entomologist*, 96:792 (1964)].
28. Ayala, F.J. *Science*, 162:1453 (1968).
29. Ira Rubinoff, in discussing the proposed sea-level canal joining the Atlantic and Pacific oceans [*Science*, 161:857 (1968)], calls for a "control commission for environmental manipulation" with "broad powers of approving, disapproving, or modifying all major alterations of the marine or terrestrial environments. . . ."
30. See Kahl, M.P. *Ecol. Monographs*, 34:97 (1964).
31. The late Aldo Leopold remarked long ago [*Symposium on Hydrobiology*. Madison: University of Wisconsin Press, 1941, 17] that man does not perceive organic behavior in systems unless he has built them himself. Let us hope it will not be necessary to rebuild the entire biosphere before we recognize the worth of natural systems!
32. See Cooper, C.F. *Sci. Amer.*, 204:150 (April 1961).
33. See "Proceedings Oyster Culture Workshop, Marine Fisheries Division, Georgia Game and Fish Commission, Brunswick" (1968), 49–61.
34. See Odum, H.T., in *Symposium on Primary Productivity and Mineral Cycling in Natural Ecosystems*, ed. H.E. Young. Orono, Maine: University of Maine Press, 1967), p. 81; _____, in *Pollution and Marine Ecology*. New York: Wiley, 1967), p. 99; Watt, K.E.F. *Ecology and Resource Management*. New York: McGraw-Hill, 1968).
35. Redfield, A.C. *Amer. Scientist*, 46:205 (1958).
36. Ardrey, R. *The Territorial Imperative*. New York: Atheneum, 1967.
37. Hardin, G. *Science*, 162:1243 (1968).
38. Murphy, E.F. *Governing Nature*. Chicago: Quadrangle Books, 1967.

EARLY MAN AND
HIS ENVIRONMENT

John Napier

During the past 25 years thousands of fragments of protohuman fossil remains
have been dug from cave floors and hunting camps in Africa, Asia, and Europe.
Though not without its heralds, this extraordinary trove of prehistory has accumulated quietly in the shadow of worldwide crisis and turmoil. It is ironic that
a species threatening to destroy itself should simultaneously find and recognize
clues to its own origins.

The new information is not only anatomical; it is environmental as well. To
paraphrase Winston Churchill, the environment made us human, and humans
thereafter made the environment. But we wonder whether the environments we
created have also enhanced our humanity. The levels of archaeological diagnosis,
says John Napier, run from single bones and functional structures to behavioral
patterns, and finally to ecological status. Perhaps paleontologists are better prepared than anyone else to see the connections between our structure and our environment, to recognize the archaic core of our behavior, and to perceive that
the relationship between our bone-deep selves and our environment runs both
ways, each requiring the other as a complementary part of a whole. Do our bones
hold the ultimate architectural secrets?

The large cerebrum is the glory of mankind. A late development in human
evolution, it arrogantly presumes to direct functions of the body over which it
has no jurisdiction, meddle in the body's essential homeostasis and the wisdom
of instinct, plague the adrenals, regulate the bowels, and mold the emotions. And
it makes environments: not only incomparable cathedrals, but garbage landscapes
as well. Our works threaten to isolate us from the past too quickly and too fully,
to alienate our inner architecture from the wisdom of the fossil bones.

It was Bernard Shaw who said that man is only an amoeba with acquirements.
This is just one of the many attempts to define *Homo sapiens* which range from
broad generalizations to the micro-detail of "Gray's Anatomy." Definitions have
come from philosophers, behaviorists, sociologists, psychologists, physiologists
and anatomists. From this wealth of fact and hypothesis, palaeo-anthropologists
must select their criteria for the study of early man.

J. R. Napier, "Early Man and His Environment," Discovery, *24 (March, 1963), 12–18.* Reprinted by courtesy of Science Journal *(incorporating* Discovery*), London.*

The basic problem of palaeo-anthropology is one of identification. Does the fossil material in question belong to an extinct anthropoid ape or to an hominid— a member of the family of man? If an hominid does it belong to the genus *Homo* (or man), or to some extinct genus on a collateral branch, a first cousin so to speak, whose descendants have failed to survive to modern times?

Obviously, not all the criteria by which man can be identified are applicable to fossil bones. Fortunately, however, bones are not the only things that can be discovered by digging. Information on climate, vegetation and even behavior can be obtained from excavations. It is in the emphasis placed on these particular fields of study today that the methods of palaeo-anthropology are rapidly changing.

However, the diagnosis of fossil man depends mainly on the identification and analysis of his remains. These may constitute an entire skeleton, or just a skull or even one bone—often in the form of a number of incomplete and broken fragments. In these circumstances one of the first tasks is to settle down to the time-consuming, though satisfying, occupation of solving a bony jigsaw puzzle that is unlike a real jigsaw in several particulars. Firstly it is three-dimensional, secondly it is incomplete and thirdly there is no guarantee that the pieces don't belong to several different puzzles.

The ultimate aim of this kind of research is to determine the structural, functional and behavioral characters of an early population, to establish firstly its position in a natural Order (*Taxonomic status*) and secondly its relationship to its environment (*Ecological status*). We are concerned here with ecological status.

To investigate ecological status we need to analyze fossil remains at a number of different *levels*—we must assess their anatomical importance, their functions and eventually try and reconstruct the behavior of the fossil concerned. This requires the help of numerous other sciences, and Figure 1 shows the sciences which can be drawn upon at various stages of the investigation.

Single characters must inevitably be the starting point (R.I. level). Scientists are well aware of the limited value, in general, of assessments based on individual characters and of the misjudgments which they may engender. This danger lies in a failure to appreciate the extent of variability within populations. Variability, which is apparent at functional and behavioral as well as structural levels, may arise during the lifetime of the individual (due to some occupational feature such as the callosities on the hands of heavy manual workers) or may be determined by a gene change or mutation. Genetic variability is extremely important in evolution, for it is through variability that natural selection operates; without it there would be nothing to select.

The true significance of individual characters is not always apparent when they are studied in isolation. In fact many such characters have in the past been canonized by scientists who regarded them as "non-adaptive"—independent of environmental influences and therefore of crucial significance as taxonomic markers. It is doubtful whether any character can be truly "non-adaptive"; the more likely explanation seems to be that "non-adaptive" is a synonym of "not understood."

ecological status

ethology and ecology
paleo-ecology
stratigraphy
geochronology
zoogeography
ethnology

R4 behavioural pattern

ethology and ecology
paleo-ecology

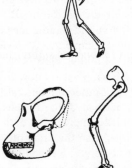

R3 total functional pattern

primatology
human anatomy
comparative anatomy

R2 functional complexes

primatology
human anatomy
comparative anatomy

R1 single structures

Figure 1
*Different levels at which fossil remains can be
analyzed. The final aim of all fossil study is to
establish its total relationship to the environment.*

The precise patterns of the meeting place of the sutures of the skull, the pterion, was once regarded as non-adaptive but it is now clear that the pattern of this region is a reflection of the different growth rates of skull bones—rates which themselves are highly adaptive. The 'simian shelf,' the notorious bridge of bone uniting the two sides of the lower jaw of anthropoid apes, is another structure that has little taxonomic value in isolation—it merely reflects the mechanical stresses exerted on the jaw by a particular form and arrangement of teeth. Again the massive bony prominences of the face and skull of anthropoid apes are the result of dental mechanics.

Some features, such as the buttressing elements of the skull, are not always comprehensible at an R1 level, but become meaningful at R2 level when collected into 'functional' complexes. The principal complexes that are recognized in the diagnosis and identification of *Homo* are (1) the brain; (2) the masticatory apparatus; (3) the upright posture and bipedalism; and (4) the manipulative functions of the hand. Functional complexes like these are ideal objects of study because it is upon them that natural selection operates. In the evolution of early man it was the quicker thinker, the more enduring walker, the better chewer and the more effective maker of tools and weapons that survived to breed.

R3 reconstruction is a major advance on the R2 level. The total structural and functional pattern of a fossil hominid is more meaningful than the sum of the separate units of the functional complexes (R2 level). For example, we know that the South African group of middle Pleistocene hominids, the australopithecines, were upright bipedal forms; we also know that their teeth and jaws, though massive, were similar to those of modern man. Taking these functional complexes together we are already half persuaded that the australopithecines were essentially manlike. If we now add the third complex, that of the brain, which we know to have been extremely small—no larger than the brain of a gorilla—a totally new picture of these South African forms emerges; we see them as they were—in many ways more like apes than men. We have only an imperfect idea of the manipulative ability of the hands of australopithecines but study of the closely related East African hominids from Olduvai Gorge indicates that their hands were unlikely to have added a particularly *Homo*-like quality to this prehuman phase of hominid evolution found in South Africa.

Thus far the anthropologist has relied largely on his knowledge of human and comparative anatomy to attain an R3 level of reconstruction. In order to proceed to the behavioral pattern (R4 level) information is required from a number of other branches of biology. These include *ethology* or the study of animal behavior in natural habitats; *ecology*, the study of plants and animals in relation to each other and their physical environment, and *palaeo-ecology* or ecology of the past, embracing past-geography, past-climatology, past-botany and past-zoology. The problem at the behavioral level is to relate the total function of an organism to its environment; this is what is meant by behavior. Environment acts on the genetic pattern of a population by eliminating those forms—structural and behavioral—which are inappropriate. The selection pressures thus set up ensure the

survival of an adequate type for existing conditions. Efficient morphology alone
is not enough for survival—there must be efficient behavior as well. As Nissen
has stated: "Behavioral incompetence leads to extinction as does morphological
disproportion or deficiency in a vital organ."

Obviously the behavior of an extinct population can only be inferred, for behavior, as such, does not fossilize. However, some aspects of behavior, such as
locomotion and food-getting, can be inferred from fossil forms. In both cases,
however, confirmatory evidence is required that the environment of the time
was appropriate for these particular kinds of behavior. For example, *Proconsul
africanus*, a possible candidate for remote human ancestry, was discovered in
Miocene deposits representing an ancient lake bed. Much of the associated fossil
fauna indicated a savannah type of environment—hardly appropriate for the tree-
living characteristics of the ape revealed by a comparative study of its limb-bones.
However, fossil flora from the same beds included fruits and seeds and sections
of thick lianas indicative of a tropical rain forest environment. It was deduced
that in this particular area of Kenya the vegetation was largely grass savannah
interspersed with belts of tropical rain forest fringing water-courses draining into
the lake. Many highly arboreal monkeys live in similar terrain to this day, including *Colobus*, a group of monkeys with a locomotor pattern that serves as a rough
model for the sort of locomotion deduced from the skeletal remains of *Proconsul*.

Another example comes from South Africa where C. K. Brain has investigated
the climate associated with the occupation of the Sterkfontein Valley by the
australopithecines in the lower-Middle and Middle Pleistocene periods. Brain
studied the ratio of the grains of chert and quartz found in the solid deposits of
breccia in the dolomitic caves that contained australopithecine remains. The
chert grains are of dolomitic origin but the quartz grains are intrusive, and must
have been blown there. An increase in the proportion of quartz grains, therefore,
indicates a period of dry windy conditions, while a low proportion suggests wetter
conditions. From this and other methods climatic curves for the period covered
by these cave deposits can be constructed.

During the dry phase at the beginning of the middle Pleistocene the genus
Australopithecus occupied the Sterkfontein Valley; the disappearance of this
form from the sites coincided with the arrival of a more advanced hominid form
that may have emigrated south from East Africa where the climate was probably
even more arid. During the succeeding wetter period, a third form, *Paranthropus*,
appeared on the scene. There is some evidence (relating both to the teeth and to
the post-cranial skeleton) that the behavioral pattern of *Paranthropus* was distinct from that of *Australopithecus* and that he was in fact better adapted to the
forest conditions than to savannahs. The wetter period, which heralded his arrival, no doubt brought forest into special regions such as the valley floors—thus
there is a certain amount of supporting evidence for the functional deductions
derived from morphology.

In recent years field studies of behavior, particularly of baboons and chimpanzees, have predominated in the field of primate research. Baboon studies are of

special importance to human evolution for it is possible to see in the behavior of modern baboon troops something of the group organization necessary for the survival of savannah-living Primates. It is possible that the ancestors of both baboons and man broke away, at much the same time, from the somewhat parochial life of the forest to move out into the open savannahs, where the struggle for existence is altogether a tougher proposition but which, at the same time, offers almost limitless horizons for subsequent evolution and multiplication. No doubt this radical step was related to the major climatic changes which produced an increase in the world's grasslands at the expense of forests during the Miocene epoch. Although the subsequent evolution of the two groups was so entirely different, the basic problem of survival facing ancestral baboons and early hominids must have been much the same. There is a vast gap between the social organization of the most primitive of living human races—the hunter-gatherer communities still living without agriculture—and that of baboons, which represent the highest expression of social organization among nonhuman Primates. The chief reason for this divergence may lie, according to Dr. S. L. Washburn of the University of California, in hunting, which promotes in a group such behavioral traits as cooperation, sharing of food, and defense of territory—traits not found in baboons who neither hunt cooperatively nor alone. Hunting, of course, implies firstly a carnivorous diet and secondly access to adequate hunting grounds. But baboons obtain their food off the land by roaming daily over their home range which may not exceed a few square miles. There have been a number of reports of the carnivorous habits of baboons, particularly from stock-farmers in South Africa; these reports have recently been collected and collated by Professor Raymond Dart of the University of Witwatersrand. Such sporadic meat eating is characteristic of most Primates in zoos and of many of them, including chimpanzees, in the wild, but this does not really alter the fundamental fact that the preferences of subhuman Primates are vegetarian. Incidental deviations of this sort from a rigid pattern of behavior are a characteristic feature of Primates.

Studies of baboon behavior in the wild are of great importance to anthropologists because they provide clues to the behavior of man in his prehuman phase when the foundations of modern human society were being laid. These clues provide the basis for hypothesis which can be tested experimentally by psychologists.

Behavioral patterns of the kind already discussed can only be inferred for fossil man, but there is one aspect of behavior that *can* be excavated. Artifacts—products of human technology—sometimes referred to as 'fossilized behavior,' are important indicators of man's psycho-neural evolution. Benjamin Franklin is usually credited with the concept of *Homo faber*, or man-the-toolmaker, but it was K. P. Oakley of the Natural History Museum who appreciated the significance of this concept as a breakthrough in mental development and, therefore, as a basis for an objective definition of man. As Oakley points out, many animals make use of naturally occurring objects as tools. The Galapagos Woodpecker-finch employs a cactus thorn held in its beak to winkle out insects from the bark of trees, and the sea-otter cracks open the shells of molluscs on a convenient rock. There are many recorded instances of apes and monkeys that have used tools but only man *constructs* them in a systematic manner. There is little doubt that the beginnings of toolmaking to a "set and regular pattern" can be regarded as the base line for the emergence of human culture and technology, but there is less certainty of its validity as a base line for the emergence of *Homo*.

Recent evidence in the fields of ethology and palaeontology suggests that toolmaking is a great deal older, both in the sense of absolute time and in the sense of evolutionary level, than was previously thought. From a prolonged field study of chimpanzees in Tanganyika, Jane Goodall reports the prevalence of a simple form of toolmaking in the group she studied, consisting of termite 'fishing.' The chimpanzee, after picking a number of slender stems or stalks, settles down beside a termite hill, scratches away the soil over the flight-hole with the forefinger, inserts the stick and after a few seconds withdraws it, covered with termites. The chimpanzee then passes the stick through its mouth, removing the termites. Stalks and stems may be picked some distance away and brought to the termite hill—this is clearly purposeful tool-using. If the sticks are too long, they are pruned to a convenient length and, if their usefulness is marred by side branches, these are stripped off.

In these simple but nevertheless surprising actions of a chimpanzee one can perhaps see the beginnings of toolmaking. It is possible to visualize a gradual transition from *ad hoc tool-using* to *tool-modifying* for an immediate purpose, to *tool-modifying* for a future eventuality to the full flowering of cultural *toolmaking*. There is, of course, no evidence, as yet, that this particular aspect of the behavior of a particular group of chimpanzees is practiced by any other groups, but the use of sticks for other purposes such as honey-collecting has been reported. From what we know of the intellectual capacity and of the anatomy of the hand of chimpanzees, tool-modifying for an immediate purpose probably represents the acme of their technological behavior. The essentially noncarnivorous diet of chimpanzees, furthermore, does not impose a very high selection pressure on toolmaking as a means of survival. However, this observation has shown us that some chimpanzees in the wild possess the rudiments of conceptual thinking and that the transition between tool-using and toolmaking in its simplest expression was probably not as complex as we have supposed.

A rather more advanced form of tool-modifying that may in fact overlap into toolmaking, is represented by a bone-tool culture that Professor Raymond Dart believes to have been prevalent among the very earliest known of the South African australopithecines from Makapansgat in the Transvaal. The evidence for this osteodontokeratic (bone-tooth-horn) culture is the discovery of a vast collection of broken bovid bones which appear to have been selected purposefully for use, after modification, as mallets, scrapers, knives, and scoops.

The earliest evidence of the use of stone tools comes from Olduvai Gorge, Tanganyika, where in recent years Dr. L. S. B. Leakey has made a number of remarkable discoveries that make this offshoot of the Great Rift Valley a natural museum of Pleistocene evolution. The evidence from recent potassium-argon dating is that toolmaking at Olduvai may extend back to more than a million years before the present time. At least five living sites are known throughout the 40-foot thickness of the lowest stratum, and at each site stone tools distinctive of an Oldowan pebble culture have been found.

On four of these living sites skeletal remains of hominids have been discovered—they include a skull, a lower jaw, an almost complete foot and a number of hand bones. It seems almost certain that at Olduvai we have the remains of two creatures living as contemporaries—one an australopithecine and one that may possibly turn out to be true man or *Homo*. So far only the collection of hand bones has been reported on and the findings have surprised a number of authorities. It has generally been assumed that by the time that true man started to make tools (as opposed to tool-modifying) his hands were essentially modern in form. The Olduvai hands, however, are far from modern. They were powerfully built with short, strong, curved fingers having broad tips surmounted by flat nails and, in all probability, having a disproportionately short thumb.

Considered individually (R1 level) these bones are *unlike* those of *Homo sapiens*; at an R2 level, however, there are a number of similarities that suggest a functional affinity with modern man in respect to prehensile capability of the hand. The stone tools on the living floor are of a type that *could* have been fabricated by a hand of this degree of development.

These findings, considering the technologically crude nature of the pebble-tool culture, suggest that morphological improvement in the form of the hand has played an important part in the evolution of toolmaking skill. This is an aspect of cultural evolution that will merit further investigation.

There is of course no denying the large intellectual factor in toolmaking—this is the basis of Oakley's definition—but, as S. L. Washburn has emphasized, the increase in brain size characteristic of man's evolution is more likely to have followed toolmaking than to have preceded it. The area of the cerebral cortex that interprets tactile stimuli and initiates motor activity in the hand is very extensive compared with the same region in a monkey, and increase in the size of this area would lead to substantial increase in the total size of the brain; in addition, of course, an expansive cultural life would be associated with enlargement of the frontal lobes. Once toolmaking was established at a cultural level, the evolutionary premium on efficient toolmaking would be high and the size of the brain would rapidly increase through natural selection. The evidence of Goodall's chimpanzees, Dart's osteodontokeratic culture and the Olduvai hand make it abundantly clear that toolmaking is an extremely ancient capability and that cultural toolmaking was preceded by many thousands of years of tool-using, tool-modifying and *ad hoc* toolmaking. Tools were undoubtedly 'made' many times over in different materials ranging from wood through bone to stone, and during this time local 'crazes' for toolmaking were established, lost, and established again, until finally, perhaps related to the acquisition of speech, it became established as a tradition. Cultural toolmaking "to a set and regular pattern" with its implications of an organized social pattern is still a valid criterion for the beginnings of our own kind, but we must probably accept that to start with the hand of man-the-toolmaker was somewhat less than 'human.'

Other constituents of early hominid living floors are important clues to environment and behavior. The bones of animals provide evidence of food preferences (which can be related to the characters of the dentition) and food-getting habits. Large-scale hunting was apparently not established among the Olduvai Bed hominids, for bone accumulation on the living floors is not extensive, and suggests scavenging rather than hunting. Other material, such as charcoal and charred bones, provides evidence of the use of fire and the presence of accumulations of 'imported' spherical pebbles may suggest the employment of bolas as hunting weapons.

This sort of evidence can be used to reconstruct the behavioral pattern (R4 level) which in turn may provide the basis for an assessment of the *ecological status* of a population—ecological status being the expression of the standing of a population in a particular habitat.

During the progress of evolution, man became better and better adapted to existing conditions—this was primarily the reason for his subsequent diffusion and multiplication. Eventually he was able to modify the existing environment to suit his own needs—he produced his own warmth and shelter and later grew his own crops, provided his own irrigation and tended herds of domesticated animals. Natural environment thus became less and less critical to his survival.

With the twentieth century came a radical change. Although still dependent to a limited extent on his natural environment—in particular in very cold and hot, dry climates and at high altitudes—man is erecting his own synthetic environment. Through his efforts the arctic and the desert are being made habitable, the patterns of disease are changing, and a complete new range of psychological and sociological pressures is developing as a result of his insistence on city dwelling. The wheel of evolution has turned something of a circle. Ecological status—which is the marker of survival value—is again of prime importance. But now it is against the background of an environment of his own making that man must struggle to survive.

ENVIRONMENT AND CULTURE
IN THE AMAZON BASIN:
AN APPRAISAL
OF THE THEORY OF
ENVIRONMENTAL DETERMINISM

Betty J. Meggers

Throughout the literature of the sciences, the phrase "freedom from environ-mental control," or its equivalent, appears as a recurrent motif. This shibboleth is a major theme in the historical fantasy of the technocrats and, at the same time, a cry of excelsior. Safety and comfort are ordinarily no more questioned as values than is motherhood. Half the world's people, still living in a Neolithic economy, do need something better—but is what they need truly disengagement and protection from the land and the climate, from hardship and risk?

People are protected from wet, cold, heat, and wind by buildings and by mechanical regulation of temperature, humidity, light, and sound. Food is stored, medicines consumed, distances crossed, and cultural differences diminished. And beyond these elementary steps of progress, in moments of escape, men achieve the freedom (from necessity) to be eccentric, and to "create" free, irrelevant, impractical, willed (rather than caused) objects, art, and communities. It is a freedom much insisted upon.

In spite of our own security—toward which we are helping our Neolithic brothers and the remnants of Paleolithic men—there is deepening uncertainty and frustration, both among committed environmental controllers and among con-verts. It is not simply doubt, but a feeling that we have misconstrued the nature of success, and so misused the environment that it can no longer comfort us.

Moreover, our ability to regulate our environment does not settle the issue of our relationship to particular local conditions, both geographic and biological. It would be ironic indeed to have undertaken the domestication of the planet only to discover that the rhythms of light and dark and of the seasons, the uncertainty of storm, pain, disease, and accident, are the stuff of life. We are unanimously gratified to escape early death, to ameliorate physical debility, and yet . . .

These are doubts for which the world is not yet ready. Until we have satisfied our physical needs, the virtue of need itself may remain hidden. Perhaps we should begin with the hypothesis that what we are faced with is not the accep-tance or rejection of hardship, but the discovery of the conditions and natural contours which make human industry worthwhile. We may then hope to discover—

Betty J. Meggers, "Environment and Culture in the Amazon Basin," *P.A.V.* Social Science Monographs, *3 (1957), 71–89. Reprinted from* Studies in Human Ecology, *Washington, Pan American Union, 1957, by permission of the author and the General Secretariat of the Or-ganization of American States.*

perhaps first in the straightforward examples of tropical agriculture—the harsh and necessary nutrient of raw environment.

"Culture and environment" has at least three different meanings in anthropology: 1) that all cultures exist in an environmental setting; 2) that a culture is generally adapted to the characteristics of the environment; and 3) that a culture is molded, or determined by the characteristics of the environment. The first is universally recognized and the second generally accepted, but the third is usually rejected today, although it was a leading theoretical concept in anthropology's earlier years. Its renunciation began with the demonstration that some of the environmental determinists' assertions were exaggerated. Ridicule of this over-embellishment brought about the disgrace of the theory, with little serious effort to determine whether or not the core was sound.

In recent years there has been a revival of interest in the relationship between environment and culture; and the biological concept of ecology—that the organism and its environment are interrelated—has been accepted as equally applicable to culture. There has been no serious effort to explore further and to re-evaluate the question of whether or not the environment can exert a deterministic influence on a culture. The misdeeds of the early environmental determinists have been kept fresh in the minds of each new generation of students and the mere use of the word "determinism" can still provoke a vigorous retort (Baerreis, 1956, p. 315). There is, however, the risk that the environmental determinists were on the track of a useful concept, and that we have been uncritical in discarding the whole idea along with the errors and overemphases that poor documentation and an excess of enthusiasm made inevitable. Our knowledge of both culture and environment is now infinitely greater than it was then, and we are in a position to re-examine their relationship from the point of view of determinism. It is appropriate, therefore, that this discussion of environment and culture in the Amazon Basin be directed toward such an end. If the evidence suggests that the Tropical Forest Pattern of culture is a product of well-defined environmental characteristics, then we can conclude that determinism exists. If no such relationship can be detected, we may decide either that the theory is wrong, or that the evidence is as yet insufficient to permit a final judgment.

To place the discussion on an objective footing, it is necessary to have an impartial definition of "determinism." Our authority here will be Webster's New International Dictionary of the English Language, Unabridged, 1952 Edition, which gives the following meanings for the verb "determine": "To set bounds or limits to; to fix the form or character of beforehand, to foreordain; to establish causally; to bring about as a result; to give a definite direction, impetus, or bias to; to impel; to fix the course or end of." The question to be kept in mind is, therefore: Does the environment limit, establish causally or give definite direction to the culture it supports? Can the culture be shown to respond to characteristics of the environment that fix the course it must take if it is to survive? Finding the answer will require detailed analysis of that portion of the environment most directly affecting human exploitation—the subsistence resources, and particularly the agricultural potential.

Those familiar with some of the recent books extolling the unexploited wealth of the tropics may find it strange to pick the Amazon basin as the test ground for such a theory. The luxuriant vegetation exceeds in variety and exuberance the indigenous flora of any other climate of the world. On seeing it, men have reasoned: if temperate lands with poorer natural flora can be made to yield abundant crops, how much greater must be the harvest where nature unassisted succeeds so well? There is, however, another side to the story. Soil experts, agronomists, plant ecologists and other specialists have come to the conclusion, after detailed and extensive investigations of the properties of the soil, climate and natural vegetation, that the widely held impression of exceptionally fertile soils in the lowland tropics is contrary to the facts, and that to regard such lands as needing but an ax and a plow to transform them into the bread basket of the world is to believe in a myth.

The Standard Climate of the Wet Lowland Tropics

The Amazonian rain forests form part of a belt of similar vegetation that encircles the globe between the tropics of Cancer and Capricorn, or roughly 23° on either side of the equator. Its northern and southern extension is erratic because of the intrusion of mountain ranges, plateaus, and other factors that create climatic conditions beyond the tolerance of rain forest vegetation. The three major regions of the world where this vegetation occurs—tropical America, tropical Africa and tropical Asia—are distinct in plant species but show striking similarities in forest structure, plant succession and adaptation to the standard climate (Richards, 1952, pp. 6–7). Consequently, much of what will be said here is also generally applicable to the tropical rain forest regions in Asia and Africa. However, to avoid the pitfalls that come from too wide generalization, this discussion is specifically directed toward the Amazon basin. Although this area supports the largest continuous body of tropical forest in the world, its homogeneous geological origin, its slight variation in altitude and its equatorial location result in a remarkably uniform set of conditions over some million and a half square miles. Most important of these conditions is what may be termed the standard climate [1]—the characteristics of temperature and rainfall that combine to create a well-defined and distinctive environmental situation.

[1] This term is used by P. W. Richards (1952, p. 158) to label "the climate recorded by instruments about 1 m. above the surface of the ground, exposed, according to the rules adopted by meteorologists, in more or less extensive clearings." It has been retained in this discussion as a convenient means of referring to the combination of rainfall and temperature characteristics that produce tropical rain forest vegetation. Humidity, wind velocity, evaporation and other factors are relevant, but less spectacular than temperature and rainfall. They have been omitted in the interest of simplicity because their effects do not conflict with the conclusions derived from an analysis of the temperature and rainfall pattern.

The tropics lack the extremes of both heat and cold characteristic of the temperate zone. The mean annual temperature averages 78° F (26° C), with the mean for the coldest month rarely differing from that of the warmest month by as much as 13° (Richards, 1952, pp. 136-7). At Manaos, in the center of the Amazon basin, the data on record show a maximum of 100.9° F (38.3° C) and a minimum of 65.8° F (18.8° C) (Richards, 1952, Table 10). These extremes are balanced by more moderate temperatures on other days so that over a series of years the average is 85.1° F (28.2° C) for the hottest month and 79.7° F (26.5° C) for the coldest month (ibid.). Lack of marked seasonal variation is related to the small annual variation in the length of the day and the relatively constant angle of the sun throughout the year, in contrast with the large fluctuation in both these factors at greater distances from the equator. The marked day-to-day fluctuations in temperature characteristic of temperate regions, especially in spring and fall, are also rarely met with in the tropics (Richards, 1952, p. 136).

Like temperature, rainfall has certain characteristics that contrast with its pattern in temperate regions. Three of the most distinct differences are in quantity, intensity and variability. In typical tropical rain forest localities, the average amount of annual rainfall is at least twice that of normal temperate locations or about 80 inches (200 cm) per year. Manaos, with 66 inches (165.4 cm) is near the estimated minimum requirement for the maintenance of rain forest vegetation. Toward the other extreme is the Mazaruni Station, British Guiana, where the annual average is 98.7 inches (246.9 cm) or a little over 8 feet.

The presentation of rainfall data as averages indicates the large total quantity of precipitation, but obscures the two other important characteristics of the tropical rainfall pattern: intensity and variability. Extended soaking rains of the sort welcomed by farmers in temperate regions are relatively less common in the tropics and cloudbursts are correspondingly more frequent. Technically, a cloudburst is defined as a shower "having an intensity of at least 1 mm per minute for not less than 5 minutes" (Mohr and Van Baren, 1954, p. 41). Converted into inches, this represents a minimum of 1/5 inch in 5 minutes, and tropical rains often exceed this specification in both intensity and duration. Although figures do not appear to be available for comparing the rainfall intensity of temperate and tropical areas using the Amazon as the point of reference, a study has been made using observations taken on the frequency of cloudbursts at 13 stations in Indonesia and at 13 stations in Bavaria (Germany). Analysis shows that cloudbursts furnish 22% of the total rainfall in Indonesia, but only 1.5% in Bavaria. Since tropical regions like Indonesia receive a much larger quantity of rain annually than Bavaria, it has been estimated that "the amount of water precipitated by tropical cloudbursts . . . (is) 40 times more than . . . in temperate latitudes" (Mohr and Van Baren, 1954, p. 42).

Another important characteristic of tropical rainfall is its high degree of variability. One might say paradoxically that its unpredictability is predictable. There is a wide fluctuation in both monthly and annual totals. A given month may receive 2 inches (5.1 cm) one year and 12 inches (30.4 cm) the next.[2] A wet year receives at least twice as much rain as a dry one and a difference of 400–500% is relatively common (Visher, 1923, p. 4). When one considers that the tropical averages are at least twice as great as the temperate ones, the variability in terms of actual amount of rainfall received becomes very marked.

The characteristics of temperature and rainfall outlined here constitute the dominant factors in the production of the standard climate of tropical lowland areas around the world. They have profound effects on the production and maintenance of soil fertility, and consequently on the food supply available to man. For an understanding of these effects it is necessary to examine the process by which soils become suitable for the growth of plants.

A discussion of soil fertility may properly begin with a description of the flora and fauna that inhabit the soil—earthworms, ants, algae, bacteria, fungi, etc.—because their activity creates the fertility. Of this flora and fauna, the most important and most completely studied are the microscopic plants that abound in all soils and play a major role in the reduction of organic matter to the basic elements from which it was originally derived. Bacteria, the major group of microflora both in quantity and in number of species, are the smallest. They are present by the millions in every gram of soil (Mohr and Van Baren, 1954, p. 277). Larger and less numerous are the fungi or molds, which range from microscopic size to readily visible plants like giant puffballs, and which number from a few thousand to a million or more per gram of soil (Jacks, 1954, p. 93). The activities of these and other micro-organisms result in the complete decomposition of almost every kind of organic compound so that only under special circumstances (such as those leading to the formation of peat or coal) can any organic matter accumulate.

Bacteria and fungi perform partly complimentary and partly overlapping functions in the decomposition of organic material. While bacteria are frequently specialized to perform a specific task like nitrogen fixation, cellulose decomposition or ammonia production, fungi are more versatile and act as scavengers, attacking not only wastes that the bacteria are not able to deal with but also some of the same materials that are subject to bacterial decomposition. Lignin, the main constituent of wood, is resistant to bacterial action but falls prey to the voracious fungi. When the micro-organisms themselves die, their bodies are in turn attacked and decomposed. Ultimately, everything that was taken from the soil to build a living plant or animal is returned to the soil in its original form to be reutilized by another generation of living things. However, under certain circumstances some of the organic matter is temporarily diverted from the path toward complete mineralization and converted into an amorphous colloidal substance known as humus.

---

[2] Rainfall records on the upper Essequibo River, British Guiana show December totals of 1.63 inches (4.4 cm) in 1954 and 12.03 inches (30.6 cm) in 1955. May totals were 14.53 inches (36.9 cm) in 1954 and 27.97 inches (71.1 cm) in 1955 (Records, Meterological Department, Georgetown, British Guiana).

Although soil scientists and practical farmers agree that humus is a vital component of fertile soils, its actual composition is poorly understood in spite of considerable research. This matters little here, because for our purposes what humus does is more significant than what humus is. There is general agreement that it has two important functions: 1) it increases the capacity of the soil to absorb and hold plant nutrients so that they cannot be dissolved and washed away, and 2) it combines with clay minerals to form the crumb-like texture that is both favorable to the growth of plants and resistant to erosion (Jacks, 1954, pp. 110–113). It is also generally agreed that the presence of humus is indispensable to the achievement and maintenance of soil fertility, especially under continuous agricultural exploitation. Since the major producers of humus appear to be fungi, conditions favorable to their activity will result in the maximum degree of humus production (Jacks, 1954, p. 93; Mohr and Van Baren, 1954, p. 279). Contrariwise, in situations where bacteria flourish there will be no humus accumulation, because these micro-organisms reduce organic wastes rapidly and completely to their constituent minerals and return the latter in soluble form to the soil. From this it is evident that climatic factors favoring the activity of fungi will also favor the production and maintenance of soil fertility. At this point, the characteristics of the standard climate of the lowland tropics assume major significance. The ratio of fungi to bacteria is a function of the temperature of the soil, and higher temperatures are more favorable to bacteria. Experiments have shown that temperatures below 77° F (25° C) encourage the development of fungi and that increased warmth above this point increasingly inhibits their activity. The higher the temperature rises above 77° F (25° C), the more bacterial activity will predominate over that of fungi, and the less humus will be formed. Bacterial activity is also promoted by humidity in the neighborhood of 98%, whereas fungi prefer conditions of less moisture (Mohr and Van Baren, 1954, p. 277). Since high temperature and high humidity are both characteristic of the standard climate of the lowland tropics, bacterial activity is favored over that of fungi, and without ameliorating circumstances no humus can accumulate in the soil (Richards, 1952, p. 218; Mohr and Van Baren, 1954, p. 280). In view of the important role of humus in the production and maintenance of soil fertility for agricultural purposes, this situation presents a serious problem.

The abundance and intensity of tropical rainfall compounds the difficulty by thoroughly leaching from the soil all of the soluble minerals deposited by bacterial action, some of which might otherwise remain accessible to growing plants (cf. Richards, 1952, p. 208). The fact that precipitation exceeds evaporation for the greater part of the year means that there is a continuous downward movement of water in the soil. This percolation carries nutrients out of reach of plant roots, and leaves behind little but insoluble aluminum and iron oxides. When the full force of the standard climate is allowed to exert itself, the ultimate result of this process of mineralization and leaching is the production of a compact and infertile compound called laterite, on which only a sparse and hardy grass can make an effort to survive. Much tropical savanna owes its existence to the presence of this type of soil.

The important aspects of the standard climate of the tropics, to be borne in mind as we move on to a discussion of the problem of natural and human expolitation, can now be summarized as:

1. A high and even temperature that favors bacterial activity in the soil, so that the formation of humus essential to continued agricultural utilization is inhibited;

2. Abundant annual precipitation, which exceeds the moisture lost by evaporation and results in the leaching from the soil of soluble plant nutrients;

3. Intensity of rainfall, much of which comes in the form of cloudbursts, creating a great potential for erosion;

4. Variability of the total annual rainfall, expressed in wide differences in the amounts received in wet and dry years, which subjects agricultural crops to uncertain water supplies.

The success of any utilization of a tropical area with this standard climate can be measured by the degree to which this utilization is able to minimize or inhibit the undesirable effects the climate produces.

The Standard Climate and the Natural Vegetation

A visitor from the temperate zone requires only one look at the lush growth of a tropical rain forest to find himself doubting or opposing the suggestion that the soil may be infertile. Statistics are as impressive as the sight itself. Tropical rain forest is the most exuberant, luxuriant and varied of all flora. Trees average 50% taller than those in temperate woodlands, and a comparable area of ground will support many more species. Tropical forests are often so diverse in composition that it is difficult for the expert to locate two trees of the same kind. To the untrained eye, however, the same forest gives an effect of monotony because diversity of species is masked by uniformity of appearance. The trunks are nearly all straight and slender, the base is often expanded into prominent buttresses, the bark is smooth, and the leaves are dark green, leathery, oval and of similar size. Since such a forest is evergreen, not even a change of season does much to vary its appearance.

The dense canopy of foliage formed wherever the sun sheds its light is composed not only of trees but also of quantities of climbing plants, many of which are epiphytic and trail their roots like streamers down from the treetops. An impenetrable-appearing shield of vegetation is presented to the viewer whether he looks from an airplane in the sky or from a dugout on the waterways. This dense and compact surface has led to the mistaken impression that a similar condition exists in the depths of the forest. On the contrary, in a primary forest the canopy of shade is so complete that undergrowth is kept at a minimum and a traveler can frequently pass through on foot with little clearing of the way.

Forests of this sort flourish where the conditions of temperature and rainfall have all the detrimental features described for the standard climate of the lowland tropics. In explaining this apparently contradictory situation, it may be well to begin with the words of P. W. Richards, an outstanding authority on the tropical rain forest: "The most important common characteristic of all rainforest soils . . . is . . . their low content of plant nutrients. This being so, it seems paradoxical that rain-forest vegetation should be so luxuriant. The leached and impoverished soils of the wet tropics bear magnificent forest, while the much richer soils of the drier tropical zones bear savanna or much less luxuriant forest. This problem has been considered by Walter (1936) and Milne (1937) for African forests, and by Hardy (1936) for those of the West Indies, and all these authors reach a similar conclusion. In the rain forest the vegetation itself sets up processes tending to counteract soil impoverishment and under undisturbed conditions there is a closed cycle of plant nutrients. The soil beneath its natural cover thus reaches a state of equilibrium in which its impoverishment, if not actually arrested, proceeds extremely slowly" (Richards, 1952, p. 219).

Among the processes favoring the maintenance of soil fertility, which are furthered by the rain forest in spite of obstructing features in the standard climate, is the formation of humus. Although the conditions of high temperature and high humidity work to inhibit its development, the shelter afforded to the soil from rain and sun by the dense mass of foliage mitigates their full expression sufficiently to permit some humus accumulation. The amount is very slight, usually not exceeding 1-2% of the soil content (Richards, 1952, p. 218), but even this small quantity exerts considerable effects on soil development by holding plant nutrients where they can be returned to the vegetation and by retarding leaching. As a result rain-forest soils never reach the point of complete laterization that renders savanna soils barren and agriculturally useless.

In addition to creating a microclimate that promotes continuing soil fertility, rain forest vegetation plays an important role in moderating the destructive potential of the precipitation for leaching and erosion. This it does in two ways: 1) by reducing the quantity and intensity of the water that strikes the surface of the ground, and 2) by obstructing the erosional action of the runoff. Reduction in quantity and intensity is accomplished by the foliage. Data collected in Surinam show that when the daily rainfall is .04 inches (1 mm), 80% of the moisture is absorbed before it reaches the ground. As the quantity of precipitation increases, the percentage retained by the vegetation declines, but even when the amount is as high as 1.6 inches (40 mm) per day, about 20% fails to penetrate the vegetation shield. On the basis of these and other similar observations, it has been estimated that tropical forest vegetation allows only about 75% of the annual precipitation to reach the ground surface (Mohr and Van Baren, 1954, p. 96). In view of the fact that such rainfall generally amounts to 80 or more inches annually, a reduction of 25% is a significant mitigating influence on erosion. Furthermore, what does penetrate to the ground comes in a fine spray rather than a heavy shower because of the deflection provided by the leaves, further reducing the erosion potential. A more familiar erosion-controlling mechanism of forests is their root system. This is so effective that forest soils do not develop the kind of erosion-resisting structure characteristic of less protected soils, with the consequence that they are highly subject to erosion once the forest cover is removed (Jacks, 1954, p. 180).

In spite of this considerable role played by the vegetation in shielding the soil from the direct and total effects of the precipitation, a great deal of soil erosion occurs in rain forest areas. Its extent may be illustrated by contrasting the Amazon with the Rhine. Whereas the silt carried by the Rhine amounts to an average lowering of the land surface in the drainage area by only 0.002 inches (0.06 mm) per year, that carried by the Amazon amounts to 0.03 inches (0.8 mm) per year, or about 14 times more (Richards, 1952, p. 207). This is still a very minute amount, but it raises a question: if this degree of erosion is possible with the maximum protection provided by forest cover, what would be the consequences of any considerable amount of deforestation, which would expose the soil to the full effects of the standard climate?

The adaptation of the natural vegetation to the requirements of the standard climate of tropical lowland South America can be scored according to the success with which it mitigates or counteracts the unfavorable results of high temperature combined with high humidity. The double plus mark opposite each of the 6 major factors in Table 1 indicates that bacterial breakdown of the humus, leaching, and erosion are all markedly reduced, and in some cases brought to a standstill. The extravagant language often employed in the description of the luxuriant vegetation is thus deserved, not for the more obvious characteristics usually described but because of the marvelous adaptation to stringent climatic conditions that it represents.

The Standard Climate and Agricultural Exploitation

When man turns his hand to making a rain forest like that of the Amazon basin agriculturally productive, he faces the same standard climate with the same problems of soil conservation that nature has faced and solved. To the extent that this standard climate is unalterable and uncontrollable, the bounds within which man makes his adaptation are preordained. Numerous obervers have characterized slash-and-burn agriculture as wasteful, inefficient, unproductive and primitive, and have stigmatized groups who practice it as lazy, ignorant or too stubborn to abandon a practice whose only justification is to be found in tradition. On this basis, the fact that no advanced civilization has developed in the tropical rain forest is attributed to human failure rather than to the existence of a low level of agricultural potential in the environment. We have already seen that visitors

Table 1
Relative success of rain forest vegetation, slash-and-burn agriculture and total clearing (temperate zone technique of agriculture) in counteracting the detrimental effects of the standard climate of the wet, lowland tropics

Environmental Requirements (Conditions for Permanent Production)	Rain Forest Vegetation	Slash-and-Burn Agriculture	Total Clearing
Retardation of Humus Destruction:			
Minimum Exposure of Soil to Sun	++	+	–
Minimum Aeration (Cultivation)	++	++	–
Mitigation of Erosion Potential:			
Diminution of Quantity of Precipitation Reaching Soil	++	+	–
Deflection of Intensity of Precipitation Impact	++	+	–
Reduction of Runoff Erosion	++	++	–
Retardation of Leaching	++	+	–

++ approaching complete protection
+ partial protection or brief exposure period
– no protection

from the temperate zone are inclined to evaluate the natural vegetation in terms of their own experience and consequently to pronounce the soil wondrously fertile, although quite the opposite is true. It seems possible that the deprecation of tropical shifting cultivation may spring from a similar misunderstanding of the kind of problems that confront an agriculturalist in the tropics.

First, what is the aboriginal situation? In tropical rain forests around the world, the most common agricultural technique is a variety of shifting cultivation, known in South America as slash-and-burn agriculture. By this method, a patch of forest is cut and the fallen trees are allowed to dry for a period varying from a few months to a year. At the beginning of the rainy season they are burned, a process that frequently consumes only the smaller branches. Some of the unburned wood is removed before planting, but the prepared field remains thickly strewn with trunks and large limbs, which gradually decay where they fell. Immediately after burning, manioc and other crops are planted in the bare spots with a hoe or digging stick. There is no cultivation of the soil and little if any weeding. Such a field will produce rather well the first year, less the second, and by the third is generally so unproductive that the clearing of a new field is begun, although bananas, papayas and other tree crops continue to be exploited until killed out by secondary forest growth. The field may be used again in 25, 50 or 100 years, or never. This method of agriculture requires a high ratio of land per person, with the consequence that only a small fraction of the forest is cleared at any one time. It has been recently estimated that only about 500 square miles out of more than a million square miles in the Amazon Basin are agriculturally productive today (Osborn, 1953, p. 143), when farming is still carried on with aboriginal methods. The main characteristics of slash-and-burn agriculture as practiced in South America are the small size of clearing, retention of stumps and root mat of the natural vegetation, minimal period between burning and the growth of the crops during which the soil is exposed to rain and sun, return to the soil of some plant nutrients from slashings left to decay, minimal cultivation and aeration, and short interval between the destruction of the forest and the beginning of its regeneration.

Turning now to the effects on the soil of removing the natural vegetation, we find the following sequence of events: "The removal of the forest cover at once changes the illumination at ground-level from a small fraction to full daylight. The temperature range greatly increases. . . . There is a change from the complicated system of microclimates characteristic of high forest to conditions closely approximating to the standard climate of the locality. Exposure to sun and rain very quickly alters the properties of the soil. Where the slope is sufficient, erosion will begin to remove the surface layers or their finer fractions. The rise in soil temperature leads to a rapid disappearance of humus" (Richards, 1952, p. 401).

The length of time that this situation continues affects the length of time required for recovery. If the growth of the secondary forest is allowed to begin immediately, a vegetation cover will totally shield the soil within a few weeks and there will be a minimum of soil damage to be repaired. It is generally agreed that the longer the onset of secondary succession is postponed, the longer it will take for the soil to return to its original condition of fertility. The length of time required to complete the transition back to primary forest is not well established, but former agricultural land along the Brazilian coast is still occupied by secondary vegetation 150–200 years after clearing (Richards, 1952, pp. 399–400).

Under these circumstances, slash-and-burn agriculture seems reasonably well suited to the demands of the standard climate. The small size of the cleared area, and the fact that the stumps are not uprooted, keeps the erosion damage at a minimum. The absence of plowing or other cultivation, and the short time during which the soil surface is exposed to the sun keep humus destruction to a slow rate in comparison with what would result from the kind of extensive clearing and preparation of the soil practiced in temperate regions. Leaving the debris in the cleared area permits the return to the soil of some of the nutrients taken up by the former vegetation during growth, whereas all would be lost if the field were completely cleaned off. Finally, the short period of agricultural exploitation keeps modification of the soil at a minimum and facilitates recovery of the original fertility with the return of primary forest. Marking these adaptive features on the same chart (Table 1) used to score the adaptation of the natural vegetation shows that slash-and-burn agriculture is not as successful as the forest in counteracting the damaging effects of the standard climate. However, it minimizes some and allows others only a brief period of operation before the forest cover returns.

To conclude that slash-and-burn agriculture is relatively well adjusted to the requirements of the standard climate in the Amazon Basin does not end the discussion of this form of agriculture. The disrepute in which it is held does not stem from a conservational effect on the landscape, but rather from the conservative influence it exerts over the local culture. It is these cultural characteristics that concern anthropologists most because they represent evidence of environmental determinism if they can be shown to stem from the character of the agricultural exploitation, which in turn is dictated by the requirements of the standard climate.

It has been noted many times that the centers of development of civilization lie outside the boundaries of the tropical rain forests. Various explanations have been offered, but the one most pertinent to this inquiry is that the limitations of the subsistence resources in tropical rain forest areas prevent cultural development from advancing beyond a relatively simple level. Just as the standard climate has features to which the vegetation must adapt, slash-and-burn agriculture has characteristics to which a culture must adapt. The most significant of these derive from the short period of time that a garden remains productive, which means 1) that a relatively large amount of land per capita must be available for agricultural use, and 2) that the settlement cannot remain permanently in one place. Let us consider the manner in which these two requirements affect cultural development.

The amount of land under cultivation at any time must always be slight in comparison with that held in reserve because of the long period required after use for recovery of fertility before reclearing is profitable. This situation exercises a strong control over population density and also over population concentration (cf. Palerm, 1955, pp. 30–31). Since the amount of agricultural land in an accessible radius of the village is limited by the irregularity of the terrain, by and large the smaller the community, the longer it will be able to remain settled in one spot. Differences in local hunting and fishing resources sometimes make local exceptions and permit larger population concentrations than could be supported were agriculture the only important food resource. However, generally speaking 1000 individuals is a large population for villages in the South American tropical forest, and settlements with less than 300 people are typical.

Such a low level of population concentration allows little room for occupational specialization. If we note in our own culture how occupational specialization increases with the size of the urban population, it is readily understood how its absence is normal and inevitable in the small settlements characteristic of Tropical Forest life. Specialization provides a favorable atmosphere for the acquisition of detailed knowledge and for improvement of technical skill, and the archeological picture in the centers of civilization around the world shows an advance in all fields of endeavor under its influence. Where specialization is absent, and each generation transmits what it has learned in much the same form as it was received, the normal result is slight variation but no marked increase in the scope or quality of techniques or products. One does not need to search for psychological explanations or to point to geographical isolation from centers of diffusion. The answer seems to be adequately provided by the series of causes and effects just described—without occupational specialization, progress in technology is slight and slow; without population concentration there is little specialization; with shifting cultivation, there can be no large permanent settlements.

In addition to a low population concentration, dependence on slash-and-burn agriculture necessitates periodic moving of the village. While it might be feasible in a temperate climate to exploit fields at a considerable distance from the settlement, this solution is not practical in the tropics. The staple root crops do not mature for seasonal harvest as do temperate crops, and cannot be stored in the humid, warm climate without sprouting or rotting. Harvesting must be daily or several times a week. If the fields were not readily accessible, the time needed to exploit them would be so great that agriculture would provide little more return for the labor than wild food gathering. Hence, shifting of the village periodically is not simply a matter of choice but an adaptation to a subsistence base whose most effective utilization is continuous rather than seasonal.

The inability to settle long in one spot has certain cultural effects that can be most effectively indicated by recalling a saying current in our own culture: "Three moves are as good as a fire." Even with all the opportunities for accumulation of material goods afforded to us, frequent moving inhibits their full realization. It is often more convenient and economical to reacquire an object than to move it. How much less incentive is there for preserving and transporting goods in a culture where everyone can make what he needs from materials freely available in the forest. If equipment is expendable, it also is not normally lavishly made, so that the expertness provided by specialized artisans finds no market. This factor reinforces the small size of population concentrations in inhibiting the growth of occupational specialization. Since property ownership is an effective basis for social differentiation and the concentration of power, the absence of incentive for property accumulation helps to maintain social organization on a simple, unstratified level, largely dominated by kinship.

Environmental Determinism

The picture that emerges from this analysis shows a complex interrelationship between climate, agriculture and culture in the Amazonian rain forests. Agriculture must take account of climatic factors, and the culture must be adjusted to the requirements of the subsistence exploitation. This conclusion is supported not only by theoretical analysis of the processes promoting or inhibiting cultural advance, but by the fact that no advanced culture has developed in the Amazon basin or has been maintained there by a subsistence pattern dominated by slash-and-burn agriculture. In the sense of Webster's definition of determinism—namely, to set bounds to, and to give definite direction to—it seems acceptable to conclude that the Tropical Forest Type of culture characteristic of the Amazon Basin shows the effects of environmental determinism.

To the extent that a culture is a functional whole, this determinism may be felt even in aspects remote from the subsistence sphere. There is a difference between this concept and the earlier determinists' tracing of everything to environmental causes. The statement that thatch houses are built because of the abundance of thatching materials is easy to refute by pointing to wattle and daub or even stone as equally available. However, if thatch houses are associated with slash-and-burn agriculture, it can be argued that quickly made structures of short term utility represent the least expenditure of effort for the maximum in effective shelter, and are therefore a secondary reflection of an environmentally determined way of life. This is not to argue that all cultural traits can be traced to environmental causes, even secondarily removed. Certain types of human cultural activity place so little burden on subsistence that they are relatively free from its restraints. However, it is probable that a larger proportion than is generally suspected is the direct or indirect reflection of an environmental characteristic.

It can be shown that the environments of the world do not offer equal potential for human exploitation (Meggers, 1954). Reciprocally, all environments are not equally deterministic. In areas where the agricultural potential is absent or limited, the boundaries within which a cultural adaptation must be made are circumscribed. There is little latitude and successful alternative methods of exploitation are few. In areas where agricultural potential is naturally high or can with simple techniques be greatly increased, the boundaries are wide and environment is more permissive than deterministic in its action. In such situations, both greater range of cultural development and greater variety of result might be expected. It would be easy to express this difference by saying that where the environment is strongly deterministic (i.e., offers little latitude) a culture must remain simple, but where the environment is permissive it may remain simple or it may advance. However, the fact that all the areas of the world with great natural agricultural potential served as cradles of civilization suggests the environment plays an active rather than a passive role even when it is most indulgent.

The strong emphasis currently placed on man's influence on his environment (Heizer, 1955; Princeton Symposium, 1955) has tended to obscure those situations where man conforms rather than dominates. Changes wrought by hunters, gatherers and primitive slash-and-burn agriculturalists are comparable to those effected by birds, animals and other natural forces: all scatter seeds, selectively kill other creatures and make similar minor alterations in their habitat. Such modifications are inevitable by-products of remaining alive. However, man alone has evolved the capacity to alter his environment purposefully, on a large scale and in a permanent way, and the development of this capacity is a crucial factor in cultural evolution. To say that all human beings modify their environment is to lose sight of the fundamental difference between transporting a seed and flattening a mountain or extinguishing a forest. All cultures have not been equally successful in achieving this mastery, which is another way of saying that all environments are not equally malleable; modifications that some environments reward, others resist. Those that resist may not necessarily be less plastic, but only have their plasticity in directions that cross-cut rather than parallel human needs. In view of the diversity of climate and topography, it would be remarkable if man found all parts of the world equally congenial, equally easy to master, equally unresistant. In the Amazon basin he has conspicuously failed to make more than a fleeting mark, and denial of the environmental obstacles does not make this failure less real. Recognition of the deterministic quality of environment, on the other hand, provides one more tool for the solution of our ultimate problem—the understanding of how and why culture develops when, where and as it does.

Tropical Forest Agriculture in the Future

The recognition that there is a cause and effect relationship between environment and culture, far from being a defeatist doctrine, establishes a realistic basis for the evaluation of the potential of the Amazon Basin for future human exploitation. If any important alteration in culture depends on the eradication of the inhibiting aspects of slash-and-burn agriculture, then the problem is to find a means of retaining fields in more permanent agricultural production so that increased sedentariness and increased population concentration can be achieved. Keeping in mind the requirements of the standard climate, let us examine a few of the solutions that have been proposed.

One suggestion involves the use of alluvial land, whose fertility is renewed by the annual deposition of silt, and which provides the basis of agricultural production in many other parts of the world. A certain amount of native use of the low river banks exists in the Amazon Basin (Smith, 1954, pp. 96-7), but the pattern of exploitation is at present no more stable than that associated with slash-and-burn agriculture. Expansion of the flood plain usage has a number of drawbacks, some of which stem from the characteristics of the river. Although the Amazon is vast, its flood plain is not proportionately large. Survey has shown that it is typically narrower than that of the Mississippi below its junction with the Ohio River. The total area occupied by recently deposited alluvium amounts to only about 10% of the entire Amazon Basin (Marbut and Manifold, 1925, pp. 622 and 632) and most of this is subject to annual inundation. Furthermore, the flood plain is not continuous, but is subdivided by innumerable lakes and sloughs into isolated and irregularly shaped patches. Engineering attempts to consolidate these into larger units must contend with the river at flood, a mass of water that makes the raging Mississippi seem small and docile by comparison, and whose harnessing seems unlikely (Pendleton, 1950, pp. 120-1). Plans for expansion of this type of agriculture must also take into consideration the dietary requirements of the local population. A major factor limiting its aboriginal use is its unsuitability for growing manioc and other staple tropical root crops. Food habits are highly resistant to change and people often prefer to go hungry rather than eat something they do not consider fit for human consumption. It matters little that what they refuse may form a major part of the diet in another part of the world.

Preparing manioc for planting in the Brazilian Amazon. Photo from USOM.

A second solution that has been mentioned also raises the question of consumption. This takes cognizance of the fact that tree crops are ideally suited to the requirements of the tropical lowland climate. However, tropical tree crops do not figure prominently in world subsistence, and there seems to be no prospect of making bananas, for instance, a staple food on a large scale. The failure of plantation rubber in the Amazon Valley, furthermore, illustrates one of the undesirable factors encouraged by the standard climate, but not allowed full expression by the scattered distribution of species of plants in the natural vegetation. The continuously high temperature and humidity favors rapid multiplication and dispersal of diseases such as the one that wiped out plantation rubber in Brazil.

The absence of a dormant winter period of cold makes such invasions more difficult to combat than in the temperate zone, and the possibility that similar epi-
demics may defeat other attempts to develop plantation agriculture looms large.
That the problem is not physically insuperable is shown by promising results of
attempts to produce blight resistant strains of rubber plants. However, this development has taken several decades, and in the interim synthetic rubber has been
perfected so that there is little demand for the hard won solution.

A third possibility is the development of a synthetic substitute for humus that
will be resistant to breakdown at high temperatures, so that soil fertility can be
maintained with complete clearing of the land. This problem seems near solution
(Jacks, 1954, p. 113), but there is still the irregularity of the rainfall to contend
with and the problem of erosion control. When these are solved, the question remains as to what crops can be raised that will be in sufficient demand on the
world market to justify and repay the tremendous expense involved in achieving
their production on a large scale. For, when all is said and done, successful agricultural exploitation in the lowland tropics requires more than good will; it must
meet the hard test of competition in the world market.

What may we conclude, then, about environment and culture in the Amazon
Basin? First, the evidence suggests that environment and culture are not independent variables, but intimately related to one another. The climatic conditions
characteristic of this tropical region present well defined problems to agricultural
exploitation. To date, no better solution has been found than that developed by
the indigenous population, namely, slash-and-burn or shifting cultivation. This
type of food production has a conservational effect on soil and soil fertility,
which is desirable, but also exercises a conservative influence on the culture, keeping it in a relatively simple level of development. Just as attempts to alter the
agricultural pattern that do not recognize its environmental adjustment are
doomed to failure, so attempts to maintain a more highly developed type of culture on a subsistence base of slash-and-burn agriculture have not had permanent
success. The existence of these interrelationships indicates that efforts to understand how and why culture has developed to different levels of complexity in
various parts of the world must literally work from the ground up.

Recognition of determining factors in the environment places the Tropical
Forest Area of South America in a new perspective. Instead of being a backward
region, whose cultural development was retarded or stagnated by isolation, war-
fare or psychological barriers, we see it as an area in which the culture is in equilibrium with the environment, having made a remarkably efficient adjustment to
extremely difficult conditions for agricultural exploitation. The recognition of
this cause and effect relationship helps not only to understand the development
of culture in the Amazon Basin in the past, but opens the door to a more realistic
attack on the problem of improving the cultural potential of this area in the future.
If we accept the premise that the standard climate determines that agricultural
exploitation must have certain features, then man's problem is to find a solution
that fulfills these requirements and in addition meets the demands of modern

civilization. The recognition of the existence of environmental determinants shows us the direction in which we should look, but unfortunately only the future will tell whether or not a satisfactory solution can be found.

REFERENCES

Baerreis, David A. Review of *New Interpretations of Aboriginal American Culture History*. (75th Anniversary Volume of the Anthropological Society of Washington). *American Antiquity*, 21 (1956), 314–316.

Hardy, F. "Some Aspects of Cacao Soil Fertility in Trinidad," *Trop. Agriculture Trin.*, 13 (1936), 315–317.

Heizer, Robert F. "Primitive Man as an Ecologic Factor," *Kroeber Anthropological Society Papers*, 13 (1955), 1–31.

Jacks, Graham V. *Soil*. London: Thomas Nelson & Sons, Ltd., 1954.

Marbut, C. F., and C. B. Manifold. "The Topography of the Amazon Valley," *Geographical Review*, 15 (1925), 617–642.

Meggers, Betty J. "Environmental Limitation on the Development of Culture," *American Anthropologist*, 56 (1954), 801–824.

——————. "The Coming of Age of American Archeology," pp. 116–129 in *New Interpretations of Aboriginal American Culture History* (75th Anniversary Volume of the Anthropological Society of Washington). Washington, D.C.: the Society, 1955.

Milne, G. "Essays in Applied Pedology. I. Soil Type and Soil Management in Relation to Plantation Agriculture in East Usambara," *East Afr. Agric. J.*, July, 1937.

Mohr, E.C.J., and F. A. Van Baren. *Tropical Soils: a Critical Study of Soil Genesis as Related to Climate, Rock and Vegetation*. The Hague and Bandung, 1954.

Osborn, Fairfield. *The Limits of the Earth*. Boston: Little, Brown and Company, 1953.

Palerm, Angel. "The Agricultural Basis of Urban Civilization in Mesoamerica," *Irrigation Civilizations: a Comparative Study*. (Pan American Union Social Science Monographs.) 1 (1955), 28–42.

Pendleton, Robert L. "Agricultural and Forestry Potentialities of the Tropics," *Agronomy Journal*, 42 (1950), 115–123.

Richards, P. W. *The Tropical Rain Forest*. Cambridge, England: Cambridge University Press, 1952.

Smith, T. Lynn. *Brazil, People and Institutions*. Baton Rouge: Louisiana State University Press, 1954.

Stamp, L. Dudley. *Land for Tomorrow*. Bloomington: Indiana University Press, 1952.

Visher, Stephen S. "Tropical Climates from an Ecological Viewpoint," *Ecology*, 4 (1923), 1–10.

Walter, H. "Nährstoffgehalt des Bodens und natürliche Waldbestände," *Forstl. Wschr. Silva*, 24 (1936), 201–5, 209–13.

THEME OF PLANT
AND ANIMAL DESTRUCTION
IN ECONOMIC HISTORY

Carl O. Sauer

*The "discovery" of the environment which characterizes the close of the third
quarter of the twentieth century is undeniably bound up with the sudden high
visibility of offal. We are being inundated with chemical wastes, fertilizer concentrations, and pesticides. The environmentalists of the Seventies cannot be
mistaken for those idealists generally disparaged as "nature lovers."*

*Nor can the new environmentalists be confused with their immediate prede-
cessors, who were obsessed with forest destruction and soil erosion. The older
conservationists' discovery of the "dark obverse" to the primacy of man was not
a response to the stink of air or to chemical attacks on their bodies; they saw the
antiphonal signs in the land itself. Now the older generation has become a part of
history, along with its unheeded warning that the price of technical mastery was
the disruption of planetary processes.*

*Urban men suffering in a failing environment—both social and natural—are
not likely in their frenzy and frustration to care much about the long slow sweep
of geological and evolutionary events. Even the soil is beyond their concern.
More and more the sense of crisis diverts the mind from essential long-term
planetary operations. Perhaps this is the way the environment collapses: not in a
sublime cataclysm but in fixation on immediate problems. Has our economic
transition from an agricultural nation to an urban one given rise to an assumption that only farmers depend on the soil? By 1971 the subjects of the erosion
of topsoil and the loss of native plants and animals seemed almost to have vanished from debates on world survival.*

Our Zeitgeist is congenial to debate and to the planning of our future by resolution. Perhaps such a mood marks the beginning of a great era, but even though
we be far better social engineers than I think we are, it is still most important to
keep track of the present as to its position on the long graph of history, to see
where we stand on the trend curves of social change. We have neglected dreadfully,
in our impatience to get at universals, the "natural history" of man, which is also

Carl O. Sauer, "Theme of Plant and Animal Destruction in Economic History," Journal of
Farm Economics *20 (1938), 765–775. This article was originally presented as the presidential address at the Eighth Annual Meeting of the Social Science Research Conference of
the Pacific Coast.*

expressed as *die Weltgeschichte ist das Weltgericht*. Institutions and outlooks have their origin in time and place; they spread from one group to another; with lapse of time and shifts of place they undergo change; they meet competition and resistance. Origins, derivations, and survivals are the basic determinations of social dynamics. How much of social science have we that has meaning apart from relations of space and time? We are not metaphysicists, we know even the Logos only as a term in culture history. Today's triumph in social theory is tomorrow's footnote to culture history. The facts we dig up may find permanent place in human learning. The constructions we place upon them, if they survive, survive as data of history.

In social science interpreted as culture history there is a dominant geographic theme which deals with the growing mastery of man over his environment. Antiphonal thereto is the revenge of an outraged nature on man. It is possible to sketch the dynamics of human history in terms of this antithesis.

We have traced the beginning of our direct lineage back about 25,000 years, when *Homo sapiens* makes his appearance as an apparently finished product of evolution. More than half, perhaps two-thirds, of human history has passed before we come to the tremendous achievement of plant and animal domestication. This marks the major step forward by man in his use of nature. It is carried out for a long time without any disturbance in the relation of man to his environment. Though growing steadily in cultural grace and stature, man long remains in symbiotic balance.

Perhaps as far back as Neolithic time, the first ominous discordance develops. The dry interiors of the Old World from Cape Verde to Mongolia are today a far more meager and more difficult human habitat than was true in early Neolithic. We know that their deterioration is much greater than can be accounted for by climatic change. Under similar physical conditions, the New World steppes and deserts bear a varied and useful cover of vegetation, whereas the Old World dry lands show tremendous wastes of shifting sand and denuded rock surface. Moisture values are not at all minimal in some of the bleakest parts of the Sahara and Arabia, for instance. There are successful drought tolerant plants aplenty in the Old World. The inference, therefore, is that the discrepancy between vegetation and climate in the Old World is due to cultural influence. Specifically, ancient overgrazing by herding peoples is blamed for the bareness of much of the great interior of the Old World. The damage developed perhaps three or four thousand years ago. Lapse of time has brought no repair of this destruction. The dry lands of the center of the Old World are permanently and sadly diminished in their utility.

The next major destruction of habitat values is associated with the Mediterranean lands and is assigned to the latter days of Rome or to the disordered period immediately following. Here again we know that modern productivity and known condition of land at the beginning of the Christian era do not coincide. The upland landscapes of the Mediterranean are not in line with their geomorphologic situation. Bare rocks obtrude themselves on slopes where they do

not belong. Normal soil profiles are wanting. The vegetation shows many characteristics of regressions. Destructive exploitation has damaged seriously and permanently a great share of the lands about the Mediterranean. In spite of the lapse
of many centuries, we have no evidence of significant regeneration of resource,
but probably rather that of continued physical degeneration.

With these two major exceptions, we know of scarcely any record of destructive exploitation in all the span of human existence until we enter the period of
modern history, when transatlantic expansion of European commerce, peoples,
and governments, takes place. Then begins what may well be the tragic, rather
than the great, age of man. We have glorified this period in terms of a romantic
view of colonization and of the frontier. There is a dark obverse to the picture,
which we have regarded scarcely at all.

Much has been made of the disastrous impact of Spain on the New World.
The polemics of Las Casas were carried on by Spain's political rivals and his theme
of the Spanish destruction of the Indies lives on in popular misconceptions of the
Spanish colonies. The first half century, following the discovery, was indeed destructive. Then a desolation of the Indies by depopulation appeared imminent.
These expectations, however, were realized only in part, partly because the
severity of Old World epidemic diseases diminished and partly because of an increasingly effective governmental protection of native population and natural
resources. The Spanish government developed and applied principles of conservative stewardship, for which we find no parallels in other colonial countries at the
time.

In the late 18th Century the progressively and rapidly cumulative destructive
effects of European exploitation become marked. They are indeed an important
and integral part of the industrial and commercial revolution. In the space of a
century and a half—only two full life-times—more damage has been done to the
productive capacity of the world than in all of human history preceding. The previously characteristic manner of living within the means of an area, by use of its
actual "surplus," is replaced at this time by a reckless glutting of resource for
quick "profit." The early outstanding illustrations are the wearing out of Virginia
by tobacco planting and the effects of the China trade. The westward movement
of Virginians was conditioned largely by the destruction of the land through
tobacco. The development of the China trade via Cape Horn and the Chinese demand for furs and other animal products led quickly to a spoliation of pelagic
mammals from the Falkland and South Orkney Islands to the Bering Sea. The
opening of the 19th Century, with the initiation of upland cotton planting, set
our South definitely on its way to the permanent crisis in which it now is. In
1846 Charles Lyell described graphically the great gullies near Milledgeville,
Georgia, and stated that they had not been in existence twenty years before.[1] In
1864 George Marsh, distinguished jurist and forgotten scientist, wrote the first

[1] A Second Visit to the United States of North America, II (1849), 28–29.

description and analysis of the destruction of our basis of subsistence.[2] In the early nineties the washing out of western grazing lands became notable, a decade after the last great herd of buffalo was exterminated. At the outbreak of the World War the last passenger pigeon was dead and the last important stand of the white pine of the Great Lakes was being cut. In the present decade the top soil of the wheat fields of the Great Plains is being carried by dust storms as far as the Atlantic. These are a few notes toward a history of the modern age. The modern world has been built on a progressive using up of its real capital.

The apparent paradox results that the lands of recent settlement are the worn and worn-out parts of the world, not the lands of old civilization. The United States heads the list of exploited and dissipated land wealth. Physically, Latin America is in much better shape than our own country. The contrast in condition of surface, soil, and vegetation is apparent at the international border between the United States and Mexico. For a reconstruction of upland soil profiles and normal vegetation cover of California we must go to Lower California. Chihuahua shows us what New Mexico was like a generation ago. The other parts of the world that have been opened to commerce in the last century and a half show parallels to the destructive exploitation of the United States. South Africa and Australia are well aware of their serious problems of conservation. South Russia is now becoming an active field for the study of soil erosion. Increasingly troublesome dust storms are sweeping the pampas of the Argentine (which is not characteristically Latin American in its economy), whereas more primitive Uruguay still has its land capital almost undiminished.

California is still in reasonably good condition as to physical resource. On the debit side we can cite the advanced destruction of redwood stands which are not able to restock, the brief expectation of life of our oil fields, the abandonment of unnumbered hillside farms in the Coast Ranges and Sierras, the worn soils of the old barley and wheat districts on the west side of the Great Valley, and the general heavy loss of soil through overpasturing in hill lands. An excursion through the dairy country of Marin County, for instance, will show in almost every pasture serious evidences of soil stripping. Fortunately our primary agricultural resource lies in broad, smooth valleys that cannot wash away, and the safety of the mountain forest lands is assured in large measure by the great extent of public forest land. California has sufficiently serious problems of conservation, but they are not life and death matters as is the case in many states and they can be solved without desperate expedients.

The overdraft on the young colonial lands has serious implications for the older regions of the North Atlantic. These depend on a flow of raw materials which probably cannot be maintained indefinitely. They doubled their population in this period of extractive commerce. Their own balanced agriculture is balanced only because intensive animal husbandry is made possible by the supply

[2] Man and Nature; or Physical Geography as Modified by Human Action. London.

of overseas feedstuffs such as bran, meal, and oil cake, and of commercial fertilizer, which imply continued extraction of resources overseas. The whole occidental commercial system looks like a house of cards.

Some of the losses which the world has thus sustained are the following:

1) The extinction of species and varietal forms. The extinction of large predators and grazing animals may perhaps be checked off as failure to survive in environments altered by economic needs. This does not apply, however, to a long list of other animals. The seas and their margins have been wantonly devastated of many mammals and birds without compensating substitutions. The killing off of our sea otter, for instance, has simply removed from our coasts the most valuable of all fur-bearing animals, whose presence would not diminish in the least any fishing or other marine activity of man.

The removal of species, moreover, reduces the possible future range of utility of organic evolution. This may be illustrated by the domesticated plants. Primitive plant breeders developed a very wide range of useful plant forms from a great number of wild ancestors. Our commercial plants are only a small fraction of the primitive domesticated species and varieties. Commercial corn growing, for instance, utilizes only two subspecies of maize and of them only a small part of the range of genes that have been fixed by primitive plant breeding. Yet the qualities on which we have standardized for present-day commercial corn growing may not be the same that will be desired a century from now.

Meanwhile, the extension of commercial agriculture is causing a rapid extinction of the primitive domestic forms. Many species and far more numerous genetically fixed varieties have been lost irrevocably in late years. Of the great varietal range of upland cotton only a very few enter into the commercial forms. The extension of cotton in the United States, Egypt, and India has resulted in its disappearance over much of its primitive area of cultivation in Mexico and Central America, where the full range of varietal forms was developed. Yet these primitive forms hold by far the greater range of plant breeding possibilities for future, as yet unrecognized needs. Some years ago we secured from southern Mexico seeds of a type of cotton, called Acala, which made possible the current development of cotton-growing in the San Joaquin Valley. Had the plant explorer missed this particular spot in the State of Chiapas or come a few years later, we might not have a successful cotton industry in California. No one knows how many domestic varieties of cotton survive or have been lost.

In the case of most domesticated plants and animals the greatest range of genes lies in non-commercial varieties. Until the late extension of commercial production the age-long tendency of the native husbandry was to continue and expand this range. Primitive husbandry was engaged in enlarging steadily the evolutionary process. Commercial production has caused and is causing a steady and great shrinkage of forms, because suddenly restricted standards of utility are introduced. Unfortunately, immediate and prospective utility may be very different things. This applies equally in criticism of the effect of our commercial civilization on wild and on domesticated forms of life; in both cases we have drastically impoverished the results of biologic evolution.

2) The restriction of useful species. Often we have effected local rather than total extermination. There are still fur seals of one species on the Pribilov Islands, but we know no means of repopulating the many island rookeries from which they are gone. The eastern white pine is not extinct in the Great Lakes, but it has been removed entirely from large areas where it once flourished. Its reestablishment may involve uneconomic costs of seeding or planting, or may be economically impossible because their place has been taken by inferior species that filled in the cut-over pine lands. Also ecologic associations, once seriously disturbed, may be very difficult or impossible to reestablish. Overgrazing has caused sagebrush to increase hugely in the cooler steppes of the west, and the equally unpalatable yucca and sotol on the hot steppes of the Southwest. If overgrazing were stopped at once on such lands, an indefinitely long time would still be required for the grass to replace the useless brush even if no damage to the soil has been involved. Ecologic successions often are very slow and once a degenerative plant succession has set in a restoration is very uncertain. Fires, for instance, may reduce for a long period of years the utility of a site, by altering soil quality.

3) Soil destruction is the most widespread and most serious debit to be entered against colonial commercial exploitation. Only a brief statement is made of this dreadful problem, for which there is never an easy solution, and often none at all. Under natural conditions—given a specific climate, vegetation, relief, and rock structure—there will be a characteristic soil as to depth and profile for any given position on a slope. Soil and slope are in genetic relationship. Neither is static. Both naturally are changing very slowly. In the majority of cases the slope gradually grows less and the soil on it weathers more deeply, because it forms a bit more rapidly than it is removed at the surface. Soil formation and removal are either balanced, or formation exceeds removal, or, more rarely, removal exceeds formation. Soils develop slowly by weathering. The mechanically comminuted rock flour of our glacial lands has acquired approximately optimum characteristics in the course of about 25,000 years. This does not involve weathering that starts from solid rock but from the crushed materials of the glacial mill.

The Old World peasant agriculture, by placing animal products first, has maintained a condition of the soil in which cover crops and animal manuring have kept the soil profiles reasonably intact. Parts of our Northeast show similar maintenance of natural balance by culture.

Prevalently, however, we have not provided in our cropping systems any means for maintaining an adequate absorptive cover on the soil, as has the general farming-animal husbandry of northwest Europe and the northeastern United States. Row crops and bare fields in the off season have resulted in the diminution of absorptive organic matter in the soil. The surface has been exposed to the sluicing action of rains. Film after film is stripped by rain, diminishing steadily the depth of the top soil, which is normally the most productive and most absorptive part of the soil, in some soils the only part that is fertile. Full soil sections are almost impossible to find in many parts of the South. The red color of southern uplands and of their streams is derived from the subsoil which is now widely exposed at the surface. Southern farming in large measure is farming of the subsoil, made to yield crops only by liberal dosages of commercial fertilizer. The Ohio and Mississippi are becoming yellow rivers, which indicates that the yellow subsoils of that part of the country are now widely exposed. It is in the gradual and too commonly unnoticed loss of the true soil that the greatest damage is effected. The product of uncounted centuries of weathering and soil development is removed by a few decades of farming. The much publicized destruction of land by gullies is only the final dramatic removal of the surface. The major and irreparable damage is done beforehand.

This loss of the soil horizon by rain wash is not confined to steep slopes, nor is it even most characteristic of the hillier lands. It has reduced many gentle uplands of Piedmont and Coast Plain to briar-grown pastures. It has destroyed in the main the old Black Belt of Alabama for cotton growing, with minimal slopes, many of less than one degree. It is invading the Black Prairies of Texas and has made amazing headway in the past ten years on the smooth plains of central Oklahoma. All that is needed is a slope sufficient for muddy water to run. Even the great Corn Belt is becoming very badly frayed about the edges. The once rich counties of northwestern Missouri have been reduced to widespread distress. Serious damage is claimed for one-fourth of the area of Iowa.

Sheet and gully erosion, caused by June rains, on a South Dakota cornfield. Photo from United States Department of Agriculture.

Wind erosion is not bound to slope at all; it operates best in fact on level land. The baring by plow of the dry margins of our farming land has there resulted in rapidly accelerated wind transport whenever there is a marked dry spell.

These losses are in many cases irreparable. Engineering devices are in the main palliatives that reduce rate of loss, but which under extreme weather conditions may increase the risk. The saving of worn land requires more labor, more skill, and more capital than the farming of good land, and then is of uncertain results. If one could place the best farmers on the worst used land, some headway could be made. The cycle of degeneration is very, very difficult to break, and there is no salvation by any brilliant device.

To this summary review of some of the suicidal qualities of our current commercial economy the retort may be made that these are problems of the physical rather than of the social scientist. But the causative element is economic; only the pathologic processes released or involved are physical. The interaction of physical and social processes illustrates that the social scientist cannot restrict himself to social data alone. We cannot assume, as we are prone to do, an indefinitely elastic power of mind over matter. We are too much impressed by the large achievement of applied science. It suits our thinking to rely on a continuing adequacy on the part of the technician to meet our demands for production of goods. Our ideology is that of an indefinitely expanding universe, for we are the children of frontiersmen. We are prone to think of an ever ample world created for our benefit, by optimistic anthropocentric habits of thinking.

Let us admit for the moment that the supplying of the world with primary goods is simply a matter of the expenditure of energy, and that there is no lack of energy and no loss thereof. Even this optimistic assumption encounters the difficulty of the geography of population. The two billion inhabitants of the world have a very unequally localized distribution. It is going to be bitterly hard to arrest the declining capacity of many well populated areas, as for instance our Old South. It is going to be difficult to find the means of shifting large numbers of people from crisis areas into areas of opportunity. Our Resettlement Administration has no trouble in discovering crisis areas, but it had slight success in finding areas that were ready to receive immigrants in number. The current national attitudes toward foreign immigration (witness Canada, Australia, Latin America) proceed in large part from a lately hardened conclusion that the resident populations are adequate to make use of the national opportunities. This attitude has become well-nigh world wide. Decline in productivity is becoming characteristic of larger and larger areas. The generalization that the total productivity of the world might be maintained or raised gives no comfort to increasingly large numbers of people who are trapped in lands of fading economic resource. India may be suggested as an example, on a huge scale, of a country in which occidental political economy stimulated population growth and in which an overdraft on land resources will develop a major population crisis. What is to be done about such specific maldistributions?

Let us accept once more the view that the physical scientist will be able to make the requisite syntheses of matter to provide laboratory-made substitutes for the exhausted natural resources. There still remains the problem of the cost of distribution imposed by the geography of land and sea and climate. Freight must continue to be hauled and costs incurred in the movement of goods. The dream of the growth of staggeringly great laboratories to give us synthetic products will involve also great changes in comparative advantage of location. If we appeal to the sun for our salvation, we must build our visionary factories in deserts, along mountain fronts, and in great tidal bays, that fail to coincide with present distributions of dense and advanced populations, and which introduce additional charges in transport of power and goods.

The easy denial of our dilemma by referring it to the technologist is in large measure wishful thinking. It derives mainly from the successful, but relatively easy, experience in syntheses of hydrocarbons. We expect a lot from the laboratory technician when we ask him to supply the great range of bio-chemical compounds, for which we are recklessly destroying the natural plant and animal laboratories, or even if we only expect him to come near meeting their cost of production from natural sources. But we demand a good deal more. Actually, we ask that chemistry become alchemy, that it achieve the transmutation of elements. The classical but far from singular illustration of this is the problem of the phosphates. Phosphorus is well known to be a very minor constituent of the earth's crust, too rare as a primary mineral to be recoverable in quantity. The loss of accumulated and available phosphorus from soils by destructive cropping is enormous and forms one of our most acute problems. We are getting along by cleaning up the last of the guano deposits, which have been under exploitation for a century, and by using up the secondary mineral phosphates. The latter are highly localized fossil accumulations in certain ancient marine graveyards. These are pretty well known as to occurrence, and the reserves are not large. What then? The question, sharply asked by Cyril Hopkins, as to how civilization will survive the dissipation of this element critical to animal life, remains unanswered.

The doctrine of a passing frontier of nature replaced by a permanently and sufficiently expanding frontier of technology is a contemporary and characteristic expression of occidental culture—itself an historical geographic product. This "frontier" attitude has the recklessness of an optimism that has become habitual, but which is residual from the brave days when north European freebooters overran the world and put it under tribute. We have not yet learned the difference between yield and loot. We do not like to be economic realists.

WORLD AS VIEW
AND WORLD AS EVENT

Walter J. Ong, S.J.

Every element of American society expresses concern for the environment. That the issue should bear the imprimatur of the Establishment as well as that of the Counter-culture testifies to its universality and to the various possible ways of perceiving it.

Recognition that social and ecological problems have a common basis is more frequently expressed by the disenchanted young. Generally speaking, the older, more powerful, and more comfortable segments of society do not want to confront the revolutionary implications of the environmental issue. It is not easy to accept the painful consequences implied in the view that these are more than matters of policy and management, that war, social injustice, and environmental destruction spring from a common sickness. It is Bad News to those in power that the environmental crisis is not a result of failure in planning, organization, priorities, engineering, or allocation—these are symptoms, not causes—and that youth is insisting on the far more difficult task of changing our attitudes and sense of the world.

Such a radically-altered sense of things challenges more than convention, affluence, and the status quo, striking as it does at the roots of personal identity and social interaction. The issue is not conservation as against exploitation, but an experience of the natural world quite distinct from those two alternatives: a sense participatory rather than manipulative, a sense of the world as presence rather than object; a universe moving in vast cycles and rhythmic harmony instead of the serial stages of beginning, progression, decay, and end.

Such a cosmos has not been newly invented by the young and the disengaged—it has been rediscovered. It is an ancient form of intelligence, its tools dance and oration, song and history, its receptacles human memory rather than books or computers. It opens the senses more fully to nonvisual communication. It is a world where everything is vital and polemic, where ideas are experienced as part of one's being, where psychosis is expressed as frenzy and riot rather than as schizophrenia and delusion.

Walter J. Ong, S.J., "World as View and World as Event." Reproduced by permission of the American Anthropological Association from the American Anthropologist: Vol. 71, 1969, pp. 634–647. This paper was originally prepared for and presented at Wenner–Gren Foundation Burg Wartenstein Symposium no. 41, "World Views: Their Nature and Their Role in Culture," August 2–11, 1968.

*For so many born in the civilized world between 500 B.C. and 1950 A.D.,
such a world view is unfamiliar—even threatening. The dominant powers within
society are likely to respond to it violently, protecting not simply the* status quo
but their own sense of reality and personal orientation.

*What are the possible consequences of such a new–old world view? If this
different form of contact with the world, mediated by touch and sound as well
as by vision, should become a predominant mode, it would radically alter the
character of modern life in ways that cannot be foreseen (for there is no way to
"go back" to an earlier time). But it is closer to human and ecological reality, a
regeneration counteracting the tragic consequences of existential manipulation
and solitude, and of our war against nature and ourselves.*

As a concept and term, "world view" is useful but can at times be misleading. It
reflects the marked tendency of technologized man to think of actuality as
something essentially picturable and to think of knowledge itself by analogy with
visual activity to the exclusion, more or less, of the other senses. Oral or non-
writing cultures tend much more to cast up actuality in comprehensive auditory
terms, such as voice and harmony. Their "world" is not so markedly something
spread out before the eyes as a "view" but rather something dynamic and relatively unpredictable, an event-world rather than an object-world, highly personal,
overtly polemic, fostering sound-oriented, traditionalist personality structures
less interiorized and solipsistic than those of technologized man. The concept of
world view may not only interfere with the empathy necessary for understanding such cultures but may even be outmoded for our own, since modern technological man has entered into a new electronic compact with sound.

I

This paper is addressed to the question of whether there are differences in kind
between the problem of discovering the world view of a technologized contemporary society and the problem of discovering the world view of other societies.
It appears that there may well be such differences. Our very use of the concept
"world view" advertises the likelihood. This concept is of recent formation, part
of the equipment of the postromantic historicism that, somewhat surprisingly,
grows up with technological culture. Its ready applicability to all cultures of the
past or of the future can hardly be taken for granted.

Many cultures have never generated this particular concept. I suspect that no
early culture has. In ancient Greek and Latin, for example, there appears to be
no way to express "world view" short of circumlocutions so vast as to be surely
misleading. It is a waste of time to look for an entry under "world view" in most
English-Latin word lists, and if we try for something approximating it, such as
"outlook," we find that the best Latin equivalent offered is *spes*, hope, which is

refinable into *bona spes*, good hope, and *nulla spes*, no hope. This conjures up an atmosphere entirely different from that of "world view." We can grope for other terms—*conspectus*, perhaps, or *contemplatio* or even *animus, opinio, sententia de mundo, consilium de orbe terrarum,* or *propositum*—but they all prove remote from our twentieth-century concept. The curious Latin word *saeculum*, which yields our English "secular," comes closest of all perhaps in its sense of "spirit of the age," but it lacks sufficient subjective reference: one can hardly refer to the *saeculum* of an individual. Ancient Greek offers *theōria*, but that too lacks adequate subjectivity: it suggests either abstract theorizing or a public spectacle.

"World view" is an elusive term, but when we speak of someone's world view in any of its senses, we do not mean simply the world impressing itself upon his passive receptors, sensory or intellectual. A person does not receive a world view, but rather takes or adopts one. A world view is not a datum, a *donné*, but something the individual himself or the culture he shares partly constructs; it is the person's way of organizing from within himself the data of actuality coming from without and from within. A world view is a world interpretation. This makes it evidently a romantic or postromantic formulation that suggests Coleridge's idea of the imagination as giving form to material otherwise disorganized.

M. H. Abrams (1953) has shown that, by and large, preromantic concepts of man hold that the art he creates imitates or mirrors nature, whereas romantic and postromantic concepts hold that it throws light onto nature, interpreting the world. This romantic concept depends, as hinted above, on technology. The reason is that it implies a degree of control over nature unknown to early man, one achieved only by the growth of technological skills and physical sciences that accelerates so remarkably during the period running from the high Middle Ages through the Enlightenment. This growth in technological skills not only vastly enlarges technological control over the external world but also enables knowledge to expand at unprecedented rates through the development of writing (which needs technology for its materials) and of print, as well as through the increase of leisure time. For early man the world was something he could only participate in, not an object to be manipulated in his consciousness.

On the face of it, a concept so dated would appear probably more applicable to the cultures out of which it arose than to earlier cultures. Discovering a world view in cultures that talk of world views and in cultures that do not possess the framework for such a concept might well be undertakings differing in kind. I do not mean to suggest, however, that speaking of the world view of an early culture is illegitimate. It would be idiotic to rule that we may study a given culture only in terms the culture itself provides. That would freeze thought for good. Nevertheless, the limited distribution of the concept suggests that the term itself needs close study, especially when it is applied to cultures removed from those where it is current. Such study can become very complex, and I shall undertake it here in only a limited way, attending to some noetic implications of the term with relation to the conditions of knowledge storage and retrieval in contrasting cultures.

II

However we break it down or specify it, the term "world view" suggests some sort of major unifying perception, and it presents the unification as taking place in a visual field. "View" implies sight, directly or analogously. The concept is of a piece with many other spatially grounded metaphors we commonly avail ourselves of in treating perception and understanding: "areas" of study, "field" of investigation, "levels" of abstraction, "fronts" of knowledge, "waves" of interest, "movements" of ideas, "trains" of thought, "grounds" for analysis, and so on indefinitely. We are used to these conceptualizations by now and have found them productive, so we often forget how thoroughly metaphorical they are and how remote from actual cognitive experience. Studying anthropology or anything else gives one no experience at all of moving one's mind over an "area." We become aware in various ways of changed interests, but we do not directly experience a change of interest as a wave, whether we take a wave as visually or as kinesthetically perceived. Nor does anyone ever directly experience ideas of his as taking part in a movement. Ideas are neither moving nor static; they simply are not that sort of thing, although we can consider them analogously as one or the other.

These metaphors and others like them are useful and beyond a doubt worth keeping. Many of them have roots deep in the past. There is nothing new in taking the physical universe as somehow a model for conscious intellectual activity. The macrocosm-microcosm notion is an old one and an inevitable one. But the metaphors just noted here, including that of "world view" itself, present both macrocosm and microcosm in a distinctive fashion. In a way characteristic of modern technologized man, they take the physical world to which they relate consciousness as something visually perceived. The senses other than sight do not count here or count very little, with the exception of touch insofar as it is allied to vision in presenting extension and insofar as visual perception itself perhaps never occurs without some admixture of the tactile imagination. (Touch, as both medieval scholastics and modern psychoanalysts remind us, is the most basic sense, lying at the root of all the others.) But touch enters into these concepts of the physical world unobtrusively or even subconsciously, however really and inevitably. Essentially, when modern technological man thinks of the physical universe, he thinks of something he can visualize either in itself or in terms of visual measurements and charts. The universe for us is essentially something you can draw a picture of.

The history of this assertive and on the whole marvelously productive visualism is, in the main, fairly well known. Habitual resort to visual models or analogues is of a piece with the modern stress on "observation" (a concept referring essentially to sight; you cannot "observe" a sound or a smell but only listen to the one and sniff the other). Visualism grows to its present strength under the aegis of modern science, particularly with the application of mathematics to physics from the seventeenth century on. It has, of course, earlier roots too, which can be discerned in ancient Greece but grew much sturdier in the European Middle Ages. Elsewhere (1958) I have tried to show in some detail how medieval scholasticism, most particularly arts scholasticism rather than theological scholasticism, fostered quantification and visualization as nothing before ever had, and how scholasticism gave birth to the movement (there we are again!) known in the sixteenth and seventeenth centuries as Ramism, after Peter Ramus (1515-1572). Ramism gratified the growing desire for quantified, diagrammatic treatment of actuality. But the Ramist kind of quantification is related to actuality only obliquely at best. Instead of applying measurements to carefully observed physical phenomena, Ramists set up diagrammatic arrangements of knowledge itself in dichotomized divisions and subdivisions ad infinitum.

Nevertheless, despite the aberrancy of Ramist efforts, history from Ramus's time on shows that thinking of the universe as essentially something seen (and to a degree touched) is highly rewarding in the physical sciences. Whether it is equally rewarding in philosophy or anthropology is a question seldom, if ever, raised. Whatever the case with anthropologists, most philosophers from Locke through Kant and many down to the present day not only accept the physical universe in exclusively visualist terms but also treat understanding itself by analogy with visual knowledge to the virtual exclusion of analogies with any of the other senses (Ong 1967:66-74). The success of vision (observation) and quantification in the physical sciences has charmed the modern mind into considering its own activity as essentially like that of sight. Until the past decade or so, there was little awareness that there are any other options. Hence we are likely to take for granted that the presence of the world to man or of man to the world should be thought of in terms of a world "view."

Recent studies of oral or preliterate cultures, however, have brought out the fact that other options are indeed open. In particular, the work of psychologists and psychiatrists reported by J. C. Carothers (1959), Marvin Opler (1956), and others whom they cite, provides evidence of "auditory synthesis." There are cultures that encourage their members to think of the universe less than we do as something picturable and more than we do as a harmony, something held together as a sound or group of sounds, a symphony, is held together. Modern theological and biblical studies have made it a commonplace that the ancient Hebrew concept of knowing expressed by *yadha'* takes knowing as something like hearing—personal and communal—whereas the ancient Greek concept expressed in *gignōskō* takes knowing as something like seeing—impersonal, fractioning, and analytic. Leo Spitzer (1963) showed, however, that the ancient Greeks also quite commonly thought of the world as a harmony, something heard rather than something seen; the universe was something one responded to, as to a voice, not something merely to be inspected. So did many other early peoples. We are seldom aware of how strongly audile the sensibility of early man could be or that of modern nontechnologized man often still is. Of the many rural cosmological concepts well known in nontechnologized cultures, that of the harmony of the spheres is perhaps the only one generally familiar today to technologized man, even in learned circles.

Of course, the physical universe is both seen and heard and is touched, smelled, and tasted as well. But each of the various senses has an economy of its own, and each impinges on the human life world differently, particularly with regard to awareness of interiority and exteriority.

> Sight presents surfaces (it is keyed to *reflected* light: light coming directly from its source, such as fire, an electric lamp, the sun, rather dazzles and blinds us); smell suggests presences or absences (its association with memory is a commonplace) and is connected with the attractiveness (especially sexual) or repulsiveness of bodies which one is near or which one is seeking ("I smelled him out"): smell is a come-or-go signal. Hence "It stinks" expresses maximum rejection or repulsion: do not even go near—the farther away the better—do not even think about it. Taste above all discriminates, distinguishing what is agreeable or disagreeable for intussusception by one's own organism (food) or psyche (aesthetic taste). . . .
>
> Sound, on the other hand, reveals the interior without the necessity of physical invasion. Thus we tap a wall to discover where it is hollow inside, or we ring a silver-colored coin to discover whether it is perhaps lead inside. To discover such things by sight, we should have to open what we examine, making the inside the outside, destroying its interiority as such. Sound reveals interiors because its nature is determined by interior relationships. The sound of a violin is determined by the interior structure of its strings, of its bridge, and of the wood in its soundboard, by the shape of the interior cavity in the body of the violin, and other interior conditions. Filled with concrete or water, the violin would sound different [Ong 1967:117–118].

Touch attests "objective reality" in the sense of something outside that is not myself.

> Dr. Johnson made this clear when he undertook to refute Berkeley tactilely— once one felt contact with a stone one kicked with one's foot, idealism, Johnson thought or pretended, was doomed. His state of mind persists and no doubt will always persist. "Real as this stone," we say, feeling ourselves clutching it with our fist, in actuality or in imagination. By touch we assure ourselves that the stone is there, is objective, for, more than other senses, touch indeed attests to existence which is objective in the sense of real-but-not-me.
>
> And yet, by the very fact that it attests the not-me more than any other sense, touch involves my own subjectivity more than any other sense. When I feel this objective something "out there," beyond the bounds of my body, I also at the same instant experience my own self. I feel other and self simultaneously [Ong 1967:169-170].

III

These examples may remind us of "worlds" we often neglect in our scientific commitment to vision. What was the "world" like to a culture that took actuality in more auditory, less visual, terms than those to which we are accustomed? Relying for support on a much longer treatment of my own (1967) that in turn draws upon the work of many others, I shall attempt a summary listing and description of four salient features. (When I say "salient features," that is, features that "stand out" or, more accurately, "leap out," I betray my own visual or visual-tactile bias. A more aural expression might be "assertive qualities.")

Dynamism

The world of a dominantly oral or oral-aural culture is dynamic and relatively unpredictable, an event-world rather than an object-world. What we are getting at here can be understood in terms of the nature of sound as compared to other sensory perceptions. Sound is of itself necessarily an event in the way in which the object of no other sense is.

> Sound signals the present use of power, since sound must be in active production in order to exist at all. Other things one senses may reveal actual present use of power, as when one watches the drive of a piston in an engine. But vision can reveal also mere quiescence, as in a still-life display. Sound can induce repose, but it never reveals quiescence. It tells us that something is going on. In his *Sound and Symbol*, writing on the effect of music, Victor Zuckerkandl notes that, by contrast with vision and touch, hearing registers force, the dynamic. This can be perceived on other grounds, too. A primitive hunter can see, feel, smell, and taste an elephant when the animal is quite dead. If he hears an elephant trumpeting or merely shuffling his feet, he had better watch out. Something is going on. Force is operating [Ong 1967:112].

Moreover, voice is for man the paradigm of all sound, and to it all sound tends to be assimilated. We hear the voice of the sea, the voice of thunder, the voice of the wind, and an engine's cough. This means that the dynamism inherent in all sound tends to be assimilated to the dynamism of the human being, an unpredictable and potentially dangerous dynamism because a human being is a free, unpredictable agent.

Traditionalism

The world of a dominantly oral or oral-aural culture is traditional. Its traditionalism is closely related to the problems of acquiring, storing, and retrieving knowledge in a voice-and-ear or oral-aural economy of thought and communication, operating without the use of records.

Recent studies, many involving massive recordings of oral performances, have revealed the noetic processes or oral cultures as never before. We can only summarize here some relevant points in the new discoveries, points that will be found explicated in more detail in lengthier works (Lord 1960, Havelock 1963, Yates 1966, Ong 1958 and 1967, Chadwick and Chadwick 1932–1940).

An oral culture, we must remind ourselves, is one in which nothing can be "looked up." Words are sounds, and sounds exist only as they are going out of existence. I cannot stop a word as I can a moving picture in order to fix my attention on an immobilized part of it. There are no immobilized parts of sound. If I stop sound, I have only its opposite, silence. An oral culture is deeply aware of this evanescent quality of words. Homer expresses this awareness when he sings of "winged words." At the same time, oral cultures consider words more powerful than we do, probably in the last analysis because whereas we interpret movement as instability, they are keenly aware of the moment of sound as signaling use of power. Words fly, which means that they not only move but do so energetically.

How to keep knowledge stable is thus a major problem in an oral culture. We know now the general lines along which the problem is solved. Basically, the solution is to standardize utterance, making it highly "traditional." By contrast with verbal expression, which is composed in writing, oral verbalization is thematic and formulary, filled with epithets (standard, expected qualifiers), prolific of heroic figures (fixed, "heavy," more or less symbolic individuals, predictable in performance, almost entirely free of any character development). When writing takes over from oral verbalization but before writing fully develops its own economy of noetics and expression, these heroic figures become quasi-scientific abstract types (writing makes science possible). Such are the virtues and vices of medieval morality plays or the related figures of Ben Jonson's drama and eighteenth-century comedy. Stability of character helps anchor knowledge for retrieval in an oral world. If Nestor is always wise, around a story about Nestor can be clustered what Greeks knew and could later treat more scientifically as wisdom. So wily Odysseus serves to store and retrieve what was known about wiliness, Achilles what was known about bravery, and so on. In the interest of stabilizing knowledge, oral cultures make a great deal of commonplace statements enshrined in popular adages or proverbs and of apothegms attributed to famous persons. Oral folk want to and need to hear the treasured utterances of the past. "Tell us something from the tales of old." Highest marks are given to superlatively skilled performance of the expected, and there is little if any interest in "originality" or "creativity," such as grew up with the late typographical phenomenon called the Romantic age.

Accustomed as we are to noetic conditions, where virtually everything that men have ever known can be "looked up" on a designated page in a locatable book on a specified shelf in a library, we forget how natural and inevitable the oral exploitation of commonplace material is. In a society in which articulate utterances or statements about a subject cannot be "looked up" (although visual aides-memoire such as wampum belts or winter-count pictures may be used), even the expected is not so expected as it is for us. It is on hand only when it is being recited. And one needs to be assured that it can be retrieved by recitation on demand. Under such conditions the role of a poet in, for example, preliterate Homeric Greece, as Eric Havelock (1963) has shown in beautiful detail, is not simply that of an entertainer. The poet is also a recaller and a repeater; if he and others like him were not around, what knowledge the society has would simply disappear. The orator participates in the role of the poet. He must likewise deal in the commonplace, the expected, the already known, as well as in the particular issues with which individual forensic or deliberative problems engage him.

We are now aware of just how conservative, just how fixed, just how essentially repetitive the poetry and the oratory of an oral society are. Homer, recent studies (Lord 1960 and others cited there) have shown, is made up almost completely of cliches. Everyone is familiar with his "wine-dark sea" and "rosy-fingered dawn." These are among the most heavily worked epithets. But close tabulatory study of the text shows that virtually every image in Homer, line after line, is of that sort. Epic poets sing of standard themes—the arrival of the messenger, the summoning of the council, the feast, the arming of the hero, the description of the hero's shield or sword or other armor, the journey, the challenge, the combat, the despoiling of the vanquished foe, and so on. And they sing of those themes in formulas or formulaic elements that they have accumulated by the thousands. A horse, to fabricate an English example that makes the point clear, is a "coal-black steed," a "roan-red steed," a "snow-white steed," a "fast gray mare," a "dapple-gray mount" (one extra syllable), a "dapple-gray stallion" (two extra syllables), and so on. If a rider needs a horse, the singer has a number of options he can trot out of his memory, all metrically harnessed and ready to go. And so with everything else he deals in.

That is why, as Albert B. Lord (1960), carrying on Milman Parry's work, found with oral epic singers of modern Yugoslavia, a singer can repeat an epic of an hour's duration after hearing it only once. Essentially all the singers have the same thematic and formulaic equipment—although each will have his own peculiarities in his management of it—and it is simply a matter of putting the equipment to work on a new set of characters and situations. (Of course, even today all narration is always thematic, including the most sophisticated kind of present-day historiography, for the only way to cut verbally into the unbroken web of history is to lift out certain themes; but the themes of the oral epic are much more fixed and limited in number than those of today's writers.)

Memory in an oral noetic economy is never verbatim on any appreciable scale. Lord (1960) has shown this as an indisputable fact in the case of the prodigiously skilled memory of the Yugoslavian epic singers; recordings show that they never sing any epic exactly the same way twice, despite their protestations (also recorded) that they do. I have reviewed elsewhere (1967) the evidence—or, better, the utter lack of it—that leads us to believe that no oral culture in the world achieves verbatim memory for lengthy passages of anything. But oral memory is nevertheless tenacious and accurate; it is locked in the themes and formulas. And it is extensive. Innocent hearers from chirographic and typographic cultures, who themselves generally memorize verbatim from texts, are likely to think that a person capable of reciting ex tempore thousands of lines in a highly complex meter must have memorized the material word for word. The fact is that such persons have in their store of expressions thousands upon thousands of phrases that fit into the standard metrical pattern. They are "rhapsodizers" or "stitchers," as the Greeks called them (*rhaptein*, 'to sew together,' from which *rhapsōidein* derives). It is significant that this kind of composition features complex meters but not rhyme, which would be much more unmanageable.

Even today the "feel" of an oral tradition for unchanging themes and formulas is still accessible to the post-typographic man who is familiar with the telling of fairy stories to children. Here there is no question of an original author or of originality or of telling the story each time in exactly the same words. But the story remains in its basic elements quite stable, and the audience expects the story as a whole and its formulary elements to be the same each time it is told. Anyone who in repeating the story of *The Three Little Pigs* to a youthful audience varies the number from three to four or seven will immediately meet with resistance from his hearers. And formulas, once uttered, are sacrosanct. I myself was pulled up by a five-year old some years ago for saying, "He huffed and he puffed, and he huffed and he puffed" instead of the expected, "He huffed and he puffed, and he puffed and he huffed."

Oratory, the other great oral art form, remained an oral improvisation or rhapsodizing ("stitching") long after the appearance of writing (Ong 1967). Cicero wrote his orations only after he had delivered them, that is, performed them. Oratory as an oral form proceeded in much the same fashion as epic, exploiting the set commonplaces or *loci communes* relentlessly, such as Cicero's "O tempora! O mores!" which was his "things-are-going-to-pot" bit, and other comparable prefabricated purple patches on dishonesty, valor, a dark night, a long time, and so on. Traffic in the commonplaces persisted as oral residue through the age of Shakespeare (who is quotable because he is made up of quotations tooled and retooled and given their final resonance by his master voice) and pretty strongly into the nineteenth century. It endures in some political oratory even today, particularly in nontechnologized cultures, where "capitalist warmongers," "colonialism," and similar themes, whatever their validity, are repeated with a persistence nauseating to technologized man but completely in accord with the older oral noetic patterns.

The noetic procedures illustrated by epic and oratory extend through the entire economy of a completely oral culture, as Havelock (1963) has pointed out. Oral Homeric Greece contrasts here with Lord's modern Yugoslavia, where oral epic poets constitute only a subculture in a society administered by literates—and a dwindling subculture, as Lord notes (1960), since growing literacy is destroying it. An oral poet must be illiterate or he will take to matching written or printed texts, thereby destroying the entire oral economy of performance. In contrast to modern Yugoslavia, Homer's Greece not only included a population of illiterate, highly skilled epic singers but also was administered from top to bottom by illiterates. In such a society the stitching or weaving of thematic and formulary elements that the epic singers practiced was a skill needed by public officials too, although not to the same specialized degree. If an official wanted to get a substantial message from Ithaca to Argos, he would have to cast it up in some mnemonic form or an illiterate messenger would never be able to deliver it.

The fixed-formula economy of an oral culture of course governs not only what it can repeat but also what it can know. Man knows what he can recall—all else is so ephemeral as to be negligible. In an oral culture this means that he knows what is cast in fixed thematic and formulary patterns. Anything else will seem unreal, nonknowledge, reprehensible, and dangerous. This is the noetic foundation for the traditionalism stemming from oral cultures. What is not traditional—cast in recognized themes and formulas—is dangerous because it is slippery and unmanageable. Oral-aural man does not like the nontraditional because, beyond his limited means of control, it advertises the tenuousness of his hold on actuality. Only when recordkeeping, first by chirography and then much more effectively by print, anchored knowledge in space for facile visual retrieval could traditionalism yield to a more flexible relationship to the world and a more flexible understanding of what the world is.

Polemicism

The world of a dominantly oral-aural culture is highly personal and polemic, at least in part because of its orality. Although this does not mean that polemic qualities in early cultures cannot also be related to other features besides orality, it is not entirely impossible that all the other features in some way or other relate significantly to orality, making it the major component in a complex of causes.

Without records, oral cultures have quite limited means of storing knowledge by categorization in what we may call scientific or highly abstract fashion. The development of bodies of knowledge of the sort we call arts and sciences has to wait on the advent of writing. Although it is fortunately out of date to say that primitive man has no idea of causality, it is true that complex chains of causality elude him. A is caused by B, B by C, and C by D, but D happens because Zeus was peeved at Athena. This means, in effect, "I pass." When divine causality is later analyzed in a sophisticated Christian tradition, it is no help at all in accounting physically for physical phenomena. It operates at another level.

The larger conceptual and verbal structures in which oral-aural man stores what he knows consist in great part of stories that turn on human action and on the interaction of man and man. Thus the *Iliad* and the *Odyssey* function not merely as entertaining stories but also as encyclopedias to an extent we often fail to appreciate . The list of the ships in the *Iliad* (ii. 494–875) is probably the closest thing to a national directory that an oral culture could produce. Where else would such material be verbalized? Similarly, the description of shipbuilding in the *Odyssey* (v. 225–261), when Odysseus is getting away from Circe, is the closest thing to a shipbuilding manual that an oral culture would know. Where else in a culture without writing would the method of building a ship be articulated? Perhaps in an oration, but orations were constructed in much the same way that epic poems were. What we find in Homer or a shipbuilding manual today would hardly be recited by a shipwright who learned and taught his trade by an apprentice system.

Whether in an epic narrative or in an oration built around some expected personal response, factual material and even technical description thus was stored and retrieved by being built into the human life world. Objects and objective fact did not inhabit an isolated section of actuality purportedly altogether screened off from contact with human "subjectivity" or personal relevance, as they do for modern technologized man. Everything was part of human activity, more or less objective and subjective simultaneously.

By the same token, in one way or another everything was caught up in the polemic of the human life struggle. The action of the heroic figures generated in an oral economy of narration would naturally at root consist of a battle between forces of good and evil. When so much of the lore of a culture was retained through narrative tales or songs about great heroes, even what would otherwise be completely neutral material thus acquired a moral flavor by association with the polemic or *agonia* of the hero and his adversaries. The entire world thereby tended to be polarized in terms of "good guys" and "bad guys" and later in terms of abstract personifications of virtues and vices (at least in Western European cultures around the Middle Ages, when writing was encouraging abstraction but had not yet crushed dominantly oral structures). In the highly moral climate of heroic song the *Iliad's* catalogue of ships is thus not merely a national directory, but, from the technically rhetorical point of view, it is also an encomium or "praise" of the Greeks: the Greek leaders and their followers are "good guys." Learning itself takes place in an agonistic setting under these oral-aural conditions. Puberty rites of early societies correspond in many ways to academic education in more developed cultures. Through puberty rites the young men are initiated into the lore of the tribe, its myths and intellectual heritage, as well as into its various skills. In this lore objective fact and man's subjective world interpenetrate. In the process of learning the youths are often subjected to excruciating physical torment, which gives their new knowledge its requisite agonistic tone.

By an extension of oral practices into literate society and even for a while into early typographical society, the agonistic element in learning is perpetuated through the arts of rhetoric and dialectic, which governed all academic practice from antiquity through the Renaissance. During that period no one was ever formally taught neutral objectivity, although many doubtless did achieve it in their own way. A scholar was taught to defend a stand he had taken or to attack the stand of another; rhetorical performance and dialectical debate governed all subjects. Truth was a human possession, to be defended as one's own life. This long persistence of agonistic frames of reference suggests how thoroughly polemic had been oral man's life world.

More could be said about the polemic frame of mind and its connection with an economy of scarcity, with the linguistic situation that fragmented most of mankind into small groups hostile to outsiders, with the common acceptance of war as the permanent state of human existence, with the incredibly harsh punishments, including execution even for minor offenses, found in early conquest states and some other early societies, including the residually oral societies of medieval and Renaissance Europe. But enough has been retailed here from the more substantial studies to give some indication of the noetic roots of polemic in oral cultures.

It was against the personal world inherited from preliterate Greece that Plato's philosophy took form, as Havelock (1963) has circumstantially shown. Plato's expulsion of the poets from his Republic and his touting of the "ideas" are the two sides of the same coin. His expulsion of the poets was his rejection of the old *paideia*, in which learning was basically oral, only slightly modified by writing; the *Iliad* and *Odyssey* were learned from a written text. The pupil was made to identify with heroic figures in a life world in which all things, even objective fact, were caught up. Plato's ideas launched the new world, the opposite of the old, which his attack on the poets proscribed. The old world had made much of man's activities and of human struggle as the focus or axis of all reality. Where the old world had been warm and human, Plato's "ideas" or "forms" (Greek *idea*, 'outline': a concept based on visual perception) were cold and abstract; where the old world had been mobile, event-full, visualized as narrative is often visualized, but not visualized in explicatory, analytic fashion. The vision of narrative was a swirl of exciting activity. In contrast, Plato's new ideas were motionless, ahistorical; where the old view had held all knowledge in a concrete human setting, the new traced everything to the abstract, the other-worldly, the totally objective, the fixed, modeled on an immobile figure visualized on a motionless field.

Structuring of Personality

In oral cultures the external world sets up and impinges on personality structures quite different from our own. The clinical studies reported by Carothers (1959) and Opler (1956) correlate definite psychological or personality structures with differences between illiteracy (studied pretty well across the globe) and literacy (as represented only by alphabetic writing, not character writing such as Chinese, which might produce a third, intermediate personality structure). The difference in psychological structures can be summarized by noting that in oral cultures schizophrenia virtually never manifests itself by delusional systematization, that is, by systematic day dreaming, by constructing a private, imaginary, unreal world in which one's problems are solved or non-existent. When subject to the kind of strain that produces schizoid behavior, the illiterate from an oral culture (illiterates from literate cultures are not quite total illiterates, for they experience the effects of literacy vicariously) reacts, too, by losing contact with actuality. But his typical pattern is an outbreak of intense anxiety and hostility and psychic disorganization that shows itself in extreme violence toward others and sometimes toward himself; Carothers attributes the pattern to a lack of ego defences due to tribal reliance on the group. The outbreak of anxiety and hostility is rioting, which is a regular phenomenon in many oral cultures and which is represented by the ancient Scandinavian warrior who goes berserk or the southeast Asian warrior who runs amok as well as by more recent Congolese rioters, whose behavior is interpreted by their own culture as regrettable but inevitable. The absence of schizophrenic delusional systematization appears to be the correlative of the individual's inability to isolate himself and his thought processes from the group, from the tribe, in the ways that become possible for the first time with reading. (The shift to reading, however, does not make withdrawal the only recourse of schizophrenics: in literates, too, violence can occur, perhaps as a more primitive response.) Just as physical personal privacy is at best a rare luxury in oral, tribal cultures, so psychological withdrawal is infrequent or even impossible in such cultures. Thought is not advanced by Aristotles or Einsteins or other individual discoverers but rather moves ahead with glacial slowness; everyone must advance together. We must remind ourselves that in an oral culture there is no private study. Learning is communal, unless it is achieved at the hands of that most dangerous and worst of teachers, raw experience.

IV

Script and print, with all that they entail, have transformed the oral world into the one we know today—or at least into the one we have known up to the past few years. Script, and particularly the alphabet, converted the dynamic event-world in which oral-aural man stored his knowledge into a world of static visual record. Many, perhaps even all, primitive peoples make much of sight, but the alphabet warped sound itself into a visual mold. The alphabet triumphed only slowly and never entirely, but inexorably. Print, by locking words into the same place in thousands of copies of a book and thereby making indexing and retrieving information possible to a degree utterly unknown in pretypographic manuscript culture, consolidated the work of the alphabet in reducing evanescent sound to the repose of space.

The conversion from totally oral to largely visualized vocalization took a long time, though its success was inevitable. Three thousand years and more after the invention of the first script (around 3500 B.C.) and a thousand years after the invention of the alphabet (around 1500 B.C.), classical antiquity remained largely oral. Its modes of composition were still largely based on the commonplaces and the oration, even in genres such as historiography. Its stance was polemic, its educational goal the training of the *rhetor*, the *orator*, the public speaker, outfitting him for verbal combat. The Middle Ages were far more textually oriented than antiquity and yet by our standards still impossibly oral. Their universities applied themselves to texts as man never had before, and yet the testing of

intellectual achievement was never by writing but always by oral *agonia* or dialectical debate. Even the Renaissance, which culminated the medieval drive
toward the written word by producing the printing press and modern textual
scholarship, still felt itself committed in principle and to a surprising degree in
actuality to the oratorical culture of classical antiquity. As I have undertaken to
spell out in great detail (1967), all Western culture remained significantly oral
until well into the Romantic age, only slowly relaxing its hold on the traditionalism and the polemicism marking oral society and personality structure.

V

In the light of the foregoing explanation, which is uncomfortably sketchy but
cannot be enlarged on here, we can reflect on the applicability of the concept of
world view to earlier cultures. Is an oral world unduly distorted by having applied
to it the concept of "view"? Are the very differences that mark it off from our
own thereby obscured? The visual synthesis the concept endorses certainly makes
the concept congenial to the psyche developed in a context of writing and print
and technological design. We take very readily to synthesizing "world" as some
kind of picture. But does this very type of synthesis somehow vitiate what we
make of earlier man's life world?

Perhaps we cannot do otherwise. Freudians have long made the point that for
thought and civilization itself to advance, man must minimize the proximity
senses of touch, taste, and smell and maximize the senses of hearing and sight.
The latter are more abstract in that they report on objects that can be and to a
degree must be at a greater distance from the perceiver. Touch requires contact,
which the eyeball cannot tolerate. Thus hearing and sight keep the individual
and the object of perception nicely distinct. (Touch includes a perception of
self-as-touching far more than hearing includes a sense of the self-as-hearing or
sight a sense of the self-as-seeing.) Of the two, sight is the more abstract and thus
the more "objective." The latter-day history of civilization has entailed a marked
movement from the aural to the visual world sense.

Specialization in visually based concepts thus appears to be a sign of progress
because they afford preferred information of a sort otherwise unavailable. It does
not make much sense to say that we should not examine an oral culture in terms
of our concept of a world view because an oral culture tended to synthesize less
in terms of view and more in aural terms than we do. For the same reason, oral
culture was in fact quite incapable of analyzing itself or anything else in the ways
that have become feasible and even mandatory for us.

Nevertheless, we can ask whether we are not too exclusively and unreflectively
exploiting visual models today to the neglect of analogs from the other senses.
Insofar as understanding of the life world of a given culture requires participation
in it, or a kind of empathy for it, the hypervisualism of our sensorium may to a

degree disqualify us for understanding whatever unity an earlier culture may have known in its relationship to actuality.

VI

Finally, our hypervisualism may already be outmoded. It may hinder our understanding of our own life world as it is reorganizing itself today and for the immediate future. If it is true, as I have suggested elsewhere (1967; see also others there cited), that we are moving into a new era of sound, we can ask ourselves whether the term "world view" alone is adequate to conceptualize the kind of unification man of coming generations will experience or undertake to realize. The new era into which we have already entered is marked by an unprecedented augmentation of sound-communication devices. We live each succeeding day in an increasingly oral world. Telephone supplements letter-writing, radio makes voice present all over the world simultaneously, television (much more an aural device than its name suggests) does the same, rapid transportation has multiplied personal confrontation in conventions, discussion groups, and assemblies of all sorts. Sonar is even used to catch fish. As sound gains, in certain ways sight is downgraded. With radio telescopes and interplanetary television mediated through codes of binary numbers, the use of all kinds of complex nonvisual probes in physical and chemical analysis, and other similar developments, the direct use of sight is on the wane in science. Our oralism profoundly differs from that of pre-literate man, for it is programmed by means that include writing and print. But at the same time we are often more effectively oral than early man, who could not make an individual's voice heard in every quarter of the globe simultaneously.

How far does our new oralism make our culture like that of early oral-aural man, man before the advent of writing? Marshall McLuhan's statement that we live in a "global village" has become a commonplace. But it is a gnomic and paradoxical commonplace. For what is global cannot be a village, with the village's feeling of an in-group affording shelter from the larger outside world. There is no longer an outside world.

When we examine the present situation for evidence of the four features of early oral-aural culture we noted above (there are other features, of course, in addition to these), we find some striking correspondences and some striking differences. First, our present world has become an event-world to a significant, self-conscious degree. Preliterate cultures were immersed in an event-world because of their inability to structure knowledge other than around human beings. We construct an event-world self-consciously and programmatically to strengthen the human in a world filled with objective structures of the mind. And we do so, as I have attempted to show elsewhere (1962:223–229, 1967:87–110), by massive exploitation of sound.

On the other hand, our world is certainly not traditional in the way in which the old oral-aural world was. We rely on too many records and too exhaustive historical knowledge to need this sort of support. But is there some kind of new traditionalism among us? Faddism, perhaps? Are beatniks and hippies traditionalists of a new kind? Or of a reverse kind? Their drive to conformism is marked.

Further, the personal and polemic cast of preliterate oralism is represented only partially in the present situation. Personalism is indeed stressed. The protest against overmechanization is one of the many manifestations of attention to the person as such; other manifestations are the growth of counseling in all its forms, the proliferation of discussion groups of all sorts, the cult of the outsider, the study of group dynamics and group relations, and so on. Again, in contrast to earlier spontaneous or unreflective personalism, ours is reflective and programmatic. This makes it in one way less human and in another way more human. But the polemic associated with older, feudal, personalist structures is missing. Despite our much publicized strife, the irenic quest marks our age. We are still distressingly warlike, but being so troubles our collective consciences as it seldom if ever troubled the collective or even most individual consciences of earlier man. Strong in their feeling for in-groups, earlier cultures believed quite generally that war, though perhaps regrettable, was an inescapable part of life.

Finally, are we entering into the older pattern of schizoid behavior, with rioting replacing schizophrenic withdrawal? Perhaps to a degree. It is probably significant that much rioting centers in groups who are either largely illiterate in tradition or ill at ease in centers of literacy, such as universities. Elsewhere (1958, 1962) I have attempted to detail the connections the alphabet and alphabetic printing have with a sense of order. It would appear that these connections are being shaken up in our present stage of oralism.

The foregoing is no more than a sketch of the present state of oralism, but it shows that the world ahead of us, like the world of the distant past, may call for new tools of analysis. Man's experience of the "world" organizing itself today may to a significant degree elude us if we unthinkingly equate "world" with some sort of canvas spread out before us, as something of which we have primarily a "view."

The concept of world view of course need not and should not be discarded. But how can it be supplemented? We can perhaps start from a more generic concept, thinking of not merely a world view but a world sense. In fact, such a generic concept would seem to be demanded by the terms we use, or are likely to use, in analyzing various world views. Although the concept of view is visually grounded, it is also quite metaphorically interpreted, and analyses of world views do not in fact commonly restrict themselves to the use of visually grounded terms. We can analyze a world view in terms of texture, which is based patently on the sense of touch, or in terms of tonality or concordance, which refer to hearing. We might, however, gain a good deal if we reflected more on the sensory field or fields in which the various concepts we use are grounded. Perhaps it would be productive to cultivate some aurally based concepts, such as those just mentioned as well as "harmony," "cacophony," and "melody," although doing so might seem to suggest a certain affectation.

But I believe that another productive way to supplement our concept of world view is to move from the concept of world sense to the concept of world-as-presence. By presence I mean the kind of relationship that exists between persons when we say that two persons are present to one another. Presence in the full sense of the term entails more than sensation. Insofar as it is grounded in the senses, it appears to be grounded in all of them simultaneously. We speak of a "sense" of presence, rather than a sight, sound, smell, taste, or touch of presence. There is some special relationship, of course, between presence and touch; probably because with touch is associated our sense of reality and presences are eminently real, we can say that we feel someone's presence. There is also some special relationship between presence and smell, presumably because of the relationship of smell to memory. A particular odor can conjure up a presence or presences very effectively, although it may leave the impression very vague. Still, the sense of presence appears not to be founded on any one sensory field in particular.

What happens if we think of world presence or the world-as-presence rather than of the world as something viewed, something toward which we have an outlook? We do suffer some disabilities. In terms of presence we cannot achieve the precision we achieve by resort to the visual imagination for models representing the structures in consciousness. But by thinking of world-as-presence we gain in immediacy and in a certain kind of relevance.

The conditions in which we find ourselves today call for consideration of the world as a kind of presence chiefly because of what Teilhard has called quite aptly the hominization of the globe. The ambiance in which man finds himself today is made up of human beings more than ever before. For the first time in man's history the globe is pretty well covered with men all of whom are in contact with one another, at least in the large. Nature is more and more subjected to man's management and is becoming a kind of extension of humanity. Our environment is more and more a peopled environment in which things themselves exist in a context of people. This is the kind of world the concept of presence expresses. Presence applies most directly to persons. If I am in a room with a chair, a plant, a cat, and a human being, it is the human being who normally will be felt as a presence, not the other things. In the strict sense only persons are real presences. A world conceived of in terms of presence is a hominized world.

Thinking of the world as a kind of presence is, of course, not entirely new. There is a good deal of evidence that in the past it was thought of this way after a fashion. First, as has been noted earlier, oral-aural cultures predispose man to personalize even impersonal phenomena because he has to store knowledge in narrative rather than abstract scientific categories. Secondly, as phenomenologists like to remind us, intersubjectivity is a primary mode of human experience. When I walk alone through a dark wood at night and hear what I know is the branch of one tree rubbing against another in the breeze, I cannot keep my imagination from persistently suggesting that the noise is the voice of some living being, and indeed of some person who, being otherwise unknown and of uncertain intent, may well wish to harm me. My imagination wants persons around. Every infant is initiated into an awareness of himself from the beginning in a context of persons who mediate the exterior world to him, and he can never after release himself from that context. Where persons are missing, he projects them. Animism exists in primitive cultures for a variety of reasons, no doubt, but one reason would appear to be the relative emptiness of the primitive universe. Since there are very few persons around, personal presences are projected into the otherwise empty world. Animism can persist for a while in urban populations, but it is more typically a phenomenon of loosely dispersed groups.

We no longer need animism today. The wood nymphs vanished as the woods filled with trailer camps. Water sprites have been crowded out by submarines and scuba divers. We need no longer project presences into the world, for they are already there. Besides the persons just down the street or in the next room or at our elbow, there are all the others permanently available on television. For dealing with our superpeopled environment we seem to need some attention to the notion of presence if we are to think of the world in post-Cartesian terms. We must, of course, refine our various visual models of the universe as never before. But we also need some nonvisual concepts, including even some that have not yet been born. In the present situation, this paper can pretend to be no more than maieutic.

REFERENCES

Abrams, M.H. *The Mirror and the Lamp*. New York: Oxford University Press, 1953.

Carothers, J.C. "Culture, Psychiatry, and the Written Word," *Psychiatry*, 22:307–320.

Chadwick, H. Munro, and N. Kershaw Chadwick. *The Growth of Literature*, 3 vols. Cambridge, England: Cambridge University Press, 1932–1940.

Havelock, Eric A. *Preface to Plato*. Cambridge, Mass.: Belknap Press, 1963.

Lord, Albert B. *The Singer of Tales*. Cambridge, Mass.: Harvard University Press, 1960.

Ong, Walter J. *Ramus, Method, and the Decay of Dialogue*. Cambridge, Mass.: Harvard University Press, 1958.

_____ . *The Barbarian Within*. New York: Macmillan, 1962.

_____ . *The Presence of the Word*. New Haven: Yale University Press, 1967.

Opler, Marvin K. *Culture, Psychiatry, and Human Values*. Springfield, Ill.: Charles C Thomas, 1956.

Spitzer, Leo. "Classical and Christian Ideas of World Harmony: Prolegomena to an Interpretation of the Word '*Stimmung.*'" 1963.

Yates, Frances A. *The Art of Memory*. Chicago: University of Chicago Press, 1966.

THE ROLE OF THE
NONHUMAN ENVIRONMENT

Harold F. Searles

The traditional approaches of psychology and psychoanalysis have been nearly as antiseptic as a hospital surgical unit. This is so both because the enormous complexity of the human mind imposes limitations on such young disciplines and because all scientists must study difficult subjects in their simplest operations and settings. They well know that omissions and errors are likely to occur.

The problem of what to eliminate in order to simplify is crucial. By characterizing a species as social (e.g., termites and men), we imply that the nonsocial aspects of its environment have secondary importance in its development and normal functioning. But, in recent years, such problems have been approached in many fields in terms more of processes *or* systems *than of hierarchies. The sciences of the mind are now moving rapidly toward a similar approach, emphasizing the study of whole beings and the interpenetration of total functional entities. One of the results is increased attention to man's relationship with his natural environment. After all, even if the environment is socially filtered, it is indisputable that it exists independently and cannot be understood adequately by studying the filter alone.*

Deprivation of contact with all species but one's own—mirrors of oneself—impairs the individual psyche and physiology, and may be regarded as an ecological disaster resulting from impaired structural relationships. Perhaps man is uniquely vulnerable, his relationships to the environment being not only chemical and physical, as are termites', but also necessary as experienced and felt kinship, as a conscious awareness of other presences. *What is impaired in the absence of a rich ecology is the individual's knowledge of himself not only as a person (a presence in his own right) but as a member of a species. A psychology which disregards the nonhuman environment is incapable of recognizing and diagnosing ecological deprivation.*

Probably for everyone who has found life to be more kindly than cruel, the land of his youth is a golden land. Certainly for me the Catskill region of upstate New

Harold F. Searles, "The Role of the Nonhuman Environment," Landscape, 11 (Winter, 1961–62), 31–34. Adapted from Nonhuman Environment; in Normal Development and in Schizophrenia *(New York: International Universities Press, Inc., 1960). Copyright by International Universities Press, Inc., 1960. Reprinted by permission.*

York possesses an undying enchantment, a beauty and an affirmation of life's goodness which will be part of me as long as I live. For as far back as I can recall, I have felt that life's meaning resided not only in my relatedness with my mother and father and sister and other persons, but in relatedness with the land itself—the verdant or autumn-tapestried or stark and snow-covered hills, the uncounted lakes, the rivers. In subsequent years, the so-different life in cities—Boston, New York, San Francisco, Washington—has shown me that the "nonhuman environment" here is equally enchanting and profoundly meaningful to one's living. Whether in surroundings that are largely natural or largely manmade, I have found that moments of deeply felt kinship with one's nonhuman environment are to be counted among those moments when one has drunk deepest of the whole of life's meaning.

My thesis is that this environment, far from being of little or no account to human personality development, constitutes one of the most basically important ingredients of human psychological existence. It is my conviction that there is within the human individual a sense *of relatedness to his total environment*, that this relatedness is one of the transcendentally important facts of human living, and that if he tries to ignore its importance to himself, he does so at peril to his psychological wellbeing. The data I have in mind consist in our love of gardening; our love of frequenting familiar haunts of nature; our enjoyment of active sports—golf, hiking and so on—which in their pursuit bring us physically closer to nature; the very real and important places which pets have in the lives of many of us; the fascination in going to zoos, the appeal of beautiful landscapes in motion pictures, in paintings, in literature, and, not uncommonly, in the very dreams that well up from our innermost being.

It is my conviction, moreover, that we need to extend the focus of our psychoanalytic investigation to include more than mankind alone. But I would not draw the limit, as Schweitzer does, regarding the concern of ethics, to include only that wider sphere of all that lives; I believe that psychoanalysis needs to concern itself with the *total* nonhuman environment, including the inanimate as well as the living elements in it.

There is, I believe, an additional dimension involved here which many writers on psychiatry touch upon only fleetingly. The crucial phase in normal infancy when a sense of separateness from the mother is achieved involves the infant's becoming aware of himself as differentiated not only from his human environment *but also from his nonhuman environment*. My whole theme, in fact, is that the human being is engaged, throughout his lifespan, in an unceasing struggle to differentiate himself fully, not only from his human but also from his entire environment, while developing an increasingly meaningful relatedness with it as well as with his fellow human beings.

The role of the nonhuman environment in the life of the healthy human individual is too vast a subject for me to hope to deal with it in any comprehensive way. It seems to me unnecessary, moreover, to elaborate upon the obvious point that the personality of the healthy human adult in our culture cannot be considered entirely apart from the individual's car, his home, his clothing and all his manifold other material possessions, nor apart from the particular skills which he possesses in dealing with his nonhuman environment. But the very fact that it proves so difficult to define the mature person's attitude here is itself of deep significance; it may well be that maturity involves a *readiness to face the question* of what is one's position about this great portion of one's total environment. I believe that there is one basic attitude which is of general validity here, one central emotional orientation to which the mature human being returns, *vis-à-vis* his nonhuman environment, and this basic emotional orientation in one word: relatedness. By "relatedness" I mean a sense of intimate kinship, a psychological commitment to the structural relationship which exists between man and the various ingredients of his nonhuman environment. This experience of relatedness involves a maintenance of our own sense of individuality as a human being, a knowing that however close our kinship, we are not *at one* with it. The mature human being knows that he is irrevocably, irreversibly a member of the human species, and can rejoice as well as despair in this knowledge. It seems inevitable that the human being will experience varied and conflictual feelings about his nonhuman environment, for mankind's position in regard to this environment is existentially a conflictual position. He is grounded in nature, and yet is unbridgeably apart from it.

Thus far I have dealt with this subject in terms of the human individual. But the subject can be discussed in a different and broader scale or frame of reference: that of the effects which the institutions of various cultures have upon human beings' relatedness to their nonhuman environment.

The degree to which any particular culture fosters, or, on the other hand, interferes with and distorts, the members' healthy relatedness with their nonhuman environment is doubly important because it has repercussions, for good or ill, upon the members' relatedness *with their fellow human beings*. To give some inkling of the variety in this regard, among various cultures, I shall touch very briefly upon a culture other than our own.

First, in this following glimpse into a "primitive" culture we catch something of how intimate a relatedness may exist between the individual and an environment consisting predominantly of the elements of nature in a state only minimally altered by man's own hand. This quotation is from a work by Robert Ranulph Marett:

"Said a Vedda cave-dweller . . . 'It is pleasant for us to feel the rain beating on our shoulders, and good to go out and dig yams, and come home wet, and see the fire burning in the cave, and sit around it.'"

Such a glimpse lends conviction to the anthropologist Paul Radin's opinion that "it is one of the salient traits of so-called primitive man . . . that he allows a full and appreciative expression to his sensations."

When we come to consider our own culture, we find that it fosters a distinctly unhealthy psychological estrangement from the nonhuman environment, whether part of nature or manmade. As farming grows rapidly more mechanized, even here man becomes increasingly separated, by his own artifacts, from the nonhuman manifestation of the larger nature of which he is a part. Similarly, those other inhabitants who wrest an existence from nature—lumbermen, miners and so on—make contact with environing nature in an increasingly indirect way, through the medium of increasingly abundant and complex machinery. The formerly greatly valued domesticated animals have been largely relegated to a position of little significance to man's labors; he has, therefore, little occasion to experience his erstwhile sense of respect, of meaningful kinship, toward these nonhuman creatures.

The steadily increasing majority of the population who live in large cities have, of course, still vastly less daily contact with nature. They work, and many of them have their homes, in buildings whose architecture is minimally expressive of the special beauties of the environing nature of the city's geographical region. The advancement of our technology has made for a psychological distancing of man not only from his home and land but from innumerable other elements of his nonhuman environment. Not only has man in our culture lost, to a large degree, contact with nature; he does not view the manufactured substitutes in his possession as cherished objects with which he has had, as it were, a richly meaningful shared experience.

When one works with schizophrenic patients, to whom these matters are so important that they can no longer remain disguised, one sees clearly how deeply a human being can cherish things that have accompanied the person through a great deal of life experience. It is not, I believe, that the "normal" culture member is so very different from the schizophrenic in this regard; it is that the "normal" person continuingly underestimates, or entirely overlooks, a fact which the schizophrenic simply cannot afford to ignore: the material objects in one's life are an emotionally meaningful part of it. The culture member who repeatedly discards his material possessions—his house, his car, and so on—for more prestigious ones probably is not only unwittingly keeping his own emotional life impoverished to a significant degree, but is inflicting upon any small children in his family an emotional impoverishment, a continuing series of losses, of a much more traumatic degree. This point is readily believable to one who has come to know, as I have, schizophrenic adults who have been the children of rapidly socially advancing, highly prestige-conscious parents.

Optimism is seldom heard in descriptions of the state of social and psychological life in our culture. Much more often, the voices register not exuberance but deep concern. Paul Tillich, for instance, finds that modern life, for the individual of our culture, is permeated with a profound sense of meaninglessness. The particular point which I wish to emphasize at the moment is that Tillich at least implies, when he speaks of "man's separation from the whole of reality," that this so-prevalent meaninglessness derives not only from impairment of man's relationship to himself and to his fellow men, but also from impairment of his relationship to his nonhuman environment. When one recalls that in terms of sheer volume, the vast preponderance of one's total environment is nonhuman, one can believe that culture-fostered impairment of relatedness to this vast section of our environment can have a significant effect upon our relatedness to our fellow human beings, and an effect which is in the direction of similar impairment.

It seems to me that, in our culture, a conscious ignoring of the psychological importance of the nonhuman environment exists simultaneously with a (largely unconscious) *overdependence upon* that environment. I believe that the actual importance of that environment to the individual is so great that he *dare* not recognize it. Unconsciously it is felt, I believe, to be not only an intensely important conglomeration of things *outside* the self, but also a large and integral *part* of the self.

If such a psychodynamic process goes on in our culture to a large extent, as I believe it does, then it becomes understandable that we are inordinately vulnerable to the anxiety lest we become, or stand revealed, as nonhuman. Our personalities have become so greatly invaded by elements of the nonhuman environment with which we have unconsciously identified, or, to put it in a more accurate way, the institutions of our culture have so greatly hindered us from psychologically differentiating ourselves from the nonhuman environment, from growing out of that state, normal in infancy, of subjective oneness with the totality of the environment that, in a real sense, we *are* less than fully human.

I believe that this psychodynamic formulation illuminates certain features of one of the most important and pressing situations in our culture: our living under the imminent threat of atomic annihilation. Our basic fear is that the most alien portion of our nonhuman environment (the inorganic portion of it, in the form of the atomic bomb) will rise up and destroy us, along with the rest of humanity and much of all the rest that is animate in our environment.

It seems to me that the members of our culture (and likewise, the members of cultures in the other highly technological nations, including Russia) tend to *project* the "nonhuman" part of the self and perceive it as a nonhuman thing which threatens the conscious self with destruction; it is too threatening to let oneself recognize the extent to which the nonhuman environment has, as it were, already invaded and become *part of* one's own personality. The real threat of atomic annihilation readily lends itself, then, to becoming the bearer of this paranoid projection, and thus, I think, the danger that we will indeed be destroyed by the atomic bomb becomes intensified. That is, clinical experience with paranoid patients shows clearly enough that the patient, after projecting onto the outer world an attitude which is sensed as an inner danger, threatening to the integrity of the self, unwittingly sets about behaving in such a way as indeed to bring upon himself that threat which, he is convinced, looms in the outer world.

Finally, I believe that our culture fosters, actually, an unconscious *identification with* the ingredients of our nonhuman environment, to such a degree that we are barred from experiencing either the fullness of the realization of our own uniqueness or the rich sense of relatedness with that environment. I believe there is at work here a culturally fostered pathological process which one unquestionably encounters in the exploration of a deeply ill patient's *interpersonal* relations. It is maturational development, I think, which the institutions of our culture make it difficult for us to achieve with respect to our nonhuman environment.

Thus far I have referred to the advances made by physical sciences chiefly in terms of their negative effects upon our relationship with the nonhuman environment. On the other hand, through these advances we have become largely free, over the past few centuries, from many of the animistic distortions which caused ancient man, and which still cause the people of the so-called primitive societies today, to react to the nonhuman environment with irrational fear and awe.

The achievements of the natural sciences can help man to develop a richer ego than was ever possible in prescientific times. Modern means of transportation and communication, which have been brought into existence by these sciences, enable the average member of our culture to come into contact with his nonhuman environment on a vastly broader, and, therefore, much more varied scale than was ever attainable by his predecessor of several hundred years ago.

The crucial issue, I believe, is whether the members of our culture are able to *integrate their experiences* of this vastly broader, richer and more varied nonhuman environment which science has opened up within, particularly, the past two hundred years. Insofar as one can assimilate these experiences, to that extent they enrich the ego. They help one to become literally a greater human being.

But, insofar as one is exposed to these experiences in too great a variety and abundance, and at too rapid a rate, for one to be able to integrate them, to that extent they tend instead to overwhelm the ego.

As an example, an airplane trip, which to an Anne Morrow Lindbergh, or to an Antoine de Saint-Exupery, can be a beautiful and even glorious experience of personal participation in relatedness with the nonhuman environment, is to the average airline passenger of today, apparently, little if anything more than a mode of getting with time-saving rapidity from one place to another; incredibly enough, he may barely glance out of the window during the whole trip, but instead may bury himself, with a kind of world-weary nonchalance, in his newspaper. Ostensibly, this phenomenon of our culture is due simply to the fact that the novelty of air travel has worn off; actually, I believe it is due also to the fact that the traveler has unconscious anxiety about his nonhuman environment's shifting at such a great rate that he cannot assimilate this experience as a personally meaningful one. He reacts in a very similar way, too, I believe, during the train and automobile trips which are so very prominent a part of the lives of the people of our culture, and which used to be, a few decades ago, relatively rare and personally cherished experiences.

A note of healthy skepticism, of searching for ever more meaningful answers rather than settling for lesser ones, should certainly characterize the individual who aspires toward unceasingly deepening personal maturity in a mid-twentieth-century world made up of not only human beings and the face of nature, but also of increasingly awesome scientific devices. But it is still rightful, I believe, to point out a circumstance of his life which will always be there, and which can help him find the courage to face his future with open eyes: his relatedness with nature, a relatedness which, though raised to increasingly complex levels which bear less and less similarity to Thoreau's relatedness with his homely environment at Walden, will always be there for him to feel if he will but open his heart to it. It is there, for him to feel and know, in the working of man's proudest scientific achievements.

One can sense this relatedness between man and nature when one stands on the darkening land at twilight and sees, high above the sunset, a transcontinental jet-liner drawing its golden vapor trail, thin as a pencil line and straight as an arrow, slowly at this vast distance across the sky. Here is beauty which man could not create alone, and which nature could not create alone; here is beauty which man and nature, working through man's increasing knowledge of nature's processes, can create only in their mutual relatedness.

THE
CROSS VALLEY SYNDROME

Paul Shepard

Perception of the body as landscape and of the natural terrain as a body is as
fundamental to psychology as it is to mythology. The ancient concept of the
Earth Mother belongs to that realm of experience which is generally regarded as
primitive or obsolete. It is considered inappropriate as a subject to the various
departments of modern knowledge, being at once subjective and objective, personal and social, individual and universal.

  Merely to identify it explains little, however. Does the concept develop from
an infantile projection of one's mother onto the world? Or is it an expression
of some more general construct in human consciousness? Do the magnification
of the individual and the miniaturization of the terrain as anatomy have a reciprocal or proportional relationship? What account must we take of the mother/
nature analogy, and what does it really mean? Does this preverbal notion of the
world as living presence prefigure philosophical organicism? How is it related to
the illusions (?) of anthropomorphism? Of homocentrism?

  In some ways the idea is simply quaint and primitive. We expect the infant to
refine its interpretations as it grows, to distinguish people from animals, mother
from other women, and the living from the nonliving. We expect the growing
child to classify with greater precision, to differentiate ideas from dreams—in
short, to recognize metaphor. We know very little about the value and role of
myth, but it may be seriously inquired whether some fundamental injury is done
to life by these severe rationalizations.

  In a time of widespread violence and environmental destruction we may well
wonder whether the microcosmic and the macrocosmic are not related by more
than chance, and whether both are not united at the root.

Cross valleys are streams or rivers that cross ridges or mountains. They result
from at least four situations: from the overflow of a basin, from being gently
lowered across a buried ridge as the stream removes materials by erosion, from
the stream's capacity to maintain its position as the ridge rises by uplift at right
angles to it, and from erosion into the hillside until the crest of the hill is notched.

Paul Shepard, Jr., "The Cross Valley Syndrome," Landscape 10:3 (Spring, 1961), 4–8.

There are refinements and combinations, of course, but in a given set of conditions a geologist may predict where streams would be likely to breach mountains.

In terms of human geography, these water gaps provide passageways. They tend to become historical and economic landmarks. In the settlement of America, for instance, water gaps were especially important because the westward movement of settlers was at right angles to the general, north-south lineaments of the continental ranges. Cities and roads developed in definite spatial relationship to these passages. The water gap might be cited as the classic example of the topographic passage.

Another characteristic of the water gap is that it is usually admired as scenery. It is frequently described as a sublime spectacle of great forces at work. The valley is narrow and the current speeded. The rough walls and rocky débris seem evidence of upheaval and destruction, or scars of former gigantic earth movements. The slopes are too sharply inclined to cultivate and may be covered with forest, except where there are cliffs. Forest and cliff are conventional signs of natural catastrophe and wildness; they have evoked some of the most rapturous descriptions in travel literature. From a distance the cross valley has an emotional impact, since, unlike most mountain-valley landscapes, it may be observed looming above a horizontal foreground.

The Discovery by Tourists and Artists

The water gap was intimately associated with the discovery of American scenery in the first half of the 19th Century. Although travelers had described New England from the time of settlement, a genuine enthusiasm for its landscapes matured only in the general intellectual and artistic renaissance that began in the 1820s. The water gaps of New England are particularly associated with the rise of landscape painting, travel literature, nature poetry and the sentiments for the outdoors that was to lead in one of its branches to the conservation movement.

Evidence for this linkage between water gaps and an intensified American attitude toward nature may be found in the history of some of the principal examples. About 100 miles north of New York the Hudson valley, here about ten miles wide, lies in the afternoon shadow of the spectacular escarpment of the Allegheny Plateau. This rocky outcrop, rising 3000 feet above the valley floor, is the extreme eastern point of an upland, the Catskill Mountains. This escarpment is deeply dissected at intervals along its face of sediment rocks. In the glens draining from it toward the Hudson, Washington Irving set many of his tales, drawn from Dutch folklore. Sleepy Hollow is part of a mountain stream valley, a clove, (or "kill") working headward into the face of the escarpment. James Fenimore Cooper used this immediate area as a setting for some of Leatherstocking's adventures. The steep ravines on the face of the escarpment next attracted poets and painters. Asher Durrand, Thomas Doughty and Thomas Cole came up the river on the heels of William Cullen Bryant, and were pursued in turn by admirers, aspiring artists, people of taste and tourists. The esthetic enjoyment of this area precipitated new popular interest in the scenery of the Hudson and focused it in the Catskills. This burst of awareness of the native landscape may be considered, ecologically, to mark a revolution in the American sensitivity to the habitat.

Access to New England scenery proper was up the Connecticut River valley. In southern Massachusetts the river crosses the axis of an igneous trap ridge; the peaks on either side of the breach are Mount Tom and Mount Holyoke. Immediately above the passage is a wide lacustrine fill upon which the river has formed an oxbow, a landmark on the river. The panorama of the valley with its oxbow from Mount Holyoke evoked the construction of one of the first and most popular of the New England mountain houses. The mountain house tradition was, in fact, an integral part of the 19th Century effort to absorb the benefits of grand scenery. From shacks to luxurious hotels, they marked the most prized viewpoints in the region.

In the Mount Washington area of the White Mountains are the Franconia and Crawford Notches. These incipient gaps were, from the time of Timothy Dwight, highly prized for their scenery. Here, as in the glens of the Catskills, glaciated notches and their associated drainages are developing cross-axial patterns.

What is the Explanation?

It is one thing, however, to claim that these cross valleys, including the Delaware Water Gap, the gaps on the Susquehanna and other rivers, catalyzed American ideas of scenic beauty, and quite another to uncover the nature of their peculiar attraction. We can detect something of the motivation of the paintings of these water gaps that were made during the period of esthetic discovery by comparing the paintings with the sites themselves, by using the same basic approach used in distorted mirror studies in psychology (see Paul Shepard, "They Painted What They Saw," *Landscape*, Vol. 3, No. 1).

Another way of gaining insight into this motivation is to consider the response of travelers to the first sight of such gaps in another, newer, environment: *i.e.*, the semi-arid west. About half way along the Oregon Trail between Independence, Missouri, and Astoria is a remote water gap which has been seen and has been recorded in their diaries by hundreds of west-bound Americans before 1850. As Bernard DeVoto has pointed out, these people had few visual expectations of the West, for at that time almost no pictures of it had been published. If the cross valley has unique evocative qualities, gaps like the Devil's Gate on the old trail can be unusually interesting; they are removed from the tame context of familiar surroundings: the temperate forest openings with the town and country patterns of Western Civilization are, as it were, stripped away.

The Devil's Gate

The Devil's Gate is a spur of the Granite Range transected by the Sweetwater River of South-central Wyoming. The walls are less than four hundred feet in height above the stream, and the passage is only about a hundred yards in length. At this point the Oregon traveler was a thousand miles from civilization and had been weeks in what seemed a "desert." The way had been along the Platte and now the Sweetwater. There was an easy detour around the gap, so that wagons were not forced to go through it. But many of those travelers who kept journals found it awe-inspiring, and lingered to climb, sketch, measure, explore and engage in geological speculation. The conventional figure of an harassed, plains-weary, fearful emigrant is scarcely consistent with the name-carving, rock-collecting, scenery-hunting tourist which he occasionally became.

This vaguely familiar landform was unaccountably fascinating in its novel surrounding; but why should it have been called Devil's Gate? Father Louis De Smet, who stopped to sketch the Gate in 1841, believed that it should have been named "Heaven's Avenue." Referring to the distant mountains, he wrote, "If it resembles hell on account of the frightful disorder which frowns around it, it is still a mere passage, and it should rather be compared to the way of heaven on account of the scene to which it leads." He noted its perpendicular walls, the tree trunks caught in the rocks, the overhead masses of shadow and gloom where dark pines and cedar grew. "Lofty galleries" could be seen among the rocks. "In the midst of this chaos of obstacles, the roaring waves force a passage," the water coming first furiously, then with majesty, and finally gently. The gate itself was horrid, but it led to paradise. Thus the gap is characterized by contradictions and by the contrasts of barrier and penetration. De Smet's account of the Devil's Gate was probably in some measure influenced by the 18th Century esthetics of the Sublime; but the esthetic was itself merely a means of formalizing and sorting out spontaneous responses to the landscape. De Smet refers to a geomorphic feature, but there is—for want of a better term—fantasy in his description of it. His encounter with the Devil's Gate is what might be called an ecological event.

Certain aspects of this cross valley syndrome are unusually distinct in this strange habitat. We may examine them further by turning to a wholly fantastic description in a story by Edgar Allan Poe.

Poe's "Domain of Arnheim" is a first-person narration of a mysterious journey. The narrator is enroute to visit the estate of a wealthy friend. The way is by water. In a beautiful and elaborate skiff he glides along a heavenly avenue. "The channel grew more narrow; the banks more and more precipitous . . . clothed in richer, more profuse and more sombre foliage." Past the walls of foliage the voyageur entered a gorge in which "intertwining shrubberies overhead gave the whole chasm an air of funereal gloom." Suddenly the boat entered a large basin of great "softness" and "voluptuousness" with slopes whose flowers look like precious gems. Transferring to another fairy canoe propelled by an unknown force, he floats through a gigantic gate of burnished gold, "elaborately carved and fretted, and reflecting the direct rays of the now fast-sinking sun with an effulgence that seems to wreathe the whole surrounding forest in flames." Then "the whole paradise of Arnheim bursts upon the view" with its melody, sweet odors and amphitheater begirt with purple mountains and a gleaming river, flocks of golden birds, meadows full of blooms, lakes, tall slender trees, and "a mass of semi-Gothic, semi-Saracenic architecture, sustaining itself as if by miracle in mid-air, glittering in the red sunlight with a hundred oriels, minarets and pinnacles; and weaving the phantom handiwork, conjointly, of the Sylphs, of the Fairies, of the Genii and of the Gnomes." This paradisiacal garden with its ornate hanging structures, preternatural light, fragrance, flowers, birds and parks belongs to a class of landscape images that frequently recurs in eschatological and epic lore. It is worth noting that these images are almost identical with those of hallucinatory and visionary landscapes. Studies of induced hallucinations strongly suggest that spontaneous visions of this sort are not uncommon, especially under conditions of physiological stress. Even the perception of the normal individual who seldom or never has traumatic visions can be affected by hallucinatory sense experiences. Aldous Huxley has pointed out in *Heaven and Hell* that, given sufficient doses of certain chemical agents, the normal observer perceives objects in his daily life in terms of a truly visionary landscape; they are then reminiscent of something not remembered. Among the geographical forms which play a compelling part in these visions is the cross valley—the defile or precipitous pass or ravine.

An Archetypal Landscape

How are we to explain this recurrent vision, and the elation of travelers, tourists and artists when confronted with this type of scenery? One answer, I believe, is to be found in our deep-seated, if unconscious, tendency to liken earth forms to human forms; to think of the earth itself as a body.[1] The prevalence of the primordial image of the earth-mother is a familiar instance. There are primitive societies which reject work in the fields because the body of the earth-mother is not to be injured; where stones are likened to the bones of the earth, soil to her flesh, plants to her hair. The passages of the body have long been recognized by anthropologists as having special significance in primitive orientation.[1] "If the earth is thought of as a living and fecund mother," Mircea Eliade observes, "all that she produces is both organic and animated, not only men and plants, but also stones and minerals. . . Such concepts are extremely ancient. Mines, like the mouths of rivers, have been likened to the matrix of the earth-mother. The word *bi* in Egyptian is translated as vagina or shaft of a mine. . . And the same symbolism can be applied *a fortiori* to grottoes and caves; it is recognized that caves have

---

[1] Carl Jung, *Psychology of the Unconscious*, New York: Dodd, Mead & Company, 1925.

played a religious role from paleolithic times. To penetrate a labyrinth or a cave was the equivalent of a mystic return to the Mother—the object of rites of initiation as well as funeral rites."

If this correspondence is no longer part of our conscious perception of the landscape, it is nevertheless still part of the vision of artists; such persons retain the power to apprehend and symbolize what others only vaguely sense. To this first group belong prophets, story-tellers and legend-makers as well as painters.

The river issuing from the cloven stone or from a mountain in paradise is, in fact, part of an ancient core of myth. The Grail legends and the Tannhaeuser epic contain such earthly paradises; the deep gorge with its gloomy forest and torrent, the importance of such obstacles as bridges and gates. The ornate castles and parks beyond the defile are consistent themes. Tannhaeuser's goal was the Venusberg, and many persons in the Middle Ages actually searched for the Venusberg in Germany, Italy and elsewhere. Nor did the Arthurian or Tannhaeuser quests end with the Middle Ages; both remain with us in a modified, scarcely recognizable form. In an age of easy transportation and egalitarian culture every man may set out on such an errand. It survives to this day in the search for wild and remote places, passes through forbidding mountains, hidden landscapes beyond barriers.

It is in this light that much of our American agitation for wilderness preservations can be interpreted. The rationale for the preservation of Yosemite Valley in 1864 was based less on scientific than on esthetic grounds. The articles and diaries of early travelers to Yosemite contain many pseudo-psychological expressions; observers attributed their feelings to spiritual transcendence, to formal esthetic responses or to the unexplained virtues of a natural Wonder. Yet, however rationalized in the extensive travel literature which has developed since the discovery of the Yosemite in 1851, it is permissible to believe that the attributes of the valley owe at least part of their allure to a profound and unarticulated recognition that their morphology reflected an inner image of a fundamental kind.

Yosemite was the first wilderness in history to be preserved for its scenery by an official act of the government. Public interest in the Dinosaur National Monument is a more recent example of the same geopsychic experience. Within this area along the Colorado-Utah boundary is a junction of the Green and Yampa Rivers. As part of the Colorado River system it was included in a valley development program which came before Congress early in the 1950s. The ensuing controversy over the construction of a dam in the Monument recently drew to a close after six years of dispute in Congress, in magazines and newspapers, and among a mélange of private organizations and individuals. Opponents of the dam won, and Echo Park Dam was omitted from the legislation passed by Congress in 1956.

The public debate serves in its way to illustrate the prevalence of the cross valley (or in this case, canyon) syndrome. Although Dinosaur had been little visited, much money and energy was expended in opposing the dam. It was claimed by the dam proponents that this particular piece of desert was not greatly

*The ancient streams on what is now the Sierra Fault
block ran in north-south patterns. With the tilting of
the block up along its eastern side, the general slope
was down toward the Pacific and the present streams
developed at right angles to the old valley-and-ridge
pattern. Photo by Bill Sears from Western Ways.*

unlike much of the rest of the Basin country. But this section of the Green River in
Dinosaur is a cross valley transecting a spur of the Vinta Mountains, and the exciting passage through the turbulent cayon waters was publicized by pictures
showing whole families—children, old ladies, ordinary persons—as they emerged
from rubber boats onto the green, gardenlike fringe at the mouth of the canyon.
Their triumph over the perilous mountain valley had been possible because of
strong young men who, like Tannhaeuser, had forsaken the humdrum world.

If the application of this hypothesis to the Dinosaur controversy appears highly speculative, it should be recalled that an unconscious identification between bodily image and geological form is a widely held theory however it may be explained. The early history of geographical exploration includes many extraordinary examples of the delicate interplay between a complex psychic image and its geomorphic correspondent. It was an experience particularly common in the early Renaissance, when Christianity had lost some of its ascetic character and had adopted (or was invaded by) pagan, magic and mystic elements. In the present century we are not accustomed to allegorical art forms; we do not consciously see the natural world as symbol. Positivism and materialism have all but overwhelmed the art and myth which in the past seemed at times even more real than objective experience. Perception of the landscape as anatomy now seems primitive and irrelevant; in our culture, where technology rather than affirmation connects man to nature, it is merely a romantic anthropomorphism— it would be difficult to say much in its praise that would be accepted happily.

Yet the Dinosaur episode suggests that these attitudes continue to operate in the formation of personal and collective ideas of the landscape, in the evaluation of scenery, and in the motivation of much tourism.

A New Landscape Interpretation

One might venture further and suggest that the study of the relationship between psychological processes and their geomorphic or ecological components is a potentially fruitful approach to the broader areas of man's relationship to nature. This brief examination of a cross valley syndrome—a persistent theme of a mountain barrier and sundering stream in vision, romance, art and in travel and exploration—is a provisional effort in this direction. Even the underlying concept, that of the earth-mother, merits in this connection a far closer study. "The obscure memory of a pre-existence in the womb of the earth" (to quote once more from Eliade) "has had considerable consequences. It produced in man a sentiment of cosmic relationship to his environment. One might say that at a remote period man was less aware of belonging to the human species than of a cosmobiological participation in the life of his surroundings. . . This sort of experience established a mystic solidarity with the *place*, the intensity of which extends to our day in popular traditions and in folklore. . ." We have not yet begun to explore the benefits of such "illusions." The ecological interconnections of the living members of a landscape have an organic fragility needing protection. We must even appreciate the tenuous projection of the human form into the environment if that is part of the process by which we acknowledge the world as living and perishable.

PART **TWO**

SOCIETY

AND

ITS

CREATIONS

THE SANE COMMUNITY — A DENSITY PROBLEM?

P. Leyhausen

One of the slowest-dying lies we tell about ourselves is that human behavior is characterized by a rationality and freedom of choice not prefigured in other forms of life. This notion has long impeded the study of man and animals. Such distinctions, created by understandable acts of historical imagination, have forced us to see dichotomy where none existed. But at last their intellectual under-pinnings have dissolved.

Vertebrate animals have traditionally been regarded as either social and rank-tight or solitary and territorial. What appeared to be opposites, however, now seem, at least in some animals, to be reciprocal expressions of a social relation-ship that changes according to particular conditions of time, place, and popula-tion density. Moreover, all species seem to have an optimal combination of fixed and flexible status related to population density, and all show neurotic and psychotic symptoms when they are stressed socially. Further, the social structure of all higher animals is apparently dependent on individual recognition and familiarity.

Surely this kind of information will prove aesthetically as well as scientifically satisfying to a species that has regarded itself as singular and alone, without prece-dent for its actions and without counterpart in the natural world. A species in serious environmental trouble will find the posture of biological alienation un-suitable grounds for a claim on dignity, and existential dignity poor compensa-tion for unnecessary isolation.

Man is supposed to be the all-round-adaptable animal. Yet in modern times an ever-increasing number of medical, psychological and social workers is concerned with the care, and if possible the cure, of an ever more rapidly growing number of socially ill-adapted, maladjusted individuals. According to common belief, Man is also an essentially social animal. However, beliefs vary widely as to how Man as a social being should behave. Thus it is hard to define conclusively the individual's place in the community.

In an attempt to find out something which might also throw light on the fabric of human societies, no animal species living in some sort of social

P. Leyhausen, "The Sane Community—A Density Problem?" Discovery, 26 (September, 1965), 27–33, 51. Reprinted by courtesy of Science Journal (incorporating Discovery), London.

organization has been spared comparison, from ape and wolf down to bee and ant. On such findings—the value of which cannot be doubted—a variety of theories has been based. At present the prevailing opinion is that there is always some kind of cooperation between or combination of nature and nurture as the two possible sources of human social behavior, with the emphasis heavily on nurture, especially learning. However, the argument continues, and as more detailed data and facts are amassed, we seem to get further from a comprehensive understanding of the patterns and forces underlying the social life and development of our own species.

Under the circumstances, it may seem odd to expect any new clue to be gained from the study of solitary animals instead of those living in a community. Certainly, when Dr. Rosemarie Wolff and I, at first independently and not knowing about each other, started to investigate the behavior of free-ranging domestic cats, we did not envisage this surprising result.

Basis of Social Structure

First let me recall some facts about the ranking order or dominance hierarchy which the Danish psychologist T. Schjelderup-Ebbe discovered some forty years ago in the domestic fowl and which, with very slight variation only, seem to apply to almost all vertebrates which live in social groups. Schjelderup-Ebbe found that the hens of a barnyard do not by any means have equal rights, but establish among themselves a 'peck-order' in which each individual is allocated a definite place on the social ladder which it is normally unable to alter. Usually a subordinate does not even try to fight a superior animal even if grossly provoked. When it does, it is almost invariably quickly subdued. Very rarely, and only after prolonged and bitter fighting, does an inferior animal succeed in improving its social position by degrading a formerly superior one. The resulting ranking order is mostly linear: hen A pecks B but is not pecked by her, B pecks C but is not pecked by her, C is thus automatically inferior to A, and so on throughout the whole flock. Quarrelling usually occurs only between individuals separated by not more than one step of the social ladder; an inferior animal never dares so much as to look straight at an animal two or more steps its superior; and an animal so vastly superior cannot be bothered to notice the existence of the ones far below—she has enough to do to keep her nearest rival in check and to avoid the relentless attacks of her immediate superior, by which she is punished if she inadvertently comes too close. Occasionally, relationships may be somewhat more complicated, as for instance in a triangle where A may peck B and B may peck C, but C in turn pecks A. However, this does not alter the main principle: the resulting social hierarchy is very rigid, and it is *absolute*, meaning that the ranking between any two given individuals of the flock, once established, is observed *at all times, in all places, and under all circumstances.* Throughout this article, therefore, it will be called "absolute social hierarchy." The main prerequisite of its proper functioning is, of course, that all the members of a community know each other individually.

This kind of social hierarchy prevails largely in communities of animals normally living together as adults and in families which break up as soon as the young are capable of looking after themselves—the parent(s) always holding the top position(s). Since the social habits of most, if not all, vertebrates living in communities have evolved in that they ceased to break up their families after the young had reached maturity, the evolution of absolute social hierarchy has its roots in family life itself.

Solitary animals would not seem to need any kind of social order. They occupy a piece of land, a so-called territory, on which they will not allow any other member of the same species to stay, the only exception being a mate during the reproductive season. Within his territory the owner is—with very few exceptions which we need not go into here—superior to all strangers, and easily wins if an intruder should actually choose to stay and fight. His courage and self-assurance diminish as the distance from the center of his territory increases. Thus, neighboring individuals soon find a line of balance between them, and once such a boundary has been established neither will go beyond it. Territories of this kind were first observed in birds by B. Altum and H. E. Howard independently. It is in birds that they have since been best and most extensively studied, with the result that bird biology and bird behavior have largely framed the whole concept of territory.

Professor Hediger of Zurich Zoo was the first to realize that the original concept had to undergo certain adaptations if it was to be of good use when studying solitary mammals. He pointed out that a mammalian territory consisted not so much of a solid area as of a number of places—first and second order homes, spots for sunbathing and resting, lookout posts and feeding areas—connected by a network of pathways (*see Figure 1*). The owner of the territory moves along the paths to his various points of interest and activity according to a more or less fixed timetable, and the spaces enclosed by the pathway network are seldom or never used.

In defending their territories, most solitary mammals are at a great disadvantage as compared with birds. They cannot lift themselves onto the highest perch and from there survey the whole of their territory, and most mammals do not 'mark' their presence acoustically as songbirds do. Thus they often fail to notice trespassers. The border areas of domestic cat territories overlap considerably in the sense that pathways and places of interest are shared even if the first order homes are well spaced out.

'Sharing' in this context does not necessarily mean that the animals concerned are on good terms with each other. When they meet on disputable ground they may fight. But with territorial behavior being dependent on proximity to the territory center (first order home) the victorious cat will not extend its pursuit of the defeated one too far into unknown territory and too far away from its own home. Thus, unlike dominance in a group governed by absolute social hierarchy,

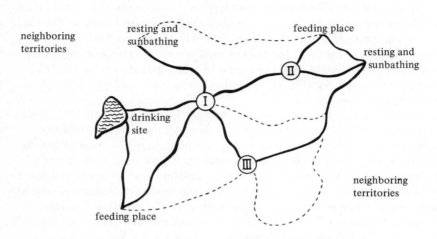

Figure 1
*Mammalian territory in simplified diagrammatic
form. The continuous lines within the territory
show pathways used regularly while dotted lines de-
pict those used rarely. The roman numerals stand
for the animal's first-, second-, and third-order
homes. Unlike birds, which can survey their entire
territory, mammals restrict themselves to a number
of specific places and connecting pathways.*

superiority gained through territorial fighting is from the start more or less confined to the locality of the fight and, after a series of such fights at different
localities, the ranking between the neighboring individuals still applies only in
the border area and may even be reversed from one spot to the next according to
the distance from their respective first order homes.

Nor is this the only condition limiting the ranking order resulting from territorial fighting. The timetable of an animal's movements about its territory is
constant enough to enable one formerly beaten in a territorial fight over a certain
spot or path to adjust its schedule with regard to that spot so as to avoid the risk
of an encounter with the victorious opponent. The time schedules may become
so fixed that an animal supposedly superior in a certain locality will not press the

point or may even lose its superiority when for some reason turning up at the 'wrong' time.

From all this, it will have become apparent that, quite unlike absolute social hierarchy, any ranking between two individuals based on the outcome of territorial fighting is largely subject to *locality and time*. I therefore call it 'relative social hierarchy.' It will also be apparent that relative social hierarchy depends as much as absolute hierarchy does on the individuals knowing each other personally, but over and above this, other individuals become mentally associated with the places where they have been encountered. Thus, as Gustav Kramer pointed out, any given individual may be defined more by such localities than by its own personal characteristics.

Both types of social hierarchy can be present in the same animal species. The chaffinch for instance, as the extensive studies of Peter Marler have shown, changes seasonally from one type to the other in correlation with its reproductive cycle. In the cat, absolute ranking order is normally established among the siblings of a litter, and also among the adult male cats of a region. Males keep less strictly than females to a defined area surrounding their homes, and when rutting they tend to wander well beyond what may be considered as their territory proper. Accordingly they frequently meet at places which none of them claims as territory. The result, after some serious fighting, is a fixed ranking order between the males of quite a wide area, and then the serious fighting practically ceases.

Yet there is one striking difference as compared with the absolute ranking order within a group which lives together all the time: the tom cats, after meeting outside their own territorial grounds, return to their homes and into their territorial rights where their supremacy is not challenged, whatever their rank may be 'outside.' Here they heal their wounds and regain their confidence, and thus are never as totally and utterly subdued as the lowest-ranking in a permanent social group. If in a region there are several tom cats almost evenly matched, they have it out with each other and afterwards are very careful not to provoke any more serious fighting, which might only endanger their position. At first this relationship resembles an armed truce, but as the animals gradually become accustomed to each other it leads eventually to friendship, in the limited sense that the animals may like being together for a while and even keep company in their pursuit of love and . . . novice males.

Such a loose and temporary association of adult males I have called a brotherhood. Their competition for females attains a pro-forma quality, and it is largely the females who make the choice. Hard and continued fighting ensues, however, when somewhere in the brotherhood's region there is a young tom just reaching maturity and setting out to battle his way into the brotherhood. Singly or together, the 'brethren' walk up to the youngster's home and summon him to fight. Since the adolescent will not accept defeat as any sensible adult would, he will continue to challenge any member of the establishment until he has either won his place among them or is finally defeated and either driven out of the neighbor-hood or even killed.

It would, however, be entirely wrong to deduce from the foregoing that fight-ing and mutual repulsiveness are the only factors forming the basis of the social structure of so-called solitary mammals. It has frequently been observed in song-birds, and even some fish, that, after fighting initially over the boundaries of their territories, they eventually come to tolerate neighbors coming close to the boundary and occasionally even trespassing, but still drive off all trespassing strangers. With cats, relations between neighbors need not stop at sharing border areas by mutually avoiding all encounters. They may tolerate each other within seeing distance or even greet each other in a friendly manner before separating again. At times the inhabitants of a region may even meet regularly in some place, sit around a certain distance apart, some individuals even greeting and grooming each other, then disperse again after a while. In one little square I ob-served social gatherings of this type almost every night over a long period. This was definitely not in connection with any reproductive activity. Thus, solitary animals are certainly not asocial and some form of friendly neighborliness may develop.

Population Density and Hierarchies

It will be evident by now that relative social hierarchy, being associated as it is with territorial behavior, is inseparably linked to the spacing out of the indi-viduals of a population, that is to population density. Density as a factor in the inner machinery of absolute social hierarchy is not so obvious at first glance. Its importance is shown best by the fact that species which under normal free-ranging conditions show no recognizable signs of any ranking within the group, for example the Brown Rat or the Night Heron, will establish absolute social hierarchy when crowded.

The influence of the density factor can be easily studied by keeping groups of animals of either social type under conditions where density can be manipu-lated. The effect of increasing density on absolute social hierarchy is invariably to emphasize the tyrannical aspect of the system until life becomes practically unbearable for everyone in the group except the overlord, and in time the strain and stress of having to assert himself begins to tell even on him, whether the species under observation be doves, or wolves, or goats. Hence absolute social hierarchy is also dependent on density and room for maneuver if it is to work without lasting detriment to the group.

With relative social hierarchy, results do not seem quite so clearcut at first. Again, cats provided us with the first clues. Other investigators as well as myself found that any given group of cats kept in close confinement did not seem to develop an unvarying rank order, although as density increased one animal, usu-ally a male, might emerge as undisputed overlord, and one other animal or even two as 'pariahs' who eventually could not make the slightest movement without provoking attack from some other animal in the group. Yet between overlord and pariahs the rest of the group seemed to form a rather amorphous crowd with no clearly definable and permanent ranking order.

Since the only known kind of ranking order at that time was the one described here as absolute social hierarchy, these observations were explained by assuming that cats, being solitary animals by nature, simply lacked the potentiality for forming a stable ranking order. Only after observation of free-ranging cats had suggested to me the existence of a second principle of ranking, namely relative social hierarchy, and after I had realized that cats are quite capable of establishing absolute hierarchy, within the litter as well as the tom cat brotherhood, it dawned upon me that what we observed in the caged cats might simply be a mixture of the two kinds. In short, *with increasing density absolute hierarchy becomes more and more prominent and the manifestations of relative hierarchy dwindle away*.

Another idea arose from this: since even in animals commonly regarded as solitary and asocial some traces of communal life could be found which are governed by absolute social hierarchy, perhaps in animals normally living in large groups ostensibly governed by absolute social hierarchy there were marginal parts of their social life in which relative hierarchy prevailed? In between these two extremes there might be many animal species habitually showing some signs of both kinds of hierarchy?

There is at least some indirect evidence pointing in that direction: some species, like the African lion and the grizzly bear, have a faculty for living either as solitary, territorial animals, or in groups more or less determinedly defending group territories, according to habitat or season. Herding animals like the wapiti deer show territorial behavior in some regions but not in others. These observations show that both kinds of social organization are potentially present in these and other mammalian species. Taken with the results obtained from captive communities, they also suggest that the proportion of the two forms of social hierarchy has a different optimum in each species. Moreover, the balance is not rigidly fixed and may be shifted within certain limits before any distinct, outward signs of behavioral disorder become manifest. This point seems to be of the greatest importance, because it indicates the probability, if not certainty, that *well within* the apparent or obvious limits of density tolerance there are *latent tolerance limits* beyond which damage is surreptitiously done long before it becomes apparent.

Quite obviously such a species-specific balance of hierarchies will determine an individual's tolerance of others and the diurnal and seasonal fluctuations of this proximity tolerance. This balance is therefore one of the factors controlling the population density in a given species. Professor Wynne-Edwards recently put forward the hypothesis, and corroborated it by an overwhelming mass of facts, that density regulation, and through this, control of numbers, is the main function of all forms of social organization in animals. He claims that the advantage to the species (the selection pressure) is that social competition ("conventional competition" as he calls it) limits the number of individuals to a level which not only prevents the species from exhausting its resources through direct competition, but actually keeps the numbers of both exploiter and exploited at an optimum level. This is especially true of those species which have a life cycle several times as long as that of the organism(s) on which they depend for food, and which therefore cannot quickly adapt their numbers to the latter's fluctuations.

From Animals to Man

People undoubtedly show territorial behavior in many forms and in many spheres of their lives. Professor Bayr-Klimpfinger of Vienna has shown that it starts in the nursery. Garden walls, no-trespassing posters, the "my home—my castle" attitude of mind, the way people and especially children are quick to stake out their claims on the holiday beach and resent all "intruders," are clear examples of this all-pervading tendency to territorial behavior. There is, on the other hand, hardly any need to point out examples of absolute social hierarchy in human societies, ancient or recent, primitive or evolved: chieftains, princes, kings and the carefully elaborate hierarchies of their courts, armies and the management of modern big business, as well as teenager gangs, are only a few.

Dr. A. H. Esser, observing autistic patients in a New York clinic, and not knowing anything about my theories, found a dichotomy of absolute and relative hierarchy practically identical to what I observed in crowded domestic cat communities. As such patients have practically none of the social inhibitions which prevent normal people from giving vent to undisguised aggressiveness, their display of dominance and territoriality (Dr. Esser's terms for absolute and relative hierarchy respectively) was almost brutally uninhibited, though this does not mean that the basic mechanisms involved are in themselves abnormal.

Nearly five years in prisoner-of-war camps taught me that overcrowded human societies reflect the symptoms of overcrowded wolf, cat, goat, mouse, rat or rabbit communities to the last detail and that all differences are merely species-specific; the basic forces of social interaction and of organization are *in principle* identical and there is true homology between Man and Animal throughout the whole range of vertebrates.

To recognize such an internal balance in man between absolute and relative social hierarchy, brought about by evolution as part of a density-control mechanism, *which limits the adaptability of the individual*, is not to deny that adaptability. What it does mean, however, is that the mental health of the individual is in danger and will eventually break down if adaptability is stretched too far beyond the limits set by evolutionary adaptation. If this happens to enough individuals to constitute a sizeable proportion of a community, then that community ceases to be stable, healthy and fit for humans to inhabit. Density surreptitiously creeping beyond the tolerance limits (for in a species like ours there is certainly also a minimum limit, though this is not of such general importance at present because we are not in acute danger of underpopulation) may create symptoms which cannot be directly and easily traced back to it as their cause but are often attributed to factors which are merely contributory or symptomatic in themselves. The resulting constant subliminal tension will lower the individual's resistance toward other disturbing factors. Thus I have no doubt whatever that a great number of neuroses and social maladjustments are partially or totally, directly or indirectly, caused by overcrowding.

Professor Calhoun and others have shown that crowded conditions seriously disturb maternal care in rats and mice. Likewise human mothers, according to Professor René Spitz, are deeply influenced by population density: they often cannot form and maintain the proper emotional bonds toward their babies; this in turn interferes with the child's "ego formation," with its whole character development in which early youth and proper maternal care and affection are so vastly important. Nothing shows better than this what far-reaching damage can be done indirectly to future generations by the parent generations being too densely packed.

This is our situation now, and we have already been in it a long while. What every normal man wants for himself and his family is a detached house in an adequate garden, with neighbors close enough to be found if needed or one feels like a social call, yet far enough away to be avoided at other times. What we see instead is the cancerous growth of the huge blocks of flats of so-called satellite cities creeping out into the countryside, and very soon we shall reach the point where individuals simply cannot any longer be allowed to acquire a piece of land of their own and erect a single family house on it: in the interest of the Common Good the block of flats will have to become compulsory. Our civilization is marching with banners flying from battery hen to battery consumer.

Population Problem in Perspective

In recent years there has been growing concern about the so-called population explosion and the measures to be taken to avoid overcrowding. However, this is mostly understood to mean that an attempt should be made only to slow down the population increase so that the production of supplies, predominantly food, can catch up, and if this is achieved everything will be fine—or so many of those in authority seem to think.

Reasoning on these lines makes it look as if controlling the population growth were mainly a problem of the underdeveloped countries: our own affluence distracts from the fact that we *are* already overcrowded. We recommend birth control to the underdeveloped nations, but in our own overpopulated countries we still encourage large families with tax relief and even handsome allowances.

Contrary to current discussion, the danger of overpopulation does not rest solely on the need for food and shelter. It lies in whether the population will exceed the limits of human tolerance toward the presence of other humans. These limits have been set by evolutionary processes over millions of years. They cannot, therefore, be altered or trained differently within a few generations, nor can they be neglected, repressed or overstepped without seriously disrupting the internal harmony of the species.

It will be argued that my assertions run contrary to almost everything which is regarded as scientifically safe in modern psychology and sociology. The concept of adjustment is almost invariably understood as pertaining to the adjustment of individuals to environment, especially social environment. Hence, where disharmony between individual and social environment is found, this is generally explained as failure of the individual to adjust. True as this is in some cases, it overlooks the fact that in many respects the environment fails to be adjusted to the proper needs of the individual. Modern psychologists have, in many instances at least, been so amazed and overwhelmed by the enormous range of variation found among human personalities and behavior patterns that they have largely forgotten that all variations are but variations on the one theme, the species. Nothing can happen to or become of the individual which is not within the range of the characteristics defining the species. But today most psychologists are so sure of the omnipotence of individual adaptability and learning that they are blind to the facts which would help to reveal exactly what is the role of genetic— that is, phylogenetic—information in all the different types of human behavior.

Yet along with the learning psychologist, our social psychologists and sociologists are so convinced that everything in social behavior can, and therefore must, be trained, learned, institutionalized, that they fail to see a very plain fact: traditions and institutions would never be stable if they did not rest on an innate behavioral basis. To the student of evolutionary processes, all changes in cultural, traditional, educational, religious, philosophical and institutional attitudes appear to stir the surface only. The very core of human nature and conduct has evidently remained unchanged throughout known human history.

One of the age-old characteristics of the human species is that it is adapted to social life in a small group where each member knows each of the others personally, having a need for larger social gatherings from time to time but not too often, feeling a need to be by himself quite often, and reacting to continued oversocialization with all sorts of frustrations, repressions, aggressions and fears which soon develop into genuine neuroses. As it is a species characteristic it does not matter whether we like or regret the fact. *We have to live with it* and find conditions which allow us to live with it in comparative health, wealth and sanity.

That it is, for instance, possible to rear and train children so that they become habituated to oversocialized conditions until they are unable to feel safe and happy outside a crowd of their own kind certainly does not invalidate my point. Children and even adults can be trained or habituated to avoid everything good and healthy, to see their only source of contentment and even happiness in regularly overeating all sorts of palatable but unbalanced food, in continually seeking unsuitable and demoralizing amusements, in all kinds of perversions and addictions, and similarly in living continuously in a crowd. Robbed of these conditions, the afflicted individual will feel thoroughly dejected and miserable. Yet this "adjustment" to mass communities does the human species no more good than drug addiction or alcoholism.

As mentioned earlier, all *structurally* organized vertebrate communities depend for their internal structure and function on the individuals being personally acquainted with each other. This is the most fundamental difference between such communities, which therefore rightly deserve to be called societies, and the highly organized communities of bees, ants and termites, in which individuals in the sense of known personalities are wholly unimportant and, as a matter of fact, not to be found: any given individual will do for a certain function provided it is of the right "caste" or in the right phase of its life cycle. In a vertebrate community, however, which is not solely governed by absolute social hierarchy, the individual not only acquires personality, he also has some place, some preserve, where he is superior to all other members of the community. No matter how big or small the territory may be, and no matter what the ranking of the individual in the various absolute hierarchies of the community, as a territory owner he is equal among his equals. In this capacity, and in this capacity alone, the human individual is able to enter, as a responsible, participating, cooperating, independent, self-respecting and self-supporting citizen, the type of communal organization we call a democracy. Overcrowded conditions are thus a danger to true democracy which it is impossible to exaggerate. Tyranny is the almost inevitable result, whether it be exercised by personal tyrants or by an abstract principle like the Common Good, which is no longer any good at all to the mass of individuals. *For this is an unalterable law*: as long as density is tolerable, sacrifices made for a common cause will, one way or another, pay dividends to the individual and contribute to his own fulfillment. Beyond this point, however, the demands of the Common Good rise steeply, and what is taken away from the individual is gone for good; he cannot even see that it goes in any sizeable amount to others, for they are likewise robbed without reward.

If, in accordance with Wynne-Edwards' theories, the innate balance of relative and absolute social hierarchy once served as density control mechanism and thus ensured that social life did not develop into unbearable social pressure, why has it now apparently ceased to function in man? To the biologist the answer is obvious; hardly any biological mechanism works independently of others and faultlessly. Thus density tolerance in humans is adapted to a certain level of child mortality, to a "natural" percentage of people dying prematurely of diseases and plagues, and so on.

Scientific and technical progress has altered all this, but it could not and has not altered the basis of human social behavior and happiness which has been built into each individual by at least five hundred million years of vertebrate evolution. This cannot be altered in harmony with the whole except by that same, slow process of evolution, taking countless generations, and any attempt to force it will only result in the destruction of our own species. But the density control mechanism described here at length can be revived and brought into its natural and beneficial function again if we use our rational powers to restore the equilibrium, and use them swiftly and efficiently. It is no longer a question of forestalling future overpopulation: we must not only call a halt to further increase, we must find ethically and psychologically acceptable means of slowly shrinking numbers back to less than the present, to a sane density level. There is no time to be lost.

At present most people seem paralyzed by fear of The Bomb, but the bomb in itself is no danger. The only real danger to Man is men, too many men. Statisticians have forecast that by 2040 the world population will have reached 22 billions. By then production may possibly be capable of feeding, clothing and battery-keeping these numbers; but then nobody will be able to move without being impeded by numbers of other people moving, and without interfering irritatingly with their movements. At least half the population will have to be psychiatrists tending the neuroses of the other half. To this future population, the bomb will no longer be a threat but a temptation: it will appear as the salvation from all evil.

I think we all agree that we want neither the extinction of our species, or at least of many future billions, through the bomb, nor the re-establishment of the old, cruel methods by which nature balanced our numbers. Thus the only way remaining is humane density control—birth control. It can be done. Automation, if properly used, can allow us to keep and even enhance our living standard with a slowly decreasing number of young working people. At present, under the influence of an economic theory which regards ever-growing expansion as the aim of all economy and automation as a means of stepping it up even farther and faster, it can end only as all unchecked positive feed-back mechanisms end: in catastrophe. The choice is still ours: do we want rational regulation and—for some time—reduction of numbers, or unrestricted procreation and the Bomb as Ultima Ratio?

FURTHER READING

Leyhausen, P. *Verhaltensstudien an Katzen*. Berlin, 1956. English edition in preparation.
Russell, C., and W.M.S. Russell. *Human Behaviour*. London, 1961.
"Social Organization of Animal Communities," *Symposium of the Zoological Society of London*, 14 (1965).
Spitz, R.A. *A Genetic Theory of Ego Formation*. New York, 1959.
Wynne-Edwards, V.C. *Animal Dispersion in Relation to Social Behaviour*. London, 1962.

PSYCHO-ECOLOGICAL ASPECTS OF POPULATION

John B. Calhoun

It is ironic that altruism as a social stance and practical idealism as a political ideology (as exemplified by the Peace Corps) are customarily directed toward peasant agricultural societies, while our own people are stricken with the diseases and deprivations of affluence. The herdsman's lands have indeed been damaged— the soil, the water, the health of plants and animals—but in our own territory injury has been done to the total surround, of which the vast poisoned sky and sea are simply the most tangible aspects.

With five percent of Americans suffering from anxiety neuroses, with physical and biochemical strain manifested as organic failure and cancer, with the hazards of the automobile, with the quiet desperation of meaningless time-filling, we are still preoccupied like no nation before us with the problems of others.

Perhaps it is the quintessence of selflessness, perhaps guilt. But, more likely, digging wells in dry villages and transporting wheat to the hungry are visible solutions. Add moral conscience to money and effort and—presto!—you solve a problem, provided you can first find it.

No such easy magic can cure the strange maladies of post-industrial men: acedia and hubris, "encounter" difficulties and identity vacuums, excess leisure and rootless family life, existential funks and inability to cope with the prevailing high-contact social style, freakouts and withdrawal from the nonlife of the daily grind, and the psyche-lag and future-shock which characterize the millraces of change.

Since these ailments cannot be treated directly—because we don't even understand them—it is no wonder that we look for the merely homeless or diseased to help. Perhaps our so-called "environmental crisis" is the visible, ecological symptom of a sick society: stressed overnumerous organisms vibrating at an accelerating rate, for whom pollution is not so much a source of sickness as a response to it.

The very title I have selected reflects my rejection of the body and its nutrition as the ultimate concern of the adjustment man must make in the face of the very

---

John B. Calhoun, "Psycho-Ecological Aspects of Population," Unit for Research on Behavioral Systems, National Institute of Mental Health, URBSDOC No. 62, rev.

obvious fact that the world population will become much greater than at present before its growth can be brought under control. By this rejection I do not imply that we will be able to avoid some very serious questions regarding production and distribution of food during the next century. Serious local famines may take place. Mayer (*52*) contends that food production will keep up with population growth. This contention assumes that there will be curtailment of the rate of population growth, and that as the world population approaches a stable, relatively unchanging level, greater equity in the distribution of food will gradually be achieved.

Recently, the RAND Corporation (*36*) analysed the independent assessments of a number of "experts" regarding the future trend of world population growth. Their consensus indicated a leveling off at about 8 billion a century from now. This is less than half what projections from present trends indicate by that time. In fact, Gordon and Helmer, who coordinated this RAND study, concluded that the participants in this study appeared overly optimistic in their projections with regard to man being able to curtail world population growth at such a low level. Instead, we might do well to consider the possibility that world population might not be brought to a stable level under 12 billion even if a concerted effort toward curtailment of population growth does evolve within the world community. Taking this number of 12 billion as the minimum stable level that may be achieved, we can now begin to inquire what may be its impact upon man's life.

In this connection Boulding (*11*) presents two theorems: 1) If the only thing which can check the population growth is misery, then the population will grow until it is sufficiently miserable to check its growth. 2) If the only thing which can check the population growth is misery, then the ultimate result of any technological improvement is to enable a larger number of people to live in misery than before and hence to increase the total sum of human misery. In these two extensions of the Malthus' theory, Boulding originally said, "starvation and misery," but, if Mayer is right, we can drop out starvation and leave only misery in these two theorems. Here is Boulding, an economist, focusing on misery as the critical factor in population regulation. Or, again, turning to another economist, we find Galbraith (*34*) saying that henceforth our primary prescription must be for what may broadly be called the quality of life. This must now be our primary goal. We can no longer rely solely on measures of annual increase in production of goods for private consumption as an indicator of national vigor. In addition to the index of Gross National Product, he implies that we need a measure, which might be called the Gross National Service, as an indicator of the effort made to increase the quality of life. As he sees it, increasing population and increasing density of population does increase both the friction of person upon person and the outlay that is necessary for social harmony.

From studies on animals (*15,20*) it is quite apparent that misery, as reflected by the social stresses of living under crowded conditions, can markedly interfere with the ability to conceive, bear, and rear young. Likewise, we are led to suspect that comparable processes operate on the human level as indicated by Kincaid (*44*)

A New York City subway. Photo by Charles Gate-wood.

who reports that the prevalence of stillbirths and comparable phenomena are negatively correlated with social class. Although this ultimate impact of misery on curtailing population growth might be expected to operate on the human scene at some very high density, we can anticipate the possibility of a much more proximal effect operating through fear and hope. First, there is the rational fear of the consequences of uncontrolled reproduction to the extent that a fuller understanding of the broader meaning of misery becomes appreciated. Then, second, there is the rational hope for enhancing human potentialities (59) or for permitting continual self-renewal (35). Murphy (59) and Gardner (35) both recognize that the increasing massing of man hinders the realization of such hopes. And yet, it is the very awareness of unrealized hopes that can provide an acceptable avenue whereby individuals can come to decide on limiting the size of their families sufficiently to stem the tide of increasing population. Thus it is that my search focuses on the knowledge of misery and the meaning of increasing the quality of life.

U Thant (*101*) has emphasized the need for such a search when he remarked about population and related problems: "These are problems which never present the kind of dramatic ultimatum that questions of peace and war present. They slowly build up their crushing weight of misery until the human tragedy becomes overwhelming. We know all of this and we can, together, do something about it. We need new approaches and new ideas for our new world."

We may well ask: "What new approaches; what new ideas?" Julian Huxley (42) points the way. He says: "We must take a new look at the problem. We must stop thinking in terms of a race between production and reproduction, a race that never can be won. We must realize that our aim is not mere quantity, whether of people or goods or anything else, but quality—quality of human beings and of the lives they lead. Once we have grasped this, things begin to fall into place." Note the phrase, "quality of life," used here by Huxley, and above by Galbraith. This phrase is being used with increasing frequency in relation to population by persons from quite different professional backgrounds (e.g.: *21, 27, 41, 47, 52, 53, 55, 67, 76*). I am coming to believe that this patently very general phrase is, through usage, acquiring fairly specific meaning. Some might argue that in "mental health" we already have a phrase adequate to encompass what many are now feeling is *the* critical aspect of population. Speaking strictly logically from an etymological point of view this is so. However, as Knutson (*45*) has noted, there has been an Orwellian twist made to the point that mental health means mental illness, and so carries a negative aura. In contrast, the phrase "quality of life," though it too might be anticipated to encompass a range from the negative to the positive, seems to be highly weighted toward the positive. Furthermore, from the context in which quality of life is used more nearly equal emphasis is placed upon realizing the potentialities of the individual, increasing the effectiveness of social organization, and placing man in perspective to all life of all kinds to the point that we can no longer pursue human population problems without being imbued with Schweitzer's reverence for life.

Following Huxley's lead, we need to know more precisely what is meant by: "things begin to fall into place." Qualities of man fitting him for the transition demanded of contemporary cultures form one such set of "things." In the following five sets of paragraphs I have summarized some major constellations of these qualities as they are revealed by authors who, in general, are quite aware of their relevance to problems which, in part, have their origin in the growth of the human population.

Awareness, Consciousness of Self

Royce (*71*) has developed a figure of speech which helps to focus on this issue. He speaks of man being "encapsulated" by his experience; that each of us must attempt to get outside of ourselves, our culture, and our time, to break out of the bonds of conformity; to extend oneself by searching with sensitiveness into new domains of experience which constitutes the essence of adaptability to cultural change. Simpson (*80*) emphasizes this same viewpoint, but in a longer time perspective, when he points out that we must be aware of the process of our entire biological and social evolution in order that we may move from the strictures of the present to control our future evolution. But, this very awareness as one consciously strives for freedom beyond present circumstances creates anxiety as individual intent becomes thwarted by personal shortcomings or opposing forces in the environment (*89*). Thus, in a way, increasing the quality of life, through increasing awareness, makes life more difficult by demanding a greater understanding and tolerance of anxiety.

Concern and Service

The individual must free himself from utter self-preoccupation without losing his individuality in the process, but instead place himself in the voluntary service of some larger objective. In doing so he must develop the quality of empathy, the capacity to identify one's own feelings and needs with those of another person, the ability to look inward so as to obtain the insight which is necessary for the foresight to work for the good of others as well as for oneself. There is here the fusion of oneself and others, where oneself becomes the whole human species. Such meaningful relationship between the self and the values beyond the self make the free man capable of tolerating the rigors of freedom. This concern possesses an intrinsic religious orientation, a commitment to serve, which becomes a generic attitude of tolerance and compassion for fellow mortals, accompanied by charity, mercy, forbearance, and benevolence; as each individual improves his ability to give positive assistance to the adequate performance of others (*3, 9, 35, 49, 79*).

Happiness, Creativity, and Leisure

Happiness here forms more than the gratification experienced in the satisfaction of creature comforts, important though they are. Rather, happiness is here considered in the sense of the aesthetic experience, that Eureka exaltation, as the creative process, operating through an ego extending beyond its own boundaries, leads to new visions of pattern, values, and meaning, emerging out of anomaly, conflict, and dissonance (*37, 73, 78*).

Five capacities seem essential for an individual to be creative (*23, 35, 39, 71, 80, 90, 99*). There is first an unconditional *openness and receptivity to stimuli* from the external world and the inner self which preserves a freshness of perception and an unspoiled awareness. Then there is the capacity to free oneself from the web of social pressures which tend to bind us into a cocoon of conformity or withdrawal. This *independence to take risks* derives not from arrogance but from humility. It entails *flexibility of learned responses* in which one maintains the capacity to alter customary concepts and values in the face of altered conditions of the environment. Flexibility is the cultural analog of genetic diversity which permits animals to adapt to new niches. Perhaps the most difficult quality to achieve is what has been called *the tolerance of ambiguity*. It is the capacity to tolerate the internal conflict engendered by a transient or even long-persisting inability to make a rational judgment between alternative opportunities of decision. And yet, this tolerance of ambiguity does not mean avoidance of decision. Rather, it means that the individual is willing to take the risk of making a decision on "thematic grounds" (*39*), on intuition. Such a decision, such a suspected best choice in the face of conflicting and uncertain relationships, reduces the anxiety inherent in any confrontation with ambiguity, and thus contributes to the feeling of aesthetic exhaltation. Finally, creativity requires *the capacity to impose order on experience*; to replace old order with new order; to develop a rational hypothesis or a rationalized value system compatible with justifying the new order.

Creativity is closely bound to leisure. According to Martin (*51*) leisure differs from the mere filling up of free time with banalities in that it "is both the occasion and the capacity of the whole personality to open up to all stimuli from within and without. . . . In the creative cycle, work and leisure complement each other. . . . In work there is a focusing, a contraction of faculties and an acuteness of consciousness. During leisure, there is an unfocusing, a relaxation of faculties, a greater diffusion of consciousness. . . . With this relaxation, the field of consciousness widens to include what previously had been peripheral, subconscious, and suddenly, great unifying patterns are recognized and the great 'inductive leap' occurs. . . . In childhood we naturally possess and freely exhibit this capacity for leisure in its various manifestations. . . . A great part of this capacity suffers undue suppression and is lost during our development. . . . Hans Selye deplores this loss of leisure we had as children and attributes much of man's over-stressful life to it. . . . We are crossing the threshold of a totally new world, equipped with an obsolete philosophy. . . . Where, yesterday, our concern for mental health led us to those who were underprivileged, exploited, overworked, and 'poverty-stricken,' today, we are forced to turn our attention to those who are 'leisure-stricken.' . . . Now we must also serve to make men more fit for leisure, with the firm belief that only those fit for work and leisure will survive as creative individuals."

Considering the increasing capability of producing material goods, the demand for human skills falls primarily "in the creative and humanistic types of services, such as teaching, social work, entertainment, government, health services, scientific and aesthetic activities" (7). In this sense life becomes art, all organized expression of experience in significant and aesthetically effective form, where art is not a *thing* but rather, in Julian Huxley's words, it is a "type of human activity and its products" which permits us to escape upwards to 'new levels of being' (86).

Blain (10) has summed up these characteristics of the new type of man who is dissatisfied with mere quantity, but searches for quality. He speaks of him as the "novalescent" man, one who is devoted to the pursuit of excellence, to the development and maintenance of creativity, and who retains the capacity for self-renewal by persisting in the youthful capacity to break out of closed systems he has entered. And, though the novalescent man breaks out of the neurotic bonds of defenses and distortions by thus freeing his energies for self-realization, his creative act gains social meaning only to the extent that it arises in the context of some mature and tender concern for human values and needs and becomes the sublimated love of creative power, agape (70,73).

Moral Responsibility

There must be alternative modes of action available, but among them man, guided by humanistic ideals and goals he considers ethical, must exercise self-discipline in the use of his freedom of choice while aware of the consequences of his actions, and as he assumes responsibility for them, even as they extend to later generations (35, 78, 79, 80).

Diversity, Choice, and Change

We move here to conditions external to the individual or to differences among individuals. Individuality has become the hallmark of man. Its realization implies the opportunity to be different as a consequence of one's unique heredity and the opportunity to become different as a consequence of the ability and opportunity to express choice (42, 67). Ability to choose, the personal freedom to choose, becomes the process whereby the individual activates the impulse to gather information about a decision relative to his self-protection (59, 62). But the opportunity to express choice, or even to recognize the opportunity for choice, becomes largely an ecological problem, one in which the opportunity for choice is highly influenced by the conditions of the system within which the individual lives. Increasing complexity of organization *can* increase the range of choice, provided the network of communication which it sustains functions effectively (*35, 57, 68, 100*).

In this "provided-that" we find lurking the dark genie of social malaise affecting the individual. Eiseley (*30*) sums it up this way: "As a kind of shadow-accompaniment of technological advance, man has brought about an evolution of contingency itself. Chance—dangerous, irrevocable chance—plays a constantly increasing role within human society and, indeed, within our whole natural environment. Thus, while man has become the most adaptable creature on earth, he is unwittingly forcing this adaptability in all directions. Choice, even intelligent choice, becomes increasingly hard to make among an infinite number of diverging pathways, some of which show signs of leading into new and dangerous corners" such as: "Infant mortality, fantastically curtailed, produces in its wake a desperate struggle to reduce a locust swarm of human beings." To which point Mumford (*58*) remarks: ". . . every new baby is a blind desperate vote for survival: people who find themselves unable to register an effective political protest against extermination, do so by a biological act." Such recognition of the effect of the increasing population on the freedom of choice (*25, 55, 77*) has led Wood (*100*) to emphasize the need for "fail-safe mechanisms" in social as well as atomic affairs to counteract the consequences of "the so-called 'encounter' problem—the expanded and unintended consequences of acts, when carried on among a great number of people and things."

Change theoretically produces more choices, and adaptation to change through ethical choices thus enhances the opportunity for ethical life as the rate of change increases (*80, 86*). Change should, therefore, be a desirable aspect of life. Querido (*67*) points out that change causes "dis-ease," negative feelings, which only disappear when a new social organization demonstrates that the individual can exist in a better way than before. Every change causes a reorganization of personality (*88*) during which anxiety is generated and persists while the individual's coping mechanism, and the supportive mechanisms provided by society, facilitate final readjustment.

Here lies the basic issue of current times. Cultural changes, induced by the interaction of an ever more rapid pace of technological change with the increasing population, are now demanding an ever-increasing rate of change in personality structure (*1, 7, 14, 30, 53, 63*). We can visualize the present dilemma something like this: If, at any moment of contemporary life, T is the time it takes to accommodate to a unit change in culture, and t is the time elapsing between successive units of change in culture requiring an adjustment in personality, then we seem to be in the unenviable situation in which t is less than T; we are never able to complete one unit of change in our personality before one or more additional changes are demanded. So, it comes about that we have entered an era of the lagging psyche (*14*) and sustained anxiety.

Platt (*63*) describes the developing condition as a "kind of cultural 'shock-front,' like the shock-fronts that occur in aerodynamics when the leading edge of an airplane wing moves faster than the speed of sound and generates the sharp pressure wave that causes the well-known sonic boom," and, he continues, "I think our present transitional crisis is a similar shock-front for the human race, buffeting us about as sudden changes in every direction come thick and fast. It is a multiple shock-front, with each type of exponential change reinforcing all others." This analogy "suggests that after the shock-front has passed, we will have reached larger powers and interactions—higher temperatures and pressures!—but, that the buffeting of change will be reduced, and times will perhaps become psychologically and socially calmer than anything this generation or this century has known. . . . Life will go on being different, . . . but it will also be different in a different way, because the approach to a steady state is something rare in the history of the world. We see that humanity is on the verge of a new kind of life." Murphy (*59*) and Teilhard de Chardin (*22*) have all made significant contributions to our understanding of the nature of this transition and the life ahead. Both they, and many others who attempt to grapple with problems related to population increase and cultural change, single out creativity and capacity to adjust to change as primary capacities required of men to make this transition during the century ahead.

During this transition, most are agreed that there must be a curtailment of the headlong increase of the numbers of man on the earth. Emphasis has been placed on mechanisms for reducing family size with no clear concept as to what the ideal optimum population might be. Some argue that it eventually should return to a level lower than that of the present. On the other hand, we must accept the fact that the world population will become considerably greater than at present, and, furthermore, we must not close our eyes to the possibility that the evolution of the human species may require a considerably larger population than now exists. We must begin working for that understanding which will lead us to better criteria for judging the size of this optimum population. Querido (*67*) provides a guideline for such criteria; he says: "If and when, therefore, organizational responses encroaching irretrievably on the individual poetentialities and characteristics of society members seem to be the only possible answer to population problems, the upper limit in population figures must be considered to be reached. Obviously, this limit is a psychological one. . . . 'Too much' exists, if the person is forced to subject to the collectivity to such an extent that he loses essential individual attributes. He becomes an infra-individual; he is less than a man." Thus, the population problem is ultimately a psychological one, but its solution involves the organization of society, the entire ecology of man as the realization of his potential become influenced by the entire matrix of the biological and cultural systems in which he is enmeshed. From this orientation comes the title of this paper, "The psycho-ecological aspects of population."

Despite this increasing focus on the positive side of the balance of life, concern with the pathological still provides a powerful lever in uncovering the insights which can assist us in increasing the quality of life, as we push the misery of life into the background. For example; there is now a voluminous literature (*20, 87, 98*) delineating the physiological pathology which accompanies crowding in animals. In general pathology increases with density and may be attributed to an inability of the pituitary-adrenal system to accommodate sufficiently to the stresses arising from increased density. Few of these studies have attempted to focus down upon the independent variables of more direct involvement than density per se. On the human level the kinds of pathologies, observed to be related to increase in density among animals, have usually been investigated without regard to the question of crowding. And yet, as Hinkle and his associates (*38*) have found, such diverse phenomena as precipitation of the diabetic reaction and increase in nasal congestion become accentuated following periods of unsatisfactory social interaction. Such studies of physiological malfunction help us to appreciate that there is, in fact, an hierarchy of levels of processes involved in the misery-quality spectrum.

Overriding the lower levels we have the entire ecosystem involving all forms of life with their manifold interactions and dependencies along with the impact they have on the physical environment and, in turn, the influence exerted by the physical environment upon all these forms of life. Below that comes man's culture itself involving all the processes of communication, social organization, and technology which both generate and facilitate the realization of his continually rising expectations. As individual members of the human race each of us, in our natural egocentric concern with our own welfare, often finds it difficult to recognize the primacy of these more complex processes over that third level from the top, the level of processes involving the interations of each of us with our associates. Lastly, comes the level of physiological changes within the individual, as these become consequences of the processes within the three higher levels. Except for the prior brief paragraph, this last level falls outside the scope of the present paper. Rather, I shall proceed back up through the three higher levels only to the extent of providing an indication of their relationship to the increasing human population.

Two attempts have been made to develop logically useful formulations of the relationship between population and the disruption of the equilibrium between the comforts and discomforts (gratification and frustration) arising from an increase in population. The one comes from psychoanalysis, the other from animal behavior. René Spitz (*83*) couches his formulation under the rubric of the "derailment of dialogue." He says: "Behavior patterns consist of *anticipatory, appetitive,* and *consummatory* phases we call action cycles. Interrupting action cycles prior to consummation produces unpleasure in various forms, only one of which is anxiety. We frequently also speak of this unpleasure as *frustration.* Consistent interruption of action cycles leaves a residue which is cumulative."

"There comes a point at which the compensation of the accumulated un-discharged appetitive readiness cannot be carried through without seriously interfering with the normal functioning of the organism. A conflict arises now between the need to compensate and the requirements of normal everyday functioning. At this point a vicious circle begins for the need to compensate conflicts with the consummation of normal functions and creates an increasing quantity of unconsummated action cycles. These now will cumulate in their turn and lead to the disorganization and disruption of the compensatory attempts. The culmination of this process is what I call *derailment of dialogue*."

Our technology permits us to overcome a host of obstacles in the physical sphere. This, says Spitz, "thus imperils man and his survival at a much more vulnerable point, in his organ of adaptation, in his ego." And he continues: "I have yet to hear anyone raising his voice about the dangers of overpopulation to man himself, I would be inclined to say to man's very essence, about the danger to the ego, the one agency in man which possesses the resources to cope with these hazards—but when damaged, cannot cope with them."

On the animal side my empirical studies of social behavior have led to a somewhat comparable formulation (*16, 19*). Every species finds optimum satisfaction from social life within a very narrow range of variability of group size. The larger the optimum group size the less intensely do its members react to each other upon encounter. Each individual from time to time feels the need to interact with an associate. When two such individuals meet, their interaction places each in a state of gratification for some period of time during which each may be said to be refractory with reference to appropriate interaction with some other associate. If perchance some individual, who is in the need state for social interaction, happens to meet an associate who happens to be in the gratification refractory period, the resultant interaction will be unsatisfactory to the individual which had need of social intercourse. Such an individual is thrown into a refractory period of a frustrating nature. No individual in a refractory period, regardless of kind, can react appropriately to the needs of another. Any individual which is so frustrated, will have had his social approach unrewarded, that is unreinforced. Therefore, in its next approach to another individual its behavior is likely to be slightly deviant. Retaining a normal repertoire of behavior demands a fairly high frequency of approaches culminating in gratifying refractory periods. Thus it is that the greater the proportion of an individual's encounters are frustrating, the more deviant will be its behavior and, furthermore, the more it will withdraw physically and psychologically from social contact until, at the extreme, all contact with social reality is lost. Furthermore, even in the best of all possible worlds, membership in an optimum sized group, the stochastics of the social system is such that every individual must anticipate becoming frustrated in at least half of its encounters. But, as the group size increases the proportion of frustrating encounters must increase until, at not much greater than the square of the optimum group size, every individual becomes essentially out of contact with all of his associates despite their frequent close approaches to each other.

Both theories recognize that where increasing frequency of interaction accompanies increases in population, marked disorganization of normal behavior must transpire. Both similarly recognize that the group or population size is still not the critical variable. Each formulation makes clear what Querido (67) stated in general terms; that the degree of satisfactoriness of the relationship between pairs of individuals is the crucial variable. Insofar as man goes, he likely still retains a physiology and social responsiveness whose genetic base varies little from that of millenia ago, when semi-isolated closed social groups probably did not vary greatly from 12 adults. And yet, through cultural history, one of man's continuing greatest achievements has been that he has been able to develop appropriate mechanisms whereby each individual could be members of several groups, but at any moment in time he would operate in one whose numerical characteristics differed little from those of his culturally more primitive ancestors.

Despite this culturally buffering process we know all too well, from many avenues of research, that interpersonal relationships do break down for a variety of reasons. If we are to gain an adequate comprehension of how population increase may affect man with regard to both his psychopathology and the quality of his life, we must begin to seek a more adequate basis for the connection between population and the effectiveness of interpersonal relations.

Spitz (83) considers the primary point of effect: "It should be remembered that inappropriate mother-child relations can arise for a variety of reasons, only one of which is overpopulation; at present, it still surely is not a major one. However, up to now it has not been described and we are unaware of the dangerous potentialities of overpopulation. In view of present demographic trends we will do well to keep these possibilities in mind. . . . For when the dialogue breaks down in infancy, ego formation is inhibited, ego functions distorted and atrophied; ego apparatuses are crippled and the integrity of the ego, of the principal organ of adaptation, is in jeopardy. Compensation functions will be developed which have little or nothing to do with the givens of reality. Such an ego, if it survives, will show monstrous deformations, and probably will never be able to achieve the capacity to develop into a well-integrated partner in any kind of dialogue."

Adults too must face integration into existing social groups. Such adjustments accompany any change of residence or change of place of work. Malzberg (50) showed that immigrants into the State of New York exhibited a marked increase in incidence of hospitalization for mental disorders, which did not decline to the level of long-term residents until after five years had elapsed. Though the definite causal relationship is here unknown, it is at least certain that these initial years of new residence form a period fraught with the uncertainties and frustrations accompanying acceptance into the several kinds of groups essential for participation in our modern complex way of life.

Many changes other than those of residence or place of work can affect interpersonal relationships. The whole fabric of society appears to be changing at a faster rate even than that of population increase. So far, we cannot separate these two kinds of changes—population and social—insofar as their effects are concerned.

Spengler (*82*), from the viewpoint of economics, has presented a mathematical formulation having much in common to those of Spitz and Calhoun. His essential conclusion holds that, as population increases, there must come a point beyond which freedom of choice must decrease. It is very interesting to note the growing emphasis of economists upon behavior, sociology, and ethics as the critical area of concern in adjusting to increasing population. For example: Gabor (*32*), in examining freedom of choice as it relates to opportunity for employment, concludes that as populations increase, hereditary limitations to learning capacity will increasingly limit opportunities for work, whether relating to production or service. This recognition of the prime importance of capacity for educability, of the problem of human learning in coping with conditions arising from population increase, and the pace of cultural and technological change, is forcing man to consider how he may assume rational control of his genetic evolution (*11, 24, 40, 43, 54, 60, 63, 97*) as well as his cultural evolution.

Even though guidance of genetic change, to increase capacity for educability, may gradually become a necessity, Salvadore (*72*) and Doxiadis (*27*) have pointed out that in the here and now and near future, the increase in the general level of educational experience, and the enhanced consciousness of most individuals of the world about them, has the effect of increasing the psychological mass of each individual. Thus, we must consider "psychological density" as well as population density. This leads us beyond the concept of density to that of population potential (85, 96). This concept of population potential holds that every individual is affected by every other individual in proportion to the reciprocal of the distances separating them. Furthermore, the greater the psychological mass of any individual the greater will be his effect upon every other individual. Thus, even with a constant sized population and an unvarying distribution of its members through space, the population potential at any individual will increase in so long as the psychological mass of every individual is, on the average, increasing. So, it is not enough to become more cognizant of the consequences of a simple population explosion; the "psychological population potential" explosion is of even greater magnitude. Urbanization increases the force of this latter explosion by bringing larger numbers of individuals closer together and by increasing more rapidly the psychological mass of each individual as a result of the generally more effective means of education found in urban areas.

The above attempt to focus on the level of interaction between individuals rapidly forces consideration of relations involving many individuals. This takes us directly to the institutional level of social organization, where we can ascribe an "institutional morality" to those processes which enhance the quality of life (*9, 11, 35, 67, 90*). Such institutional morality must be based on that knowledge of organization which enhances freedom and which provides for freedom on a higher plane to compensate for freedom given up for collective security; it maintains a balance between the values of the individual and of society. Institutional morality increases when cultural institutions increase the probability of the consequences of the responses or acts of the psychologically creative individual spreading beyond his own self's situation. That is, society must provide the ground, the climate, and the cultivation without which such seeds of creativity would remain socially unfruitful. By such processes of organization society can encourage the development of the "noosphere" (*22*) by improving every individual's ability and opportunity to give positive assistance to the adequate performance of others, and thus to maximize the "mental-health potential" (*9*). Muller-Thyme (*57*) defines a prime characteristic of such organization when he says that every level and every center of organization should have free and easy communication with every other level or center; that hierarchical organization will no longer suffice. In the absence of such organized and yet untrammeled communication the misery of socio-pathology arises; the environment is missing which can provide for the full scope and diversity of society and human personality (*84*).

Protest is the sign that such misery exists; protest of adolescents toward their elders; protest of students and even faculty against the system of university organization and administration; protest for civil rights; protest of developing nations against the slowness of realizing their rising expectations; protest against impending and ongoing armed conflict; all these and many others highlight the breakdown of dialogue and the conflict of values. Protest denotes an absence of dialogue, an absence of institutional means for promoting the dialogue necessary for deciding what it is we wish to do and why, for arriving at value decisions to bolster our intent. Vickers (*91*) designates as "appreciative systems" such institutional organization of dialogue which increases our freedom of decision. He sees development of effective appreciative systems as the prime prerequisite to adjusting to the pace of cultural and technological change and to the increasing population, and says (*92*): "The changes of the next thirty-five years, far more even than those of the last thirty-five years, will require of us a radical exercise in learning and relearning—not merely learning new ways of doing, but also new ways of seeing, and valuing, and organizing. And if we are to keep any control over the way the world develops, we must not wait to be taught those lessons by events. We must be moved to learn by our anticipation of things to come, moved not only to technical learning but to political learning and ethical learning. This is something we are very ill-equipped to do, both biologically and—at present— socially." Statements by others, who are concerned with this issue, clarify it:

Brain (*12*): "Is man too intelligent, or perhaps not intelligent enough? The world population crisis, as I suggested, may illustrate a lack of social integration of the intelligence of individuals."

Burhoe (*13*): "Not only is science as a discipline more important to society than the subsequent technological applications of it, but there is a matter of prior importance still, and that is the value attitudes and orientation of a population and their integration with the scientific world view. If the crisis of a split culture (cf. the two cultures of C.P. Snow) of the Western and more developed nations in the last half of the twentieth century is threatening to disintegrate them, how much more so will it disrupt the viability of individual personalities and social groups in peoples who have not even lived with some value integration around an earlier level of scientific advancement. This means for me that the primary problem of world society and peace is that of an integration of our values with the scientific world view, and this is as much a problem for the developed as for the less developed nations."

Potter (*64*): "If we are to preserve the dignity of the individual, and if the human species is to survive and prosper, we need to cultivate the world of ideas and perfect the techniques for arriving at value judgments in areas where facts alone are not enough."

Murphy (*59*): "Freedom is largely a function of the availability of relevant information in the decision-making process, and reflection on our part will increase rather than decrease the freedom of those who in later years will have to make the decisions for which we are as yet unready. . . . Part of this conception is that man can and will understand himself and his society. A still more concrete exemplification of the idea is that all men in the science-dominated modern era can learn to understand one another despite colossal gulfs established by political, economic and military cleavage; and that it is only through a common discovery of all men striving to understand that a 'one world' fit to live in can be discovered."

Mead (*53*): "In the present crisis, the need to establish a shared body of assumptions is a very pressing one—too pressing to wait for the slow process of educating a small elite group in a few places in the world. . . . Speed in working out new solutions is essential if new and more disastrous fragmentations are not to occur—but we also need an appropriate framework."

Laswell (*46*): "In Julian Huxley's classical phrase, man is taking evolution in his own hands; and the critical process is the rehearsal of the entire range of imaginable options. The self-discipline involved in exposing the focus of attention to these options is an act of rational choice, since no terminal selection can be justified unless all major categories of value have been considered in relation to each alternative. By building various value orientations into computer societies it will be possible to explore the consequences of renovating the value systems to which we are accustomed." Though this dialogue which is the appreciative system ultimately involves man with man, we must in the process join forces with computers, see them as collaborators, not as antagonists, or in the words of Ross Ashby (as quoted by Dryer, *28*) we need to link computers with men as "intelligence amplifiers."

Brain (*12*): "As individuals we are all receptors, capable of supplying the higher centers with information. What information they get, therefore, depends upon us. We are also the motor nerves, and what society does is done by us. But we are again, collectively, ourselves the higher centers, the forebrain, which mediates for the social mind the difficult task of receiving the information, learning from past experience, reacting to it emotionally, yet controlling its emotions; and, above all, looking into the future." (Also see 75.)

Eiseley (30): "Today a new analogy has excited attention on the part of the public and many scholars. It lies in a rough comparison with the evolutionary growth and increasing complexity of that spheriod known as the brain, with the increase in human numbers and the extension of a nerve net of communications over a similar sphere of limited dimensions; it is, namely, the world. Human society, like the convolutions of the individually evolving neopallium, should lead to a heightened, reflective consciousness on the part of the human masses. 'Man,' in the words of Teilhard de Chardin, 'is building his composite brain before our eyes.'"

Lest we become disheartened we can note with encouragement that the rate of emergence of this consciousness is proceeding at a far faster rate than that of population increase.[1] One can best grasp the magnitude of this emergence by examining Jacques Ellul's *Technological Society* (31). In it, written first in 1954, but not translated into English until 1964, we find a dismal picture of the inextricable misery of modern society with its de-humanization produced by the elaboration of "technique," of "know-how," (or as Vickers, 91, calls it, "regulatory systems") which proceeds without plan with only the criteria of efficiency, power, and yield marking its progression and domination. The very emergence of the concept of the appreciative system and the predominant focus of recent writers on the quality of life reveals the tremendous upsurge of consciousness over the past ten years.

Vishniac (93) precisely sums up the "calling" we must assume: "Only the power of the mind, of our spirit, can conquer misery. We are now coming to a very dangerous spot, and we must feel the responsibility. We have not the right to make mistakes. This can mean the end of civilization; the end of everything. . . . We are trying to establish a great society. This is a great step forward. Behind it lies the next step: the family of man; one humanity. We have no choice: go this way or go no way at all." Going "this way" demands more than awareness, more than intent; it demands a rational knowledge of social organization and the process of communication, and it requires moral institutions for the implementation of the related processes. All about us we can see disconnected empirical efforts at establishing facets of appreciative systems, for developing channels of dialogue to replace protest. Beyond this we can begin to detect emerging theoretical structure from an elaboration of the concept of the isolated "invisible college" (11, 65) into a dialogue among a network of them (17) to an adaptation of the general principles of cybernetics to such social processes of communication (23).

What is it about our times that engenders this remarkable process of expanding consciousness? It can be summed up in what may be called the "modern prophecy" which holds that man is entering a period of transition, more dramatic

[1] See comment at end of paper.

than any at least since his emergence as a biological genus, and that whatever transformation this transition will entail, it will be well on its way by the time another century has elapsed. Among the leading prophets we find Teilhard de Chardin (*22*), a Roman Catholic, Julian Huxley (*42, 43*), a biologist and humanist, Kenneth Boulding (*11*) an economist and Friend, Gardner Murphy (*59*), a psychologist, John Platt (*63*), a physicist, and von Foerster (*102*), an electrical engineer. They lead the creative ecumenical movement of the day, the movement toward increased consciousness, realization of the human potential, and readiness for the as yet unknown character of the transformation ahead. They have responded to the twin forces of the "avalanche" (*5*) of human numbers and the acceleration of cultural change. Their meaning may be summed up (*18*) in the following fashion: Over recorded history, and apparently extending far back into the murky past, each doubling of the world population has required only about half the time as the immediately preceding doubling. We are now approaching a point where continuation of past trends would for all practical purposes culminate in near instantaneous doublings. Furthermore, if we list the major revolutions along the course of the human lineage as the successive establishment of *Homo habilis, Homo erectus*, and *Homo sapiens* on the biological level; followed by settled agricultural life, the major religious philosophies, the scientific revolution, and the current electronics revolution on the cultural level, we may note that the interval of time between any two revolutions is less than one fifth the duration of the prior interval. Again, this process cannot continue for long before the interval between revolutions would be far shorter than the span of generations. Such is the source of the modern prophecy. Our role now becomes one of reacting to it with increasing consciousness, which may well take us through the last revolution of this two million year long domain of evolutionary epochs, through its final epoch which might be termed the revolution of compassionate understanding (*18*) with its emphasis on compassion, communication, and creativity.

Even the conservative medical profession is beginning to react responsibly and progressively to the forces which have precipitated the modern prophecy. In part this response arises from guilt, much in the fashion that creation of atomic bombs led to an increased social conscience by physicists. In medicine the source of guilt has arisen from their creation of that "other bomb," the precipitous increase in human numbers made possible through the effective death control "invented" by medical sciences and medical practice. Much to the credit of the medical profession it is not limiting its attention solely to the questions of birth control and family planning. Most encouraging is the whole process of reevaluation of the role of medicine in society. This ranges from the reexamination of the role of the clinician toward making his personal relations with patients more effective (*61, 66, 69*), through a search for the role for what Watts (*94, 95*) calls "the physician to society," to a reorganization of medical education (*4, 6, 26, 33, 74*) including the perspectives of ecology, the behavioral sciences and evolution.

In fact it is this enlarging view of man in his context of a more encompassing ecosystem even than his own culture that reflects the growing state of consciousness. At both the level of institutional organization and of the ecosystem the complexities of structure and process, and the long term nature of the processes and their effects are necessitating the systems approach to analysis and long-term planning in order to cope with anticipated contingences as they begin to emerge (*2, 8, 29, 48, 56*). This approach, including those processes more directly related to population, have become necessary for the growth and survival of social systems. Deutsch (*23*) designates social systems which are most likely to grow and survive as "self-developing or self-enhancing systems, which are able to increase their probability of survival and their ranges of possible action over an increasing variety of environments." And he says further: "An essential characteristic of any human organization, in contrast to an anthill, is the interplay between the dimensions of growth of the organization and the growth of the individuals and of the more or less autonomous subgroups which compose it. In this sense, the growth of human organization is always the growth of several levels of autonomous systems, and the autonomous growth and self-determination of individuals is one of its touchstones." This statement must be broadened to include the highest level, the entire ecosystem of the earth. Only through its inclusion in the overall process of analysis and planning may we maximize the probability of enhancing the potentialities of the individual human being.

The extension of consciousness required for this inclusion takes us into an elaboration of Schweitzer's "reverence for life." We are indebted to Deutsch (*23*) for a definition of reverence appropriate to the present discussion: "Reverence always implies the openness to, and the higher value put on, any information concerning that which is outside and greater than ourselves." I am here concerned with a reverence applied to the entire ecosystem, a reverence for life then that is greater than that relating to any individual human, other animal, plant or social or biological system. In closing I wish to focus on the irreverence accompanying the population growth of the human species, most particularly in recent years.

This brings us face-to-face with the problem of evolution, not just of man as the now dominant species, but of other forms of life as well. To Slobodkin (*81*) evolution is an existential game in which the only payoff "is in the continuation of the game," a game organisms play with their environment "making certain adjustments only when there is reasonable assurance that the risks associated with these adjustments have been covered. Neither efficiency, nor complexity, nor power, nor even destruction of one's opponent, can serve as a goal itself." The question here pertains to the opportunity of playing this game, which becomes several kinds of games including that of the game of the growth and survival of "self-developing and self-enhancing systems" discussed by Deutsch for man but open to other organisms.

Once upon a time, really not too many years ago, certainly no longer ago than the beginning of settled agriculture, the earth was something like a chess board in that it consisted of a mosaic of lesser areas, each cell of which was formed by a community of plants and animals which differed somewhat in composition from those in adjoining cells. Some cells harboring similar communities were often separated from each other by differing communities, bodies of water or other physiographic or climatic barriers. Despite these barriers, or because of their occasional breakdown, there has been a flow of organisms between similar cells, or their invasion of cells somewhat less appropriate to their existing heredity. Both the isolation, the later mixing, and the invasion of less hospitable habitats have all contributed to every organism playing the existential evolutionary game. But look at the "board" now. Large portions of most cells, and the entire area of some cells, are now filled with cities. Arteries of highways, railways, and agricultural lands connect the urban areas and sometimes fill the entire area between arteries. If this process of fragmentation continues while the human population increases to three or four times its present numbers all surviving forms of non-domesticated life will be restricted to small completely isolated cells. With the exception of bats, and birds and a very few very mobile insects—such as the monarch butterfly—evolution will have come to a halt for most terrestrial organisms. We can paint a canvas in black and white of the earth at that not too distant date. If we paint the continents and islands black where human occupancy nearly totally excludes all non-domesticated forms, we will have before us a nearly totally black canvas with only a few minute and isolated dots and splotches of white representing the final refugia of other forms than man.

We can paint another picture, one in which the white areas form a connected network of cells with channels between cells along which many forms of life can flow. When one of these life-channels is crossed by an artery between human centers, the artery of human communication will dip underneath the surface, or, less desirable, swing over it like the Golden Gate Bridge over the passage of the sea into the San Francisco Bay. Sustaining the multiple games of evolution by such action we can preserve many degrees of freedom of choice of the ecosystem and through it enhance the human potential.

The present treatment of psycho-ecological aspects of population has avoided pretense at establishing boundaries of the scope of a subject matter suitable for further investigation. No longer does a topographic model of compartmentalization of knowledge and investigation prove very useful. Rather, we can take the topic of population as a point of focus and couple it with any one of many specific areas of concern such as psychiatry, psychology, education, ecology, communication, creativity, sociology, philosophy or even theology, and then from one of these vantage points or centers of interest one can begin searching for connections with all the others.

The present article, published here for the first time, was completed in 1966 as an elaboration of a talk of the same title given on August 17, 1965, at the annual meeting of the Ecological Society of America at Urbana, Illinois. It represents an effort to establish a consensus of insight about the human population crisis. This consensus, in conjunction with my "field theory" of evolution of sociality (*16*), formed a springboard to a set of papers exploring the image of man and the design of his future evolution:

a. "Space and the Strategy of Life," Moving Frontiers of Science Lecture No. 3, 1968 Annual Meeting of the American Ass'n. for the Advancement of Science, Dallas, Texas (shortened version in press, 1970, in *Ekistics*).

b. "Promotion of Man," in *Proceedings of the Global Systems Dynamics Symposium*, ed. E.O. Attinger. Basel: S. Karger AG, in press 1970.

c. "Creativity and Evolutionary Design," URBS Document No. 153, November 1969 (scheduled for publication in *Proceedings of the Conference on Religion and the Future*, held November 20-23, 1969, at Crozer Theological Seminary, Chester, Pennsylvania). 14 pages.

REFERENCES

1. Ackerman, N. W. "The Family in Crisis," *Bull. N. Y. Acad. Medicine*, 40 (1964), 171-187.
2. Adelson, M. *Toward a Future for Planning*. Santa Monica: System Development Corporation, March 1965.
3. Allport, G. W. "Mental Health: A Generic Attitude," *J. of Religion and Health*, 4 (1964).
4. Arrington, G. E., and G. Hilkowitz. " 'Man and His Environment': A New Course at the Medical College of Virginia," *J. of Medical Education*, 39 (1964), 704-711.
5. Audy, J. R. "Aspects of Health in the Pacific," pp. 3-11 in *Public Health and Medical Sciences in the Pacific*. Honolulu: University of Hawaii Press, 1964.
6. _____. "Human Ecology," *Bull. Med. Lib. Assoc.*, 53 (1965), 410-419.
7. Barre, R. L. "Trends, Issues, and Social Policy," the keynote address before the Annual New York State Welfare Conference, November 17-19, 1964.
8. Bell, D. "Twelve Modes of Prediction: A Preliminary Sorting of Approaches in the Social Sciences," *Daedalus*, (Summer, 1964), 845-880.
9. Blain, D. "Organized Religion and Mental Health," *J. of Religion and Health*, 4 (1965), 164-173.
10. _____. "Novalescence," *Amer. Jour. Psychiatry*, 122 (1965), 1-12.
11. Boulding, K. E. *The Meaning of the Twentieth Century: The Great Transition*. New York: Harper & Row, 1964.
12. Brain, Lord. "Science and Behaviour," *Advancement of Science*, 21 (1964), 221-229.
13. Burhoe, R. W. Professor of Theology and the Sciences, Meadville Theological School, University of Chicago, in a letter to John B. Calhoun, dated March 6, 1965.
14. Calder, R. "Earthlings in the Space Age," *Advancement of Science*, 19 (1962), 11-20.
15. Calhoun, J. B. "A Behavioral Sink," chapter 22 in *Roots of Behavior*, ed. E. L. Bliss. New York: Harper & Brothers, 1962.
16. _____. "The Social Use of Space," pp. 1-188 in *Physiological Mammalogy*, vol. I, ed. W. Mayer and R. Van Gelder. New York: Academic Press, 1964.
17. _____. "Behavioral States and Developed Images," paper given at the 1965 annual meeting of the American Association for the Advancement of Science at Berkeley, California.
18. _____. "A Glance Into the Garden," pp. 19-36 in *Three Papers on Human Ecology*. Oakland, Calif: Mills College Assembly Series, 1965-66.

19. _____. "Ecological Factors in the Development of Behavioral Anomalies," in *Comparative Psychopathology*, ed. J. Zubin. New York: Grune & Stratton, 1967.
20. Christian, J. J., and D. E. Davis. "Endocrines, Behavior, and Population," *Science*, 146 (1964), 1550–1560.
21. David, H. P. "Editor's Preface," pp. 9–10 in *Population and Mental Health*, ed. H. P. David. New York: Springer, 1964.
22. de Chardin, T. *The Phenomenon of Man*. New York: Harper & Brothers, 1959.
23. Deutsch, K. *Nerves of Government*. New York: The Free Press, 1963.
24. Dobzhansky, T. "Evolution: Organic and Superorganic," *Bull. Atomic Scientists*, (May, 1964).
25. Dorn, H. F. "World Population Growth," pp. 7–28 in *The Population Dilemma*, ed. P. M. Hauser. Englewood Cliffs, N. J.: Prentice-Hall, 1963.
26. Dorosin, D. "Emerging Disciplines in the Health Sciences and Their Impact on Health Science Libraries: The Behavioral Sciences," *Bull. Med. Lib. Assoc.*, 53 (1965), 403–409.
27. Doxiadis, C. A. "On the Measure of Man: Challenge and Response in the Anthropocosmos," *Mayo Clinic Proceedings*, 40 (1965), 70–89.
28. Dryer, B. V. "Thinking Men and Thinking Machines in Medicine," *Jour. Medical Educ.*, 38 (1963), 82–89.
29. Duhl, L. J. "New Directions in Mental Health Planning," (paper given at Rutgers University, February 26, 1965) *Archives of General Psychiatry*, 13 (1965), 403–410.
30. Eiseley, L. "The Freedom of the Juggernaut," *Mayo Clinic Proceedings*, 40 (1965), 6–21.
31. Ellul, J. *The Technological Society*. New York: Alfred A. Knopf, 1964.
32. Gabor, D. "Technology, Life and Leisure," *Nature*, 200 (1963), 513–518.
33. Galdston, I. "Prometheus and the Gods: An Essay on Ecology," *Bull. N. Y. Acad. Medicine*, 40 (1964), 560–575.
34. Galbraith, J. K. "Economics and the Quality of Life," *Science*, 145 (1964), 117–123.
35. Gardner, J. W. *Self-renewal: The Individual and the Innovative Society*. New York: Harper & Row, 1963.
36. Gordon, T. J., and O. Helmer. *Report on a Long-range Forecasting Study*. Santa Monica: The RAND Corporation, (September, 1964).
37. Grace, H. A. "The First Stage of Inquiry," *Amer. Behavioral Scientist*, 6 (1963), 22–23.
38. Hinkle, L. E., Jr. "The Doctor, His Patient and the Environment," *Amer. Jour. Public Health*, 546 (1964), 11–17.
39. Holton, G. "Presupposition in the Construction of Theories," pp. 77–108 in *Science as a Cultural Force*, ed. H. Woolf. Baltimore: Johns Hopkins Press, 1964.
40. Hulse, F. S. "The Paragon of Animals," *Eugenic Quarterly*, 11 (1964), 1–10.
41. Huxley, A. "Education on the Nonverbal Level," an address given *circa* 1961, ditto copy, source unknown.
42. Huxley, J. *The Human Crisis*. Seattle: University of Washington Press, 1963.
43. _____. "Eugenics in Evolutionary Perspective," *Biology and Human Affairs*, 28 (1963), 4–30.
44. Kincaid, J. C. "Social Pathology of Foetal and Infant Loss," *British Med. Jour.*, 17 (April, 1965), 1057–1060.
45. Knutson, A. L. "New Perspectives Regarding Positive Mental Health," *American Psychologist*, 18 (1963), 300–306.
46. Lasswell, H. D. "The Shape of the Future," *Amer. Behavioral Scientist* 8 (1965), 3.
47. Lorimer, F. "Issues of Population Policy," pp. 143–183 in *The Population Dilemma*, ed. P. M. Hauser. Englewood Cliffs, N. J.: Prentice-Hall, 1963.
48. Luten, D. D. "NAWAPA," *Science*, 149 (1965), 133.
49. MacLean, P. "The Brain in Relation to Empathy and Medical Education," *J. Nervous & Mental Disease*, 144 (1967), 374–382.

50. Malzberg, B. *Migration and Mental Disease.* New York: Social Science Research Council, 1956.
51. Martin, A. R. "Man's Leisure and His Health," *Bull. N. Y. Acad. Medicine,* 40 (1964), 21–42.
52. Mayer, J. "Food and Population: The Wrong Problem?" *Daedalus,* (Summer, 1964), 830–834.
53. Mead, M. "The Future as the Basis for Establishing a Shared Culture," *Daedalus,* (Winter, 1965), 135–155.
54. Medawar, P. M. "Do Advances in Medicine Lead to Genetic Deterioration?" *Mayo Clinic Proceedings,* 40 (1965), 22–33.
55. Melman, S. "Behind the Mask of Success," *Saturday Review,* (July 31, 1965), 8–9, 29.
56. Michael, D. "Comments on the Conference Topic: The Impact of Science and Technology," pp. 24–33 in Proceedings of a Conference on "The Environment of Change" printed by TIME, the Weekly Newsmagazine, 1964.
57. Muller-Thym, B. J. "Comments on the Conference Topic: The Management of Business," Proceedings of a Conference on "The Environment of Change," printed by TIME, the Weekly Newsmagazine, 1964.
58. Mumford, L. *The City in History.* New York: Harcourt, Brace & World, 1961.
59. Murphy, G. *Human Potentialities.* New York: Basic Books, 1958.
60. Parkes, A. S. "Change and Control in Human Populations," *Eugenic Review,* 55 (1963), 11–16.
61. Pickering, G. "The Present Scope of Medicine," *Jour. of Medical Education,* 38 (1963), 681–687.
62. Piel, G. "Physician, Heal Thy Society!," *Bull. N. Y. Acad. Medicine,* 40 (1964), 615–624.
63. Platt, J. R. "The Step to Man," *Science,* 149 (1965), 607–613.
64. Potter, Van R. "Council on the Future," *The Nation,* (February 8, 1965).
65. Price, D. De S. "The Scientific Foundation of Science Policy," *Nature,* 206 (1965), 233–238.
66. Prior, M. E. "Science and Medicine," *Jour. of Medical Education,* 38 (1963), 765–767.
67. Querido, A. "Population Problems and Mental Health," pp. 29–39 in *Population and Mental Health,* ed. H. P. David. New York: Springer, 1964.
68. Riedl, J. O. "Comments on the Conference Topic: Social Organization," Proceedings of a Conference on "The Environment of Change," printed by TIME, the Weekly Newsmagazine, 1964.
69. Romano, J. "Requiem or Reveille: The Clinician's Choice," *Jour. of Medical Education,* 38 (1963), 584–590.
70. Rome, H. P. "On Novalescence: A Response to the Presidential Address of Dr. Daniel Blain," *Amer. Jour. Psychiatry,* 122 (1965), 13–15.
71. Royce, J. R. *The Encapsulated Man.* Princeton: D. Van Nostrand, 1964.
72. Salvadori, M. G. "Comments on the Conference Topic: The Impact of Science and Technology," pp. 16–23 in Proceedings of a Conference on "The Environment of Change," printed by TIME, the Weekly Newsmagazine, 1964.
73. Salzman, L., in N. Kelman, "Man: Creator, Discoverer, Instrument," *Amer. Jour. Psychoanalysis,* 23 (1963), 175–184.
74. Sargent, F., II. "Conference on the Teaching of Behavioral Sciences in Medical Education," *BioScience,* 15 (1965), 533–534. Also see several related articles in this issue of *BioScience.*
75. Schmitt, F. O. "The Physical Basis of Life and Learning," *Science,* 149 (1965), 931–936.
76. Sears, P. B. "The Inexorable Problem of Space," *Science,* 127 (1958), 9–16.
77. ————— . "Man or Motor," *The Atlantic,* (July, 1965), 74–78.
78. Semenov, N. N. "The World of the Future," *Bull. Atomic Scientists,* (February, 1964), 10–15.

79. Shakow, D. "Ethics for a Scientific Age: Some Moral Aspects of Psychoanalysis," *Psychoanalytic Review*, 52 (1965), 335–348.
80. Simpson, G. G. "Naturalistic Ethics and the Social Sciences," *American Psychologist*, 21 (1966), 27–36.
81. Slobodkin, L. B. "The Strategy of Evolution," *American Scientist*, 52 (1964), 342–357.
82. Spengler, J. J. "Population and Freedom," *Population Review* (Madras), 6 (1962), 74–82.
83. Spitz, R. A. "The Derailment of Dialogue," *Jour. American Psychoanalytic Association*, 12 (1964), 752–774.
84. Steigenga, W. "Urbanization and Town Planning," pp. 67–75 in *Population and Mental Health*, ed. H. P. David. New York: Springer, 1964.
85. Stewart, J. Q. "Concerning Social Physics," *Scientific American*, 178 (1948), 20–23.
86. Stuart, A. L. "Evolutionary Man," *British Jour. Philosophy of Science*, 14 (1963), 41–53.
87. Thiessen, D. D. "Population Density and Behavior: A Review of Theoretical and Physiological Contributions," *Texas Reports on Biology and Medicine*, 22 (June, 1964).
88. Thomas, C. S., and B. J. Bergen. "Social Psychiatric View of Psychological Misfunction and the Role of Psychiatry in Social Change," *Arch. General Psychiatry*, 12 (1965), 539–544.
89. Tillich, P. "What is Basic in Human Nature," *Amer. Jour. Psychoanalysis*, 22 (1962), 115–121.
90. Van Den Haag, E. "Creativity, Health, and Art," *Amer. Jour. Psychoanalysis*, 23 (1963), 144–156.
91. Vickers, G. "The Psychology of Policy Making and Social Change," *British Jour. of Psychiatry*, 110 (1964), 465–477.
92. _____. "The End of Free Fall," *The Listener*, 28 (October, 1965), 647–648, 671.
93. Vishniac, R. "From Cuneiform to Cinema," *Jour. of the University Film Producers Association*, 17 (1965), 15–17.
94. Watts, M. S. M. "Medicine in Society, Part II: Some Dimensions of Medicine in Modern Society," *Calif. Medicine*, 102 (1965), 28–32.
95. _____. "Medicine in Society, Part III: A Role for Medicine in Modern Society," *Calif. Medicine*, 102 (1965), 133–138.
96. Warntz, W. "A New Map of the Surface of Population Potentials for the United States, 1960," *Geographical Review*, 54 (1964), 170–184.
97. Weatherall, R. "Man in a Man-made World," *Biology and Human Affairs*, 29 (1963), 3–11.
98. Welch, B. L. "Psychophysiological Response to the Mean Level of Environmental Stimulation," pp. 39–100 in Walter Reed Army Institute of Research, Symposium on Medical Aspects of Stress in the Military Climate. Washington: U.S. Government Printing Office, 1965.
99. Wenkart, A. "Creativity and Freedom," *Amer. Jour. Psychoanalysis*, 23 (1963), 195–204.
100. Wood, R. C. "Comments on the Conference Topic: Changes in Living," Proceedings of a Conference on "The Environment of Change," printed by TIME, the Weekly Newsmagazine, 1964.
101. Thant, U. "New Ideas for a New World," *Saturday Review*, (July 24, 1965), 24–25.
102. Von Foerster, H., P. M. Mora, and L. W. Amiot. "Doomsday: Friday 13, November, A.D. 2026," *Science*, 132 (1960), 1291–1295.

OVERPOPULATED AMERICA

Wayne H. Davis

Several of the preceding articles have redirected our attention to new criteria for thinking about density and overpopulation. The authors have identified human actions and relationships which, although in part instinctive, also change in relation to certain environmental variables. Density is one of these variables. It operates directly by modifying the distances between individuals and the social texture of space. In an affluent society, subject neither to starvation nor to epidemic, the perception and experience of human numbers determines the quality of life.

That some societies will suffer more than others with the same densities must be attributed to cultural differences in the means of coping with numbers. Patterns of residence and work, architecture, customs of ingress and egress, types of transportation—all affect the rhythms of human contact and the distances that separate people.

The culture also mediates the effect of population density on the total environment, which is equally important in the long run. Some years ago ecologist Paul B. Sears observed that the relationship between human population and resources depends on the cultural functional variable $(R=P/r(f)c)$. We cannot say that a society with a population density of 100/square mile will have a crowd-psychosis of, say, 3 percent, because it will depend to some extent on how the particular culture copes with its numbers and what therapies are built into its activities. Nor can it be said that one acre of land will support ten people at an environmental deterioration level of zero, because the level will vary depending on the technology employed.

This does not mean that any number, large or small, can occupy the earth healthily. At the extremes the cultural cushions fail because of the species' limitations—limits defined by genetic and biological constitution. It does mean that a relatively sparse population can be environmentally overgrown while a dense one, with less food and space, may be ecologically more fit.

I define as most seriously overpopulated that nation whose people by virtue of their numbers and activities are most rapidly decreasing the ability of the land to

Wayne H. Davis, "Overpopulated America," The New Republic, January 10, 1970, 13–15. Reprinted by Permission of The New Republic, © 1970, Harrison-Blaine of New Jersey, Inc.

support human life. With our large population, our affluence and our technological monstrosities the United States wins first place by a substantial margin.

Let's compare the US to India, for example. We have 203 million people, whereas she has 540 million on much less land. But look at the impact of people on the land.

The average Indian eats his daily few cups of rice (or perhaps wheat, whose production on American farms contributed to our one percent per year drain in quality of our active farmland), draws his bucket of water from the communal well and sleeps in a mud hut. In his daily rounds to gather cow dung to burn to cook his rice and warm his feet, his footsteps, along with those of millions of his countrymen, help bring about a slow deterioration of the ability of the land to support people. His contribution to the destruction of the land is minimal.

An American, on the other hand, can be expected to destroy a piece of land on which he builds a home, garage and driveway. He will contribute his share to the 142 million tons of smoke and fumes, seven million junked cars, 20 million tons of paper, 48 billion cans, and 26 billion bottles the overburdened environment must absorb each year. To run his air conditioner we will strip-mine a Kentucky hillside, push the dirt and slate down into the stream, and burn coal in a power generator, whose smokestack contributes to a plume of smoke massive enough to cause cloud seeding and premature precipitation from Gulf winds which should be irrigating the wheat farms of Minnesota.

In his lifetime he will personally pollute three million gallons of water, and industry and agriculture will use ten times this much water in his behalf. To provide these needs the US Army Corps of Engineers will build dams and flood farmland. He will also use 21,000 gallons of leaded gasoline containing boron, drink 28,000 pounds of milk and eat 10,000 pounds of meat. The latter is produced and squandered in a life pattern unknown to Asians. A steer on a Western range eats plants containing minerals necessary for plant life. Some of these are incorporated into the body of the steer which is later shipped for slaughter. After being eaten by man these nutrients are flushed down the toilet into the ocean or buried in the cemetery, the surface of which is cluttered with boulders called tombstones and has been removed from productivity. The result is a continual drain on the productivity of range land. Add to this the erosion of overgrazed lands, and the effects of the falling water table as we mine Pleistocene deposits of groundwater to irrigate to produce food for more people, and we can see why our land is dying far more rapidly than did the great civilizations of the Middle East, which experienced the same cycle. The average Indian citizen, whose fecal material goes back to the land, has but a minute fraction of the destructive effect on the land that the affluent American does.

Thus I want to introduce a new term, which I suggest be used in future discussions of human population and ecology. We should speak of our numbers in "Indian equivalents." An Indian equivalent I define as the average number of Indian citizens required to have the same detrimental effect on the land's ability to support human life as would the average American. This value is difficult to determine, but let's take an extremely conservative working figure of 25. To see how conservative this is, imagine the addition of 1000 citizens to your town and 25,000 to an Indian village. Not only would the Americans destroy much more land for homes, highways and a shopping center, but they would contribute far more to environmental deterioration in hundreds of other ways as well. For example, their demand for steel for new autos might increase the daily pollution equivalent of 130,000 junk autos which *Life* tells us that US Steel Corp. dumps into Lake Michigan. Their demand for textiles would help the cotton industry destroy the life in the Black Warrior River in Alabama with endrin. And they would contribute to the massive industrial pollution of our oceans (we provide one third to one half the world's share) which has caused the precipitous downward trend in our commercial fisheries landings during the past seven years.

The per capital gross national product of the United States is 38 times that of India. Most of our goods and services contribute to the decline in the ability of the environment to support life. Thus it is clear that a figure of 25 for an Indian equivalent is conservative. It has been suggested to me that a more realistic figure would be 500.

In Indian equivalents, therefore, the population of the United States is at least four billion. And the rate of growth is even more alarming. We are growing at one percent per year, a rate which would double our numbers in 70 years. India is growing at 2.5 percent. Using the Indian equivalent of 25, our population growth becomes 10 times as serious as that of India. According to the Reinows in their recent book *Moment in the Sun*, just one year's crop of American babies can be expected to use up 25 billion pounds of beef, 200 million pounds of steel and 9.1 billion gallons of gasoline during their collective lifetime. And the demands on water and land for our growing population are expected to be far greater than the supply available in the year 2000. We are destroying our land at a rate of over a million acres a year. We now have only 2.6 agricultural acres per person. By 1975 this will be cut to 2.2, the critical point for the maintenance of what we consider a decent diet, and by the year 2000 we might expect to have 1.2.

You might object that I am playing with statistics in using the Indian equivalent on the rate of growth. I am making the assumption that today's [American] child will live 35 years (the average Indian life span) at today's level of affluence. If he lives an American 70 years, our rate of population growth would be 20 times as serious as India's.

But the assumption of continued affluence at today's level is unfounded. If our numbers continue to rise, our standard of living will fall so sharply that by the year 2000 any surviving Americans might consider today's average Asian to be well off. Our children's destructive effects on their environment will decline as they sink ever lower into poverty.

The United States is in serious economic trouble now. Nothing could be more misleading than today's affluence, which rests precariously on a crumbling foundation. Our productivity, which had been increasing steadily at about 3.2 percent a year since World War II, has been falling during 1969. Our export over import balance has been shrinking steadily from $7.1 billion in 1964 to $0.15 billion in the first half of 1969. Our balance of payments deficit for the second quarter was $3.7 billion, the largest in history. We are now importing iron ore, steel, oil, beef, textiles, cameras, radios and hundreds of other things.

Our economy is based upon the Keynesian concept of a continued growth in population and productivity. It worked in an underpopulated nation with excess resources. It could continue to work only if the earth and its resources were expanding at an annual rate of 4 to 5 percent. Yet neither the number of cars, the economy, the human population, nor anything else can expand indefinitely at an exponential rate in a finite world. We must face this fact *now*. The crisis is here. When Walter Heller says that our economy will expand by 4 percent annually through the latter 1970s he is dreaming. He is in a theoretical world totally unaware of the realities of human ecology. If the economists do not wake up and devise a new system for us now somebody else will have to do it for them.

A civilization is comparable to a living organism. Its longevity is a function of its metabolism. The higher the metabolism (affluence), the shorter the life. Keynesian economics has allowed us an affluent but shortened life span. We have now run our course.

The tragedy facing the United States is even greater and more imminent than that descending upon the hungry nations. The Paddock brothers in their book, *Famine 1975!*, say that India "cannot be saved" no matter how much food we ship her. But India will be here after the United States is gone. Many millions will die in the most colossal famines India has ever known, but the land will survive and she will come back as she always has before. The United States, on the other hand, will be a desolate tangle of concrete and ticky-tacky, of strip-mined moonscape and silt-choked reservoirs. The land and water will be so contaminated with pesticides, herbicides, mercury fungicides, lead, boron, nickel, arsenic and hundreds of other toxic substances, which have been approaching critical levels of concentration in our environment as a result of our numbers and affluence, that it may be unable to sustain human life.

Thus as the curtain gets ready to fall on man's civilization let it come as no surprise that it shall first fall on the United States. And let no one make the mistake of thinking we can save ourselves by "cleaning up the environment." Banning DDT is the equivalent of the physician's treating syphilis by putting a bandaid over the first chancre to appear. In either case you can be sure that more serious and widespread trouble will soon appear unless the disease itself is treated. We cannot survive by planning to treat the symptoms such as air pollution, water pollution, soil erosion, etc.

What can we do to slow the rate of destruction of the United States as a land capable of supporting human life? There are two approaches. First, we must reverse the population growth. We have far more people now than we can continue to support at anything near today's level of affluence. American women average slightly over three children each. According to the *Population Bulletin* if we reduced this number to 2.5 there would still be 330 million people in the nation at the end of the century. And even if we reduced this to 1.5 we would have 57 million more people in the year 2000 than we have now. With our present longevity patterns it would take more than 30 years for the population to peak even when reproducing at this rate, which would eventually give us a net decrease in numbers.

Do not make the mistake of thinking that technology will solve our population problem by producing a better contraceptive. Our problem now is that people want too many children. Surveys show the average number of children wanted by the American family is 3.3. There is little difference between the poor and the wealthy, black and white, Catholic and Protestant. Production of children at this rate during the next 30 years would be so catastrophic in effect on our resources and the viability of the nation as to be beyond my ability to contemplate. To prevent this trend we must not only make contraceptives and abortion readily available to everyone, but we must establish a system to put severe economic pressure on those who produce children and reward those who do not. This can be done within our system of taxes and welfare.

The other thing we must do is to pare down our Indian equivalents. Individuals in American society vary tremendously in Indian equivalents. If we plot Indian equivalents versus their reciprocal, the percentage of land surviving a generation, we obtain a linear regression. We can then place individuals and occupation types on this graph. At one end would be the starving blacks of Mississippi; they would approach unity in Indian equivalents, and would have the least destructive effect on the land. At the other end of the graph would be the politicians slicing pork for the barrel, the highway contractors, strip-mine operators, real estate developers, and public enemy number one—the US Army Corps of Engineers.

We must halt land destruction. We must abandon the view of land and minerals as private property to be exploited in any way economically feasible for private financial gain. Land and minerals are resources upon which the very survival of the nation depends, and their use must be planned in the best interests of the people.

Rising expectations for the poor is a cruel joke foisted upon them by the Establishment. As our new economy of use-it-once-and-throw-it-away produces more and more products for the affluent, the share of our resources available for the poor declines. Blessed be the starving blacks of Mississippi with their outdoor privies, for they are ecologically sound, and they shall inherit a nation. Although I hope that we will help these unfortunate people attain a decent standard of living by diverting war efforts to fertility control and job training, our most urgent task to assure this nation's survival during the next decade is to stop the affluent destroyers.

Farmer and his sons. Photo by Bruce Davidson from Magnum Photos.

MEASUREMENT AND DIAGNOSIS OF HEALTH

J. Ralph Audy

While sensitivity to the fragile and dynamic nature of the environment increased markedly as the 1970's began, a new vision of man-as-organism was emerging. The two developments were closely related. Previously the people of the machine culture had thought of themselves and their environment as reciprocal and separate entities. Health for both was defined as the lack of symptoms of acute disease.

The change in perspective on man and nature came neither from medical science nor from agriculture. (Indeed, as the Seventies began, the new thinking on and understanding of relationships generated more opposition than acceptance from those traditions. Neither was instrumental in reversing the dehumanizing processes at work in the modern world or in rescuing the planet as a habitation.) The sources of creative insight were rather those areas which focus on the study of relationships: behavioral psychology, epidemiology, anthropology, ecology, systematics, and the like.

What the new understanding of relationships promises—and this will be hard for some to accept—is a view of human and environmental health in which disease plays only a minor role. Man will be regarded not as a sack of organs with an attached mind, but as a sentient being swimming in envelopes of life and nonlife, endlessly striving toward equilibrium between insult and protection, deprivation and satiation.

It is likely that the whole concept of what it means to be well will be drastically altered. At the end of the twentieth century, if civilization survives until then, the individual will receive far more medical attention while he is "well" than at present, and disease organisms will be considered far less threatening than at present. The conditions of relationship between men and their "envelopes" will take the place of infection as a basic concern.

Definition and Application

Introduction

This is an attempt (a) to redefine health in quantitative terms so that it can be studied more satisfactorily, and (b) to outline what processes may affect a quantitative "index of health" (or indices of different types of health) during maturation from the ovum onward. Scientific medicine has hitherto paid much attention to disease and almost none to health; to causative agents rather than to the person or host, that is, to the seed rather than the soil; and to the sick rather than to people who may become sick. The greatest obstacle to understanding health has probably been the natural tendency to regard health and disease as a continuum, two ends of the same spectrum. But however closely they may be related, they should not be defined in terms of each other; otherwise the argument becomes circular.

Like Galen (*1*), laymen may view health as a condition of perfect internal harmony. But what of healthy persons at another time? How often are they in such harmony? In the Peckham Centre experiment (*2*), only one in ten people, at first overhaul, were "healthy" as determined by the absence of a detectable disorder at that moment. Diseased people can be assessed according to prognosis. Although "healthy" people are not so readily assessed, those who are accident-prone or sickness-prone can be distinguished from those less prone to trouble, through observation over a span of time.

Many efforts have been made to develop an index of health (*3,4*) but the conclusions reached refer to morbidity, disability, and mortality in the population. The World Health Organization took a great step forward when it gave the currently accepted definition of health in the preamble to its constitution in 1946: "Health is a state of complete physical, mental and social well-being, not merely the absence of disease or infirmity."[1] Nevertheless, this definition leaves much to be desired. It rightly recognizes that absence of disease is not health, and implies that social health may be distinct from physical and mental health. It also implies that a person with a disease or infirmity cannot be healthy, a view which is readily challenged, as I hope to show. Furthermore, what is meant by "complete," or any degree of measure in an unmeasurable state? What of the very healthy man leading and enjoying an active life, but with an infirmity such as a palsied leg? Bader flew fighter planes in combat after losing both legs: would he be labelled as permanently unhealthy in contrast to some miserable fellow who at this rare moment happens to have no detectable disease or infirmity? And what *is* the social health of an individual?

---

[1] Perkins (*5*) defined health more soundly, though wordily, as "a state of relative equilibrium of body form and function which results from its successful dynamic adjustment to forces tending to disturb it. It is not passive interplay between body substances and forces infringing upon it but an active response of body forces working toward readjustment." This definition describes health as both a state *and* a process. It does not, however, allow of quantitative approaches nor include a place for social health.

Quantitative Definition of Health

Health is a continuing property, potentially measurable by the individual's ability to rally from insults, whether chemical, physical, infectious, psychological, or social.

Rallying is measured by completeness and speed. Any insult may have a "training" function, and recovery will often be to a slightly *higher* level of health. The person or body learns something.

Health is thus a continuing property, a function of the efficiency of the system's homeostatic mechanisms. It does not disappear during an illness to return on recovery but continues, even though it may drop in level while the organism is adapting to the current insult. The concept of disease, necessarily modified by this concept of health, may for the moment be regarded as representing episodes during which the property of health is being challenged: most disease is an expression of the rallying, the coping process, but the measurable ability to rally is there all the time.

Insults may be positive or negative (compare overeating and nutritional deprivation). They may arise from without or within, and inappropriate responses or overreaction may add an insult from within to an insult received from without. A threat is a psychological insult that may be external and realistic or internal and neurotic.

However individualistic an organism may seem to be, it is only an open subsystem in a hierarchy of interlocking systems (6),[2] ranging from organelles inside cells to major ecosystems with their interacting living and nonliving components. Health must be considered not only relative to the environment generally, but also relative to one or more protective subsystems such as the uterus or kinfolk, discussed below as cocoons. Although Sargent (8) has regarded health and illness as "polar phases in the continuum of the life sequence," (9) he identified with the "adaptive capacity of the organism toward environmental circumstances and hazards" (10). This was independently expressed by Dubos in terms that hint at the ease with which health and disease may be confused: "States of health or disease are the expression of the success or failure experienced by the organism in its efforts to respond adaptively to environmental challenges" (11). Dubos does not, however, define health in terms of disease. The social health of a person is likewise inconceivable except in the context of his community and its culture. Other aspects of his health are similarly related to the environment. The blood-cell count normal in the high Andes is pathologically high for an inhabitant of the plains.

Man's dreams of health (12) and subjective "health" generally are outside the scope of this paper (13). Let it suffice to say that dying people may yet be serenely contented; and there are circumstances in which to be happy would indicate serious mental illness.

[2] Arthur Koestler's concept of linked *holons* (7).

Types of Health

There are four distinct but interconnected kinds of health, coping differently with insults of five kinds (see Table 1). *Physiological health* develops along well-recognized patterns. It includes the neurosecretory mechanism for dealing with stress (*14*). It is the sort most rigidly influenced by genetic constitution. *Immunological health* is developed by encounters with infective agents. The ability to respond specifically is a genetically endowed mechanism, but its education in the individual is largely a product of antigens from the environment. Autoimmunity and hypersensitivity may evoke insidious and progressive insults from within.

Mental health is here separated into *psychological* and *social health* because I have found it to improve my thinking about mental health and culture. Mental development of animals and man is largely effected by feedback from other living creatures of the same and other species. A meeting of minds (through whatever medium) is somewhat analogous to receiving or exchanging grafts and as a mind develops it virtually becomes a nexus of minds. Social health is concerned with the flexibility and adaptiveness of that nexus in its complex relations with the greater network of nexuses that is society.

Any insult, including an episode of disease, is also likely to be in some measure a psychological and perhaps a social insult—a point too frequently overlooked by scientifically minded physicians.

Cocoons[3]

If health is measurable by ability to rally, the other side of the same coin is that it is also measurable by the degree of protection needed to preserve a steady state. Throughout life there is a series of physical, physiological, psychological, and social cocoons that give various degrees of protection. It is helpful, often necessary, to consider the individual's index of health in both ways, relative to a cocoon and relative to the external world without it. The most obvious cocoon is the uterus (Figures 1 and 2), but there are other protective devices: (a) physical, such as garments, or homes and other buildings, and (b) sociopsychological, and to some extent physical, such as mother, family, and peer-group, but also social institutions such as tradition, religion, in-group membership. A most remarkable protective capsule is a person's culture, that systematic body of learned behavior and beliefs that is transmitted, piecemeal and never completely, vertically from parents to children and horizontally between cultures and subcultures in contact—and which may evolve separately among dissident groups within a broad culture.

All organisms are genetically adapted to their specific environment, even more so to their specific artifacts (ipsefacts) (*15*) such as nests and burrows which are

[3] Although a convenient term, this implies only protection. Because there is also active feedback to the individual, what I call "cocoons" might also be compared to a series of uteri with their placentas.

TYPES OF HEALTH COPING WITH INSULTS

PHYSIOLOGICAL
ontogenetically trained by all adaptations

IMMUNOLOGICAL
involving immunogenetic mechanism; trained
by every antigenic encounter

PSYCHOLOGICAL
involving the psyche

SOCIAL
involving the psyche in relation to social context;
relative to the group or society or societies
(distinguish from societal health)

MENTAL

MENTAL

KINDS OF INSULTS

CHEMICAL
e.g. alcohol, food poisoning

PHYSICAL
e.g. injury, surgery

INFECTIOUS
receiving a potential pathogen

PSYCHOLOGICAL
e.g. rejection, death of loved one,
failing exam, frightening diagnosis

SOCIAL
e.g. shift to new culture or miniculture:
culture shock (foreign appointment;
high school to megauniversity)

Table 1

genetically controlled "crystallized" or manifest behavior. Man's major adaptations have been sociocultural, both to the densities that he has encouraged by technology and to his fantastically extensive ipsefacts. He is making his own environment at high speed and with little guidance, and perpetually attempting to adapt to it. His sociocultural (mental) adaptations may be rapid but his genetic adaptations must be slow. Since, by our definition, the tolerance that is health is constantly being tried by insults that arise in or penetrate through our successive cocoons, the degree of mutual adaptation between people and their cocoons is fundamentally important. Even the maternal cocoon of the newborn is increasingly unreliable. This cocoon is subject to sociocultural whims and, we suspect, social and neurotic derangements preceded by lack of proper maternal feedback. The newborn is genetically adapted to an earlier kind of cocoon and does not yet have the sociocultural adaptiveness or flexibility that would enable it to develop properly without help in its first postuterine cocoon.

Measurement of Health

Each kind of health is best measured by challenges, much as one would test a fabric by exposing samples to repeated washing, beating, exposure—the result would be multiple indices measuring fading, tensile strengths, liability to fraying, and so on. From these indices one might derive a general index by weighting them according to circumstances (requirements). A fabric may require in one circumstance resistance to wear, in another, to attack by insects. Similarly, a laborer might greatly need physical strength and stamina while a sedentary worker with a mentally demanding job might find them relatively unimportant. One man's health can be another's weakness.

A man cannot be sampled like a fabric, nor can he be deliberately tested to destruction. In practice, parts of health are measured, or quantitatively tested, in three ways. The first is by exposure of groups to roughly the same challenge or set of insults. This may be accidental or deliberate. A group of people left at sea for a long time in a lifeboat respond very differently to the same misfortune, in both their immediate and long-term reactions (*16*). Prisoners of war, military patrols, and school children are likewise tested in groups. The protein metabolism of a proportion of students may be upset by the stress of examinations (*17*). A more specific large-scale accidental test was the exceptional London fog of 1952. Four days of this led to about 4,000 extra deaths that could be ascribed to being "tested to destruction" by insult to lungs and, secondarily, hearts (18). Many more people must have had their health permanently lowered by that episode. Any drought, famine, winter, or epidemic similarly tests groups such as the aged, the very young, the pregnant mothers. Pregnancy is a standard stress that can uncover potential hypertension and other defects.

People's health is assessed also by observing individuals over many years. This is a standard epidemiological procedure, when causes of illness may be traced by detection of differential incidence of disease in specific groups. Given roughly the

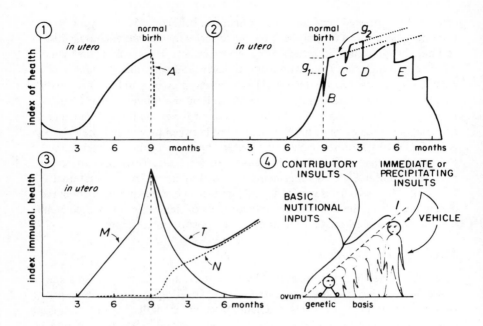

Figures 1-3. *Levels of Health.* **1.** *Physiological health relative to the uterus (cocoon #1) builds rapidly during the second trimester when the placenta is functioning and the organs have been laid down. A is a hypothetical loss of health relative to the uterus should the fetus be retained beyond the usual maximum gestation period (post-maturity).* **2.** *Physiological health relative to the outside world (cocoon #2) is nil until the third trimester, during which finishing touches greatly improve chances of survival after birth: for example, glycogen (animal starch) stored during this period increases ability to withstand the oxygen deficiency (anoxia) accompanying birth, B. After the fetus's rapid adaptation to the shocks of birth and readjustment of the circulation (32), the level of health rises considerably higher—its first and greatest gain (g_1). C, D, E exemplify lowering health while adapting to insults, with varying outcomes: a gain (g_2) as the organism learns from life's experiences (C); an indefinite or permanent lowering (D); or vulnerability to a series of insults in successively lower states of health, and shorter life expectancy (E).* **3.** *Immunological health. Protection of the fetus by maternal antibodies (IgG) lessens rapidly after birth (28), but the efforts of the newborn (N) soon compensate for the loss. Total antibodies (T) are lowest at about the fourth month.*

Figure 4. *Operation of Insults in Multiple Causation of Diseases. The quality of the individual from ovum on (1) is decided by contributory insults (both damaging and training) interacting with his genetic base. Superimposition of an immediate or precipitating insult may "cause" disease. Although these insults may be essential (only the tubercle bacillus can cause tuberculosis), they may not be obligatory, or inevitably causative (receiving the tubercle bacillus often does not produce TB). These insults may be direct or delivered by* vehicles: *water, an infected individual, an insect vector, or an intermediate host may deliver an infectious organism; and cigarettes, carcinogens.*

same insult loads in life, the healthier individual suffers fewer disease episodes and is off work or inefficient for fewer days than the less healthy one. This idea has been well expressed by Professor R. A. Black, University of Sydney, in discussion: it is the unhealthy people who get the diseases! (To be consistent with my present thesis, this should read, say, "unfit people," or "people with lowered health," since the only truly *un*healthy person is a dead person.)

Several outstanding surveys (*19*) suggest that in any urban community a small proportion of individuals (say a quarter) is responsible for most (say three-quarters) of all episodes, from accidents to infections, for which medical aid is sought. Another small proportion (say another quarter) will be found responsible for only a trivial fraction (perhaps only 1%) of all medical episodes. The age distribution of a community obviously affects such scoring, but the people in low health responsible for keeping doctors overworked and the hospitals filled are particularly the poor and those immigrants who are still in the first few years of adaptation to their new conditions. Poverty itself is thus a top priority public health problem. It is the quality of the individuals that matters. A prime responsibility of medicine is to determine what influences a man's level of health and what steps can be taken to ensure higher levels, so that fewer of the seemingly healthy will on another day become the sick. Whatever the practical difficulties in measuring individual health, dealing with it as a measurable property allows us to make a fresh approach to this vitally important problem.

The third way in which health is measured is by tolerance and provocative tests applied to individuals. An exercise tolerance test is a good example: after a person hops on and off a chair ten times, does the pulse return to its resting rate in 2, 5, or 10 minutes? Glucose tolerance and liver function tests are among the many that measure with accurate units. These are all measures of rallying after specified insults.

However desirable, defined and absolute units are not essential to deal quantitatively with properties. For present purposes we are concerned with judging changes in the levels of health of an individual at different times, such as during maturation; or with comparing one person with another in some specific respect, such as ability to work in certain ways. Simply thinking in quantitative terms and charting the progress of health, as for example in Figures 1 to 3, during the maturation of a child, encourages a new and constructive approach to health.

Qualified Health

The seemingly healthy person may be reviewed for three features: (a) for amount of physical and mental reserve the individual has at that moment; (b) for the degree of compensation for any existing defects; (c) for any predispostion to future trouble. It is useful to recognize certain states of health:

A. *Ample health*—This is the state of health, with reserves to draw upon, that we would all prefer.

B. *Health at a threshold* (with depleted reserves)—This is the time when a diabetic's last dose of insulin begins to run out. It is the time when a mother is about to scream, faint, or strike a child. Especially important it is the state of the child who is on the brink of malnutrition, in whom an attack of diarrhea and vomiting or of measles may lower the nutritional level with injurious effects. This could be disproportionately harmful if it occurs at a critical period of maturation (see below). In any community, for every single person showing some nutritional deficiency, there must surely be many whose nutritional reserves are virtually exhausted. These people are vulnerable, but it would be very difficult to detect this in a cross-sectional survey.

C. *Healthy because of compensation*—Compensation for a defect may be internal. For example, by increase in the volume of its muscle and cavities, a heart may compensate for a valvular defect and enable the person to indulge in a remarkable amount of energetic life. Compensation may also be external, as when diabetes is balanced by regular injection of insulin. Overcompensation for a defect often increases the person's general efficiency.

D. *Healthy with a predisposition*—This is often somewhat like living healthily with a bomb. The predisposition may be genetic, either expressing itself inevitably or doing so only under stress or in special circumstances as is true of many cases of diabetes or schizophrenia. A child that is genetically predisposed to grow rapidly if well fed might be harmed more by a restricted diet than a child with less genetic potential (*20*).

Or the predisposing factor could be nongenetic: a congenital arterial aneurism apt to burst at any time; a latent infection that is kept under control only until stress lowers the level of health; or a viral infection that could in complete silence one day evoke a cancer. Most of these time bombs cannot be detected. They range in nature from chemical and physical abnormalities to viruses and the specific neurophysiological or psychological effects of either positive or deprivational insults. Their common characteristic is their delayed effect.

What is generally called a "personality type" is simply a form of predisposition compounded of genetic base, cultural indoctrination, and way of life, all nurtured by circumstances. Certain personality types tend to be predisposed to particular maladies. Because of the genetic basis many of these personality types may share some common physical features and this has been the basis of many efforts at what is called somatotyping or relating liability to disease and types of behavior to physical appearances (*21*).

Maturation

Limits and Levels of Achievement

What is the least and the most that a genetically unexceptional ovum can achieve, and how far along this spectrum do most genetically unexceptional people in fact reach? Two hypothetical extremes are an individual raised to adulthood in an artificial uterus after birth by cesarian section, and one whose full potentialities have been reached through some magically felicitous and ceaseless attention. I shall call these the *simulacrum* and the *superman* (or *climax* organism, by loose analogy with a climax ecosystem (*22*)). We all fall in between these two.

The simulacrum, reared as are germ-free animals but, further, with sensory deprivation and only enough protection, nutrients, and attention to keep alive, would be highly retarded, physiologically abnormal, and probably not viable outside its artificial uterus. (We can guess at this from what is known about germ-free animals and early maternal and sensory deprivation) (*23*).

We do not know how to rear the superman: the task must inevitably be hypothetical. We do not know whether he should be given as much experience as he can tolerate, short of stress from which recovery is protracted, or for what intervals and when he should be left alone. We do not know if such a climax adult from an average ovum would be remarkable when set beside some of our best products.

What we do know, however, is that everyone falls short, probably very far short, of what he could have achieved in conditions ideal for maturation (*24*). In addition to gaining experience during his development, the ordinary individual suffers insults in the shape of deprivations, excesses, physical damage, and exposure to noxious stimuli and organisms. There is constant interplay between these and the genotype (*25*). The result is the common animal, the product of deviated or arrested *homeorhesis*.[4] According to the stage in development during which a noxious stimulus or deprivation modifies the course of optimal development, and according to the nature of the stimulus or deprivation, the effect on maturation and subsequent development may be slight or profound in degree, and general or highly specific in nature.

Levels of Health

Let us now consider broadly what happens to the index of health (IH) of the individual from the ovum to maturity. Figures 1, 2, and 4 in particular are meant to be provocative. The mere attempt to deal quantitatively with indices of health by charting them, relatively and without absolute units, forces new questions and exposes gaps in our knowledge. We do not know if the fetus's IH relative to the uterus tends to drop during postmaturity as indicated; what kinds of health should be considered through the first two trimesters *in utero* and how their levels change; or the nature, even existence, of mental health in the third trimester and the first month of life. The fetus certainly responds to stimuli, maternal and external, and there may even be imprinting of the maternal heartbeat. But

[4] *Homeorhesis* is Waddington's term for homeostasis in space-time: an orderly unfolding of events in the progress of a system toward greater complexity, whether it be ontogenic maturation or ecological succession in a sere (*26*).

we do not know whether we are at first dealing only with neurophysiological development, forming the *Anlage* of the mind, or also with mental processes such as we are familiar with in, say, the observations of Piaget. Is the neonate virtually decorticated, mindless? (That is the belief [of Frank] (27).) Or are such questions nonsensical—and why?

The uterus is an extremely efficient cocoon, but the fetus is nevertheless exposed to penetrating insults and, even more important, to deprivations. Among the insults are viruses such as that of rubella, drugs (potentially, any circulating drug can be harmful), and even metabolites, which interfere with critical periods of development and cause disproportionately great harm. The union of a normal man with a woman who has phenylketonuria (PKU) can produce a severely mentally retarded child, who apparently is the victim of maternal metabolites that penetrate the uterine cocoon and reproduce the most distressing result of PKU without conveying the genetic defect. Few antigens can pass through the placenta. But maternal immunoglobulin-G (IgG) antibodies regularly do so (Figure 3) (28) and although these benefit the newborn passively for a few months, they may include harmful rhesus antibodies when an Rh-negative mother bears Rh-positive children. Nutritional deprivations seem to greatly overshadow any positive insults to the fetus (29). Recent investigations show more and more unexpected and deeply important influences of nutrition on the fetus. Thus, it seems that protein deficiencies in the mother may affect the child's subsequent ability to handle protein metabolism efficiently. In addition, for the whole of the person's life there is a relation (usually but not always mutually exacerbating) between nutrition and infection (29).

The general IH presumably rises steadily with maturation after birth, reaches a plateau at some time during adult life, and later steadily declines because of senescence. Superimposed on this basic curve are (a) the ups and downs reflecting circadian and other physiological rhythms, (b) the ups and downs accompanying adaptations to successive insults, and (c) the gradual accumulation of what Selye (14) calls the physiological scars of adaptation, which tend to hasten (but not cause) senescence and which partly account for the plateau in IH.

Adaptation in some ways resembles the differentiation of cells: in due course it tends to lead to loss of adaptability, and the organism loses earlier potentialities as it is led along paths of specialization. This is indeed one element of normal senescence. But adaptation also tends to increase adaptability, because homeostatic competence increases with training much as physical competence and skills increase with exercise. There are many examples of such apparent paradoxes in dealing with health. They are largely due to circular processes in which a cause produces an effect that itself becomes a cause.

The rising curve of health accompanying maturation is not smooth but fluctuates according to regular physiological rhythms of circadian or other periodicity (30, 31) and also to intermittent alterations when these periodicities change phase, as when a person flies across time zones. All efforts to measure health or aspects of it, and to plan experiments for assessing adaptability or response to drugs, should take account of these rhythms. Halberg (*31*) has shown that what he calls *rhythmometry* may be carried out by self-measurement and that the results can be used to guide behavior and preventive measures.

The superimposed changes, (b) above, may best be understood if insults are regarded as potentially educative at the same time they are potentially deleterious, and if the individual is regarded as passing through a series of critical periods. The degree to which an insult trains the person or the body to withstand further insults (even if only of the same sort), set against harm it does, produces responses of the types shown in *C* and *D*, Figure 2. A succession of *C*-type responses increases the general level of health that is already rising with maturation, and this is the only way in which immunological health rises (except temporarily for maternal antibodies, Figure 3). A *D*-type response may permanently lower health.

Axiom: While a system is adapting physiologically to one insult, its adaptability to a second insult is generally reduced.[5] When a child is sick, we express this practically in our attempts to keep the external environment as uniform as possible, to preserve the body fluids and temperature; for such protection lessens the demands on the homeostatic mechanisms and hence, we argue, releases more energy for dealing with the present insult. (For example, see Cheraskin (*33*).) Therefore during, say, an episode of measles, the infant's IH drops. It is less able to tolerate another insult such as exposure to cold, a gastrointestinal upset, milk in its bottle a few degrees off temperature, or even its mother's brusqueness. After the episode, the IH usually responds as in *C* and *D* (Figure 2); but it may be an *E*-type response, and a child may take six months to die of a two-week episode of measles.

Corollary: Any protracted drop in health (IH) tends to increase the proportion of deleterious insults to training insults, and therefore, the risk of successive drops in health and a deterioration expressed by shortened life expectancy. Such an event would be most serious during broadly critical developmental periods such as intrauterine life, infancy, early schooling, and adolescence. It would be more likely in the malnourished and the motherless than in those not so deprived. Perhaps the element of self-reinforcement or positive feedback in this process is largely responsible for the saying, common to several languages, that "troubles never come singly."

A *critical period* is a limited phase during which an environmental event can most affect a developmental process (*34*). The same event before or after the critical period would have little or even no effect. Perhaps the most-studied critical period in maturation is the brief period during which an animal may become *imprinted* with an "instinctive" response or set of responses, hitherto latent, such

---

[5] This is not strictly true where mental health is concerned. New challenges may improve mental health and alleviate psychosomatic disorders. A severe involutional depression may be cleared by a coronary thrombosis. Migraine and peptic ulcers have rapidly cleared up in concentration camps. On the other hand, conditions that appear to develop after an injury may actually have existed beforehand; but their being linked with the accident makes them acceptable to both patient and society, and they may thus emerge.

as acceptance of a mother-creature. A duckling or lamb so imprinted will follow the experimenter and tend to ignore its own species. Thorpe (*35*) and others have shown that inanimate objects can be adopted in this way.

A great deal more scientific study of behavioral development, comparing many species of animals with man, is necessary, but it is obvious that (a) there are many and subtle critical phases when an individual is in a receptive state for a certain learning process, and when the lesson, once learned, is difficult or impossible to unlearn—whether the lesson be facilitation of some biochemical process or an emotional, intellectual, or social one; (b) any social lessons learned affect the individual's later response to other individuals, and therefore the course his future training will take; (c) critical periods are clustered mostly in the earliest moments, hours, and months of life, but extend beyond adolescence in the case of sexual and social maturation; and (d) critical periods not only magnify the response to insults but might encourage overreaction of defense mechanisms, a possibility inviting study (*36*).

Delivered into its first postuterine cocoon, the human newborn is even more helpless than the newborn kangaroo, which can at least climb into the mother's pouch. After the umbilical cord is cut, the infant remains as surely attached to the mother by invisible conductors through which necessary provisions flow (*37*). Before and just after birth, the supply of nutrients and the protection from noxious insults are of first importance. Within days thereafter, the input of sensory stimuli becomes almost as important as input of nutrients.[6] The infant attaches great significances to the relatively few items in its tiny world. This obvious fact and the great part played by nonverbal communication tend to be overlooked by many. For example, Harry Stack Sullivan (*39*) has classified nipples, as perceived by the puppy or the infant, into four types. The "same" nipple is two very different nipples to the infant when the mother is at one time tender and at another anxious.

The free development of the embryo and fetus, and therefore its IH, and to a high degree the IH of the newborn, depends upon genetic constitution, the proper development of the placenta, and the health of the mother. The placenta is an extraordinarily difficult organ to study, but it is a part of the fetus and deserves very careful study (*40*). It actively transmits and blocks transmission of substances to the fetus and produces its own secretions. It even carries out a useful and detectable function during the intervals between delivery and the cessation of umbilical circulation. As for maternal health, I mention in passing the possibility that the mother's IH rises during pregnancy provided she is initially healthy. It is certain, however, that if her health is already lowered, especially nutritionally, then pregnancy becomes an insult that will further lower her health. On the whole, the nutritional needs of the fetus take priority over those of the mother, but the two obviously affect each other profoundly.

[6] Comparative animal studies are now recognized as essential for full understanding of the prerequisites of psychological and social maturation (*38*).

Notes on Mental and Social Health

One cocoon normally succeeds another even though it may embrace all or part of the earlier one. The parental cocoon characteristically has a built-in obsolescence to force offspring to become independent. In many animals a sudden change in parental or maternal responses takes place when the offspring has reached a certain stage of maturity, perhaps signalled by a change in coat color. For example, the Malayan leaf-monkey infant is yellow, but when its coat changes to brown the mother no longer treats it as an infant and the young monkey is forced to break loose. If a litter of gophers does not disperse immediately after the signal has been given, those who remain are trespassers and will be killed by the parents. In man, the functioning of the parental cocoon is part of each culture. There always comes a time, however, when protection should be reduced to allow offspring to complete their maturation. Failure to loosen bonds has a neurotic origin. The first two years is when the parental cocoon is most needed and when, it seems, it can produce its own insults at critical periods of the child's life. A peculiarly human and very damaging trait is to involve one's children (as with pets) in working out personal neurotic problems. This is, of course, true in all human relations but the intensity of relations in the family makes the dominance of a parent potentially devastating. A combination of emotional deprivation and neurotic manipulation may cause gross mental and physical retardation, recognized in recent years as a form of pituitary dwarfism (*41*). Released from their parent(s), such children may grow more than an inch a month, their schoolwork improves at similar rate, and their behavior changes dramatically: they cease to be withdrawn and to have the bizarre appetites that drove them to drink dishwater or wolf a jar of mustard.

Stressors or insults should not be compared to loads, especially when mental or social,[7] since their effect may depend on how the individual perceives the insult. The same insult will be ignored by one person, but perceived as threatening by another. H. G. Wolff and his colleagues (*43*) clarify the perception of one's life-situation and the way it affects health. For example, vomiting or diarrhea does get rid of unwanted irritants; but if it is a symbolic effort to get rid of something intangible, it is ineffectual and thus tends to persist. The duration of infectious mononucleosis has been related to the ego-strength of the sufferer (*44*). Psychological factors seem to influence the course and even the incidence of infectious and noninfectious disease (*19, 45*). And we may be sure, although no experiment has been performed to support it, that the course of healing of a given fracture of the leg probably, and the clinical course certainly, will be much more satisfactory if it is caused by a skiing accident than by an uninsured drunken

---

[7] Engel (*42*) has defined psychological stress (insult): it refers "to all processes, whether originating in the external environment or within the person, which impose a demand or requirement upon the organism, the resolution or handling of which necessitates work or activity of the mental apparatus before any other system is involved or activated."

driver. In a ski accident, the fracture is almost a medal, but in an accident with a drunken driver it is strongly tied to feelings of resentment, anger, and impotence.

Hinkle (*19*) draws special attention to disturbance of people in relation to their ecological niches. Nonacceptance of one's role or niche can be stressful. Merton and others have done a great deal of work on methods adopted for dealing with the conflict presented by modern society, with its expectation that everyone must get to the top contradicted by its powerful barriers to achievement (*46*). It is both wise and healthy to know one's place.

The relations between physical disease and mental health are fascinatingly complex but very real. It is enough to note here that disease may be a way of life for many people, as Stewart Wolf has described (*47*).

Two common terms refer to aspects of mental health: stamina, a quality of the individual, and morale, usually a quality of a group shared by and applicable to each individual. There is a quality of indefeatability (*48*). Every physician has encountered patients who obstinately refuse to die—and there is a recognizable quality about these people—and others who throw in the sponge and either suffer a protracted illness thereby or even die what seems to be a psychosomatic death, that cannot be distinguished from a voodoo death except for the supernatural belief attached to the latter. A number of experiments with laboratory animals and men have shown that they can control physiological processes hitherto regarded as wholly beyond voluntary control: even such effects as subconsciously controlled lowering of blood pressure have been achieved by use of reward, and the method has been used experimentally to treat hypertension (*49*). It seems that scientific respectability is at last being accorded ancient practices such as yoga and that an exciting field is opening before us.

The WHO definition of health notwithstanding, many persons would deny the usefulness of distinguishing *social health* from *mental health*. Even more would take exception to applying the idea of health to a society, although some of these would admit that there may be "sick families" (*50*). But the definition of health presented here, being ecological, is applicable to any living system. For example, attempted acculturation to a new social environment with unfamiliar cues for behavior and without accustomed warmth of communion, whether this be on transfer to a foreign assignment, migrating from country to city, or entering a big college from a little school,[8] leads to a lowering of social health called "culture shock" (*51*). This in turn lowers psychological health which then lowers physiological health. Social health reflects the efficiency (not necessarily comfort) with which the psyche fits into the group, society, or culture—cocoons to which the individual may not be preadapted by training. However, the very security that comes with familiarity may permit nonconformity (another seeming

---

[8] If one's own cultural cocoon changes rapidly enough, its demands for acculturation resemble transfer to an alien environment. The resulting form of culture shock is one element in the current generation gap.

paradox). Some socially approved behavior is psychopathological. He who perceives this must rebel or, however reluctantly, conform.

We cannot comprehend the social health of an individual without postulating *societal health* of a group taken as a system. Simply stated, and justifiably oversimplified, the characteristics of psychological, social, and societal health are realism, flexibility (adaptability) (*52*), and, seen in retrospect, longevity. A man may enjoy a high level of social health in the cocoon of his own society but break down in almost any other (how many shamans would retain their health in New York City?). A society itself may acculturate or absorb elements of other cultures while retaining integrity (the Japanese from the Meiji era into the 1960's). Or it may not. Contrast the central Algonkian Indian tribes in the face of the European onslaught: the Kickapoo found sanctuary in Mexico, the Sauk sank into apathy and disintegrated, the Fox, resourceful like their namesake, adjusted but kept their identity, somewhat as the Tlaxcalans responded to Aztec domination (*6*). Paradoxically, flexibility can be expressed by resisting intolerable pressures to adapt.

Conclusion

"The sick are the failures in our public health effort. They must be treated, but they are not the primary object of enlightened medicine: first attention should be given to the seemingly healthy. It is the seemingly healthy who will on another day be the sick" (*53*). This paper follows that advice in attempting to quantify health and in recognizing that there are several kinds of health to diagnose.[9] Even though health is not generally measurable in absolute units, aspects of it may be; and tests administered with an eye for pattern rather than isolated results (*55*) could detect trends in health structure, before disease appears as a sign that health is being challenged. Furthermore, attempts to measure health must take account of physiological rhythms and their phase at the time of testing (*31*).

Health is measurable primarily in relation to the environment to which the species or population concerned has adapted genetically and, in the case of man, culturally. However, it is not so much the environment at large that concerns us, but a succession of close-by environments which may be likened to cocoons, sheltering the individual and comprising uterus, kindred, comrades, institutions and the cultural womb, and the manifold units of artifacts called ipsefacts (*15*). The uterine cocoon has remained stable for very long and the embryo and fetus are superbly adapted to it genetically. The next cocoon, the first to envelop the newborn, is the mother in the outside world. However, as the population avalanche descends and because of the tempo of change, the mother, almost wherever she

[9] The lowering of level of health by senescence is outside the scope of this paper. Genetic elements in the planned obsolescence of the body are presumably paramount (*54*).

may be, is a member of a rapidly changing and bewilderingly confused culture. The infant is genetically predisposed to adapt to quite another maternal cocoon, one of long ago, for molecular evolution of DNA cannot keep pace with cultural evolution of the psyche.

It is now abundantly clear that:

a. Experiences in the first two years (or five) of life lay the foundations of the future man and are more vitally important than any periods thereafter.

b. Deficiencies in specific amino acids and minerals *in utero* and infancy frequently and mostly irreversibly produce both physical and mental stunting.

c. Likewise, defective mothering produces mental, social, and to some extent physical retardation (56).

d. Much of the inferior performance of children in school, hitherto regarded as part of normal individual variation, is in fact low-grade mental retardation due to various combinations of malnutrition and emotional deprivation or stress. For the rest of their lives, such children may be unable to wrest what they need from the world around them. Some of the psychogenic damage may be reversed, for example by timely separation of the child from the parents.

e. Underprivileged people suffer, often severely, from both malnutrition and emotional deprivation. Poverty is a prime objective for enlightened preventive medicine (57), because it produces many of the unfit people who are always getting the diseases and thus throw an extra burden on medical services. The inadequacy of medical services in poverty-stricken areas further contributes to the relative lowering of health among the poor.

f. Many circular processes tend to hasten deterioration. For example, malnutrition tends to lower health and competence, to increase the chances of further deterioration due to infections, and to produce women who cannot provide the nutritional and emotional elements essential to proper mothering. Defective parenthood tends to be self-perpetuating, frequently visited on successive generations.

g. What we call the problems of youth are for the most part problems of their elders.

In many communities in developing countries, and in too many communities in "developed" countries, hardly a single child escapes such harm.

Many of those who have observed deranged behavior of animals in zoos will have independently come to the conclusion that man has created for himself the conditions of a badly run zoo to live in, with crowding, inadequate diets, and unsuitable living conditions, and a consequent disruption of social intercourse and a degradation of man (58). How well the wants and not-wants of maturation are satisfied determines the competence and total well-being of the individual. Because "it is better to make the boy than mend the man," we must learn to attend carefully to and lavish our many resources on early maturation.

REFERENCES

1. Galen, C. G. *Galen's Hygiene (De sanitate tuenda)*, tr. R. M. Green. Springfield, Ill.: Charles C Thomas, 1951.
2. Pearse, I. H., and L. H. Crocker. *The Peckham Experiment. A Study in the Living Structure of Society*. New Haven: Yale University Press, 1945. Nearly 4,000 individuals were studied. At first examination more than 90% had something wrong with them; 30% had some manifest disease (but by no means all of them were under treatment for it); 60% had "cryptic disease" masked by compensation and with apparent well-being; and only 10% were free of detectable disorder. A further example: about half of the first batch of American army recruits were rejected as unfit in 1941. According to official opinion, it was unlikely that more than a tenth of those rejected could be made fit for service.
3. U.S. Public Health Service. "Conceptual Problems in Developing an Index of Health." *USPHS Pubn*. No. 1000, Series 2, No. 17 (National Center for Health Statistics), 1966. World Health Organization. "Measurement of Levels of Health. Report of a Study Group," *Wld. Hlth. Techn. Rep. Ser.*, 137 (1957), 3–24.
4. Swaroop, S., and K. Uemura. "Proportional Mortality of 50 Years and Above. A Suggested Indicator of the Component 'Health, Including Demographic Conditions' in the Measurement of Levels of Living," *Bull. Wld. Hlth. Org.*, 17 (1957), 439–481.
5. Perkins, J. E. *To-morrow's Horizon in Public Health*. New York, 1950.
6. Caudill, W. *Effects of Social and Cultural Systems in Reactions to Stress*, Social Sci. Res. Council Pamphlet No. 14, 1958.
7. Koestler, A. "Beyond Atomism and Holism—the Concept of the Holon," in *Beyond Reductionism; New Perspectives in the Life Sciences*, ed. A. Koestler and J. R. Smythies. The Alpbach Symposium. London: Hutchinson, 1968. Reprinted in *Perspectives Biol. Med.*, *13*:131–154.
8. Sargent, F., II. "Tropical Neurasthenia: Giant or Windmill?" pp. 273–314 in UNESCO, *Environmental Physiology and Psychology in Arid Conditions; Reviews of Research*. Arid Zone Research, vol. 22, 1963. UNESCO/India symposium, Lucknow, India, December, 1962.
9. Sargent, F., II. "Ecological Implications of Individuality in the Context of the Concept of Adaptive Strategy." Working paper (mimeographed) for NAS–NRC Symposium on Physiological Characterization of Health Hazards in Man's Environment, 1966.
10. Sargent, F., II, and D. M. Barr. "Health and the Fitness of the Ecosystem," pp. 28–46 in *Environment and Man*. Hartford, Ill.: Traveler's Research Center, Inc., 1965.
11. Dubos, R. *Man Adapting*. New Haven: Yale University Press, 1961.
12. Dubos, R. *Mirage of Health. Utopias, Progress, and Biological Change*. New York: Harper and Brothers, 1959. "The kind of health that men desire most is not necessarily a state in which they experience physical vigor and sense of well-being, nor even one allowing them a long life. It is, instead, the condition best suited to reach goals that each individual formulates for himself. Usually, these goals bear no relation to biological necessity; at times, indeed, they are antithetic to biological usefulness" (Envoi, p. 233).
13. But see Soddy, K., ed. *Identity. Mental Health and Value Systems*. London: Tavistock, 1961. "Though to be mentally ill may be to be in conflict with one's environment, it does not follow that to be in conflict with one's environment is to be mentally ill" (p. 87). A person in the latter state could seem to be much less happy than one in the former.

Some outward cultural traits are well recognized, such as the smiling and happy behavior that is etiquette among Japanese and may by self-discipline be exhibited even during great distress.

14. Selye, H. *The Stress of Life*. New York: McGraw-Hill, 1956.

Wolff, H. G. *Stress and Disease*. Springfield, Ill.: Charles C Thomas, 1953. And see (6).

15. Audy, J. R. "The Environment in Human Ecology: Artifacts–the Significance of Modified Environment," pp. 5–15 in PAHO Advisory Committee on Medical Research, *Environmental Determinants of Community Well-being*. (Proceedings of the Special Session, June 17, 1964.) Washington: Pan American Health Organization (Wld. Hlth. Org.), Sci. Pubn. 123, 1965.

Audy, J. R. "The Significance of Ipsefacts." In Discussion, *The Use of Space by Animals and Man*, ed. H. A. Esser. (AAAS Symposium, Dallas, Tex., Dec., 1968.) Bloomington: Indiana University Press, 1970.

An ipsefact or "specific artifact" is a manifold unit of environment that has been physically or chemically modified by behavior.

16. Gibson, W. *The Boat*. Boston: Houghton Mifflin, 1953. In this boat, 31 of 32 people were "tested to destruction." But although the general circumstance seemed common to all, there would have been considerable differences in insults to individuals.

17. Scrimshaw, N. S., J. P. Habicht, M. L. Piche, B. Cholakos, and G. Arroyave. "Protein Metabolism of Young Men During University Examinations," *Am. J. Clin. Nutr.*, 18 (1966), 321–324.

Mayhew, P. W. "Stresses of School Examinations," *Roy. Soc. Hlth. J.* 84 (1964), 38–41.

18. *On the State of the Public Health, being the Annual Report of the Chief Medical Officer for the Year 1952*. (Report of the Ministry of Health for the Year ended 31st December, 1952, Part II.) London: H. M. Stationery Office, 1953.

19. Hinkle, L. E., Jr. "Ecological Observations on the Relation of Physical Illness, Mental Illness, and the Social Environment," *Psychosomat. Med.*, 23 (1961), 289–297.

——— . "The Doctor, the Patient, and the Environment," *Am. J. Pub. Hlth, 54* (1, suppl.) (1964), 11–17.

Hinkle, L. E., Jr., W. N. Christensen, F. D. Kane, A. Ostfeld, W. N. Thetford and H. G. Wolff. "An Investigation of the Relation Between Life Experiences, Personality Characteristics, and General Susceptibility to Illness," *Psychosomat. Med.*, 20 (1958), 278–295.

Hinkle, L. E., Jr., and H. G. Wolff. "The Nature of Man's Adaptation to His Total Environment and the Relation of This to Illness," *A.M.A. Arch. Int. Med.*, 99 (1957), 442–460.

20. Garrow, J. S., and M. C. Pike. "The Long-term Prognosis of Severe Infantile Malnutrition," *Lancet*, i(1967), 1–4.

21. Osborn, R. H., and F. V. DeGeorge. *Genetic Basis of Morphological Variation*. Cambridge, Mass.: Harvard University Press, 1959.

22. Although I can foresee the objections (it is dangerous ground), we may helpfully borrow a concept from the ecologists, that of the development of a sere to a climax. An abandoned clearing will develop stepwise until it reaches a stable limit of complexity decided by climate, soil, and dominant herbivores. The developmental series is a *sere*. The final relatively stable ecosystem is the *climax*, the most complex assemblage that local conditions can support. Thus a bare-earth clearing may finally develop (as a sere) into the climax of a particular kind of forest. Let us use *subclimax* for a climax that has been considerably stunted, remaining close to some early stage of development (as by rocky substrate), or deviated, as when shifting cultivation is followed by invasion of the fire-resistant grass *Imperata* that is burned almost annually, producing an impoverished savannah-like "fire (pyrophytic) subclimax" in a region where the normal climax is rain forest. Thinking in terms of ecological succession, the homeorhetic development of "adult" ecosystems, enriches thinking about homeorhetic development of the adult organism.

23. The temptation to equate the simulacrum with a sort of "naked living genotype" must be resisted, because the ovum and the genotype are totipotent, while the potencies for maturation of the developing simulacrum are successively reduced. So many steps cannot be retraced.

24. As one step from simulacrum to superman, consider a hypothetical intermediate type of individual who is given all his requirements but only minimally, only just enough for physical and mental maturation, but without stresses and with protection from diseases. This would require a team of people constantly at work. The minimal requirement would include allowing the brief postnatal feedback from the placenta (not cutting the umbilical cord until it has stopped pulsating), exposure to microorganisms such as are normally found on the skin and in the gut (without which the intestinal lining will not develop its normal structure (*11*)), minimal necessary feedback from the mother, and, later, peers, together with the minimum intake of all nutrients necessary to meet physiological requirements. It is very instructive to speculate on what the various minimal requirements are and on the nature of the finished product. We can only guess that we would have a person who would evoke little parental pride and would have difficulty in meeting challenges, the insults of daily life.

25. Dobzhansky, T. *Mankind Evolving*. New Haven and London: Yale University Press, 1962.
Cassel, J., R. Patrick and D. Jenkins. "Epidemiological Analysis of the Health Implications of Cultural Change: A Conceptual Model," *Ann. N. Y. Acad. Sci.*, *84* (Art. 17) (1960), 938–949.

26. Waddington, C. H. *The Strategy of the Genes*. London: Allen & Unwin, 1957.

27. Frank, L. K. "The Cultural Patterning of Child Development," pp. 408–432 in *Human Development*, ed. F. Falkner. Philadelphia and London: W. B. Saunders, 1966.

28. Allansmith, M. "Development of Immunity," pp. 582–601 in a valuable review: F. Falkner, ed. (see (*27*)). From about the time the blood forms (22nd week), maternal antibodies in the embryo and fetus rise to over 1000 mg. IgG/100 ml. blood at birth, to be approximately halved every month for the first three months. "Immunology in Relation to the Placenta [Abridged]," *Proc. Roy. Soc. Med.*, 63:57–66, 1970. This symposium deals with the conceptus as potentially a foreign graft.

29. *Nutrition and Infection*, ed. G. E. W. Wolstenholme and M. O'Connor. (Ciba Foundation Study Group No. 31.) London: J. & A. Churchill, 1967.
Malnutrition, Learning, and Behavior, ed. N. S. Scrimshaw and J. E. Gordon. (International Conference on Malnutrition, Learning, and Behavior, Massachusetts Institute of Technology, 1967.) Cambridge, Mass.: M.I.T. Press, 1968. An extensive literature has been developing on this subject.
Scrimshaw, N. S., C. E. Taylor, and J. E. Gordon. "Interactions of Nutrition and Infection," *Am. J. Med. Sci.*, 237 (1959), 367–403.

30. *Biological Clocks*. (Cold Spring Harbor Symposia on Quantitative Biology, vol. 29.) Cold Spring Harbor, L.I.: The Biological Laboratory, 1960.
Richter, C. P. *Biological Clocks in Medicine and Psychiatry*. Springfield, Ill.: Charles C Thomas, 1965.
Aschoff, J., ed. *Circadian Clocks*. (Proceedings, Feldafing Summer School, 1964.) Amsterdam: North-Holland Publ., 1965.

31. Halberg, F. "Chronobiologie: Rhythmes et Physiologie Statistique," pp. 347–411 (incl. discussion) in *Theoretical Physics and Biology. Mechanismes Physiologiques, 2me seance*. Amsterdam: North-Holland Publ., 1969.

32. Rank, O. *The Trauma of Birth*. New York: Harcourt, Brace, 1929.

33. Cheraskin, E. "The Arithmetic of Disease," *J. Dent. Med.*, 14 (1959), 71–82.
Cheraskin, E., *et al.* "The Normal Glucose-tolerance Pattern: The Development of Blood Glucose Normality by an Analysis of Oral Symptoms," *J. Periodontol.*, 31 (1960), 123–137.

Cheraskin, E., and L. Manson-Hing. "The Normal Glucose-tolerance Pattern," *Oral Surg.*, 13 (1960), 819–835.

34. The concept is derived from experimental embryology. It has been extended into the field of behavioral development, that is, from biochemical phenomena in organogenesis within the embryo, to complex emotional, intellectual, and social development within the growing juvenile. Lorenz introduced the term *imprinting (Prägung)* to stress the lasting nature of the appropriate stimulus during a critical period.
    Erikson, E. *Childhood and Society*, 2nd ed. New York: W. W. Norton, 1963.
    Beach, F. A., and J. Jaynes. "The Effects of Early Experience upon the Behavior of Animals," *Psych. Bull.*, 51 (1954), 239–263.
    Scott, J. P. "Critical Periods in Behavioral Development," *Science*, 138 (1962), 949–957.
    Sluckin, W. *Imprinting and Early Learning*. Chicago: Aldine, 1965.

35. Thorpe, W. H. "Some Problems of Animal Learning," *Proc. Linn. Soc. Lond.*, 156 (1944), 70–83.

36. Wolf, S. "A New View of Disease," *J.A.M.A.*, 184 (1963), 129–130.
    Richards, D. W. "Homeostasis: Its Dislocations and Perturbations," *Perspectives Biol. Med.*, 3 (1960), 238–251.

37. Bowlby, J. *Attachment. Attachment and Loss*, vol. 1. New York: Basic Books, 1969.
    Brody, S. *Patterns of Mothering. Maternal Influence during Infancy*. New York: International Universities Press, 1956. This important field was pioneered by René Spitz.

38. Bliss, E. L., ed. *Roots of Behavior*. New York: John Wiley, 1962.
    Christian, J. J. "Endocrine Adaptive Mechanisms and the Physiologic Regulation of Population Growth, pp. 189–353 in *Physiological Mammalogy 1* (Mammalian Populations), ed. W. Mayer and R. Van Gelder. New York and London: Academic Press, 1963.
    Etkin, W., ed. *Social Behavior and Organization among Vertebrates*. Chicago: University of Chicago Press, 1964.
    Harlow, H. F., and M. K. Harlow. "Affection in Primates," *Discovery*, 27 (1966), 11–18.
    Harlow, H. F., and M. K. Harlow. "Learning to Love," *Am. Scientist*, 54 (1966), 244–272.
    Harlow, H. F. See pp. 157–166 in Bliss, above.
    Liddell, H. S. *Emotional Hazards in Animals and Man*. Springfield, Ill.: Charles C Thomas, and Oxford: Blackwell, 1956.
    Marler, P. R., and W. Hamilton, III. *Mechanisms of Animal Behavior*. New York and London: John Wiley, 1966.
    Stone, C. P., ed. *Comparative Psychology*, 3rd ed. New York: Prentice-Hall, 1951.

39. Sullivan, H. S. *The Interpersonal Theory of Psychiatry*, ed. H. S. Perry and M. L. Gawell. New York: W. W. Norton, 1953.

40. Benirschke, K., and S. G. Driscoll. *The Pathology of the Human Placenta*. Berlin: Springer-Verlag, 1967.

41. Powell, G. F., J. A. Brazel, S. Raiti, and R. M. Blizzard. "Emotional Deprivation and Growth Retardation Simulating Idiopathic Hypopituitarism. I. Clinical Evaluation of the Syndrome. II. Endocrinological Evaluation of the Syndrome," *New Eng. J. Med.*, 276 (1967), 1271–1278, 1279–1283.

42. Engel, G. L. "A Unified Concept of Health and Disease," *Perspectives Biol. Med.*, 3 (1960), 459–485.

43. Association for Research in Nervous and Mental Disease. *Life Stress and Bodily Disease*. Proceedings of the Association, December 1949. vol. 29. Baltimore: Williams & Wilkins, 1950.

44. Greenfield, N. S., R. Roessler, and A. P. Crossley. "Ego Strength and Length of Recovery from Infectious Mononucleosis," *J. Nerv. Ment. Dis.*, 128 (1959), 125–128. Ego strength measured by two of the scores in the MMPI (Minnesota Multiphasic Personality Inventory).

45. Friedman, S. B., and L. A. Glasgow. "Psychologic Factors and Resistance to Infectious Disease," *Pediat. Clin. N. Amer.*, 13 (1966), 315–335.
46. Merton, R. K. *Social Theory and Social Structure*, rev. ed. New York: Free Press of Glencoe, 1957.
    Clinard, M. B., ed. *Anomie and Deviant Behavior: A Discussion and Critique*. New York: Free Press of Glencoe, 1964.
47. Wolf, S. "Disease as a Way of Life: Neural Integration in Systemic Pathology," *Perspectives Biol. Med.*, 4 (1961), 288–305.
48. Johnson, R. H. "Factors in Human Endurance," *Brit. Med. J.*, 1(1968), 697–700. Was Scott's death hastened by the bitter disappointment at finding Amundsen's flag at the Pole and the death of two colleagues?
49. Shapiro, D., B. Tursky, E. Gershon, and M. Stern. "Effects of Feedback and Reinforcement on the Control of Human Systolic Blood Pressure," *Science*, 163 (1969), 588–590.
50. Hess, R. D., and G. Handel. *Family Worlds*. Chicago: University of Chicago Press, 1959.
51. Ruesch, J., A. Jacobson, and M. B. Loeb. "Acculturation and Illness," *Psychol. Monogr.: General & Applied*, 292 (1948).
52. Kubie, L. S. "Social Forces and the Neurotic Process," *J. Nerv. Ment. Dis.*, 128 (1959), 65–80.
53. Audy, J. R. "Introduction: Aspects of Health in the Pacific," pp. 3–12 in *Public Health and Medical Sciences in the Pacific. A Forty-Year Review, 1920-1960*, ed. J. R. Audy. Honolulu: University of Hawaii Press, 1964.
54. Blest, A. D. "Longevity, Palatability and Natural Selection in Five Species of New World Saturniid Moth," *Nature*, 197 (1963), 1183–1186. A moth normally has no survival value for the species after oviposition and it shortly dies. One (cryptic) group of saturniid moths are palatable but protect themselves by camouflage. The females die after laying eggs. The other (aposematic) group protect themselves by foul taste and bright warning coloration from which predators learn never to try again. The females of this group stay alive a long time after oviposition. Primate (including human) social structure has to varying degrees placed survival value on individuals beyond their reproductive age.
    A symposium relevant to the present paper: The Lord Platt and A. S. Parkes, eds. *Social and Genetic Influence on Life and Death*. London: Oliver & Boyd, 1967.
55. Williams, G. Z. "Clinical Pathology Tomorrow," *Am. J. Clin. Path.*, 37 (1962), 121–124.
56. For example, great uniformity in weights of each mouse in a litter contrasts with considerable differences between mice in different litters. This remains true of "litters" formed by pooling newborns and redistributing at random. Differences between litters are related to differences in mothering behavior.
    Dubos, R. "Lasting Biological Effects of Early Influences," *Perspectives Biol. Med.*, 12 (1964), 479–491.
57. James, G. "Poverty and Public Health—New Outlooks. I. Poverty as an Obstacle to Health Progress in Our Cities," *Am. J. Pub. Hlth*, 55 (1965), 1757–1771.
    Straus, R. "Poverty and Public Health—New Outlooks. II. Poverty as an Obstacle to Health Progress in our Rural Areas," *Am. J. Pub. Hlth*, 55 (1965), 1772–1779.
58. Ratcliffe, H. L. "Contribution of a Zoo to an Ecology of Disease," *Proc. Am. Phil. Soc.*, 112 (1968), 235–244.
    Morris, D. *The Human Zoo*. New York: McGraw-Hill, and London: Jonathan Cape, 1969.

LIST OF FIRST AUTHORS IN REFERENCES

Allansmith *28*; Aschoff *30*; Assoc. Res. in Nervous and Mental Disease *43*; Audy *15, 53*; Beach *34*; Benirschke *40*; Blest *54*; Bliss *38*; Bowlby *37*; Brody *37*; Cassel *25*; Caudill *6*;

Cheraskin *33*; Christian *38*; Ciba Fdn. *29*; Clinard *46*; Cold Spring Harbor Symposia *30*; Dobzhansky *25*; Dubos *11, 12, 56*; Engel *42*; Erikson *34*; Etkin *38*; Frank *27*; Friedman *45*; Galen *1*; Garrow *20*; Gibson *16*; Greenfield *44*; Halberg *31*; Harlow *38*; Hess *50*; Hinkle *19*; International Conference on Malnutrition, Learning, and Behavior *29*; James *57*; Johnson *48*; Koestler *7*; Kubie *52*; Liddell *38*; Marler *38*; Mayhew *17*; Merton *46*; Ministry of Health *18*; Morris *58*; Osborn *21*; Pearse *2*; Perkins *5*; Platt *54*; Powell *41*; Rank *32*; Ratcliffe *58*; Richards *36*; Richter *30*; Ruesch *51*; Sargent *8, 9, 10*; Scott *34*; Scrimshaw *17, 29*; Selye *14*; Shapiro *49*; Sluckin *34*; Soddy *13*; Stone *38*; Straus *57*; Sullivan *39*; Swaroop *4*; Thorpe *35*; USPHS *3*; Waddington *26*; WHO *3*; Williams *55*; Wolf *36, 47*; Wolff *14*, (*43*); Wolstenholme *29*.

I am grateful to colleagues and students who over the past three years have commented on the first rough draft of this paper: Albert Beck, Robert Black, Yehudi Cohen, Rene Dubos, Frederick Dunn, Robert Goldsmith, C. E. Gordon Smith, Joseph Hartog, Eben Hipsley, Donald Iddins, Chauncey Leake, Victor Macfarlane, James Ransom, Joseph Rubin, Jurgen Ruesch, Frederick Sargent II, and Anselm Strauss. All responsibility for the views expressed, however, is of course my own.

Since this was written a relevant and very sound review has been published: C. M. Wylie, "The Definition and Measurement of Health and Disease," *Pub. Hlth. Rep.*, 85 (1970), 100–104. The author prefers a modification of Herbert Spencer's definition, "Health is the perfect, *continuing* adjustment of an organism to its environment." He warns that the "asymptotic or open-ended" WHO definition is one of a class of idealistic definitions that must be ineffectual when faced with a likely reality, that "health promotion will never be more than a euphemistic term for disease control." I believe this is a likelihood only so long as our approach to health is traditional (medicine's concern is with disease) rather than ecological.

THE FOUR ENVIRONMENTS OF MAN

Sibyl Moholy-Nagy

There is no escape from the city. In spite of pastoral idylls, agrarian dreams, rural utopias, and Neolithic yearning, the future of modern man—at least for the next half-century—is inseparable from the city. Not only will our values be derived from city life, but also urban forms will dominate the inhabited landscape. No amount of sociological demonstration of the virtues of the small community or of frantic idealism pitted against the complexities of the industrial state can change our direction. Ecologists, environmentalists, naturalists—and recently the disaffected young—do not always seem to recognize this, and their search for fundamental values and contact with the earth is too often distorted into a hopeless yearning for the past or for peasant life.

This does not mean, however, that the past has no lessons to offer. In spite of advances in transportation and communication, a great many city problems have not changed. Distinctions between the private and the public; the collective necessity of nutrition and waste removal; the need for a geometry which can transform the total landscape into symbols which represent social principles or externalize human structure and scale in a comprehensible and meaningful way; the accommodation by architecture of custom and climate; projective plans that allow for growth or decline: all imply questions still unanswered.

Nor does it mean that we must stand helpless before uncontrolled expansion, local decay, exploitation, and the valuation of convenience over human life. The reason that there is no escape from the city is that we refuse to have done with it. The random rural dispersal of industry is extremely expensive and destructive, as is the unregulated growth of suburbia, because both require exorbitant energy input, pollute in ways difficult to control, and waste space. Even so, our adherence to cities is less a matter of prudence than of choice; we prefer an urban existence. In the long run this can only mean the persistence of cities, and the demise of the dream of an exurban utopia with people diffused in an endless park or on subsistence farms.

When pious Indian Jains were asked by scandalized British missionaries why they went naked, they replied: "But man *is* clothed in space." Hypothetical architects,

Sibyl Moholy-Nagy, "The Four Environments of Man," Landscape *16:2 (Winter, 1966-67), 3-9.*

untouched by professional publications, if asked by the scandalized American Institute of Planners why they had no environmental theory, would probably answer: "But architecture *is* environment." For some 6,000 years man-made environment was the logical result of building, meaning of the construction of shelter for man, possessions and processes which must rate as one of the *a priori* instincts of the race because it evolved with organic life. From Jericho (7th Mill. BC) to Chandigarrh (20th Century AD) man-made environment can be judged by an unbroken continuity of challenge and response. The challenge was the single building of which all communities are made—its functional and ideological requirements of individual ownership; the response was the architect's syncretic vision to see the self-image of man in relationship to the social image of a community. The balance achieved by the architect between the impact of personality on the perceptual environment, and the waves, spreading outward from that impact into sector, community, region and ecumene, could be successful or mediocre or a dismal failure. Whatever it was that was realized, it never occurred to any man or age to doubt the architect's domain as the sole creator of man-made environment.

This millenial order of design responsibility was thrown into confusion when science succeeded in converting two human beings into programmed, totally predictable instruments, rotating around the earth in a fraction of Outer Space. I don't know what happened to other professions. The environment builders suffered a collective brainstroke from that event which afflicted the older practitioners with a form of Schizophrenia, known as *dementia praecox*:

Loss of contact with environment.
Negativistic stereotyped actions reproduced without variation and undistinguished by individual marks.
Cataleptic symptoms of total rigidity retaining any assumed form without the ability to change.

The younger group started to display all the symptoms of Paranoia:

Systematic delusions of persecution of one's greatness, accompanied by Messianism and hallucinations—perception of objects without reality.

The schizophrenic split produced the city planner who did not make it in architecture; the paranoiac stroke hit the architect who did not make it in city planning. The planner's "loss of contact with environment" assumes that cities are two-dimensional grids of real estate values, density and ground-use patterns and communication frequencies. "Master solutions," resulting from negativistic computer calculations of minimum everything, produced stereotyped renewal projects whose cataleptic shapes cannot change because economic and political rigor mortis has set in. The real city as an assembly of shapes and meanings has receded beyond the mental horizon.

The architects in the paranoiac ward have taken refuge from the space-science-induced inferiority complex by producing doodles of hallucinatory grandeur that liquidate gravity, statics, man's biological limitations and requirements, his territorial instincts binding him to the surface of the earth and his need for esthetic gratification and constant interchange with contrasting environments. Common to both types of inmates, otherwise so distinctly different, is a total disregard for argumentative logic that characterizes, according to psychiatry, all forms of mental aberration. The Dementia Praecox planners insist on the most sublimated social conscience as their motivating power whose only aim is to provide the poor of the world with decent minimum shelter; yet they hold these disadvantaged masses in such utter contempt that they eliminate from their environment the beauty, elegance and historical grandeur of nonutilitarian spaces and buildings which alone afford the welfare dweller the pride of identification with his city.

The hallucinatory architects, on the other hand, are not in the least deterred by the fact that their visionary plug-in cities are untouched by the architectural prerequisites of selective environment, form composition and space variation, but are machines whose construction can only be the job of the engineer and whose inhabitants must be conditioned to act as automated machine parts. Both the cataleptics and the delusionists assert themselves as the only competent interpreters of contemporaneousness—the makers of an environment for men whose solutions are projected into a future—nothing closer than the Year 2000 and beyond—that is supposed to represent a case of arrested development.

At the root of the psychopathic spectacle of our environmental frenzy lies a total disregard for the historical process. Historical illiteracy is an old American affliction. It became a national disease when the old historical nations became American dependents and when space science produced results for which there exists no historical precedent. Brainstruck and demoted, the environment makers were ashamed of a profession whose essence is the crystallization of the human potential through selection and revision of traditional forms. In their frantic attempts to gain admission to the space club by pretending that planning is an objective science and architecture a "technical optimum per pounds of invested resources," to quote Buckminster Fuller, they cut themselves loose from *energeiai*, the concrete state of human possibilities realized, which is challenged continually by *en dynamei*, the unrealized energy pressing toward concretization.

Science creates its criteria by laboratory experiments; architecture derives its selective standards from the accumulated building history of the race. Every change and revision in the matrix of human life will be judged by comparative memory and the conceptual imagination that sees the completed building in relationship to existing social, moral, esthetic and economic standards. It is and always has been the calling of the architect to anticipate imminent modifications of these standards with the antenna of his talent. His form-giving personality has to rise above the merely form-imagining individuality of the client.

These revisions, or, as a progress-obsessed time will have it, these advances of the historical environmental process can be barely perceptible variants: from Georgian to Federal row housing, for instance, or from "the tall office building artistically considered," to quote Sullivan in behalf of Mies van der Rohe, to the collectively condemned curtainwall elevation. Other modifications are momentous, indicating profound social reorientations within one or two generations: the siting of Greek temples in the Classical and the Hellenistic Age; or from French to English public parks. The astonishing fact is that in the largest context of the continuous environmental process, in the community as a planned concept, the crystallizations of the human condition have been few and of great constancy. Despite an inexhaustible variation of details, the societies of man have adhered to four environments only. These four man-made environments are according to their physical shapes:

    geomorphic
    concentric
    orthogonal
    clustered

of which the geomorphic one is rural, the concentric and the orthogonal ones are urban and the clustered one regional. All four modes of human settlement had fully emerged by the time Western Civilization grew from the cross-fertilization of Mediterranean culture and Northern European primitivism, and each one still flourishes in the 20th Century AD.

The geomorphic community is conditioned by the given earth on which it depends for survival. It is not a product of nature. A much respected author, Robin Boyd, thought he had solved "The Puzzle of Architecture" when he postulated:

> Every reasonably sensitive and experienced architect knows what architecture is . . . It is the creation of a microcosm of Nature, of truth, by the arrangement of functional and material components of building.

Architecture is nothing of the sort. There are few more overt antitheses to Nature than architecture, even at its most primitive level. Science is an extension of natural laws from the most arcane astrophysical formula to the computer, fashioned after the human brain. The permanence and statics of walls and roofs, of artificial heating and lighting create an environment that is entirely unnatural. Rural environment evolves on many levels from the human challenges to Nature. Each part of the farmstead or village community contributes to the taming control over Nature by interacting with the whole. Seeding, harvesting, storing, preserving are part of an organic cycle that is invariable and endlessly repetitive. There is no specialization and no escape from the organic cycle. This is why geomorphic environment is static, uniform and nonhierarchical.

The rural town, the *villaticus* of the Romans, grew either from villages or from village needs. It hardly differs from geomorphic environment, save in a limited adjustment to specialization. Trade and market are as uniform as the village whose cycle they share. There might be a contraction of small crop and service land within the settlement that gives to villages their random layout; but the interdependence of town and village in the struggle of man to make nature serviceable is clearly visible in the similarity of planning and building concepts.

Social reformers of the Garden City Movement conceived in innocence and ignorance a modern village and country town environment. In the tradition of Physical Determinism, they hope to restore mental health and pure morals to the city worker. The bogus farmhouses and village greens of Unwin's England, and Stein's America, were middle-class versions of Marie Antoinette's Petit Trianon. Their only social impact was to furnish prototypes for greedy developers. The purposeless uniformity of house types, and the lack of social and economic specialization without the conquest of nature, prove that village environment has become zero environment.

The only legitimate survival of geomorphic settlement is that much maligned "prima donna creation"—the country house. It is at its best when the purely humanistic art of architecture asserts a contrapuntal relationship between the given earth and the organic life of man, and it is at its worst if it pretends to be product and part of nature.

No villages, ancient or new, ever grew into cities and none ever will, because urban environment was developed by Neolithic man on totally different premises at the same time at which he started to build villages. Excavations in Anatolia have furnished proof that walled cities, separated from cultivated land, existed in the 7th Millenium BC. The planned unity of Hacilar, Catal Hüjük, and Palestinian Jericho expresses an urban concept of the city as an extended building whose houses equal an enfilade of rooms of great variety in shape, furnishings, mural decorations and artifacts. Public plazas and alleys clearly distinguish between communication and assembly; and an astounding assortment of tools, weapons and utensils in styles and materials not indigenous points to foreign trade as principal economic system. Perhaps nothing else shows so clearly the primordial origin of village collectivism and city individualism as the ceramic plaques of Catal Hüjük which, in a pre-literary age, marked each house with a different pattern.

Revivalists among urban historians have tried to prove that it was the sole purpose of cities, prior to our own wicked age, to serve God. This is true, but for different reasons. Man invented anthropomorphic Gods as idealized self-images on whom he could measure the extent of his ambitions and the success of his competitive aggressiveness. The earliest cities of which we have documentary evidence, those of Sumer and Akkad in the 4th and 3rd Millenia BC, derived their concentric plan and their centrifugal spirit from the symbolic identification of each citizen with the *temenos* and the world mountain—the ziggurat (Figure 1). All urban values derived from there and all communication spread outward from a single source. The urban spirit resided in the *omphalos*, the city navel, and from there dispersed and specialized into the many-faceted creature that is urban man. The concentric rings of totally anonymous row dwellings were equidistant from the source of their strength and their justification. The ledger of their sins and achievements was kept in the cosmos where it was outside the fierce contentiousness and rivalry for power over destiny, knowledge and wealth that gave impetus to the formation of cities. Among the great wealth of legend and epos which the

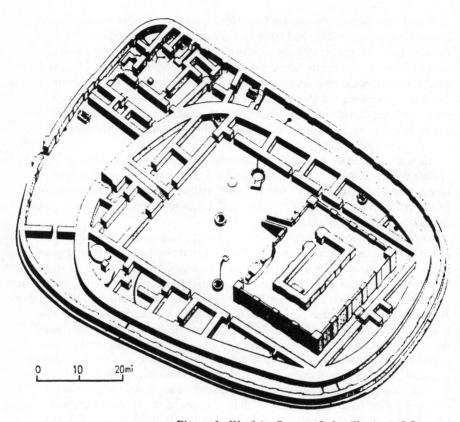

0   10   20mi

Figure 1. *Khafaje, Sumer. 3rd millenium, BC.*

Sumerian scribes left to posterity as a record of the concentric, centrifugal, cosmos-oriented city is one that should finish the argument whether the citizen of the 20th Century is "a new species" for better and for worse, or the historical continuation of his ancestors of 5,000 years ago. S. N. Kramer has translated the Sumerian epose: *Inanni and Enki: The Transfer of the Arts of Civilization from Eridu to Erech*. It tells how Inanna, protectress of Erech, contrives to transfer the urban supremacy of ancient Eridu to her city. With great cunning she finally obtains from Enki, the Lord of Wisdom, "the divine decrees that are fundamental to civilization." Among more than 100 of these civic essentials are leadership and libel, prostitution and marriage, power and envy, falsehood, art, truth, scribeship, sexual intercourse, the destruction of cities and their holy purification. The establishment of the total city in all its tensions as the *imago profanis* ranks second only to the invention of writing as the greatest Sumerian contribution to man-made environment.

The essence of the centrifugal city is the symbolic core which reappears over the milleniums whenever a society creates an environment in willed contrast to existing sociopolitical conditions. The implications of the concentric plan are always cosmological, no matter whether it is the return to the Cosmic Order of Zoroastrism of the Sassanians after Hellenistic rationalism had failed, or the sacred geometric order of Arabian Geometry based on symbolic prototypes so ancient and so worldwide that similar concentric plans are found in Central Asia, the Andean strongholds of the Incas and the tomb of Augustus in Rome.

The city of God of the Middle Ages is centrifugal and concentric and so are the uncounted "Ideal City" plans that follow first the discovery of Vitruvius, and after the Copernican Revolution, the heliocentric cosmology of modern man (Figure 2). The utopian dreams of 19th Century reform urbanists are concentric

Figure 2. *Plan for Karlsruhe, Germany.*

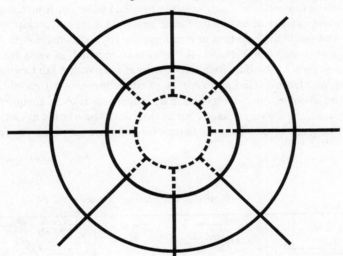

and centrifugal, and so are Israeli Kibuzim and New Towns of the recent past. The overwhelming majority of cities of the future: Taut's alpine city images, Mazet's Cité Pyramidale Gigantesque from 1947; and the recent crop of circular settlements in the ocean and on the moon, chronicled by Michel Ragon, are concentric, centrifugal and oriented toward an extra-mundane cosmological ideal.

The organic village society had celebrated its own power to force nature into human sustenance by worshipping its sources of supply. The single-focused urban society invented the invisible arbitrator, hovering axially above his own territorial realm whose destiny was unrelated to other realms claiming different leadership prototypes for cosmological protection.

The orthogonal city which challenged the ascendency of the concentric single-focused environment, by then 3,000 years old, grew from a revision of the urban self-image. The 1st Millenium BC added to the quest for divination, knowledge and wealth the quest for power over the people of the world. Imperialism, as it developed from tribal expansion of Babylonians and Assyrians into full-fledged Alexandrian world dominion, created nodes of centripetal urban centers in which the spoils of conquest were collected. The ideological perspective underwent a 90-degree shift from a vertical focal point in the sky to an open-ended vista parallel to the expansion of conquerable land. In the great age of the centrifugal city the movements of trade and war had been dependent on rivers, and the barbarian hordes falling like locusts on the conspicuous wealth so conveniently stored in one place, needed no roads. The dynamic rulers of empires had to move from city to city to destroy what hampered their world dream and rebuild what represented their victories. The emphasis of city building shifted from the monumental building to the monumental road, which in turn had to be fed from a network of secondary and exterior access roads. Public spaces were treated architecturally as containers of power and symbols of meaning. The royal decumanus—in Alexandria, Seleukia, Antioch, Palmyra—is the aorta from which all veins are fed the life of the empire. In the Babylonia of Nabopolassar from the 7th Century BC (Figure 3), which must stand as prototype of all orthogonal centripetal communication cities to come, the triumphal road no longer comes to an unequivocal stop at Etemenanki, the Tower of Babel, but cuts through the whole city. And it is here that the great alliance between conqueror and merchant is for the first time

Figure 3. *Babylonia, 7th century, BC.*

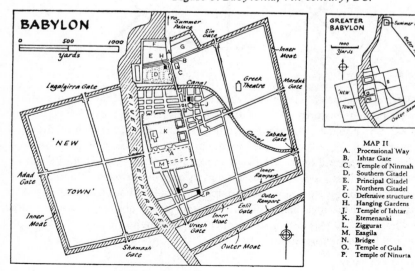

MAP II

A. Processional Way
B. Ishtar Gate
C. Temple of Ninmah
D. Southern Citadel
E. Principal Citadel
F. Northern Citadel
G. Defensive structure
H. Hanging Gardens
J. Temple of Ishtar
K. Etemenanki
L. Ziggurat
M. Esagila
N. Bridge
O. Temple of Gula
P. Temple of Ninurta

fully expressed in the city plan. The merchants, shunned and confined to their own cluster as will be seen shortly, are given a whole town of their own with spacious plazas and wide blocks that equal the royal city across the river. The four gates in the direction of the compass points that had served the centrifugal city are multiplied into dozens and, if legend is right, into hundreds in Iranian Parthia, for instance. The gigantic marble colonnade of Palmyra's Main Street was lined with memorial trophies of particularly successful caravans registering the profits made, no different from Wall Street or London's City where dividends and capital reserves inform the pedestrian as he moves from bank building to bank building.

"The merchant pleases God only with difficulty," sighed St. Jerome at the height of the Hellenistic Age whose temples had turned into stock exchanges and thereby increased in size and number. But he pleased the emperors who allotted him the freedom of the highways that covered the territory between cities like a dragnet. Both their businesses—the emperor's and the merchant's—were with the affairs of man's physical presence which changed the anonymous row dwellings of the Bronze Age into testimonials to the hierarchy of wealth. The ecumenical dream of world dominion was cosmopolitan and tolerant. The barriers were not racial or religious but materialistic. Each group of citizens had its specific focal point in the city plan around which spun the competitive drive for success. The orthogonal city was multifocal—*temenos* and temple, palace and barracks, assembly and law court, theater and circus, stoa and market, villas, palaces, shops, tenements and slums. What forged this permanence of change into an urban pattern was the street.

The difference between abortive and successful Imperialism rested with civil service and the administrative unit. It is not clear whether the Chinese learnt this from the Romans, or—more likely—the Romans imported this basic assumption along the Silk Route. Its urban expression was the modular labor camp for workers, soldiers or administrators, which constitutes a curious subspecies of the orthogonal multi-focused environment. This is not the place to argue the absurd insistence that it was Hippodamus of Miletus who in the wake of the Persian War "invented" the gridiron plan, which then is impartially called Hippodamian even where it is evidently not modular but orthogonal. The three authentic Hippodamian plans are clearly expressions of Pythagorean geometry of which their planner was an avid disciple. The other modular grid plans go back to the oldest known administrative units, the merchant citadel of Harappa from 2500 BC, for instance, where workmen's barracks and granary have the same module because, as John Stuart Mill said: "Given parts in given combinations must act alike." Their broadest application is found in the Roman civitas which is an extension of the field centuriation with which it fuses into a global grid overlaying the Roman Imperium like an iron grille.

The urban amnesia of the Great Migration and the Early Middle Ages amputated the world road system. What was left of cities reverted to the concentric pattern seeking protection from the ancient cosmological forces rather than from fallible empires. A new city building age that starts toward the close of the 12th Century recoined the secular ecumenism of the Hellenistic Age. It was now the Catholic church which covered the known world with urban nodes and connected them with pilgrimage routes whose freedom was given to merchants and crusaders. By the time the Christian Imperium reached its zenith of power in the Roman papacy, the street, the triumphal road, the multishaped plazas of churches and fairs had regained their Hellenistic importance. The new concept lay in the importance given to the continuous street elevation that is no longer separated from the buildings of the city by arcades, colonnades and porticoes. The orthogonal environment of Renaissance and Baroque received its worth or unworthiness from the street block designed as a single building. Its esthetic-symbolic importance was so great that in 17th Century Paris, for instance, the monarch agreed to pay for the elevation of the Places Royales, while the citizens handled the interior spaces.

Balances of national power, imposed by the destructiveness of firearms, curtailed the ecumenical vista of religious and secular imperialism. With it disappeared the city wall and the architectural triumph of the great gates. In its place moved the finite linear perspective, focusing on the monumental public building. When the railroad replaced the road net it was entirely logical within the imperialistic environmental concept that railroad stations were conceived as public monuments and railroad magnates as "empire builders."

The via triumphalis of Timgad differed merely in style from Williamsburg (Figures 4A and 4B) or Berlin's Unter den Linden or the Champs Elysées; and there is not even a trace of environmental modification between the palace axis of Constantinople and the hypnotic power display approached axially in Costa's Brasilia. The deviation from a 2,500-year-old prototype is ideological. No imperialistic orthogonal city would have pretended to democracy while building power; and none would have confused its modular grid-patterned civil service camps with the body of the city itself.

Perhaps it has some significance that the fourth environment of man which is clustered, exurban and regional is so demonstratively evident in a failed orthogonal city like Brasilia (Figure 5). Throughout the long genesis of village environment and territorial and imperial cities, the cluster as the barnacle on the flanks of cohesive plans had played a minor role. In the second half of the 20th Century it suddenly assumes an importance that might very well decide the death or life of great cities, American and otherwise. The cluster is a splinter of the urban unit, without context to its environmental order but dependent on it for all aspects of existence. 3,500 years ago Assyrian Karums or trading posts squatted at a safe distance from the cosmological focal point of the concentric cities by whom they made their living, and later it was the Phoenicians, the Greeks and the Venetians whose introverted shapeless clusters formed the "place of the foreign people" outside the walls of all great cities. Celtic oppidums and Germanic burgums clustered outside the geometric rigidity of Roman castrums, and later it was the monasteries in the West and the caravanserais in the East which made up nuclei

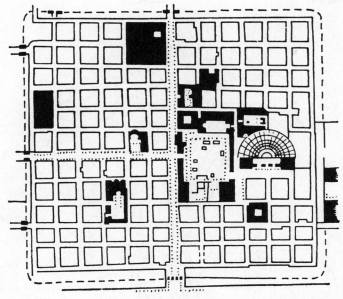

Figure 4a. *Via Triumphalis, Timgad, North Africa.*

Figure 4b. *Williamsburg, Virginia.*

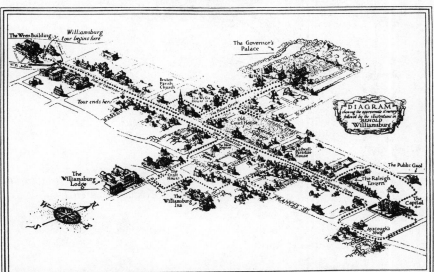

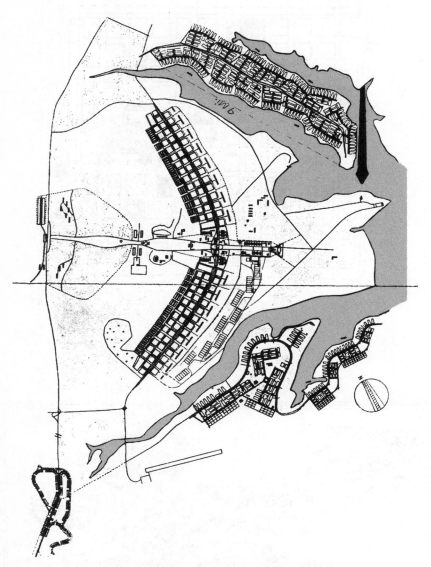

Figure 5. *The orthogonal environment: Brasilia, the prize-winning plan by Costa, executed 1954–1961.*

without parturition. In modern times the two extremes of the social scale cluster outside the orthogonal city of dominion and wealth: derelicts and squatters in the ranchos and favellos, which are not confined to South America but float in New York Harbor and along the beaches of California; and the clusters of the socially elect whose romantic exurbias started to break the identification of class and city when their own factories covered the old urban status symbol with soot.

These specks on the face of the region turned into blotches some fifty years ago. The cluster invaded the urban body like a cancer disrupting the continuity of street elevations and plazas with welfare housing ghettos which turn their bare backsides to the community and hold a piece of tattered lawn in front to hide their ugliness. With the windfall of publicly financed land clearing, private enterprise caught on to the profitable possibilities of the cluster. Philadelphia's Society Hill, New York's Kips Bay, Mies van der Rohe's Detroit Lafayette Park and uncounted other projects turned social segregation into social distinction by creating city-alienated communities whose only self-sufficiency is the contemplation of each other's navels through floor to ceiling windows. Cataleptic public and individually designed clusters are in the process of eliminating any distinction between city and region by denying the street as the definition of the city.

The question confronting us at the conclusion of the briefest possible survey of man-made environment as historical continuity is after a potential synthesis of the four environments of man. The more pompous the denouncements of the individual house and its "irresponsible prima donna architects," to quote Walter Gropius, the more assured is the rebellious quest of young designers to find a geomorphic spot on which to experiment with structural truth and challenge vision against nature. The concentric focal point of the urban core is still the biblical "tower whose top reacheth unto heaven to let us make us a name," whether it is the Chase Manhattan Bank or a Space Needle. This vertical reach beyond gravity will retain its centrifugal magic if the orthogonal matrix of civic *actum* provides the horizontal balance through street elevations and plazas. The ill-smelling contempt of the "enclosure systems" technocrats for architecture as the art of environment-making might stunt but will never kill the peripatetic delight in the linear experience of a contrasting streetscape. The new dimension beyond the orthogonal city limit is the region and the cluster as residential halo around the luminous city core. Its urban justification is the designed continuity from public to private existence. Modern life is urban, and only tightly maintained urban contact can save half of our population from turning into suburban village idiots. The line of communication is the road—not the maelstrom of concrete ribbons blighting forever what they adjoin, but the architecturally conceived transition from the ahuman city scale to the individual dimension of the clustered habitat.

Neither gravitational nor atmospheric conditions nor man's biological adjustments to them have changed; nor will they change. The compensations designed to overcome this terrestrial bondage were and are both basic and infinitely variable.

The judgment of history rests on the architect's implementation of this First Cause. There is no progress in man-made environment, only in mechanical equipment. And who cares today about the efficiency of low cost housing in Angkor Wat or how the plumbing worked in Peking as long as they feed our imagination with the creative impetus of historical continuity?

THE ECOLOGICAL CITY

Mort and Eleanor Karp

"The first house, the tomb, became the outer casing for the dead soul, just as the first house proper (its windows breathing like lungs) was a case for man—as indeed his mother's body had been a case to house the water-rocked embryo. But from all this to the temple—what an imaginative jump! . . .

"Finding that an average foot measured one-sixth part of a man's height they applied this to their column by laying off its lowest diameter six times along the overall length, the capital included. Thus did the Doric column begin to mimic and represent the proportions and compressed beauty of the male body in temple building. . . .

"But what, you will ask, of the diurnal man? What of his housing? We can of course see that the individual house bears the shadowy narcissistic image of himself embedded even in its most utilitarian forms. The head, the stomach, the breast. The drawing room, bedroom, the kitchen. I will not enlarge on this. All the vents are there. . . .

"There is no doubt in my mind that the geometries we use in our buildings are biological projections, and we can see the same sort of patterning in the work of other animals or insects, birds, spiders, snails and so on. Matter does not dictate the form but only modifies it in order to make sure that a spider's web really holds the fly, the bird's nest really cherishes the egg. . . .

"Reflect how quarters tend to flock together—birds of a feather. Buildings are like the people who wear them. One brothel, two, three, and soon you have a quarter. Banks, museums, income groups, tend to cling together for protection. Any new intrusion modifies the whole. . . .

Perhaps we have finally seen how arbitrary is the distinction between the "natural" and the "artificial." It is perhaps time we drop conceptual dichotomies which were once necessary crutches—relinquishing nothing of what has been won, but understanding that abandoning outworn modes of thought is the only means of knowing our earth estate, and is the true inauguration of dominance.

Mort and Eleanor Karp, "The Ecological City," Landscape 13:1 (Autumn 1963), 4–8.

During the past forty years there has been a development, an elaboration and a building of all that was inherent in the revolution known as modern architecture. The basic statements have been made about clarity of structure and use of material, and what we now have is a rewording and reworking into finer detail. The glass, steel and concrete parents and grandparents of the buildings in next year's architectural magazines surround us, and it is the most talented and distinguished architects who have themselves stated in print their own reservations about their work. Thus Minoru Yamasaki worries about the eclectic prettiness of his buildings. It is, however, the very best he can do, and is certainly on a much more significant level than the large plateau of mediocre building that is the general standard of architecture in the world. And so naming names is, I think, a gratuitous punishment of the few people who are honestly trying to be creative. The same holds true for the other examples that spring to mind. Skidmore, Owings and Merrill, who popularized the steel and glass boxes that now decorate downtown in every city of this country, have, in their recent projects, been looking and trying for other solutions and other forms, without any idea of where the new solution should lie. The late Eero Saarinen (who was so much an architect's architect that only another architect could appreciate the staggering amount of care and painstaking intelligence that he put into every detail, every joining of material in every one of his buildings) in his very integrity played around with a different modern esthetic in each building he did—shiny glass, or free-form concrete or formed stone walls as Frank Lloyd Wright first used at Taliesen West.

This is the beginning of a dead, an historical style. Vitality, which is the essence of any art, must come from a new source. The life of art is discovery, and to find this life we must turn our backs on what we know. The past can offer no more than sophistication.

Where to look? Novelty for its own sake is only esthetic entertainment and is of passing interest—last year's cliché. To design the merely interesting building is simple, a matter of recipe. Take some form that exists in a small scale (for instance) and enlarge its principle to the building scale. Anything will do: a safety pin, a bubble, a bamboo shoot. There is no limit to the sources available. A direct adaptation on a scale large enough to walk through will give the shock value of genuine creation. Or we can take the scheme of something which is large in scale and reduce it to building size—a spiral nebula, a cyclone. Even easier is to take a familiar shape and turn it upside-down or inside out, and the pitched roof becomes a butterfly. Make a building that is a sculptured, prostrate female figure, two hundred feet long in concrete, the organs of the body hollow for rooms, the entrances to be the natural fissures of the body. Living in *that* would be an intense emotional experience.

In this sense being creative in architecture is simple. The problem is not, however, how to be merely creative, but how to create something of value. Now the idea of *value* is a serious one, and strongly limiting. Because what is there of value in our lives? Only a very small portion of our existence on this earth, minutes here and minutes there that stand out in a slough of time. Although there may be a great variation in the way that individuals spend the waking part of their lives, what is meaningful is for everyone very much the same: moments of love, moments of awareness of one's own oneness with the universe. Where to look for the expression of these values? It is possible (and it has been done) to carve a white marble cube with a hole for a door and say—"This expresses man's oneness with nature." I do not think so.

The purpose of architecture, as of every art, is the creation of significant form. Providing merely functional shelter is engineering. In a painting, the complex of form cannot extend beyond the frame. This is the boundary. A sculpture terminates in the volume of air that surrounds it. But where is the boundary in architecture? We design a room, a group of rooms called a building, and in arbitrarily placing the boundary of architecture at the edges of the building we have neglected and omitted to make sufficiently explicit the relation of the building to those around it. Every architect is taught that a room exists in relation to the other rooms in a building, and that the relationship between rooms is what determines how the building is lived in. Yet no building exists in a vacuum. The most isolated farm is a complex of structures—a city in microcosm. It is the city that is the basic creation of man, the physical expression and background of his life. In the city the buildings themselves are rooms and the whole city, taken together, is no more than the single, collective house we inhabit.

Architecture is therefore continuous, and the work of architecture is not the building but the city. If the modern city is a mish-mash of discordant chaos, this is primarily because the architect's attention is limited to the individual building, to the discrete element, because he is often unaware that there is no frame around the building and that, in a single glance anywhere, the eye sees not one but a tangle of buildings side by side, in front of and behind each other as well as pavement, cars, signs and people. A building conceived without relation to the world around it is not architecture but sculpture. As all the streets and highways of the world form one continuous road, so it is this continuum that is the subject for design.

Let us begin without finished solutions in mind, with what is most immediate and most simple—ourselves, as we are: a bag of more or less used flesh, wrinkled and knobbed, a hollow, folded and twisted tube on legs, functioning in spurts and spasms, decay and smells. We are dying on our feet, and feel this to be the basic tragedy of life. *This* is the man who can feel at one with the world around him, the natural world as it really is—constantly changing, moving, living and dying, a texture of loose-stranded skies, grainy crumbling rock, the yellow green grass and water. This world is in us, as much as we are in it, though, because of its very poignancy, we are eager to forget and deny its presence and significance with chromium plating, false eyelashes and white marble cubes. The paraphernalia of civilization gives relief but only of a temporary kind, since at some time in everyone's life the truth itself looks into our eyes, and, if we are unaccustomed to this, there is absolute terror. Thus the purpose of an architecture can be to make the relationships of our life on the earth apparent, familiar, ordinary and, therefore, friendly.

There is an old and simple dream, common to all the peoples of the earth, and as old as mankind itself, that describes a life lived as a part of nature, without effort or stress, called variously the Garden of Eden, Paradise, the Happy Hunting Ground and so on. In contrast to this imagined ideal was the hostility of the real world, the pressing immediacy of hunger and cold. All energies were concentrated in simply keeping alive. For us, this is no longer true. A constantly decreasing part of our population is required to feed, clothe and house all of us. In the thousands of years of history, the physical problems have been solved to the extent that at last we *may* freely inhabit the earth. The Garden has no end; no walls and no gate.

Seeing the world from our strictly human point of view, we tend to exaggerate our presence in it. People live in clots, look at one another's faces all day, and worry that the earth is crowded and overcrowded with cities, with the works of man. Similarly, bees must feel that the earth is covered with beehives. Yet there are very few places in the world from which, in an hour, in a car, you cannot find wilderness; and there are the vast land areas where people have never lived permanently at all. The earth exists very much as it always has—a broad continuous inert surface, folded and undulating, crumbled into rocks and stones and sand into which the twisting roots of living things push down so that they may stand up and feel the air upon them. These are the simple basic facts of the living and the dead which underlie the fantastic, the marvelous, the unbelievable variety of expression in shape and color and consistency surrounding us, so that each handspan of land is unique and yet an integral part of the whole. Here is a vocabulary of forms, in rocks, trees and plants that must be of lasting and untiring significance. In what is most simple and devoid of affectation, we can escape the necessity for successively changing architectural styles. We always become bored with the forms of our own devising. As a column is an abstract tree, and the interior of a Gothic cathedral, an abstraction of a grove of trees, the forms we invent are too limited to be more than temporarily satisfying, although they too must refer to some aspect of nature. You can't invent a form that does not exist—that has never existed. You can make one that *you* have never seen, and, if you do, it is because that possibility of nature, of the world, is in you. But once the form is drawn on paper, you will find that it has already existed elsewhere, as the nuclear physicists find that the particles they require for their equations can then be found in reality. In this sense, there is no originality, no imagination, only receptivity—which may be the same thing.

Let us then go directly to the source for the only forms which are of permanent meaning to us, for those forms in which lie all delicacy, all strength. The forms of buildings should be the forms of the world in which they exist, so that, instead of obtruding, they will be a continuous part of the landscape, indistinguishable and integral. We can then leave the "History of Architecture" to bury itself as a shallow geometrical abstraction of this real world in which we find ourselves, and where we must find our peace.

Can such forms be built? After all, airy manifestos have no place in architecture.

The work consists of real materials that must be put together by ordinary laborers for a reasonable cost. Can we do this? Nothing simpler. We have the tools in the very technology we feel has divorced us so completely from the natural world. *Using* means, instead of being used by them, we can cut into the earth and shape it, form rocks as nature does, set the living things to grow and add warmth and light, fresh water and waste disposal, invisibly. The technical problems already have their technical solutions.

There would be as many city forms as there are places in the world. The city *on* and *in* the sand dunes would be completely different in appearance and mood from the city on the glacier, or in the Sierra forest. Monument Valley in Arizona is, in its form, a magnificent natural city with fantastic wind-carved cliff buildings in a deep red stone surrounding large open plazas in which groups of eroded sculptured figures, two hundred feet tall, occur.

It is easy to think in terms of the spectacular. But, instead, let us visit an ordinary sort of city in very ordinary surroundings; a city as little inspiring in its functional requirements and natural setting as, let us say, Jersey City. Approaching it in a car on a stabilized-soil right-of-way, not different in color or appearance from the land on either side, you pass the grasslands and outlying truck farms. The subterranean factories line the river, looking like the groves of trees that surround them, mixed with warehouses whose roofs are covered with earth and grass to continue the contour of the earth around them. No smoke stacks, of course; all power is electrical, all transmission lines are buried.

The city proper lies before us. Low rolling hills covered with trees: these are the houses where the people live. The hills gradually rise in height as they approach the stone cliffs of the city center offices and stores. As we move into the center of the city the right-of-way widens and opens up into a series of large open spaces, scaled to the size of the cars that move directly to their destination. Houses are grouped in neighborhoods with their schools, churches, shops and light manufacturing facilities. Ideally, people should be able to work close to where they live, since commuting is not an uplifting experience. An individual house will appear as a group of trees and rocks. Inside the floor level varies to provide couches, chairs, tables and beds. The equipment is an integral part of the building.

As we near the center of town, the neighborhoods grow more concentrated, being composed of row houses and apartments. In the center, the hotels, theaters and restaurants form an enclave, contiguous to one comprising the shopping area, which in turn opens into the groups of office buildings which form the city center. Each of these central enclaves consists of long, low hills of horizontally stratified rock, the outer rims of which are for vehicular approach and parking, while the inner side, with living or work space, faces on a series of open pedestrian plazas and parks. Sloping ramps with moving sidewalks and trees and planting connect each stratum (or floor or story) with both the vehicular and pedestrian plazas on both sides, and it is these sloping stone strata with foliage trailing down their faces that form the characteristic structures of the city. As the city grows, additional strata are added so that the core is even more cohesive.

This is the form of the city, based on the way we are now trying to live in, and use, the cities we have inherited. Instead of building urban renewal projects that do not renew, and enormous highway construction that increases the congestion it is meant to alleviate, we can solve these problems, and others equally inherent in our lives, by means of a city built as a continuation of the landscape, so that the hills and valleys, forests, fields and waterways, instead of being destroyed are adapted to human uses, retaining for each place its own natural character, giving us a variety of city form that changes as the world does and affirming that our place on the earth is as a conserver rather than a destroyer.

THE EXPERIENCE OF
LIVING IN CITIES

Stanley Milgram

Moralists and naturalists have vilified the city for so long that it is no surprise to find it cynically abandoned to the vested interests, whose political and economic spoils dominate a scene relieved only by tiny patches of esthetic cosmetics. The consequent social and environmental desolation seem only to confirm the Theocritan view of the city's inherent evil.

Planning as such does not guarantee relief from this vicious circle. Some Scandinavian efforts, for example, however sweetened with fountains and trees, are known by the local word for "dullsville," and the young cannot wait to get out. Design undertaken without knowledge of psychological and perceptual processes, of the relationships of organized space and group dynamics, of the different needs of sex and age groups, of the developmental and behavioral necessity of play, nonhuman organisms, the seasonal cycle, and weather, cannot hope to improve conditions. It can only play old geography games, seeking a counterpoise between the rural and the urban, or try to provide for the future demands of traffic, commerce, and housing within a finite space.

How refreshing it is to see an essay like this one by Stanley Milgram, which punctures simplistic explanations for the failure of human compassion. For how long has man's inhumanity to man been the subject of polemic preaching, appeals to guilt, and exhortations to "be good"? Milgram finds that anonymity and disengagement are adaptive mechanisms which the human organism, in its unconscious wisdom, develops to survive the ecological wastelands we have allowed expediency and machines to produce. It is impossible to read his essay without suspecting that the same processes are at work in the world at large. Do we destroy the soil, air, and ocean? Are we not constantly implored to mend our ways, as though we were merely stupid and selfish? Has anyone considered that it may be impossible to do so within the structure of a consumer society? We know even less about the psychological relationship of man to nature than we do about relationships among men. Nor do we understand the overlap of the two kinds of relationship. The balance between strangers and familiars in our social lives may be related, as part of a total spectrum of mental health, to the number and kind of nonhuman organisms that we encounter. If men treat other men as

Stanley Milgram, "The Experience of Living in Cities," Science, 167 (March 13, 1970), 1461–1468.

nonhuman, does this not in some way reflect on the poverty of their conception of nonhuman life?

The disappearance of the rural countryside is widely bemoaned, and the suburbanite chronically pursues what remains of it. But it may be that city men, with their overheated dreams of rural bliss, need a different kind of urban life, instead of a total retreat from the city.

When I first came to New York it seemed like a nightmare. As soon as I got off the train at Grand Central I was caught up in pushing, shoving crowds on 42nd Street. Sometimes people bumped into me without apology; what really frightened me was to see two people literally engaged in combat for possession of a cab. Why were they so rushed? Even drunks on the street were bypassed without a glance. People didn't seem to care about each other at all.

This statement represents a common reaction to a great city, but it does not tell the whole story. Obviously cities have great appeal because of their variety, eventfulness, possibility of choice, and the stimulation of an intense atmosphere that many individuals find a desirable background to their lives. Where face-to-face contacts are important, the city offers unparalleled possibilities. It has been calculated by the Regional Plan Association (*1*) that in Nassau County, a suburb of New York City, an individual can meet 11,000 others within a 10-minute radius of his office by foot or car. In Newark, a moderate-sized city, he can meet more than 20,000 persons within this radius. But in midtown Manhattan he can meet fully 220,000. So there is an order-of-magnitude increment in the communication possibilities offered by a great city. That is one of the bases of its appeal and, indeed, of its functional necessity. The city provides options that no other social arrangement permits. But there is a negative side also, as we shall see.

Granted that cities are indispensable in complex society, we may still ask what contribution psychology can make to understanding the experience of living in them. What theories are relevant? How can we extend our knowledge of the psychological aspects of life in cities through empirical inquiry? If empirical inquiry is possible, along what lines should it proceed? In short, where do we start in constructing urban theory and in laying out lines of research?

Observation is the indispensable starting point. Any observer in the streets of midtown Manhattan will see (i) large numbers of people, (ii) a high population density, and (iii) heterogeneity of population. These three factors need to be at the root of any sociopsychological theory of city life, for they condition all aspects of our experience in the metropolis. Louis Wirth (*2*), if not the first to point to these factors, is nonetheless the sociologist who relied most heavily on them in his analysis of the city. Yet, for a psychologist, there is something unsatisfactory about Wirth's theoretical variables. Numbers, density, and heterogeneity are demographic facts but they are not yet psychological facts. They are external to the individual. Psychology needs an idea that links the individual's *experience* to the demographic circumstances of urban life.

One link is provided by the concept of overload. This term, drawn from systems analysis, refers to a system's inability to process inputs from the environment because there are too many inputs for the system to cope with, or because successive inputs come so fast that input A cannot be processed when input B is presented. When overload is present, adaptations occur. The system must set priorities and make choices. A may be processed first while B is kept in abeyance, or one input may be sacrificed altogether. City life, as we experience it, constitutes a continuous set of encounters with overload, and of resultant adaptations. Overload characteristically deforms daily life on several levels, impinging on role performance, the evolution of social norms, cognitive functioning, and the use of facilities.

The concept has been implicit in several theories of urban experience. In 1903 George Simmel (3) pointed out that, since urban dwellers come into contact with vast numbers of people each day, they conserve psychic energy by becoming acquainted with a far smaller proportion of people than their rural counterparts do, and by maintaining more superficial relationships even with these acquaintances. Wirth (2) points specifically to "the superficiality, the anonymity, and the transitory character of urban social relations."

One adaptive response to overload, therefore, is the allocation of less time to each input. A second adaptive mechanism is disregard of low-priority inputs. Principles of selectivity are formulated such that investment of time and energy are reserved for carefully defined inputs (the urbanite disregards the drunk sick on the street as he purposefully navigates through the crowd). Third, boundaries are redrawn in certain social transactions so that the overloaded system can shift the burden to the other party in the exchange; thus, harried New York bus drivers once made change for customers, but now this responsibility has been shifted to the client, who must have the exact fare ready. Fourth, reception is blocked off prior to entrance into a system; city dwellers increasingly use unlisted telephone numbers to prevent individuals from calling them, and a small but growing number resort to keeping the telephone off the hook to prevent incoming calls. More subtly, a city dweller blocks inputs by assuming an unfriendly countenance, which discourages others from initiating contact. Additionally, social screening devices are interposed between the individual and environmental inputs (in a town of 5000 anyone can drop in to chat with the mayor, but in the metropolis organizational screening devices deflect inputs to other destinations). Fifth, the intensity of inputs is diminished by filtering devices, so that only weak and relatively superficial forms of involvement with others are allowed. Sixth, specialized institutions are created to absorb inputs that would otherwise swamp the individual (welfare departments handle the financial needs of a million individuals in New York City, who would otherwise create an army of mendicants continuously importuning the pedestrian). The interposition of institutions between the individual and the social world, a characteristic of all modern society, and most notably of the large metropolis, has its negative side. It deprives the individual of a sense of direct contact and spontaneous integration in the life around him. It simultaneously protects and estranges the individual from his social environment.

Many of these adaptive mechanisms apply not only to individuals but to institutional systems as well, as Meier (*4*) has so brilliantly shown in connection with the library and the stock exchange.

In sum, the observed behavior of the urbanite in a wide range of situations appears to be determined largely by a variety of adaptations to overload. I now deal with several specific consequences of responses to overload, which make for differences in the tone of city and town.

Social Responsibility

The principal point of interest for a social psychology of the city is that moral and social involvement with individuals is necessarily restricted. This is a direct and necessary function of excess of input over capacity to process. Such restriction of involvement runs a broad spectrum from refusal to become involved in the needs of another person, even when the person desperately needs assistance, through refusal to do favors, to the simple withdrawal of courtesies (such as offering a lady a seat, or saying "sorry" when a pedestrian collision occurs). In any transaction more and more details need to be dropped as the total number of units to be processed increases and assaults an instrument of limited processing capacity.

The ultimate adaptation to an overloaded social environment is to totally disregard the needs, interests, and demands of those whom one does not define as relevant to the satisfaction of personal needs, and to develop highly efficient perceptual means of determining whether an individual falls into the category of friend or stranger. The disparity in the treatment of friends and strangers ought to be greater in cities than in towns; the time allotment and willingness to become involved with those who have no personal claim on one's time is likely to be less in cities than in towns.

Bystander Intervention in Crises

The most striking deficiencies in social responsibility in cities occur in crisis situations, such as the Genovese murder in Queens. In 1964, Catherine Genovese, coming home from a night job in the early hours of an April morning, was stabbed repeatedly, over an extended period of time. Thirty-eight residents of a respectable New York City neighborhood admit to having witnessed at least a part of the attack, but none went to her aid or called the police until after she was dead. Milgram and Hollander, writing in *The Nation* (*5*), analyzed the event in these terms:

> Urban friendships and associations are not primarily formed on the basis of physical proximity. A person with numerous close friends in different parts of the city may not know the occupant of an adjacent apartment. This does

not mean that a city dweller has fewer friends than does a villager, or knows fewer persons who will come to his aid; however, it does mean that his allies are not constantly at hand. Miss Genovese required immediate aid from those physically present. There is no evidence that the city had deprived Miss Genovese of human associations, but the friends who might have rushed to her side were miles from the scene of her tragedy.

Further, it is known that her cries for help were not directed to a specific person; they were general. But only individuals can act, and as the cries were not specifically directed, no particular person felt a special responsibility. The crime and the failure of community response seem absurd to us. At the time, it may well have seemed equally absurd to the Kew Gardens residents that not one of the neighbors would have called the police. A collective paralysis may have developed from the belief of each of the witnesses that someone else must surely have taken that obvious step.

Latané and Darley (6) have reported laboratory approaches to the study of bystander intervention and have established experimentally the following principle: the larger the number of bystanders, the less the likelihood that any one of them will intervene in an emergency. Gaertner and Bickman (7) of The City University of New York have extended the bystander studies to an examination of help across ethnic lines. Blacks and whites, with clearly identifiable accents, called strangers (through what the caller represented as an error in telephone dialing), gave them a plausible story of being stranded on an outlying highway without more dimes, and asked the stranger to call a garage. The experimenters found that the white callers had a significantly better chance of obtaining assistance than the black callers. This suggests that ethnic allegiance may well be another means of coping with overload: the city dweller can reduce excessive demands and screen out urban heterogeneity by responding along ethnic lines; overload is made more manageable by limiting the "span of sympathy."

In any quantitative characterization of the social texture of city life, a necessary first step is the application of such experimental methods as these to field situations in large cities and small towns. Theorists argue that the indifference shown in the Genovese case would not be found in a small town, but in the absence of solid experimental evidence the question remains an open one.

More than just callousness prevents bystanders from participating in altercations between people. A rule of urban life is respect for other people's emotional and social privacy, perhaps because physical privacy is so hard to achieve. And in situations for which the standards are heterogeneous, it is much harder to know whether taking an active role is unwarranted meddling or an appropriate response to a critical situation. If a husband and wife are quarreling in public, at what point should a bystander step in? On the one hand, the heterogeneity of the city produces substantially greater tolerance about behavior, dress, and codes of ethics than is generally found in the small town, but this diversity also encourages people to withhold aid for fear of antagonizing the participants or crossing an inappropriate and difficult-to-define line.

Moreover, the frequency of demands present in the city gives rise to norms of noninvolvement. There are practical limitations to the Samaritan impulse in a major city. If a citizen attended to every needy person, if he were sensitive to and acted on every altruistic impulse that was evoked in the city, he could scarcely keep his own affairs in order.

Willingness to Trust and Assist Strangers

We now move away from crisis situations to less urgent examples of social responsibility. For it is not only in situations of dramatic need but in the ordinary, everyday willingness to lend a hand that the city dweller is said to be deficient relative to his small-town cousin. The comparative method must be used in any empirical examination of this question. A commonplace social situation is staged in an urban setting and in a small town—a situation to which a subject can respond by either extending help or withholding it. The responses in town and city are compared.

One factor in the purported unwillingness of urbanites to be helpful to strangers may well be their heightened sense of physical (and emotional) vulnerability—a feeling that is supported by urban crime statistics. A key test for distinguishing between city and town behavior, therefore, is determining how city dwellers compare with town dwellers in offering aid that increases their personal vulnerability and requires some trust of strangers. Altman, Levine, Nadien, and Villena (8) of The City University of New York devised a study to compare the behaviors of city and town dwellers in this respect. The criterion used in this study was the willingness of householders to allow strangers to enter their home to use the telephone. The student investigators individually rang doorbells, explained that they had misplaced the address of a friend nearby, and asked to use the phone. The investigators (two males and two females) made 100 requests for entry into homes in the city and 60 requests in the small towns. The results for middle-income housing developments in Manhattan were compared with data for several small towns (Stony Point, Spring Valley, Ramapo, Nyack, New City, and West Clarkstown) in Rockland County, outside of New York City. As Table 1 shows, in all cases there was a sharp increase in the proportion of entries achieved by an experimenter when he moved from the city to a small town. In the most extreme case the experimenter was five times as likely to gain admission to homes in a small town as to homes in Manhattan. Although the female experimenters had notably greater success both in cities and in towns than the male experimenters had, each of the four students did at least twice as well in towns as in cities. This suggests that the city-town distinction overrides even the predictably greater fear of male strangers than of female ones.

The lower level of helpfulness by city dwellers seems due in part to recognition of the dangers of living in Manhattan, rather than to mere indifference or coldness. It is significant that 75 percent of all the city respondents received and answered messages by shouting through closed doors and by peering out through

Table 1
Percentage of entries achieved by investigators for city
and town dwellings (see text)

Experimenter	Entries achieved (%)	
	City *	*Small town†*
Male		
No. 1	16	40
No. 2	12	60
Female		
No. 3	40	87
No. 4	40	100

* Number of requests for entry, 100.
† Number of requests for entry, 60.

peepholes; in the towns, by contrast, about 75 percent of the respondents opened
the door.

Supporting the experimenters' quantitative results was their general observation that the town dwellers were noticeably more friendly and less suspicious
than the city dwellers. In seeking to explain the reasons for the greater sense of
psychological vulnerability city dwellers feel, above and beyond the differences
in crime statistics, Villena (8) points out that, if a crime is committed in a village,
a resident of a neighboring village may not perceive the crime as personally relevant, though the geographic distance may be small, whereas a criminal act committed anywhere in the city, though miles from the citydweller's home, is still
verbally located within the city; thus, Villena says, "the inhabitant of the city
possesses a larger vulnerable space."

Civilities

Even at the most superficial level of involvement—the exercise of everyday civilities—urbanites are reputedly deficient. People bump into each other and often do
not apologize. They knock over another person's packages and, as often as not,
proceed on their way with a grumpy exclamation instead of an offer of assistance.
Such behavior, which many visitors to great cities find distasteful, is less common,
we are told, in smaller communities, where traditional courtesies are more likely
to be observed.

In some instances it is not simply that, in the city, traditional courtesies are
violated; rather, the cities develop new norms of noninvolvement. These are so
well defined and so deeply a part of city life that *they* constitute the norms
people are reluctant to violate. Men are actually embarrassed to give up a seat on
the subway to an old woman; they mumble "I was getting off anyway," instead
of making the gesture in a straightforward and gracious way. These norms develop
because everyone realizes that, in situations of high population density, people

cannot implicate themselves in each others' affairs, for to do so would create conditions of continual distraction which would frustrate purposeful action.

In discussing the effects of overload I do not imply that at every instant the city dweller is bombarded with an unmanageable number of inputs, and that his responses are determined by the excess of input at any given instant. Rather, adaptation occurs in the form of gradual evolution of norms of behavior. Norms are evolved in response to frequent discrete experiences of overload; they persist and become generalized modes of responding.

Overload on Cognitive Capacities: Anonymity

That we respond differently toward those whom we know and those who are strangers to us is a truism. An eager patron aggressively cuts in front of someone in a long movie line to save time only to confront a friend; he then behaves sheepishly. A man is involved in an automobile accident caused by another driver, emerges from his car shouting in rage, then moderates his behavior on discovering a friend driving the other car. The city dweller, when walking through the midtown streets, is in a state of continual anonymity vis-à-vis the other pedestrians.

Anonymity is part of a continuous spectrum ranging from total anonymity to full acquaintance, and it may well be that measurement of the precise degrees of anonymity in cities and towns would help to explain important distinctions between the quality of life in each. Conditions of full acquaintance, for example, offer security and familiarity, but they may also be stifling, because the individual is caught in a web of established relationships. Conditions of complete anonymity, by contrast, provide freedom from routinized social ties, but they may also create feelings of alienation and detachment.

Empirically one could investigate the proportion of activities in which the city dweller or the town dweller is known by others at given times in his daily life, and the proportion of activities in the course of which he interacts with individuals who know him. At his job, for instance, the city dweller may be known to as many people as his rural counterpart. However, when he is not fulfilling his occupational role—say, when merely traveling about the city—the urbanite is doubtless more anonymous than his rural counterpart.

Limited empirical work on anonymity has begun. Zimbardo (9) has tested whether the social anonymity and impersonality of the big city encourage greater vandalism than do small towns. Zimbardo arranged for one automobile to be left for 64 hours near the Bronx campus of New York University and for a counterpart to be left for the same number of hours near Stanford University in Palo Alto. The license plates on the two cars were removed and the hoods were opened, to provide "releaser cues" for potential vandals. The New York car was stripped of all movable parts within the first 24 hours, and by the end of 3 days was only a hunk of metal rubble. Unexpectedly, however, most of the destruction occurred during daylight hours, usually under the scrutiny of observers, and the leaders in the vandalism were well-dressed white adults. The Palo Alto car was left untouched.

Zimbardo attributes the difference in the treatment accorded the two cars to the "acquired feelings of social anonymity provided by life in a city like New York," and he supports his conclusions with several other anecdotes illustrating casual, wanton vandalism in the city. In any comparative study of the effects of anonymity in city and town, however, there must be satisfactory control for other confounding factors: the large number of drug addicts in a city like New York; the higher proportion of slum-dwellers in the city; and so on.

Another direction for empirical study is investigation of the beneficial effects of anonymity. The impersonality of city life breeds its own tolerance for the private lives of the inhabitants. Individuality and even eccentricity, we may assume, can flourish more readily in the metropolis than in the small town. Stigmatized persons may find it easier to lead comfortable lives in the city, free of the constant scrutiny of neighbors. To what degree can this assumed difference between city and town be shown empirically? Judith Waters (*10*), at The City University of New York, hypothesized that avowed homosexuals would be more likely to be accepted as tenants in a large city than in small towns, and she dispatched letters from homosexuals and from normal individuals to real estate agents in cities and towns across the country. The results of her study were inconclusive. But the general idea of examining the protective benefits of city life to the stigmatized ought to be pursued.

Role Behavior in Cities and Towns

Another product of urban overload is the adjustment in roles made by urbanites in daily interactions. As Wirth has said (*2*): "Urbanites meet one another in highly segmental roles. . . . They are less dependent upon particular persons, and their dependence upon others is confined to a highly fractionalized aspect of the other's round of activity." This tendency is particularly noticeable in transactions between customers and individuals offering professional or sales services. The owner of a country store has time to become well acquainted with his dozen-or-so daily customers, but the girl at the checkout counter of a busy A & P, serving hundreds of customers a day, barely has time to toss the green stamps into one customer's shopping bag before the next customer confronts her with his pile of groceries.

Meier, in his stimulating analysis of the city (*4*), discusses several adaptations a system may make when confronted by inputs that exceed its capacity to process them. Meier argues that, according to the principle of competition for scarce resources, the scope and time of the transaction shrink as customer volume and daily turnover rise. This, in fact, is what is meant by the "brusque" quality of city life. New standards have developed in cities concerning what levels of services are appropriate in business transactions (see Figure 1).

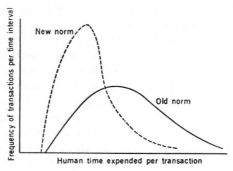

Figure 1
*Changes in the demand for time for a given task
when the overall transaction frequency increases in
a social system. [Reprinted with permission from
R. L. Meier,* A Communications Theory of Urban
Growth, *1962. Copyrighted by M.I.T. Press, 1962.]*

McKenna and Morgenthau (*11*), in a seminar at The City University of New York, devised a study (i) to compare the willingness of city dwellers and small-town dwellers to do favors for strangers that entailed expenditure of a small amount of time and slight inconvenience but no personal vulnerability, and (ii) to determine whether the more compartmentalized, transitory relationships of the city would make urban salesgirls less likely than small-town salesgirls to carry out, for strangers, tasks not related to their customary roles.

To test for differences between city dwellers and small-town dwellers, a simple experiment was devised in which persons from both settings were asked (by telephone) to perform increasingly onerous favors for anonymous strangers.

Within the cities (Chicago, New York, and Philadelphia), half the calls were to housewives and the other half to salesgirls in women's apparel shops; the division was the same for the 37 small towns of the study, which were in the same states as the cities. Each experimenter represented herself as a long-distance caller who had, through error, been connected with the respondent by the operator. The experimenter began by asking for simple information about the weather for purposes of travel. Next the experimenter excused herself on some pretext (asking the respondent to "please hold on"), put the phone down for almost a full minute, and then picked it up again and asked the respondent to provide the phone number of a hotel or motel in her vicinity at which the experimenter might stay during a forthcoming visit. Scores were assigned the subjects on the basis of how helpful they had been. McKenna summarizes her results in this manner:

People in the city, whether they are engaged in a specific job or not, are less helpful and informative than people in small towns; . . . People at home, regardless of where they live, are less helpful and informative than people working in shops.

However, the absolute level of cooperativeness for urban subjects was found to be quite high, and does not accord with the stereotype of the urbanite as aloof, self-centered, and unwilling to help strangers. The quantitative differences obtained by McKenna and Morgenthau are less great than one might have expected. This again points up the need for extensive empirical research in rural-urban differences, research that goes far beyond that provided in the few illustrative pilot studies presented here. At this point we have very limited objective evidence on differences in the quality of social encounters in city and small town.

But the research needs to be guided by unifying theoretical concepts. As I have tried to demonstrate, the concept of overload helps to explain a wide variety of contrasts between city behavior and town behavior: (i) the differences in role enactment (the tendency of urban dwellers to deal with one another in highly segmented, functional terms, and of urban sales personnel to devote limited time and attention to their customers); (ii) the evolution of urban norms quite different from traditional town values (such as the acceptance of noninvolvement, impersonality, and aloofness in urban life); (iii) the adaptation of the urban dweller's cognitive processes (his inability to identify most of the people he sees daily, his screening of sensory stimuli, his development of blasé attitudes toward deviant or bizarre behavior, and his selectivity in responding to human demands); and (iv) the competition for scarce facilities in the city (the subway rush; the fight for taxis; traffic jams; standing in line to await services). I suggest that contrasts between city and rural behavior probably reflect the responses of similar people to very different situations, rather than intrinsic differences in the personalities of rural and city dwellers. The city is a situation to which individuals respond adaptively.

Further Aspects of Urban Experience

Some features of urban experience do not fit neatly into the system of analysis presented thus far. They are no less important for that reason. The issues raised next are difficult to treat in quantitative fashion. Yet I prefer discussing them in a loose way to excluding them because appropriate language and data have not yet been developed. My aim is to suggest how phenomena such as "urban atmosphere" can be pinned down through techniques of measurement.

The "Atmosphere" of Great Cities

The contrast in the behavior of city and town dwellers has been a natural starting point for urban social scientists. But even among great cities there are marked differences in "atmosphere." The tone, pacing, and texture of social encounters are different in London and New York, and many persons willingly make financial sacrifices for the privilege of living within a specific urban atmosphere which they find pleasing or stimulating. A second perspective in the study of cities, therefore, is to define exactly what is meant by the atmosphere of a city and to pinpoint the factors that give rise to it. It may seem that urban atmosphere is too evanescent a quality to be reduced to a set of measurable variables, but I do not believe the matter can be judged before substantial effort has been made in this direction. It is obvious that any such approach must be comparative. It makes no sense at all to say that New York is "vibrant" and "frenetic" unless one has some specific city in mind as a basis of comparison.

In an undergraduate tutorial that I conducted at Harvard University some years ago, New York, London, and Paris were selected as reference points for attempts to measure urban atmosphere. We began with a simple question: Does any consensus exist about the qualities that typify given cities? To answer this question one could undertake a content analysis of travel-book, literary, and journalistic accounts of cities. A second approach, which we adopted, is to ask people to characterize (with descriptive terms and accounts of typical experiences) cities they have lived in or visited. In advertisements placed in the *New York Times* and the *Harvard Crimson* we asked people to give us accounts of specific incidents in London, Paris, or New York that best illuminated the character of that particular city. Questionnaires were then developed, and administered to persons who were familiar with at least two of the three cities.

Some distinctive patterns emerged (*12*). The distinguishing themes concerning New York, for example, dealt with its diversity, its great size, its pace and level of activity, its cultural and entertainment opportunities, and the heterogeneity and segmentation ("ghettoization") of its population. New York elicited more descriptions in terms of physical qualities, pace, and emotional impact than Paris or London did, a fact which suggests that these are particularly important aspects of New York's ambiance.

A contrasting profile emerges for London; in this case respondents placed far greater emphasis on their interactions with the inhabitants than on physical surroundings. There was near unanimity on certain themes: those dealing with the tolerance and courtesy of London's inhabitants. One respondent said:

When I was 12, my grandfather took me to the British Museum . . . one day by tube and recited the *Aeneid* in Latin for my benefit. . . . He is rather deaf, speaks very loudly and it embarrassed the hell out of me, until I realized that nobody was paying any attention. Londoners are extremely worldly and tolerant.

In contrast, respondents who described New Yorkers as aloof, cold, and rude referred to such incidents as the following:

I saw a boy of 19 passing out anti-war leaflets to passersby. When he stopped at a corner, a man dressed in a business suit walked by him at a brisk pace, hit the boy's arm, and scattered the leaflets all over the street. The man kept walking at the same pace down the block.

We need to obtain many more such descriptions of incidents, using careful methods of sampling. By the application of factor-analytic techniques, relevant dimensions for each city can be discerned.

The responses for Paris were about equally divided between responses concerning its inhabitants and those regarding its physical and sensory attributes. Cafés and parks were often mentioned as contributing to the sense that Paris is a city of amenities, but many respondents complained that Parisians were inhospitable, nasty, and cold.

We cannot be certain, of course, to what degree these statements reflect actual characteristics of the cities in question and to what degree they simply tap the respondents' knowledge of widely held preconceptions. Indeed, one may point to three factors, apart from the actual atmospheres of the cities, that determine the subjects' responses.

1) A person's impression of a given city depends on his implicit standard of comparison. A New Yorker who visits Paris may well describe that city as "leisurely," whereas a compatriot from Richmond, Virginia, may consider Paris too "hectic." Obtaining reciprocal judgment, in which New Yorkers judge Londoners, and Londoners judge New Yorkers, seems a useful way to take into account not only the city being judged but also the home city that serves as the visitor's base line.

2) Perceptions of a city are also affected by whether the observer is a tourist, a newcomer, or a longer-term resident. First, a tourist will be exposed to features of the city different from those familiar to a long-time resident. Second, a prerequisite for adapting to continuing life in a given city seems to be the filtering out of many observations about the city that the newcomer or tourist finds particularly arresting; this selective process seems to be part of the long-term resident's mechanism for coping with overload. In the interest of psychic economy, the resident simply learns to tune out many aspects of daily life. One method for studying the specific impact of adaptation on perception of the city is to ask several pairs of newcomers and old-timers (one newcomer and one old-timer to a pair) to walk down certain city blocks and then report separately what each has observed.

Additionally, many persons have noted that when travelers return to New York from an extended sojourn abroad they often feel themselves confronted with "brutal ugliness" (13) and a distinctive, frenetic atmosphere whose contributing details are, for a few hours or days, remarkably sharp and clear. This period of fresh perception should receive special attention in the study of city atmosphere. For, in a few days, details which are initially arresting become less easy to specify. They are assimilated into an increasingly familiar background atmosphere which, though important in setting the tone of things, is difficult to analyze. There is no better point at which to begin the study of city atmosphere than at the moment when a traveler returns from abroad.

3) The popular myths and expectations each visitor brings to the city will also affect the way in which he perceives it (see *14*). Sometimes a person's preconceptions about a city are relatively accurate distillations of its character, but preconceptions may also reinforce myths by filtering the visitor's perceptions to conform with his expectations. Preconceptions affect not only a person's perceptions of a city but what he reports about it.

The influence of a person's urban base line on his perceptions of a given city, the differences between the observations of the long-time inhabitant and those of the newcomer, and the filtering effect of personal expectations and stereotypes raise serious questions about the validity of travelers' reports. Moreover, no social psychologist wants to rely exclusively on verbal accounts if he is attempting to obtain an accurate and objective description of the cities' social texture, pace, and general atmosphere. What he needs to do is to devise means of embedding objective experimental measures in the daily flux of city life, measures that can accurately index the qualities of a given urban atmosphere.

Experimental Comparisons of Behavior

Roy Feldman (*15*) incorporated these principles in a comparative study of behavior toward compatriots and foreigners in Paris, Athens, and Boston. Feldman wanted to see (i) whether absolute levels and patterns of helpfulness varied significantly from city to city, and (ii) whether inhabitants in each city tended to treat compatriots differently from foreigners. He examined five concrete behavioral episodes, each carried out by a team of native experimenters and a team of American experimenters in the three cities. The episodes involved (i) asking natives of the city for street directions; (ii) asking natives to mail a letter for the experimenter; (iii) asking natives if they had just dropped a dollar bill (or the Greek or French equivalent) when the money actually belonged to the experimenter himself; (iv) deliberately overpaying for goods in a store to see if the cashier would correct the mistake and return the excess money; and (v) determining whether taxicab drivers overcharged strangers and whether they took the most direct route available.

Feldman's results suggest some interesting contrasts in the profiles of the three cities. In Paris, for instance, certain stereotypes were borne out. Parisian cab drivers overcharged foreigners significantly more often than they overcharged compatriots. But other aspects of the Parisians' behavior were not in accord with American preconceptions: in mailing a letter for a stranger, Parisians treated foreigners significantly better than Athenians or Bostonians did, and, when asked to mail letters that were already stamped, Parisians actually treated foreigners better than they treated compatriots. Similarly, Parisians were significantly more honest than Athenians or Bostonians in resisting the temptation to claim money that was not theirs, and Parisians were the only citizens who were more honest with foreigners than with compatriots in this experiment.

Feldman's studies not only begin to quantify some of the variables that give a city its distinctive texture but they also provide a methodological model for other comparative research. His most important contribution is his successful application of objective, experimental measures to everyday situations, a mode of study which provides conclusions about urban life that are more pertinent than those achieved through laboratory experiments.

Tempo and Pace

Another important component of a city's atmosphere is its tempo or pace, an attribute frequently remarked on but less often studied. Does a city have a frenetic, hectic quality, or is it easygoing and leisurely? In any empirical treatment of this question, it is best to start in a very simple way. Walking speeds of pedestrians in different cities and in cities and towns should be measured and compared. William Berkowitz (*16*) of Lafayette College has undertaken an extensive series of studies of walking speeds in Philadelphia, New York, and Boston, as well as in small and moderate-sized towns. Berkowitz writes that "there does appear to be a significant linear relation between walking speed and size of municipality, but the absolute size of the difference varies by less than ten percent."

Perhaps the feeling of rapid tempo is due not so much to absolute pedestrian speeds as to the constant need to dodge others in a large city to avoid collisions with other pedestrians. (One basis for computing the adjustments needed to avoid collisions is to hypothesize a set of mechanical manikins sent walking along a city street and to calculate the number of collisions when no adjustments are made. Clearly, the higher the density of manikins the greater the number of collisions per unit of time, or, conversely, the greater the frequency of adjustments needed in higher population densities to avoid collisions.)

Patterns of automobile traffic contribute to a city's tempo. Driving an automobile provides a direct means of translating feelings about tempo into measurable acceleration, and a city's pace should be particularly evident in vehicular velocities, patterns of acceleration, and latency of response to traffic signals. The inexorable tempo of New York is expressed, further, in the manner in which pedestrians stand at busy intersections, impatiently awaiting a change in traffic light, making tentative excursions into the intersection, and frequently surging into the street even before the green light appears.

Visual Components

Hall has remarked (*17*) that the physical layout of the city also affects its atmosphere. A gridiron pattern of streets gives the visitor a feeling of rationality, order-liness, and predictability but is sometimes monotonous. Winding lanes or streets branching off at strange angles, with many forks (as in Paris or Greenwich Village), create feelings of surprise and esthetic pleasure, while forcing greater decision-making in plotting one's course. Some would argue that the visual component is all-important—that the "look" of Paris or New York can almost be equated with its atmosphere. To investigate this hypothesis, we might conduct studies in which only blind, or at least blindfolded, respondents were used. We would no doubt discover that each city has a distinctive texture even when the visual component is eliminated.

Sources of Ambiance

Thus far we have tried to pinpoint and measure some of the factors that contribute to the distinctive atmosphere of a great city. But we may also ask, Why do differences in urban atmosphere exist? How did they come about, and are they in any way related to the factors of density, large numbers, and hetero-geneity discussed above?

First, there is the obvious factor that, even among great cities, populations and densities differ. The metropolitan areas of New York, London, and Paris, for example, contain 15 million, 12 million, and 8 million persons, respectively. London has average densities of 43 persons per acre, while Paris is more con-gested, with average densities of 114 persons per acre (*18*). Whatever character-istics are specifically attributable to density are more likely to be pronounced in Paris than in London.

A second factor affecting the atmosphere of cities is the source from which the populations are drawn (*19*). It is a characteristic of great cities that they do not reproduce their own populations, but that their numbers are constantly maintained and augmented by the influx of residents from other parts of the country. This can have a determining effect on the city's atmosphere. For example, Oslo is a city in which almost all of the residents are only one or two generations removed from a purely rural existence, and this contributes to its almost agri-cultural norms.

A third source of atmosphere is the general national culture. Paris combines adaptations to the demography of cities *and* certain values specific to French culture. New York is an admixture of American values and values that arise as a result of extraordinarily high density and large population.

Finally, one could speculate that the atmosphere of a great city is traceable to the specific historical conditions under which adaptations to urban overload occurred. For example, a city which acquired its mass and density during a period of commercial expansion will respond to new demographic conditions by adapta-tions designed to serve purely commercial needs. Thus, Chicago, which grew and became a great city under a purely commerical stimulus, adapted in a manner that emphasizes business needs. European capitals, on the other hand, incorporate many of the adaptations which were appropriate to the period of their increasing numbers and density. Because aristocratic values were prevalent at the time of the growth of these cities, the mechanisms developed for coping with overload were based on considerations other than pure efficiency. Thus, the manners, norms, and facilities of Paris and Vienna continue to reflect esthetic values and the idealization of leisure.

Cognitive Maps of Cities

When we speak of "behavioral comparisons" among cities, we must specify which parts of the city are most relevant for sampling purposes. In a sampling of "New Yorkers," should we include residents of Bay Ridge or Flatbush as well as inhabitants of Manhattan? And, if so, how should we weight our sample distribution? One approach to defining relevant boundaries in sampling is to determine which areas form the psychological or cognitive core of the city. We weight our samples most heavily in the areas considered by most people to represent the "essence" of the city.

The psychologist is less interested in the geographic layout of a city or in its political boundaries than in the cognitive representation of the city. Hans Blumenfeld (20) points out that the perceptual structure of a modern city can be expressed by the "silhouette" of the group of skyscrapers at its center and that of smaller groups of office buildings at its "subcenters" but that urban areas can no longer, because of their vast extent, be experienced as fully articulated sets of streets, squares, and space.

In *The Image of the City* (21), Kevin Lynch created a cognitive map of Boston by interviewing Bostonians. Perhaps his most significant finding was that, while certain landmarks, such as Paul Revere's house and the Boston Common, as well as the paths linking them, are known to almost all Bostonians, vast areas of the city are simply unknown to its inhabitants.

Using Lynch's technique, Donald Hooper (22) created a psychological map of New York from the answers to the study questionnaire on Paris, London, and New York. Hooper's results were similar to those of Lynch: New York appears to have a dense core of well-known landmarks in midtown Manhattan, surrounded by the vast unknown reaches of Queens, Brooklyn, and the Bronx. Times Square, Rockefeller Center, and the Fifth Avenue department stores alone comprise half the places specifically cited by respondents as the haunts in which they spent most of their time. However, outside the midtown area, only scattered landmarks were recognized. Another interesting pattern is evident: even the best-known symbols of New York are relatively self-contained, and the pathways joining them appear to be insignificant on the map.

The psychological map can be used for more than just sampling techniques. Lynch (21) argues, for instance, that a good city is highly "imageable," having many known symbols joined by widely known pathways, whereas dull cities are gray and nondescript. We might test the relative "imagibility" of several cities by determining the proportion of residents who recognize sampled geographic points and their accompanying pathways.

If we wanted to be even more precise we could construct a cognitive map that would not only show the symbols of the city but would measure the precise degree of cognitive significance of any given point in the city relative to any other. By applying a pattern of points to a map of New York City, for example, and taking photographs from each point, we could determine what proportion of a sample of the city's inhabitants could identify the locale specified by each point (see Figure 2). We might even take the subjects blindfolded to a point represented

Figure 2
To create a psychological map of Manhattan, geographic points are sampled, and, from photographs, the subjects attempt to identify the location of each point. To each point a numerical index is assigned indicating the proportion of persons able to identify its location.

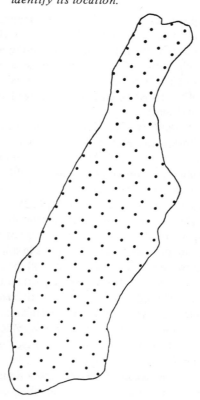

on the map, then remove the blindfold and ask them to identify their location from the view around them.

One might also use psychological maps to gain insight into the differing perceptions of a given city that are held by members of its cultural subgroups, and into the manner in which their perceptions may change. In the earlier stages of life, whites and Negroes alike probably have only a limited view of the city, centering on the immediate neighborhood in which they are raised. In adolesence, however, the field of knowledge of the white teen-ager probably undergoes rapid enlargement; he learns of opportunities in midtown and outlying sections and comes to see himself as functioning in a larger urban field. But the process of ghettoization, to which the black teen-ager is subjected, may well hamper the expansion of his sense of the city. These are speculative notions, but they are readily subject to precise test.

Conclusion

I have tried to indicate some organizing theory that starts with the basic facts of city life: large numbers, density, and heterogeneity. These are external to the individual. He experiences these factors as overloads at the level of roles, norms, cognitive functions, and facilities. These overloads lead to adaptive mechanisms which create the distinctive tone and behaviors of city life. These notions, of course, need to be examined by objective comparative studies of cities and towns.

A second perspective concerns the differing atmospheres of great cities, such as Paris, London, and New York. Each has a distinctive flavor, offering a differentiable quality of experience. More precise knowledge of urban atmosphere seems attainable through application of the tools of experimental inquiry.

REFERENCES

1. *New York Times*, June 15, 1969.
2. Wirth, L. *Amer. J. Soc.*, 44:1 (1938). Wirth's ideas have come under heavy criticism by contemporary city planners, who point out that the city is broken down into neighborhoods, which fulfill many of the functions of small towns. See, for example, Gans, H. J. *People and Plans: Essays on Urban Problems and Solutions*. New York: Basic Books, 1968; Jacobs, J. *The Death and Life of Great American Cities*. New York: Random House, 1961; Suttles, G. D. *The Social Order of the Slum*. Chicago: University of Chicago Press, 1968.
3. Simmel, G. *The Sociology of Georg Simmel*, ed. K. H. Wolff. New York: Macmillan, 1950 [English translation of Simmel, G. *Die Grossstadte und das Geistesleben Die Grossstadt*. Dresden: Jansch, 1903].
4. Meier, R. L. *A Communications Theory of Urban Growth*. Cambridge, Mass.: M.I.T. Press, 1962.
5. Milgram, S., and P. Hollander. *The Nation*, 25:602 (1964).
6. Latané, B., and J. Darley. *Amer. Sci.*, 57:244 (1969).

7. Gaertner, S., and L. Bickman (Graduate Center, The City University of New York). Unpublished research.

8. Altman, D., M. Levine, M. Nadien, and J. Villena (Graduate Center, The City University of New York). Unpublished research.

9. Zimbardo, P. G. Paper presented at the Nebraska Symposium on Motivation, 1969.

10. Waters, J. (Graduate Center, The City University of New York). Unpublished research.

11. McKenna, W., and S. Morgenthau (Graduate Center, The City University of New York). Unpublished research.

12. Abuza, N. (Harvard University). "The Paris-London-New York Questionnaires," unpublished.

13. Abelson, P. *Science*, 165:853 (1969).

14. Strauss, A. L., ed. *The American City: A Sourcebook of Urban Imagery*. Chicago: Aldine, 1968.

15. Feldman, R. E. *J. Personality Soc. Psychol.*, 10:202 (1968).

16. Berkowitz, W. Personal communication.

17. Hall, E. T. *The Hidden Dimension*. New York: Doubleday, 1966.

18. Hall, P. *The World Cities*. New York: McGraw-Hill, 1966.

19. Park, R. E., E. W. Burgess, R. D. McKenzie. *The City*. Chicago: University of Chicago Press, 1967, 1–45.

20. Blumenfeld, H., in *The Quality of Urban Life*. Beverly Hills: Sage, 1969.

21. Lynch, K. *The Image of the City*. Cambridge, Mass.: M.I.T. and Harvard University Press, 1960.

22. Hooper, D. (Harvard University), unpublished.

23. Barbara Bengen worked closely with me in preparing the present version of this article. I thank Dr. Gary Winkel, editor of *Environment and Behavior*, for useful suggestions and advice.

PART THREE
POSITIONS

THE UNITY OF ECOLOGY

F. Fraser Darling

It is now possible to travel for hundreds of miles in many parts of the United States without seeing domestic farm animals. Landscapes once animated by cows, horses, pigs, sheep, goats, chickens, and other fowl are fast disappearing. In part this is a result of the specialization, geographic localization, and individual farm economy of modern agriculture. It also marks the disappearance of such animals as the plow horse.

The absence of animals on the bulk of the land signifies more than a change in farm economics, however. As browsers, grazers, scavengers, and manure-makers, animals have been the principal agents in the creation of the rural environment for perhaps 5000 years. They have been the intermediaries, the tools, connecting men to the soil and the vegetation. As such they have carried in their genes certain behaviors and physical needs which left their mark on that environment and on the rhythm of farming and herding. In some ways these animal traits acted as a kind of restraint on the hand of man; in others, they simply limited the capacity of the human enterprise.

The pastoral countryside molded by animals was vastly different from that which is emerging now. It is common to hear the transition to "industrial agriculture" extolled in the news media as an unqualified achievement. But we know almost nothing about the long-term effects of these new procedures on rural people themselves, both on the farm and in town, or on the natural processes which are the source of agricultural wealth.

The history of husbandry is littered with geographic wreckage and its human consequences. Will we ignore its lessons on the assumption that they do not apply to us?

It is rather extraordinary to be asked by educated people, what is ecology?—the more so, as economics is a word used by everyone and the substitution of the letter 'e' for the diphthong 'œ' disturbs nobody. Both ecology and economics, so properly derived from the Greek *oikos*—the home, are concerned with the ordering

F. Fraser Darling, "The Unity of Ecology," The Advancement of Science *XX (November, 1963), 297–306. Originally delivered as a Presidential Address to Section D (Zoology) on August 29, 1963, at the Aberdeen Meeting of the British Association.*

of the habitat and income and expenditure. Both sciences deal with communities and are, at simplest, observational studies of communities. Economics has tended to deal with income and expenditure symbolized in money and the most dangerous economists have been those who have mistaken the symbol for the reality. There is now a refreshing trend to consider wealth as availability of resources, often natural and renewable and organic resources. The changes in the status of availability are subtle, depending on history, growth and movements of populations, and on technology. The resources themselves change in economic status with changes in human needs and desires, emergencies and fashions.

Ecology deals with income and expenditure in terms of energy cycles in communities of plants and animals, deriving from sunlight, water, carbon dioxide and the phenomenon of photosynthesis by which organic compounds are built. This raw definition is made more interesting by what I would emphasize as the *observational* study of communities of animals and plants. Here comes the possibility of that more general definition of ecology as the science of organisms in relation to their total environment, and the interrelations of organisms interspecifically and between themselves. The total environment includes all manner of physical factors such as climate, physiography and soil, the stillness or movement of water and the salts borne in solution. The interrelations of organisms and environment are in some measure reciprocal in influence; in animal life it is becoming increasingly clear that important environmental influences are operative in what may be called psychological factors. Social behavior can be of critical quality ecologically, and this field serves, perhaps, to show how inadequate and imperfect as yet is our observation, especially of interspecific social behavior apparent in a complex biological community which includes man. The ecologist tends ultimately to consider man as a member of the indigenous fauna if man is a primitive hunter–foodgatherer, or as an introduced species if he is buffering himself against the environment by civilization, developed technology, and an export trade in natural resources. But there is one outstanding difference between man and the rest of creation ecologically. He is a political animal and in our day and age it is quite unreal to ignore the political nature of man as an ecological factor.

I am already giving the impression, perhaps, that there is such a subject as human ecology, a matter which has called forth some tart difference of opinion until very recently. For myself, there is no such subject as human ecology; there is ecology only, which must accept man as part of the field of reference; but man can have an ecological outlook in studying his own problems, whatever they are— medical, agricultural, or those of labor relations.

Haeckel coined the word oecology in 1869 and he had animals in mind. There is something ironical in the speculation that so ecologically perceptive a man as Charles Darwin probably set back the study of ecology for half a century because after 1859 the palaeontological data concerning evolution had necessarily to be gathered. Ecology as we knew it fifty years ago was a botanical science primarily, handicapped by a certain restriction of vision associated with those whose eyes are focused on the sward. The early literature of ecology gravely neglected the influence of the biotic factor on vegetation; indeed, it was not until 1932 that the British Ecological Society published its second journal of *Animal Ecology*. Shelford was reacting to animal ecology in his studies of succession in the first decade of this century and his book on animal communities appeared in 1913, the same year in which C. C. Adams published his *Guide to Animal Ecology*.

Perhaps the First World War explains the gap between 1913 and the early 'twenties, when Charles Elton's series of papers appeared, culminating in his *Animal Ecology* of 1927, giving us the fundamental ecological ideas of cyclicism in populations, food chains of varying complexity between species, leading to the concept of what is now known as the Eltonian pyramid, and the idea of animals filling *niches* in the functions of conversion of matter. Charles Adams, to whom I have already referred, made a profound remark to the effect that ecology was a study of process—process which is not necessarily progress, although the developmental quality apparent in the slow building of biological communities was tacit in the phenomena of plant successions elucidated by the Clementian school of ecologists in America. Adams saw that the orderly thread of developmental succession could easily be broken or influenced by all manner of factors, but there was still the unbreakable thread of process or, in fact, history. There is at present some reaction against the idea of orderly succession to a climax state which is stable and continuing, because so many examples can be brought foward to show how natural phenomena such as hurricane, fire and frost-heave—each at certain moments of biological significance such as a seed year or not—can make nonsense of orderly progression within the community under investigation. But they do not make nonsense of the idea and the trend, and the plain record of process of history brings us to a perspective of reality. It is part of the thesis of this essay that man was able to civilize by being a breaker of climaxes, giving him the stored wealth of the ages in plants, animals and soil fertility with which to buttress himself against the environment and to enjoy the immense capacity for social evolution provided by the new ability to be permanently gregarious.

The concept of the dynamic biological community took a long time to mature—if we admit that it is even now much advanced beyond adolescence. Its development shows all the signs of what most of us detect some time or other in our personal investigations, inability to see much more than what we are looking for, or seeing without apprehending significance. Edward Forbes saw the concept of community clearly in his classic marine work of 1843-5, but his early death robbed Scotland and ecology of a luminous mind. The plant ecologists of the late nineteenth century, headed by Warming, made the concept of community a cornerstone of a growing science, and Tansley's famous paper of 1920 codified it and gave it greater significance. Tansley emphasized in this paper that conceptual arguments and hypotheses must be firmly based on observation of the vegetation itself and that one must constantly go back to the field. It was a necessary admonition in that laboratory era. Tansley developed then the idea of the community as a quasi-organism or organic entity, of the whole being greater than the sum of its parts. He made comparisons of plant communities with human communities, and remarked that lacking psychical awareness, instinctive cooperation did not develop—only symbioses of varying degrees—and that competition was the law of relationship. It was later, in *Vegetation of the British Islands*, that Tansley gave lengthy consideration to the biotic or animal factor in the expression of communities, realizing for example that a landscape of chalk downland, so old and English and accepted as natural, depends completely on the continued grazing of sheep. The very habitat of chalk grassland is man-produced by way of the sheep, yet it is a habitat with well-defined floristic and entomological characteristics. We see here an example of organic evolution aligning itself with the long pursuance of human activity toward development of habitat. We have much to learn in this field in Africa, one of the main cradles of humanity, where man-produced habitats such as savannah by the agency of fire, have developed their own ungulate faunas. Time has had its chance, unaffected by glaciation or major changes of climate.

Some of the shocks of human impact on biological communities may have turned the Americans the more surely to study such organic entities as inextricable webs of plants and animals; one of Shelford's pupils, W. C. Allee, expressed the notion of unconscious cooperation in biological communities, a concept so much easier to elucidate from studying plants and animals together. Some measure of the 'psychic awareness' not obvious to Tansley in 1920 was now seen to be present in the enlarged wholes of biological communities which we accept nowadays. Allee's unconscious cooperation was entirely scientific and utterly removed from the wishful thinking or pious hopefulness of Kropotkin's *Mutual Aid*. All the same, Allee brought warmth and light into a field which had tended to be chillingly botanical.

But the strings of past philosophy trail round our feet, making us conservative from a sense of prudence rather than reason. Judaic monotheism put man and nature apart, an idea strengthened by Cartesian dualism of mind and matter. The older Dionysian intuition of wholeness was heresy, and the ancient Chinese comprehension of a universe of checks and balances and compensations, in which man was essentially a part and no more, was unknown and unscientific anyway. Hence, far into our own day, man was not a proper part of the study of ecology. If you studied man you might have been an anthropologist or an archaeologist or an historian, but if you studied ecology you dealt with nature as she was conceived to be and not with man. The notion of human ecology was considered not to be scholarly, though such a man as Patrick Geddes had made most illuminating contributions to the ecology of human life and had collaborated with J. A. Thomson who held this rostrum so long. Also, there were several people in manifestly defined fields such as geography, sociology, epidemiology and social anthropology, who were jumping on this new bandwagon and calling their subjects human ecology. Ecologists would have none of it. They were aware of the wide spread of their subject and of their dependence on good taxonomy; there was some suspicion already that an ecologist might be a jack-of-all-trades and master of none, and it was academic suicide to be an ecologist except incidentally to an acknowledged position in botany or zoology. The ultimate necessity of considering the biological community as a working whole, ecology being as it were the physiology of community, produced crops of errors where good botanists were less good zoologists, and good zoologists very inadequate botanists. In such an atmosphere of the titter behind the hand, it was not easy to embrace man and his possible ecology as well.

But for several reasons the intellectual climate is changing. The archaeologist has shown in recent years that proto-civilization is several thousand years older in the Old World than we had thought, and the primitive Folsom Man in the New World was much earlier than the accepted Quaternary immigration from northeast Asia. As we have learned how man lived, what he ate, how his houses were built, and what his devotional buildings signified, what movements he made, we have been compelled to speculate on the influences man has had on his environment through many thousands of years. Also, the dynamic world of this century, particularly of the past twenty years, has made us intensely and often painfully aware of change in the landscape. We have been rather roughly pitchforked into a world of democracy, so called; into a world of human population explosion, into a world of mobility made possible by the invention of the internal combustion engine and the exploitation of fossil fuels. Land use has changed in character and so much more land has been used, often uncritically, following earlier patterns in different climates. The immense planetary buffer and reservoir of wilderness has shrunk in area and influence. Quite suddenly in these past twenty-five years and particularly since the last war there has been a shaking of confidence. The all-conquering technological man whose mind had the same characteristics as the bulldozers employed to grow groundnuts on a prodigious scale in Tanganyika is already out of date, although the breed is highly inventive and has in no way accepted defeat. There is apparent in politicians an unsureness: they look longingly and hopefully at the extreme technological man, but now it is perhaps as well to listen also to the biologists, not merely the ones who overcome noxious insects with magical rapidity, but ecologists as well.

What do ecologists offer? No panaceas or quick returns, so much as a point of view which restrains, shows the consequences of different types of action, and possibly how mistakes in land-use can be rectified, and why they were mistakes. Ecology is a science of identifying causes and consequences.

Here, I think, is where we may consider the place of history: the political situation and the changes brought about by individuals and ideas are the stuff of history and it is difficult to find out what influence man was having on his environment and what accommodations the organic world of nature was making. But it can be done to a considerable extent if we will give time to it and reconsider history in ecological terms for enrichment of our experience in making future decisions.

I would like to take as an example at random, pulling out one thread of English history, the course of sheep farming from Saxon times until the latter end of the Middle Ages. England was once a country of deep forest in the vales, with scrub on the chalk hills and wolds. Neolithic man could tackle the scrub with his tools of stone and bone, but not the forest. The Roman, better equipped, drove his roads through everything, making islands in the sea of forest. The Saxon came from forested lands, and working in his own ecological fashion soon reduced the forest to islands in a sea of cultivated or cleared land. The Saxon was a swineherd who undoubtedly valued the pig's snout in life as its hams after slaughter. Large numbers of herded swine must have been effective implements in scarifying the forest floor, disturbing or eradicating the pristine flora, influencing the physico-chemical state of the ground and preventing regeneration, so that forest with undercover would decline and open woodland with fewer and fewer standards would be left. The food-gathering, soil-working pig may be looked upon as a pioneer when present in sufficient numbers, creating conditions in which a sward of grass could form in an increasingly parklike terrain. At this stage the sheep could take over, living on the sward, maintaining it and quite surely preventing the regeneration of woodland. The cattle grazing among the sheep also helped in the establishment of permanent grassland and were creating the possibility of fairly rapid conversion into arable land when pressure of population demanded extension.

Historical research has revealed that England and parts of southern Scotland were already important wool-producing country in Saxon times. That was the main economic function of the sheep, to produce wool; mutton was welcome but incidental. Some of the wool was used at home but it was an important item of export which allowed importation of Continental luxuries and even goods from the Levant. The great early development of medieval sheep-farming did but build on the existing Saxon foundation. England was the principal European producer of fine wool. Italy, and later the Low Countries, were the large manufacturers of fine textiles. This interdependence must have helped in the unification of the medieval world. When England eventually produced her own fine cloth and cut down her export trade in wool, she inevitably crystallized more sharply. Italian bankers and merchants were prominent in the early trade and the Church was a pioneer agent in the spread of sheep-farming to new areas. The Cistercian order particularly was responsible for extension into the north and west, where flocks of several thousands were kept by each foundation, such as Fountains and Rievaulx. Lords of the manor and peasants were all in this golden age of English sheep-farming. The late Eileen Power gave a vivid impression in her Oxford series of lectures entitled *The Early English Wool Trade*. Reckoning from the number of sacks exported and allowing for some being used at home, there were probably fifteen million sheep in England in the early fourteenth century.

It has probably been insufficiently realized what effect this vast sheep-farming enterprise must have had on the landscape and wild life. Despite the patches of forest, the fringes of parklike country in transition and gorse-clad commons, there must have been extensive bald spots where open-field cultivation and sheep-farming between them would have destroyed all tree growth. The land of England was being mined of its stored fertility, but in such a favored area do we live that regeneration made good part of the loss in flora and fauna, seen and unseen, and consequently that much of the lost fertility.

Now comes the political act with its ecological consequences: this economically prosperous sheep-farming era was wrecked by taxes in wool and on wool. Edward III was on the warpath, and wars, as we know all too well, are an expensive form of dissipation. The lords of the manor began to let their plowed lands, and later their sheep also as going concerns. The rates of exploitation probably increased as the small men came in and had to create their capital. But the removal of the Wool Staple to Calais was the disintegrating blow. A system of husbandry was pretty well at an end, and before long the Reformation and the advent of American gold started a period of enclosure of land. This enclosure undoubtedly made for stabilization and a husbandry based on maintenance rather than pure extraction. The eighteenth-century introduction of leguminous crop plants and the more skilled application of the principle of rotation produced a conversion cycle of energy flow vastly in excess of that of the centuries immediately preceding. Not all of it was translated into human increase and economic prosperity. Hedges, hedge-row timber, increased leisure (for a few) for such country pursuits as hunting and shooting, which needed a varied landscape, and not least the emergence of the Romance poets in their delight in landscape, all contributed to diversification of habitat which the wild flora and fauna were quick to exploit in this favored climate.

The story in Scotland has been less happy. The more acidic soils did not withstand the sheep-farming as well as those in England, if we exclude the millstone grits of the English Pennine Chain; the Southern Uplands of Scotland are still in sheep, but are deteriorating slowly. The Highlands, poorer and wetter and steeper, suffered their hardest blow of deforestation and the coming of the sheep in the eighteenth century, and have deteriorated to an ecological decrepitude which is plain for those with eyes to see. The political situation is not yet sufficiently ecological in climate to tackle this essentially biological problem of rehabilitation in a biological and geographical manner, although, as I said at the outset, it is improving. . . .

Let us now look at an older and larger pattern of animal domestication which has profoundly influenced the characteristics of flora and fauna over a vast area of the land surface of the Old World. The development of the highly specialized husbandry known as nomadism is far from primitive, though because it shows so many examples of arrested cultural growth we are apt so to consider it. Nomadic pastoralism is one of the surest means of breaking ecological climaxes. It is an insidious means also. There is not the primary traumatic onslaught of tree-felling, brush-grubbing and plowing that agriculture demands. Pastoralism is a penetration of terrain by a relatively small number of human beings. The landscape is not altered immediately and there are no considerable works of man evident to the eye. But numbers of grazing animals and close treading place selective pressures on the vegetational complex. Where fire is used, selection is more rapid. In effect, the herbage complex is simplified, and that means gaps in the original niche structure, with consequent overall loss in biological efficiency of the community. Broadly, the vegetation moves towards the xeric.

Nomadism postdates agriculture by an undetermined period running to some thousands of years. The specialization is like that of the seafaring man, no longer content to paddle about in the shallows with primitive raft or formless dugout canoe, who has built himself a ship, beautiful in form because it is functional in crossing uncharted seas of uncertain temper, and who has developed the skill to navigate by the stars and sail the ship as if it were a live thing. Equally, the nomad did not just walk out into the sea of the steppe which stretches from the Crimea of Europe to the Yellow River of China: he was a riverside dweller, a forest edge dweller venturing no further than his domesticated animals could go and come in a day, or perhaps a little further in the season of rains. Domestication itself probably arose on religious grounds, for the animals in sight, touchable and ready for sacrifice, were the embodiment of that which was desired, life-giving and life-enhancing. One of the characteristics of nomad stock is the capacity to herd close, and to move and feed and rest as one, a matter for selection conscious and unconscious, before man could go forth with flocks and herds on to the ocean of the steppe.

The sheep is the mainstay of nomadism just as it is the mainstay of the husbandry of wild lands today. The goat provides brains for the most part. The multiplicity of mouths are wealth-gatherers activated by four times as many superbly adapted legs and feet. Water is needed in minimal quantities, and the animal itself provides man with milk, meat and warmth. But the nomad, interposing animals between himself and the generally inhospitable environment of the steppe, realized quite well that the several sorts of domesticated animals gave him different securities and desirable ends in an environment not as uniform as our school geography books would lead us to believe. Cattle are much more efficient converters as individuals, of forage into meat, milk and leather, and they can be used for traction and as weight carriers; but their heavy water requirements govern the possible nomadic routes. The camel, on the other hand, gives the nomad the greatest penetration or retreat into arid regions. Lastly, the horse was of great benefit as a producer of meat, milk and tractive power. Domestication of these animals meant their presence where and when they were wanted, their mental and even physical characteristics so far modified that they did not move as quickly as wild ones. In consequence, the animals were in general on the ground for a longer period and in greater numbers than when they were wild. The nomad society arising gradually from the more sedentary agricultural group would early realize that overgrazing hung like a sword of Damocles. The price of the life-way of grazing animals is movement, the brand of Ishmael. In the ideal, agriculture is concentration of effort, or intensification: pastoralism is conscious, well-organized diffusion.

Sheep grazing on a range in South Dakota. Photo from South Dakota Department of Highways.

Yet man does not prefer constant or random movement. Even the most highly developed nomads do not go far, no more than 150 or possibly 200 miles of farthest distance in the year, and relatively long spells of pitched tents are desired. The women wish it so, caring nothing for floristic composition of the grazing. At best the nomad was on the chernozem soils of the Ukraine or in delectable valleys: at worst in the wastes of the Gobi or the Tarim Depression. Nomadism in its highest development did not occur until after 1500 B.C. and it came with achievement of that maximum state of mobility, the mastery of riding horses, as distinct from using this animal for traction.

Horse riding seems to have arisen on the plateau of northwest Persia. If you have ever ridden a pony of stocky Prjewalski type you will know the relief of getting off it for a rest: but once you have ridden one of the delicately-controllable, long-gaited creatures of what we now call the Arab type, one's whole outlook changes on the mounted state. Man well mounted is a superior being, and the nomad soon geared his way of life to that which gave the male element swift and far range; even his eyes are a yard higher above the ground—no mean advantage. We cannot know the details of the dominant mutation which produced the dish-faced, long-necked, sloping-shouldered, fine-boned 'horse of heaven,' as it came to be called, but nomadic man quickly made use of it. Even his status changed, producing the chevalier, the caballero, and the knight, who were with us till the Land Rover came and the girls took over the pony clubs.

Now came maximum exploitation of the steppe environment, not only nomadism which, as I have said, is never over a very long distance, but in migration. The Indo-European tribes began their great easterly migrations of thousands of miles through a thousand years, by which time they reached the Ordos country of the Yellow River. Within this time the civilizations of the Near East had learned the survival value of cavalry, and the Chinese finally learned the same lesson. They became an equestrian nation in all its elite grades. Expeditions were sent into Turkestan to bring back these 'horses of heaven.' One of the Pazirik felts, so miraculously preserved in the ice of an Indo-European grave since some hundreds of years B.C. in Siberia, shows a gay cavalier with impeccable military moustache on his Arab-type steed, meeting a seated man of Mongol type in Mongol dress.

Even the bronze art of the Indo-European nomad travelled over this whole region. These people knew their animals: just as a Navajo Indian boy today does not need to look at a horse to draw it in any posture, so the Indo-Europeans thought their animals—horses, cattle, sheep, goats—in lifelike simple terms; yes, but wild animals were of immense importance to them as well, whether ungulate or carnivore, and the dramatic moment of the lion's attack on the stag or antelope is often captured in a stylized but dynamic bronze plaque. There are the Scythian bronzes of the Kuban, the animal bronzes of Luristan, and at the eastern end the bronzes of the Ordos bend, which show a remarkable sensitiveness to animal form. The involved twisting stylized representation can be found also in the Celtic and Nordic scrollwork in metal and stone on the Atlantic seaboard. Tamara Talbot Rice has brought out this wide spread of nomad art in her book on the Scythians.

The archaelogists have produced much of this material for us and set it in perspective, but zoologically they have not done so well. I suggest that it is up to zoologists to examine it with care, so that elk are not called stags, antelopes deer, or Urial sheep ibexes. The Saiga antelope also appears in these bronzes, unrecognized as such, and crested cranes seem of some significance. I myself have a complete Luristan bit, the cheek pieces of which are representations of elk. The use by the elk of the two posterior toes has been faithfully observed by this bronze-caster of nearly three thousand years ago. How did this bit get into the Zagros Mountains? Had it come from the Caucasus? I also have what must be one of the earliest surviving representations of a peacock from Amlach in the Elburz country south of the Caspian. Forgive my digression, but I hope this nomad animal art will be examined in relation to possible distribution of species in the past and to ecological history.

Once the Mongols became equestrian, the backward, westward surge began, culminating in the empire of Genghis Khan which frightened Europe and conquered

China for a spell until Kublai was himself conquered by Chinese culture. So many of the remaining nomads of Central Asia are Mongoloid, even as far west as Kazakstan, but the Indo-Europeans also survive in pockets as far east as northern Afghanistan. By the end of the Mongol Yuan dynasty it is estimated that the human population of China had been reduced by forty millions, which in itself must have had interesting ecological consequences for a generation or two.

The original fauna of this great region of the steppe survives in the mountain ranges, and the Saiga antelope is back on the plains in millions thanks to an enlightened policy of conservation by the Russians. But how long can nomadism survive? The brand of Ishmael produces this highly specialized form of society which in effect finds itself in a cultural *cul-de-sac* unable to evolve, whereas the less specialized and once handicapped societies at the edge of the steppe did evolve into the civilizations of today. Political feeling is against nomadism and the biological necessity of movement in pastoral nomadism if the habitat is to be conserved, is ignored. If there can be irrigation of the steppe, the obvious access of foods and fibers thus made possible means the nomads must change or go, and going is no longer possible in our contracting world. Farming nibbles at the alluvial river flats and the bore hole brings up fossil water also and cripples the wholeness of the habitat for the nomad. The Russians seem definitely to be eliminating nomadism, and such western nations as have any seem to be doing the same thing. Individual Britons have admired nomads and their way of life, but collectively or politically Britain is depressing nomadism: the Masai of the semi-arid East African steppe are being eased out of their culture of arrested development in favor of Kikuyu and Sukumba, rapidly increasing tribes under the Pax Britannica, which were formerly despised and harried by the nomads. The reindeer Lapps are also finding their winter grounds falling within the agricultural penumbra and there is the social urge toward education, which tends to make the winter communities static. Nomadism will die, at the expense of sterilizing large areas of back country which only nomads could utilize, as far as domesticated livestock is concerned. Whether in the future we may return to controlled cropping of wild animals on wild lands unfitted to human settlement remains to be seen, but despite the tentative experimentation in Africa and the successful Russian work on the Saiga antelope, I have the feeling that man is still going to degrade much good wildlife country in an effort to farm it, before it is fully realized that the nature of such country in its water relations and soil characteristics precludes agriculture. There is some false moral self-delusion which makes modern governments try and fail rather than consider the wholeness of land-use ecology before formulating a land-use plan.

The mention of the pastoralism of wild lands by wild animals brings me back to a form of nomadism in the New World which has several points of interesting comparison with the early development of specialized nomadism in the Old World through use of the horse. We may take it for granted that the late flowering of civilization in the Americas was the result of having fewer and less convenient domesticable plants, especially cereals, and certainly fewer and less convenient domesticable animals. At the more primitive level, the North American Indians were forest and forest-edge and river-valley people. Their beast of burden was the dog, sometimes dragging a travois—a sorry means indeed. They too were near a great central steppe of prairie where the wild bison conducted its own seasonal movements which took it away from the haunts of men. Hunting of this animal meant enticement to newly burned grazing, and stalking which even included wearing a bison mask—a most unenviable method. Nevertheless, it would seem that from about the sixteenth century man was increasing the range of the bison by burning at the forest edge.

The advent of the horse by way of Mexico and the Rio Grande far into the southwest was a major liberation for the American Indian. Horses were stolen or went feral and the terrain was that dry steppe phenologically perfect for this animal. Here man did not need to wait for the mutation which produced the 'horses of heaven,' for it was the less carefully bred examples of this type which so rapidly colonized the American steppe. The Spaniards lost their advantage when the horse went feral and spread northwards and came into the hands of the Indians, who immediately rode.

There now occurred that specialization toward nomadism. The Indian could leave the forest edge and follow the bison. Thus, from the beginning of the seventeenth century until the middle of the nineteenth there was a strong man-induced extension of the bison's range and there was a rapid specialization by certain tribes to become horse nomads, in effect pastoralizing the wild bison instead of domesticated stock. Agriculture was minimal, carried on by the women, for the water situation was generally easier than in the Old World steppe.

This situation could have gone on indefinitely as a biological continuum, for the wild animal prevented overgrazing by its migratory habits, and the enlargement of bison-inhabited country by Indian fire seems merely to have been an enlargement of soil conserving prairie grassland rather than extension of less biologically productive savannah such as we see today in South America and Africa. It was the white man overrunning the West with domesticated stock, packing it and going away with the proceeds that devastated millions of acres at a much faster rate than the Old World nomads reduced the productive potential of the Asian steppe with close-herded domesticated animals. Just as the Ukraine country of the Scythians came ultimately to wheat, so did the Middle West prairie become a bread basket. The Indians of the Middle West have gone the way of the Scythians.

We will not pause to consider the nineteenth-century calamity that befell the bison and the Indian, but what must be pointed out is that the sudden disintegration of this nomadism imposed by the wanderings of the bison hit hardest those tribes which had specialized farthest in this way of life. Even today the observer can see that the horse tribes have come off worst in social and economic adaptation. The tribes which remained in the forest or at the forest edge are now woodsmen and construction men; the Pueblo Indians of the Rio Grande valley may be anything that the white man is, because of their urban tradition; but the horse tribes who accepted the exhilaration of liberty of distance and became what we have come to call Plains Indians, have found themselves in the deepest bondage of the drastically changed economic base. Now, as pastoralists, they are finding movement cut down, and yet a dawning ecology of land use is demonstrating the old truth that the pastoralism of wild lands imposes movement of the animals. There is the continuing paradox of political tendencies to restrain the movement of people on wild lands, and scientific evidence that animals on wild lands must be kept moving. Only wild animals conduct this aspect of their lives without human direction, and on this shrinking planet of exploding humanity even the wild animals are having their necessary movements constricted. The threat to the elephant in Africa is not the killing that goes on but the merciless restriction of range and movement. Without the movement, habitat is destroyed and other species of wild animals suffer in train. A dramatic example of this trend has been the buildup of elephants in the sanctuary of the Tsavo Royal National Park in Kenya. Destruction of trees and bush by the elephants endangered the food supply of the rhinoceros, so that a period of long drought made this painfully apparent in the starvation of over two hundred rhinoceroses. They were not short of water themselves, for the river never dried, but they died with their bellies full of indigestible cellulose fiber. I saw some of these creatures die and helped in the *post-mortem* examinations. I saw the wrecked bush which would not even become a fire-climax savannah. I did not put the blame on the elephants.

I began this address with the statement that ecology was the observational study of communities of living things in time as well as space, and I repeated Charles Adams's dictum that it was essentially concerned with process. I have allowed myself to range about the world seeing man, plant communities, the communities of his own domesticated animals and some wild animals in dynamic process through some thousands of years of man's most fertile years of culture, and you may agree with me that in any synecological studies it is difficult to exclude man or to be a plant or an animal ecologist. There is only one ecology. If we are to follow an ecological approach to the study of society—be it historical, sociological, agricultural, anthropological, or economic, we must keep in mind that man's habitat and human societies are not static. The cross-section presented by a socioanthropological study needs amplification in time. Cultures are altering continually, progressing or retrogressing, and these trends, though subject inexorably to natural laws, are also the results of human behavior. Such action may have been unseeing of consequences in the past, but if ecology is to concern itself with human influences, and take its place at the council table of human affairs, it should accept the premise that our species has in many parts of the world arrived at the stage of mental evolution at which it is possible to foresee the consequences of various kinds of direct and indirect modifications of habitats and their biological communities. The well-being of the habitats and the human communities therein can be influenced and sustained by understanding the interrelationship of the biological communities in which we coexist.

I have put forward the thesis that man has been able to enjoy gregariousness and civilize as a result of learning how to tap the stored wealth of ecological climaxes—soil fertility, timber and other plants, and animals. His agriculture of annual or biennial plants sets back ecological succession and demands a high skill to maintain fertility; the general history of animal exploitation is of overuse. Are we faced with the proposition that civilization is a contradiction in terms; that civilization carries its own seeds of decay because ecologically retrogressive processes once begun cannot be checked? I believe there is some danger of this, but there need not be in an ecologically conscious world. The suffering planet has immense power of natural rehabilitation if given its chance and we are also learning how these wonderful integrated processes of healing take place. As I said earlier, ecology is the physiology of community. Understanding it we can avoid undesirable consequences. Perhaps it is necessary to say that I am not crying 'back to nature'; our growing understanding of the physiology of community gives power of planned manipulation, finding other ways round to desired ends. The history of the Nature Conservancy in this country is a vivid example of men learning how to manage biological communities in a manner simulating the natural.

Man often reminds me of the Irish Elk in that the elk's antlers could develop nonadaptatively in evolution as a byproduct of increase in body size, what Julian Huxley calls heterogonic growth. The enormous drain on the organism of growing so much nonfunctional calcium phosphate every year was too much once the prodigality of the Pleistocene had passed. Well, man conjures from his mind ways of using resources unproductively, be it pyramid building in Egypt, temple building and human sacrifice in Mexico, and now defense and nationalism. Nationalism is the modern Irish Elkism. In a world where the only hope for man is internationalism, nationalism is the political ecological factor which prevents any constructive action to curb population increase. And withal, we are faced with the ironic paradox of splintering nationalism and pseudo-national costumes, with the dismal destruction of individuality inside them, which variability is as desirable in the social system as in the ecosystem. Furthermore, I believe that the pressure of population on land is presenting us with an emergency earlier than the problem of growing enough food for the increase. Mobility by way of the internal combustion engine, vastly increased leisure by way of automation, and sophisticated modes of outdoor recreation are changing the land-use pattern far quicker than we are learning how to cope with it. Fifteen years ago the excuse of increased food production was enough to get rid of hedgerow trees in England; but at this moment the amenity value of such trees in such a populous country, needing the balm of the green leaf, far outweighs the small increase of food production which might accrue from their removal. The picture in the United States is of food surpluses but a very real shortage of recreational land. An Outdoor Recreation Bureau has been established as a department of government to help in planning the solution of this very considerable problem of land-use ecology in its widest sense, and I am glad to say ecologists have been brought in at the beginning.

It would be fantastic, nevertheless, to make the mistake now of so expanding the scope of ecology that it would become all-embracing, so that the ecologist would bog down in a morass of his own ignorance, and become the supreme irritating busybody. That, I think, was feared by those who years ago wished to exclude man from their studies and would not admit human ecology. Neither do I; there is no human ecology—only ecology—but in those sciences dealing with man, from political economy to social anthropology and archaeology, there is plenty of room for the ecological slant of mind. As a corollary, I think that ecological research must become more and more the effort of teams of workers; the single worker will continue to discover beautiful expressions of phenomena, but the synecological studies in depth of habitats and communities which we need today demand far more than what one man can compass. Ecological studies are not designed *ad hoc* to solve land-use problems but to discover truth, and this high scientific approach must be jealously guarded, but thereafter ecologists can have a social conscience and apply their discoveries to the problems of land-use by man. The teams I envisage are not collections of specialists, if they are to be successful, but, to borrow Tansley's expression, organic entities.

REFERENCES

Adams, C. C. *Guide to the Study of Animal Ecology*. New York, 1913.
Allee, W. C. *Animal Aggregations*. Chicago, 1931.
Creel, H. G. *The Birth of China*. Chicago, 1937.
Darling, F. Fraser. *West Highland Survey*, Oxford, 1955.
——————— . "Man's Ecological Dominance through Domesticated Animals on Wild Lands," pp. 778–787 in *Man's Role in Changing the Face of the Earth*, ed. Thomas. Chicago, 1956.
Elton, C. *Animal Ecology*. London, 1927.
Forbes, E. "Report on the Molluscs and Radiata of the Aegean Sea, and on their Distribution Considered as Bearing on Geology," *Report Brit. Ass. Adv. Sci.*, 13 (1843), 130–193.
Ford, C. Daryll. *Habitat, Economy and Society*. London, 1934.
Lattimore, O. *Inner Asian Frontiers of China*. New York, 1951.
Power, Eileen. *The Wool Trade in English Medieval History*. Oxford, 1941.
Shelford, V. E. "Animal Communities in Temperate America," *Bulletin Geographical Society of Chicago*, 5 (1913), 1–368.
Talbot Rice, T. *The Scythians*. London, 1957.
Tansley, A. G. "The Classification of Vegetation and the Concept of Development," *J. Ecology*, 8 (1920), 118–149.
——————— . *The British Islands and their Vegetation*, Cambridge, 1939.
Thompson, J. A., and P. Geddes. *Life: Outlines of General Biology*. London, 1931.
Toynbee, A. J. *A Study of History*. Oxford, 1934.
Warming, J. E. B. *Oecology of Plants*. Oxford, 1909 (tr. from Danish of 1895).
Wissman, H. von. "On the Role of Nature and Man in Changing the Face of the Dry Belt of Asia," pp. 278–303 in *Man's Role in Changing the Face of the Earth*, ed. Thomas. Chicago, 1956.

THE VANDAL IDEOLOGY

Scott Paradise

*Men do not stop to ponder their deeper convictions with everything they do.
Yet, every occasion on which man changes the world, whether it be starting a
motor or building a nuclear power plant, has an unspoken—usually unconscious—
philosophical dimension, involving basic assumptions, attitudes, and perceptions.*

In the chapter entitled "Nature Hating" in Man in the Landscape *(New York:
Alfred A. Knopf, 1967), the author attempted to illustrate the diverse origins
and slow sculpturing of these foundations of belief. To accuse Greek intellectual
hubris, Christian dogma, or industrial pragmatism of responsibility for the creeds
that have allowed environmental disarray and destruction was characterized as
oversimplification. The assumptions which support our present actions in the
environment are so universally accepted that they can be attributed only ten-
uously to particular segments of society.*

*What makes them enormously difficult to sort out, identify, and control is
that they are usually deeply bound up with our most cherished notions about
ourselves. The concepts of freedom, individuality, human dignity, the alleviation
of suffering, and various human rights are almost inseparable from forms of
megalomania, prejudice, and blindness. America's superlative effort toward
achieving physical well-being and political democracy can be measured in conflict and destruction. It is parallel in some ways to the high level of civilization
achieved in ancient Athens, and paid for in ravaged soils, decimated forests,
aggression, and slavery.*

*There are many differences, of course. Not the least of these is the original
European invasion of the North American continent after the fashion of the
Vandal conquest of Gaul, Spain, and North Africa 1500 years ago. Such
plundering had its rationalizations as well as its unspoken logic then as it
does now. Perhaps the most significant outcomes of the rape of America are a
high level of chronic conscious guilt, greater historical perspective, and, most important of all, deliberate exploration of our own motives and assumptions. These
phenomena amount to a considerable advantage over the self-knowledge of the
non-culture-conscious cultures of the past, for they may open the way to correct-
ing our ecological postures at a basic level.*

Scott Paradise, "The Vandal Ideology," The Nation, *December 29, 1969, 729–732.*

Some call it an ecological crisis; others admit only to a variety of serious environmental problems ranging from pollution to ugliness. In any case, the bombardment of articles, books and television programs in the past few years has made us aware that something is wrong. Exploding populations, advancing technology and economic development have joined to face us with a triple threat. But except for a few voices, the depth of the difficulty eludes expression.

We assume, rightly, that more science and technology, better planning, or more adequate political arrangements are needed; but we assume, wrongly, that a combination of these will save us. The argument runs, if we lack as yet the political will to solve the problems, a few local catastrophes will surely bring us to our senses and force us in due course to achieve general solutions. While admitting that stricter regulation of polluters and developers will be necessary, we talk as though the American industrial system could survive without really radical modification.

The contrary is true. Not only must our industrial system be changed; the system of beliefs about man's relationship with the natural world which underlies it must be corrected if we are to escape the jaws of the coming crisis. This system of beliefs might be described as an ideology. It is almost always assumed. In one way or another, its propositions are often asserted as self-evident truths. In fact, their influence on social policy and the allegiance they hold over the majority of Americans should make envious the proponents of the traditional religions.

American ideology of man and nature might be reduced to the following seven propositions:

1. *Man is the source of all value.* This is not *anthropocentrism* for that implies only that man is the center of value. Rather it is *anthroposolipsism*, which asserts that man alone has any inherent value. Everything else is valuable only as it benefits man.

2. *The universe exists only for man's use.* This proposition is a corollary of the first. If man is the single source of value, anything which men cannot use is useless and can be destroyed without compunction. Some of us broaden the idea of usefulness to include things of scientific, aesthetic and ecological value. But in practice this belief more often further narrows the meaning of value to that which has calculable economic value. Thus if the world's whaling fleets find profit in exterminating the last of the great whales, the whales must go. No argument about either the rights of whales or their ecological value will be admitted. The only argument that might possibly have effect contends that more profit might be made if whaling were limited so as to guarantee a perpetual harvest of blubber and meat.

   Since the universe exists only for man's use, man may with a crusader's zeal war against nature and bring it to unconditional surrender.

3. *Man's primary purpose is to produce and consume.* This is the heart of the good life. We sometimes define man as the tool-using animal, *homo faber.* Theologians pronounce us co-creators with God. As co-creator, man has a license also to destroy and waste. In spite of such protests as the hippies represent, the work ethic still reigns. Neither a play ethic, nor a love ethic, nor a service ethic yet challenges it. Only a consumer ethic grapples with it for supremacy.

4. *Production and consumption must increase endlessly.* Since life's primary purpose is producing and consuming, abundant life blesses us through increasing material abundance. Goods equal the good, and nothing can quench our infinite thirst for them. Growth of the gross national product defines progress and makes possible a continual and simultaneous increase in population and rise in standard of living. Those concerned with social justice see evil in that some nations have enjoyed too little economic growth; they see hope in the possibility that all nations will have more.

5. *Material resources are unlimited.* The thrust of this proposition lies not in the absurdity that the finite Earth has infinite resources but rather that we do not need to heed the warnings of those concerned with their depletion. New deposits of minerals and fossil fuels are found every decade. Our technology of extraction constantly improves and enables us to develop deposits unreachable or uneconomical a few years ago. For those resources genuinely scarce we can find substitutes. Ultimately our technology will be equal to extracting all the raw materials we need for millions of years from sea water and the granite on the earth's surface. When worried voices speak of overcrowding, they need only be referred to the vast empty spaces on the map of the world and the statistics that 70 percent of Americans are needlessly crammed together on a tiny fraction of the country's land surface. Even warnings about pollutants need not cause alarm because the human genius for short-range technical improvisation is equal to any crisis that is likely to arise.

6. *Man need not adapt himself to the natural environment since he can remake it to suit his own needs.* This assumption, sometimes referred to as "the bulldozer mentality," manifests itself most clearly when American military or business personnel live overseas. There they often create an environment more like that of continental United States than of the country in which they are stationed. We see it also in the possibility, sometimes realized through central heating and air conditioning, of never needing to spend more than a few minutes at a time in temperatures below 65 or above 75 degrees Fahrenheit from one year to the next. We see it in the vacationer who sprays his seaside acreage with DDT. On the other hand, while man need not adapt himself to the natural environment, it is assumed he can and must adjust to any stress perpetrated by his own technology. Smog, noise and ugliness come with progress, and man can and must learn to live with them.

Oil derricks on the Murphy-Coyote field in California. Photo from Standard Oil Company of California.

7. *A major function of the state is to make it easy for individuals and corporations to exploit the environment to increase wealth and power.* Ideas concerning private property stand central in this proposition. Because it has influenced the shape of the American social structures, it is easier for a lumber company to cut down redwoods than for the government to prevent it

from doing so. It is easier for a developer to destroy a beautiful old mansion to make way for new ranch houses than for the public to organize a drive and raise money to save the historic house. It is easier for strip miners to destroy a countryside than for a legislature to pass preventive legislation or the courts to enforce it. All these business initiatives increase the gross national product. The government structure and operation is biased to encourage such development rather than effectively to protect the natural and cultural heritage.

Although people often assert each of these beliefs, most Americans would perhaps not subscribe to them when stated this baldly. Nevertheless, our social policy, both public and private, operates as if these were our beliefs. And not only does this system of beliefs run in the mainstream of American culture but it is also spreading to infect societies all over the world. Any nation wanting to industrialize will find a certain usefulness in it. It tends to free a society from a veneration of places and things which might inhibit their being used for economic development. It directs attention away from personal and family relationships, away from tradition and ceremonial. It offers a moral alternative to leisure. These ideas seem necessary in order to blast most nations out of ancient ways and set them on the road of development.

But in the long run the consequences of this ideology must be disastrous— first, because no organism can endlessly multiply and exploit its environment; second, because it betrays life's meaning to elevate the economic, technical and procreative processes to absolutes. In America where this ideology has long been dominant, people tend to forget that it is not self-evident and has not always been universally accepted. It contradicts assumptions around which most cultures have organized life throughout history. Even today in the developing nations many governments are struggling with wrongheaded persistence to win the unwilling and recalcitrant people of the villages to this ideology.

The profound challenge facing America today is whether we can discover a new orientation which will preserve the necessary values and the truths in the current ideology, and yet redirect our goals so as to preserve our environment and our humanity itself.

To correct the seven propositions just stated is a good place to begin. They might be restated thus:

1. *Man is to be valued more highly than other creatures*. Such a proposition is truly anthropocentric. It puts man at the pinnacle of creation but does not isolate him as the only thing of value. Other creatures have beauty and splendor of their own.

    That this kind of assertion perplexes many in the culture is hardly surprising. A nation that coined the phrase, "The only good Indian is a dead Indian," is not likely to defend the cause of wildlife. But moral progress follows a widening awareness of the circle of fellowship. If we see it as ethical advance to discover Indians as our brothers, it is a move in the same direction to recognize animals as our cousins. Some of the most eloquent spokesmen for this perception speak out of the scientific community. Men like Loren Eiseley and Konrad Lorenz, who have spent lifetimes sensitively observing nonhuman life, can tell us without sentimentality that many animals are capable of relationship with us. Unfortunately, they cannot say with like confidence that we are interested in relating to them.

But many cannot believe that anything has value not bestowed on it by men. Those so invincibly anthroposolipsists might just understand that the human race is not an island but a part of the whole community of life. If any species disappears, man and all the rest are diminished. The extermination of animal species attendant on the growth of human population reduces the variety, fascination and stability of the biosphere. And therefore it erodes the quality of human life.

2. *Man has become the guardian of the earth.* His prerogatives to use the earth's resources are balanced by his responsibility to cherish them, protect them and use them carefully. Man does evil when he exterminates species of animals or does irreversible damage to the environment. When he does destroy life he needs to calculate the benefits he receives against the impoverishment of the living community. Man also is able to improve the environment. These changes entail disadvantages as well as benefits. Here, too, costs as well as benefits need to be carefully calculated before the project which will effect the change is undertaken.

3. *Man is far more than a producer and consumer.* Without production and consumption, of course, life cannot continue. But without singing, dancing or poetry, without loving, discovering or learning, without art, music or drama, life is hardly worth continuing. By participating in these pursuits in concert we lay hold of our humanity. The model of life as mass production and massive consumption is only one of many possible models. Most cultures throughout most of the human experience have been decidedly less obsessed than we with getting and spending. A recent study of the Kung Bushmen in the Kalihari Desert reports that on the average these people spend only three days a week food gathering and hunting. During the remaining four days they vigorously pursue noneconomic activities. Such a record, while perhaps arousing the wrath of their work-oriented fathers, would fill many of today's youth with envy and admiration. Our massive affluence should make it possible to emulate the Bushmen to some degree and so recover new dimensions of our humanity.

4. *Improvement in the quality of life takes precedence over increasing the quantity of material production.* The growth of the gross national product does not necessarily lead to an enlargement of human well-being. It may in some instances lead to the opposite. Our social goal should be to achieve a zero rate of population increase and a state of increasing human well-being with a minimum increase in material production and consumption. Herein lies

a new understanding of efficiency. In the long run this policy should lead to a state of relative equilibrium between the human race and the natural environment. But within this relative equilibrium men could make great progress in the arts, literature, sciences and human relationships.

5. *Material resources are to be used carefully and cherished.* The assumption of limitless resources breeds indifference to waste and to the likely needs of our descendants. This indifference drains us of joy and appreciation for things in the intoxication of consumption. Russell Baker observed in *The New York Times* that to transform goods into trash as quickly and efficiently as possible has become America's major pastime. On the other hand, human fulfillment comes not through an ascetic denial of the value of material things but by passionately and sensitively embracing them. Using and loving a few things long and carefully leads to a different kind of experience, a more profoundly fulfilling one, than does the careless use and abandonment of many things in rapid succession. We need a new materialism to replace the consumerism which now goes by that name.

6. *Man is to relate himself to the natural environment, remaking it according to its nature as well as for the sake of his short-term economic advantage.* Such considerations in many instances might deter us from covering superb farm land with parking lots, shopping centers and suburban subdivisions, or from carelessly filling or polluting intensely rich protein-producing wetlands and estuaries. It might save us from building expressways on some of our urban shore lines or trying to farm areas whose soil will predictably respond by becoming wasteland. Man's power to improve the world for his own use is not unlimited. His actions on it result in ecological reactions. He is part of a living web which responds when he acts and forces him to respond when it acts. Such a pattern of mutual action and reaction may be described as a relationship. In most instances man rightly claims the initiative and determines the quality of the relationship. But to make war on nature and force it to an unconditional surrender will lead to unexpected and disconcerting counterattacks. To win final victory requires that we make a desert and call it peace.

7. *A major function of the state is to supervise a planning process which will prevent the impairment of the quality of the environment.* This proposition implies a different conception of the rights of property. Land and resources cannot be seen as ours in the sense that we can abuse or destroy them for profit or pleasure. Instead, the right to hold and develop them depends on these actions contributing to the public good and preserving the quality of the environment. Of course, this principle can be applied only with complicated calculations of costs and benefits, but too often the calculations are still being made on the assumption that measures adopted for private gain usually lead to public benefit and that short-run, measurable economic advantage is an adequate criterion for determining action. The burden of proof must be shifted from those who would preserve the environment to those who would exploit it,

and from those who would limit property rights in the interest of public and environment to those who would defend such rights for private advantage.

These suggested modifications of our beliefs about man's relationship with nature are perhaps so radical as to be almost incomprehensible to many. Nevertheless, such thoughts are increasingly in the air. Conservationists, ecologists, hippies and certain groups of the New Left have created a climate in which such ideas have become more plausible than they were only a few years ago. [See "Man in Nature: Model for a New Radicalism" by Catherine Riegger Harris, *The Nation*, November 10.] Most of us, however, still doggedly embrace the hope that we can continue in the present course and save our society by tinkering. We still prefer to hope that if we reduce the military budget, develop better urban planning and pollution-control techniques, and enlarge the war against poverty, all will be well.

Technological forecasters and other futurists are still debating whether such a hope is realistic. The supposition that "something will turn up" to retrieve the situation can keep the hope alive and the argument continuing beyond the point of no return.

And, of course, it is just possible that the present system can continue on approximately its present path. But even if it can, argument can be made that it shouldn't. The perceptions and commitments suggested in the modified statement of belief serve as a far more satisfying basis for human fulfillment than does the current ideology. A society that would emerge from this new vision might have powerful appeal. Rebellious youth and growing interest in conservation may be straws in the wind to suggest that it would. In this appeal may lie seeds of revolution.

THE WISDOM OF WILDNESS

Charles A. Lindbergh

Perhaps the most curious symptom of the environmental agony of the modern world is the way we keep coming back to the notion of wilderness: coming back in the sense of returning to a subject and in the sense of historical tradition. In the U.S., at least, the preservation of wild lands (Yosemite, Yellowstone, the Adirondacks) was one of the earliest forms of social-ecological action, encouraged either by implication or exhortation in the writings of Henry Thoreau, George Catlin, William Cullen Bryant, Frederick Law Olmsted, and others.

Individual development follows a parallel course. Awareness of the interdependence of all life arrives first through the perception of wild animals and plants, nature study, or hunting. Afterwards, typically, this awareness grows to include man. The result is not the creation of a new moral analogy or metaphor—another form of false dichotomy—but a mature apprehension of a world whose inhabitants include man.

Sooner or later all environmental problems and questions are subsumed in a single question drummed in a deeper cadence—the meaning and place of wilderness in a technological society.

How persistently we have tried to leave behind the subject of "nature preservation," the protection of the primitive and nonhuman. How easy it is, in the face of food shortages among emergent nations and poisoned air in the cities, to deprecate this resurgent concern for, say, elephants and the culture of the men who hunt elephants. Like a mosquito in the dark or an insistent melody in the inner ear, this question—so distant from the concerns and occupations of the minions of power—haunts the horizon of our minds.

Until we understand its secret relationship to the whole of the human endeavor, the question of the natural will scratch and nibble in the basement of our consciousness. Could it be that there are no solutions until we make peace with wildness: wildlands as places, the wildness of most of the life on earth, and the wildness in ourselves?

The wild world is the human world. Having evolved in it for millions of centuries, we are not far removed by a clothing of civilization. It is packed into our genes.

In fact, the more power-driven, complex and delicate our civilization becomes, the more likelihood arises that a collapse will force us back to wildness. There is in wildness a natural wisdom that shapes all earth's experiments with life. Can we tap this wisdom without experiencing the agony of reverting to wildness? Can we combine it with intellectual developments of which we feel so proud, use it to redirect our modern trends before they lead to a worse breakdown than past civilizations have experienced? I believe we can, and that to do so we must learn from the primitive.

My own interest in wildness roots back to early boyhood and stories my father told me about Minnesota's frontier when he was my age. Woods were full of deer, he said, the sky often black with duck; every lake and river held its fish. Chippewa Indians built their tepees near his home. The frontier was a wonderful place for a boy to grow up. He wished I could have been there with him.

What changes a single generation brought! I saw no deer around our farm. Virgin forests had been cut. The Chippewa lived on reservations under government supervision. Even wild duck and fish were scarce. I envied my father his frontier days; but my generation had compensations—automobiles, airplanes, telephones, phonographs, thousands of scientific innovations. And still one could reach the wilderness by traveling farther west.

I learned to drive at the age of 11, to fly at 20. I made aviation my profession. Airplanes combined the elements I loved, bringing qualities of science and wilderness together without apparent conflict. Mathematics of engine and airfoil carried me over frontiers wilder and more inaccessible than my father had described. I came to know the world's geography as man had never known it before: great bends of my Mississippi Valley; sweeps of western plains; Appalachian, Rocky and Sierra ridges dividing a continent. Looking back in memory I see caribou on arctic tundra, ice fields around the northern pole, elephant herds plod African game trails, tapir scatter across Venezuelan *llanos*. Below me are New Guinea jungles, Himalayan peaks, equatorial Pacific islands set gemlike in their reefs—all pieced upon a mental sphere the progress of science has shaped within my mind.

Aviation developed so rapidly that for decades my main contact with wilderness consisted of looking down on it from cruising altitudes. I had relatively few hours to spend in isolated surface-of-the-earth environments. Metal monoplanes were needed to replaced trussed-wood and fabric craft. Engine powers had to be increased, cockpits enclosed, cabins enlarged and pressurized. Radio, automatic pilots, radar and inertial guidance, such items demanded attention in their turn. The effort required was tremendous; but increasing thousands of men and women took part, and payoffs came in safety, economy, range and speed.

My own lifetime spans the Wright Brothers' Kitty Hawk flight and manned-satellite orbiting, and scientific progress still rises exponentially. Supersonic transports will carry passengers at rifle-bullet speed. Spaceships are planned for traveling between earth, moon and nearby planets. The study of nucleonics places cosmic power in our hands, while cryobiology may suspend the human aging process. We dream of hurtling through galaxies as our ancestors dreamed of imitating birds. Obviously the development potential in all scientific fields is tremendous, extending far beyond our vision into time. I think the light of science is so dazzling that it can be evaluated only by studying its reflection from the absorbing mirror of life; and life brings one back to wildness.

Looking at the mirror of life first caused me to question our civilization's trends. During years spent flying civil air routes and on military missions, I watched changes of shade and texture on the great surface below my wings. Stumplands appeared where forests were. Lakes climbed mountainsides. Ditches gridded marshlands; dust hazed prairies; highways and power lines kept scarring ground from horizons to horizons. I watched crossroads become villages; villages, towns; towns turn into cities; suburbs spill over hills.

Wherever I landed I heard similar reports: populations were expanding, farms spreading, timber prices rising with new construction. Speedboats and four-wheel-drive vehicles carried hunters into areas previously difficult to reach, while aircraft brought every latitude and longitude within fortnight-vacation range. As a result, virgin wilderness vanished and wild animals dwindled in numbers.

Now the American eagle is verging on extinction. Even the polar bear on its ice floes has become easy game for flying sportsmen. A peninsula named Udjung Kulon holds the last two or three dozen Javan rhinoceroses. The last known herd of Arabian oryx has been machine-gunned by a sheik. Blue whales have nearly been harpooned out of their oceans. Pollution ruins bays and rivers. Refuse litters beaches. Dam projects threaten Colorado canyons, Hudson valleys, every place of natural beauty that can be a reservoir for power. Obviously the scientific progress so alluring to me is destroying qualities of greater worth.

Of course virgin wilderness had to retreat as civilization advanced. That was inevitable. But I did not consider its possible disappearance. The world seemed so large I had assumed that portions would remain in primitive state, attainable at reasonable cost in time and effort. Days spent in laboratories, factories and offices were lightened by intuitive contact with wilderness outside. Had the choice confronted me, I would not have traded nature's miracles of life for all of science's toys. Was not my earth's surface more important than increasing the speed of transport and visiting the moon and Mars?

If I were entering adulthood now instead of in the environment of 50 years ago, I would choose a career that kept me in contact with nature more than science. This is a choice an individual still can make—but no longer mankind in general. Too few natural areas remain. Both by intent and indifference we have insulated ourselves from the wilderness that produced us. Our emphasis of science has resulted in alarming rises in world populations that demand an ever-increasing emphasis of science to improve their standards and maintain their vigor.

I have been forced to the conclusion that an overemphasis of science weakens human character and upsets life's essential balance. Science breeds technology. Technology leads to infinite complication. Examples are everywhere: in the intricacy of government and in that of business corporations; in automation and labor relations; in war, diplomacy, taxation, legislation, in almost every field of modern man's routine. From the growth of cities to that of military power, from medical requirements to social-welfare benefits, when progress is plotted against time, exponential curves result with which we cannot long conform. But what action should scientific man prescribe as a result of the curves he plots? How is their direction to be changed without another breakdown and return to wildness? Suppose technologists conclude theoretically that they are destroying their own culture. Are they capable of taking effective action to prevent such destruction?

The failures of previous civilizations, and the crises existing for our own, show that man has not evolved the ability to cope with limitless complication. He has not discovered how to control his sciences' parabolas. Here I believe the human intellect can learn from primitive nature, for nature was conceived in cosmic power and thrives on infinite complication. No problem has been too difficult for it to solve. From the dynamics of an atom, nature produces the tranquillity of a flower, the joy of a porpoise, the intellect of man—the miracle of life.

In wildness I sense the miracle of life, and beside it our scientific accomplishments fade to trivia. The construction of an analogue computer or a supersonic airplane is simple when compared to the mixture of space and evolutionary eons represented by a cell. In primitive rather than in civilized surroundings I grow aware of man's evolving status, as though I were suddenly released from a hypnotic state. Life itself becomes the standard of all judgment. How could I have overlooked, even momentarily, such an obvious fact?

Walking in the day-long twilight of a high-branched Indonesian jungle, I see grotesquely twisting vines of python width tangle through multi-trunked trees that have diameters exceeding our largest redwoods. Small birds call constantly. Peacocks screech, and the heavy swish of hornbill wings overhead marks life in an unseen sky. Frequent areas of jungle floor, in their leaf shade, are clear of brush and plants. Stepping quietly over the soft loam, I watch families of wild pigs trotting, rooting about, and squealing in their quarrels. Monkeys swing overhead. A giant lizard staggers onto a log and gawks while deer bark and look at me curiously before retreating into cover. Lying on a sea edge in the evening, I watch flying foxes overhead—giant bats with wingspreads of a yard or more—dozens, sometimes hundreds at a time flapping slowly against the wind, flexing and bobbing in its gusts, sometimes dropping low enough to touch the water.

I feel transported from the modern to a Mesozoic era, freed from the blindness caused by our clocked environment of time. Ages turn to seconds as I voyage back and forth. Man becomes a recent advent among earth's contending forms, and civilization but a flash in evolutionary progress. Surrounded by wildness I become less aware of my individuality than of the life stream individuals manifest: that tenuous, immortal quality probing an unknown future and trailing, unbroken, beyond the vaguest past. Thus stripped of my culture's armor, I am an animal among various others, emerged to represent my species' progress, the momentary form and outlook of mankind.

Whether in Florida's Everglades, Tanzania's Serengeti, or Java's Udjung Kulon, I see animals about me as earthly experiments with life; and so I feel myself.

Each of us represents a life stream attempting to survive, to take advantage of every opportunity arising. The heron lengthens its legs to wade. The lion sharpens its teeth to kill. The rhinoceros thickens its skin for protection. Man develops his intellect to gain domination of the earth, and by comparison, the speed with which he has gained this domination is astounding—another of those exponential curves that mount like an explosion.

In civilization's sky-scraping cities I feel my superiority to lower animals confirmed by man's unchallenged rule. I view other creatures with a god's aloofness; for I have intellect, and they, no more than instinct. But surrounded by wildness, representing the human life stream with diverse competing life streams close at hand, I start doubting my superiority. I am struck by the physical perfection of other species in contrast to my own, amazed at the beauty, health and balance nature has achieved through instinct's influence. I ask myself what the intellect has done to warrant its prestige. As earth's most messy, destructive and defective animal, man's record gives him little cause for pride. Our present intellectual superiority is no guarantee of great wisdom or survival power in our genes. Anthropologists often warn that Homo sapiens may be only an overspecialized branch on the trunk of evolution.

Bow Valley, Banff National Park, Alberta. Photo from Canadian Pacific Railway.

For me, wildness brings out nature's basic wisdom in relationship to man's. I see the control of populations, the encouragement of coexistence, the superb juxtaposition of unity and diversity to form life's character. Above all I see an ability to choose the better from the worse that has made possible life's progress. In wildness, as in no other environment, elements of body, mind and spirit flux and fuse. Released from artificial influence, one's sensations change, and with them one's appraisals. The importance of accomplishment gives way to values of awareness. The smell of earth, the touch of leaves, sounds of animals calling, myriad qualities interweave to make one not only aware but aware of one's awareness. With stars above, a planet below, and no barrier between or after, intuition reaches out past limits of the mind into a mysticism at which man shies the name of "God." Then I think of listening to an African tribesman describe his people's culture: "We believe God is in everything," he said. "He is in the rivers, the grasses, the bark of trees, the clouds and mountains. We sing songs to the mountains because God is in them."

The primitive emphasizes factors of survival and the mysteries beyond them. Modern civilization places emphasis on increasing knowledge and the application of technology to man's way of life. The human future depends on our ability to combine the knowledge of science with the wisdom of wildness.

PART FOUR

THE

CRUNCH

PHOTOSYNTHESIS AND FISH
PRODUCTION IN THE SEA

John H. Ryther

During the 1970's, the world's nations, both separately and in concert, were expected to devote more attention to the social, technical, and economic aspects
of the uses of oceans. The political difficulties are formidable. Equally taxing is
the exercise of realism and restraint in an undertaking rapidly assuming the
tarnished image of space exploration. By this decade, although few were saying
so, it began to seem that the Americans had overreached themselves and over-
spent on the previous decade of promises to deliver the solar system. In fact, it
had become apparent that nothing could be delivered for a long time except
"glory." Expensive manned flights offered, in most cases, no greater scientific
returns than did unmanned flights.

No doubt outer and inner space are legitimate areas of human exploration.
There is a strong tendency, however, for such enterprises to be packaged by the
space industry–Congressional–news media brotherhood in the most gaudy wrap-
pings: riches for the man in the street, adventure for the young, diversion for
the hungry or bored, knowledge for the scientist, and evidence of further human
achievements for assorted intellectuals and politicians.

By 1970 newspapers were regularly reporting the imminent realization of
oceanographic science-fiction fantasies, from the construction of underwater
cities through mining gold on the sea bottom to feeding the world's millions
from sea farms. But the first millions involved would line the pockets of the
terrestrial entrepreneurs who provide the gadgetry necessary to usher in the new
ocean age. Profits from mining the sea would for some time be derived, like most
farm income and river navigation profits, from public subsidies appropriated by
Congress.

The very meaning of "the environment" as a concept involves a set of con-
tingencies. The physical conditions which are good for man are directly related
to his biological nature. What can be accomplished under exceptional circumstances, with highly trained experts using expensive and complex equipment,
should be clearly distinguished from utopian communities and grand-scale solutions to problems of man's physical and terrestrial limitations.

John H. Ryther, "Photosynthesis and Fish Production in the Sea," Science, 166 (October 3,
1969), 72–76. Copyright 1969 by the American Association for the Advancement of Science.

Numerous attempts have been made to estimate the production in the sea of fish and other organisms of existing or potential food value to man (*1–4*). These exercises, for the most part, are based on estimates of primary (photosynthetic) organic production rates in the ocean (*5*) and various assumed trophic-dynamic relationships between the photosynthetic producers and the organisms of interest to man. Included in the latter are the number of steps or links in the food chains and the efficiency of conversion of organic matter from each trophic level or link in the food chain to the next. Different estimates result from different choices in the number of trophic levels and in the efficiencies, as illustrated in Table 1 (*2*).

Implicit in the above approach is the concept of the ocean as a single ecosystem in which the same food chains involving the same number of links and efficiencies apply throughout. However, the rate of primary production is known to be highly variable, differing by at least two full orders of magnitude from the richest to the most impoverished regions. This in itself would be expected to result in a highly irregular pattern of food production. In addition, the ecological conditions which determine the trophic dynamics of marine food chains also vary widely and in direct relationship to the absolute level of primary organic production. As is shown below, the two sets of variables—primary production and the associated food chain dynamics—may act additively to produce differences in fish production which are far more pronounced and dramatic than the observed variability of the individual causative factors.

Table 1
Estimates of potential yields (per year) at various trophic levels, in metric tons
[After Schaeffer (*2*)]

| Trophic level | Ecological efficiency factor | | | | | |
| | 10 percent | | 15 percent | | 20 percent | |
	Carbon (tons)	Total weight (tons)	Carbon (tons)	Total weight (tons)	Carbon (tons)	Total weight (tons)
0. Phytoplankton (net particulate production)	1.9×10^{10}		1.9×10^{10}		1.9×10^{10}	
1. Herbivores	1.9×10^{9}	1.9×10^{10}	2.8×10^{9}	2.8×10^{10}	3.8×10^{9}	3.8×10^{10}
2. 1st stage carnivores	1.9×10^{8}	1.9×10^{9}	4.2×10^{8}	4.2×10^{9}	7.6×10^{8}	7.6×10^{9}
3. 2nd stage carnivores	1.9×10^{7}	1.9×10^{8}	6.4×10^{7}	6.4×10^{8}	15.2×10^{7}	15.2×10^{8}
4. 3rd stage carnivores	1.9×10^{6}	1.9×10^{7}	9.6×10^{6}	9.6×10^{7}	30.4×10^{6}	30.4×10^{7}

Primary Productivity

Our knowledge of the primary organic productivity of the ocean began with the development of the C^{14}-tracer technique for *in situ* measurement of photosynthesis by marine plankton algae (6) and the application of the method on the 1950–52 *Galathea* expedition around the world (5). Despite obvious deficiencies in the coverage of the ocean by *Galathea* (the expedition made 194 observations, or an average of about one every 2 million square kilometers, most of which were made in the tropics or semitropics), our concept of the total productivity of the world ocean has changed little in the intervening years.

While there have been no more expeditions comparable to the *Galathea*, there have been numerous local or regional studies of productivity in many parts of the world. Most of these have been brought together by a group of Soviet scientists to provide up-to-date world coverage consisting of over 7000 productivity observations (7). The result has been modification of the estimate of primary production in the world ocean from 1.2 to 1.5 $\times$ 10^{10} tons of carbon fixed per year (5) to a new figure, 1.5 to 1.8 $\times$ 10^{10} tons.

Attempts have also been made by Steemann Nielsen and Jensen (5), Ryther (8), and Koblentz-Mishke *et al*. (7) to assign specific levels or ranges of productivity to different parts of the ocean. Although the approach was somewhat different in each case, in general the agreement between the three was good and, with appropriate condensation and combination, permit the following conclusions.

1) Annual primary production in the open sea varies, for the most part, between 25 and 75 grams of carbon fixed per square meter and averages about 50 grams of carbon per square meter per year. This is true for roughly 90 percent of the ocean, an area of 326×10^6 square kilometers.

2) Higher levels of primary production occur in shallow coastal waters, defined here as the area within the 100-fathom (180-meter) depth contour. The mean value for this region may be considered to be 100 grams of carbon fixed per square meter per year, and the area, according to Menard and Smith (9), is 7.5 percent of the total world ocean. In addition, certain offshore waters are influenced by divergences, fronts, and other hydrographic features which bring nutrient-rich subsurface water into the euphotic zone. The equatorial divergences are examples of such regions. The productivity of these offshore areas is comparable to that of the coastal zone. Their total area is difficult to assess, but is considered here to be 2.5 percent of the total ocean. Thus, the coastal zone and the offshore regions of comparably high productivity together represent 10 percent of the total area of the oceans, or 36×10^6 square kilometers.

3) In a few restricted areas of the world, particularly along the west coasts of continents at subtropical latitudes where there are prevailing offshore winds and strong eastern boundary currents, surface waters are diverted offshore and are replaced by nutrient-rich deeper water. Such areas of coastal upwelling are biologically the richest parts of the ocean. They exist off Peru, California, northwest and southwest Africa, Somalia, and the Arabian coast, and in other more

Table 2
Division of the ocean into provinces according to their
level of primary organic production

Province	Percentage of ocean	Area (km²)	Mean productivity (grams of carbon/m²/yr)	Total productivity (10⁹ tons of carbon/yr)
Open ocean	90.0	326 $\times 10^6$	50	16.3
Coastal zone*	9.9	36 $\times 10^6$	100	3.6
Upwelling areas	0.1	3.6 $\times 10^5$	300	0.1
Total				20.0

*Includes offshore areas of high productivity.

localized situations. Extensive coastal upwelling also is known to occur in various places around the continent of Antarctica, although its exact location and extent have not been well documented. During periods of active upwelling, primary production normally exceeds 1.0 and may exceed 10.0 grams of carbon per square meter per day. Some of the high values which have been reported from these locations are 3.9 grams for the southwest coast of Africa (5), 6.4 for the Arabian Sea (10), and 11.2 off Peru (11). However, the upwelling of subsurface water does not persist throughout the year in many of these places—for example, in the Arabian Sea, where the process is seasonal and related to the monsoon winds. In the Antarctic, high production is limited by solar radiation during half the year. For all these areas of coastal upwelling throughout the year, it is probably safe, if somewhat conservative, to assign an annual value of 300 grams of carbon per square meter. Their total area in the world is again difficult to assess. On the assumption that their total cumulative area is no greater than 10 times the well-documented upwelling area off Peru, this would amount to some 3.6 $\times 10^5$ square kilometers, or 0.1 percent of the world ocean. These conclusions are summarized in Table 2.

Food Chains

Let us next examine the three provinces of the ocean which have been designated according to their differing levels of primary productivity from the standpoint of other possible major differences. These will include, in particular, differences which relate to the food chains and to trophic efficiencies involved in the transfer of organic matter from the photosynthetic organisms to fish and invertebrate species large and abundant enough to be of importance to man.

The first factor to be considered in this context is the size of the photosynthetic or producer organisms. It is generally agreed that, as one moves from coastal to offshore oceanic waters, the character of these organisms changes from large

*Hauling in a basket of fish off the coast of Kerala,
India. Photo from the United Nations.*

"microplankton" (100 microns or more in diameter) to the much smaller "nannoplankton" cells 5 to 25 microns in their largest dimensions (*12, 13*).

Since the size of an organism is an essential criterion of its potential usefulness
to man, we have the following relationship: the larger the plant cells at the begin-

ning of the food chain, the fewer the trophic levels that are required to convert the organic matter to a useful form. The oceanic nannoplankton cannot be effectively filtered from the water by most of the common zooplankton crustacea. For example, the euphausid *Euphausia pacifica*, which may function as a herbivore in the rich subarctic coastal waters of the Pacific, must turn to a carnivorous habit in the offshore waters where the phytoplankton become too small to be captured (*13*).

Intermediate between the nannoplankton and the carnivorous zooplankton are a group of herbivores, the microzooplankton, whose ecological significance is a subject of considerable current interest (*14, 15*). Representatives of this group include protozoans such as Radiolaria, Foraminifera, and Tintinnidae, and larval nauplii of microcrustaceans. These organisms, which may occur in concentrations of tens of thousands per cubic meter, are the primary herbivores of the open sea.

Feeding upon these tiny animals is a great host of carnivorous zooplankton, many of which have long been thought of as herbivores. Only by careful study of the mouthparts and feeding habits were Anraku and Omori (*16*) able to show that many common copepods are facultative if not obligate carnivores. Some of these predatory copepods may be no more than a millimeter or two in length.

Again, it is in the offshore environment that these small carnivorous zooplankton predominate. Grice and Hart (*17*) showed that the percentage of carnivorous species in the zooplankton increased from 16 to 39 percent in a transect from the coastal waters of the northeastern United States to the Sargasso Sea. Of very considerable importance in this group are the Chaetognatha. In terms of biomass, this group of animals, predominantly carnivorous, represents, on the average, 30 percent of the weight of copepods in the open sea (*17*). With such a distribution, it is clear that virtually all the copepods, many of which are themselves carnivores, must be preyed upon by chaetognaths.

The oceanic food chain thus far described involves three to four trophic levels from the photosynthetic nannoplankton to animals no more than 1 to 2 centimeters long. How many additional steps may be required to produce organisms of conceivable use to man is difficult to say, largely because there are so few known oceanic species large enough and (through schooling habits) abundant enough to fit this category. Familiar species such as the tunas, dolphins, and squid are all top carnivores which feed on fishes or invertebrates at least one, and probably two, trophic levels beyond such zooplankton as the chaetognaths. A food chain consisting of five trophic levels between photosynthetic organisms and man would therefore seem reasonable for the oceanic province.

As for the coastal zone, it has already been pointed out that the phytoplankton are quite commonly large enough to be filtered and consumed directly by the common crustacean zooplankton such as copepods and euphausids. However, the presence, in coastal waters, of protozoans and other microzooplankton in larger numbers and of greater biomass than those found in offshore waters (*15*) attests to the fact that much of the primary production here, too, passes through several steps of a microscopic food chain before reaching the macrozooplankton.

The larger animals of the coastal province (that is, those directly useful to man) are certainly the most diverse with respect to feeding type. Some (mollusks and some fishes) are herbivores. Many others, including most of the pelagic clupeoid fishes, feed on zooplankton. Another large group, the demersal fishes, feed on bottom fauna which may be anywhere from one to several steps removed from the phytoplankton.

If the herbivorous clupeoid fishes are excluded (since these occur predominantly in the upwelling provinces and are therefore considered separately), it is probably safe to assume that the average food organism from coastal waters represents the end of at least a three-step food chain between phytoplankton and man.

It is in the upwelling areas of the world that food chains are the shortest, or—to put it another way—that the organisms are large enough to be directly utilizable by man from trophic levels very near the primary producers. This, again, is due to the large size of the phytoplankton, but it is due also to the fact that many of these species are colonial in habit, forming large gelatinous masses or long filaments. The eight most abundant species of phytoplankton in the upwelling region off Peru, in the spring of 1966, were *Chaetoceros socialis, C. debilis, C. lorenzianus, Skeletonema costatum, Nitzschia seriata, N. delicatissima, Schroederella delicatula,* and *Asterionella japonica (11, 18)*. The first in this list, *C. socialis*, forms large gelatinous masses. The others all form long filamentous chains. *Thalossiosira subtilis*, another gelatinous colonial form like *Chaetoceros socialis*, occurs commonly off southwest Africa (*19*) and close to shore off the Azores (*20*). Hart (*21*) makes special mention of the colonial habit of all the most abundant species of phytoplankton in the Antarctic—*Fragiloriopsis antarctica, Encampia balaustrium, Rhizosalenia alata, R. antarctica, R. chunii, Thallosiothrix antarctica,* and *Phaeocystis brucei*.

Many of the above-mentioned species of phytoplankton form colonies several millimeters and, in some cases, several centimeters in diameter. Such aggregates of plant material can be readily eaten by large fishes without special feeding adaptation. In addition, however, many of the clupeoid fishes (sardines, anchovies, pilchards, menhaden, and so on) that are found most abundantly in upwelling areas and that make up the largest single component of the world's commercial fish landings, do have specially modified gill rakers for removing the larger species of phytoplankton from the water.

There seems little doubt that many of the fishes indigenous to upwelling regions are direct herbivores for at least most of their lives. There is some evidence that juveniles of the Peruvian anchovy (*Engraulis ringens*) may feed on zooplankton, but the adult is predominantly if not exclusively a herbivore (*22*). Small gobies (*Gobius bibarbatus*) found at mid-water in the coastal waters off southwest Africa had their stomachs filled with a large, chainforming diatom of the genus *Fragilaria* (*23*). There is considerable interest at present in the possible commercial utilization of the large Antarctic krill, *Euphausia superba*, which feeds primarily on the colonial diatom *Fragilariopsis antarctica* (*24*).

In some of the upwelling regions of the world, such as the Arabian Sea, the species of fish are not well known, so it is not surprising that knowledge of their feeding habits and food chains is fragmentary. From what is known, however, the evidence would appear to be overwhelming that a one- or two-step food chain between phytoplankton and man is the rule. As a working compromise, let us assign the upwelling province a 1½-step food chain.

Efficiency

The growth (that is, the net organic production) of an organism is a function of the food assimilated less metabolic losses or respiration. This efficiency of growth or food utilization (the ratio of growth to assimilation) has been found, by a large number of investigators and with a great variety of organisms, to be about 30 percent in young, actively growing animals. The efficiency decreases as animals approach their full growth, and reaches zero in fully mature or senescent individuals (25). Thus a figure of 30 percent can be considered a biological potential which may be approached in nature, although the growth efficiency of a population of animals of mixed ages under steady-state conditions must be lower.

Since there must obviously be a "maintenance ration" which is just sufficient to accommodate an organism's basal metabolic requirement (26), it must also be true that growth efficiency is a function of the absolute rate of assimilation. The effects of this factor will be most pronounced at low feeding rates, near the "maintenance ration," and will tend to become negligible at high feeding rates. Food conversion (that is, growth efficiency) will therefore obviously be related to food availability, or to the concentration of prey organisms when the latter are sparsely distributed.

In addition, the more available the food and the greater the quantity consumed, the greater the amount of "internal work" the animal must perform to digest, assimilate, convert, and store the food. Conversely, the less available the food, the greater the amount of "external work" the animal must perform to hunt, locate, and capture its prey. These concepts are discussed in some detail by Ivlev (27) and reviewed by Ricker (28). The two metabolic costs thus work in opposite ways with respect to food availability, tending thereby toward a constant total effect. However, when food availability is low, the added costs of basal metabolism and external work relative to assimilation may have a pronounced effect on growth efficiency.

When one turns from consideration of the individual and its physiological growth efficiency to the "ecological efficiency" of food conversion from one trophic level to the next (2, 29), there are additional losses to be taken into account. Any of the food consumed but not assimilated would be included here, though it is possible that undigested organic matter may be reassimilated by members of the same trophic level (2). Any other nonassimilatory losses, such as losses due to natural death, sedimentation, and emigration, will, if not otherwise accounted for, appear as a loss in trophic efficiency. In addition, when one considers a specific or selected part of a trophic level, such as a population of fish of use to man, the consumption of food by any other hidden member of the same trophic level will appear as a loss in efficiency. For example, the role of such animals as salps, medusae, and ctenophores in marine food chains is not well understood and is seldom even considered. Yet these animals may occur sporadically or periodically in swarms so dense that they dominate the plankton completely. Whether they represent a dead end or side branch in the normal food chain of the sea is not known, but their effect can hardly be negligible when they occur in abundance.

Finally, a further loss which may occur at any trophic level but is, again, of unknown or unpredictable magnitude is that of dissolved organic matter lost through excretion or other physiological processes by plants and animals. This has received particular attention at the level of primary production, some investigators concluding that 50 percent or more of the photoassimilated carbon may be released by phytoplankton into the water as dissolved compounds (*30*). There appears to be general agreement that the loss of dissolved organic matter is indirectly proportional to the absolute rate of organic production and is therefore most serious in the oligotrophic regions of the open sea (*11, 31*).

All of the various factors discussed above will affect the efficiency or apparent efficiency of the transfer of organic matter between trophic levels. Since they cannot, in most cases, be quantitatively estimated individually, their total effect cannot be assessed. It is known only that the maximum potential growth efficiency is about 30 percent and that at least some of the factors which reduce this further are more pronounced in oligotrophic, low-productivity waters than in highly productive situations. Slobodkin (*29*) concludes that an ecological efficiency of about 10 percent is possible, and Schaeffer feels that the figure may be as high as 20 percent. Here, therefore, I assign efficiencies of 10, 15, and 20 percent, respectively, to the oceanic, the coastal, and the upwelling provinces, though it is quite possible that the actual values are considerably lower.

Conclusions and Discussion

With values assigned to the three marine provinces for primary productivity (Table 2), number of trophic levels, and efficiencies, it is now possible to calculate fish production in the three regions. The results are summarized in Table 3.

These calculations reveal several interesting features. The open sea—90 percent of the ocean and nearly three-fourths of the earth's surface—is essentially a biological desert. It produces a negligible fraction of the world's fish catch at present and has little or no potential for yielding more in the future.

Upwelling regions, totaling no more than about one-tenth of 1 percent of the ocean surface (an area roughly the size of California) produce about half the

Table 3
Estimated fish production in the three ocean provinces
defined in Table 2

Province	Primary production [tons (organic carbon)]	Trophic levels	Efficiency (%)	Fish production [tons (fresh wt.)]
Oceanic	16.3×10^9	5	10	16×10^5
Coastal	3.6×10^9	3	15	12×10^7
Upwelling	0.1×10^9	1½	20	12×10^7
Total				24×10^7

world's fish supply. The other half is produced in coastal waters and the few off-shore regions of comparably high fertility.

One of the major uncertainties and possible sources of error in the calculation is the estimation of the areas of high, intermediate, and low productivity. This is particularly true of the upwelling area off the continent of Antarctica, an area which has never been well described or defined.

A figure of 360,000 square kilometers has been used for the total area of upwelling regions in the world (Table 2). If the upwelling regions off California, northwest and southwest Africa, and the Arabian Sea are of roughly the same area as that off the coast of Peru, these semitropical regions would total some 200,000 square kilometers. The remaining 160,000 square kilometers would represent about one-fourth the circumference of Antarctica seaward for a distance of 30 kilometers. This seems a not unreasonable inference. Certainly, the entire ocean south of the Antarctic Convergence is not highly productive, contrary to the estimates of El-Sayed (*32*). Extensive observations in this region by Saijo and Kawashima (*33*) yielded primary productivity values of 0.01 to 0.15 gram of carbon per square meter per day—a value no higher than the values used here for the open sea. Presumably, the discrepancy is the result of highly irregular, discontinuous, or "patchy" distribution of biological activity. In other words, the occurrence of extremely high productivity associated with upwelling conditions appears to be confined, in the Antarctic, as elsewhere, to restricted areas close to shore.

An area of 160,000 square kilometers of upwelling conditions with an annual productivity of 300 grams of carbon per square meter would result in the production of about 50×10^6 tons of "fish," if we follow the ground rules established above in making the estimate. Presumably these "fish" would consist for the most part of the Antarctic krill, which feeds directly upon phytoplankton, as noted above, and which is known to be extremely abundant in Antarctic waters. There have been numerous attempts to estimate the annual production of krill in the Antarctic, from the known number of whales at their peak of abundance and from various assumptions concerning their daily ration of krill. The evidence upon which such estimates are based is so tenuous that they are hardly worth discussing. It is interesting to note, however, that the more conservative of these estimates are rather close to figures derived independently by the method discussed here. For example, Moiseev (*34*) calculated krill production for 1967 to be 60.5×10^6 tons, while Kasahara (*3*) considered a range of 24 to 36×10^6 tons to be a minimal figure. I consider the figure 50×10^6 tons to be on the high side, as the estimated area of upwelling is probably generous, the average productivity value of 300 grams of carbon per square meter per year is high for a region where photosynthesis can occur during only half the year, and much of the primary production is probably diverted into smaller crustacean herbivores (*35*). Clearly the Antarctic must receive much more intensive study before its productive capacity can be assessed with any accuracy.

In all, I estimate that some 240 million tons (fresh weight) of fish are produced annually in the sea. As this figure is rough and subject to numerous sources of error, it should not be considered significantly different from Schaeffer's (*2*) figure of 200 million tons.

Production, however, is not equivalent to potential harvest. In the first place, man must share the production with other top-level carnivores. It has been estimated, for example, that guano birds alone eat some 4 million tons of anchovies annually off the coast of Peru, while tunas, squid, sea lions, and other predators probably consume an equivalent amount (*22, 36*). This is nearly equal to the amount taken by man from this one highly productive fishery. In addition, man must take care to leave a large enough fraction of the annual production of fish to permit utilization of the resource at something close to its maximum sustainable yield, both to protect the fishery and to provide a sound economic basis for the industry.

When these various factors are taken into consideration, it seems unlikely that the potential sustained yield of fish to man is appreciably greater than 100 million tons. The total world fish landings for 1967 were just over 60 million tons (*37*), and this figure has been increasing at an average rate of about 8 percent per year for the past 25 years. It is clear that, while the yield can be still further increased, the resource is not vast. At the present rate, the industry can continue to expand for no more than a decade.

Most of the existing fisheries of the world are probably incapable of contributing significantly to this expansion. Many are already overexploited, and most of the rest are utilized at or near their maximum sustainable yield. Evidence of fishing pressure is usually determined directly from fishery statistics, but it is of some interest, in connection with the present discussion, to compare landings with fish production as estimated by the methods developed in this article. I will make this comparison for two quite dissimilar fisheries, that of the continental shelf of the northwest Atlantic and that of the Peruvian coastal region.

According to Edwards (*38*), the continental shelf between Hudson Canyon and the southern end of the Nova Scotian shelf includes an area of 110,000 square miles (2.9×10^{11} square meters). From the information in Tables 2 and 3, it may be calculated that approximately 1 million tons of fish are produced annually in this region. Commerical landings from the same area were slightly in excess of 1 million tons per year for the 3-year period 1963 to 1965 before going into a decline. The decline has become more serious each year, until it is now proposed to regulate the landings of at least the more valuable species such as cod and haddock, now clearly overexploited.

The coastal upwelling associated with the Peru Coastal Current gives rise to the world's most productive fishery, an annual harvest of some 10^7 metric tons of anchovies. The maximum sustainable yield is estimated at, or slightly below, this figure (*39*), and the fishery is carefully regulated. As mentioned above, mortality from other causes (such as predation from guano birds, bonito, squid, and so on) probably accounts for an additional 10^7 tons. This prodigious fishery is concentrated in an area no larger than about 800×30 miles (*36*), or 6×10^{10} square meters. By the methods developed in this article, it is estimated that such an upwelling area can be expected to produce 2×10^7 tons of fish, almost precisely the commercial yield as now regulated plus the amount attributed to natural mortality.

These are but two of the many recognized examples of well-developed commercial fisheries now being utilized at or above their levels of maximum sustainable yield. Any appreciable continued increase in the world's fish landings must clearly come from unexploited species and, for the most part, from undeveloped new fishing areas. Much of the potential expansion must consist of new products from remote regions, such as the Antarctic krill, for which no harvesting technology and no market yet exist.

REFERENCES

1. H. W. Graham and R. L. Edwards, in *Fish and Nutrition* (London: Fishing News, 1962), pp. 3–8; W. K. Schmitt, *Ann. N.Y. Acad. Sci.*, 118, 645 (1965).
2. M. B. Schaeffer, *Trans. Amer. Fish. Soc.*, 94, 123 (1965).
3. H. Kasahara, in *Proceedings, 7th International Congress of Nutrition, Hamburg* (New York: Pergamon Press, 1966), vol. 4, p. 958.
4. W. M. Chapman, "Potential Resources of the Ocean" (Serial Publication 89–21, 89th Congress, first session, 1965)(Washington, D.C.: U.S. Government Printing Office, 1965), pp. 132–156.
5. E. Steemann Nielsen and E. A. Jensen, *Galathea Report*, ed. F. Bruun *et al.* (London: Allen & Unwin, 1957), vol. 1, p. 49.
6. E. Steemann Nielsen, *J. Cons. Cons. Perma. Int. Explor. Mer*, 18, 117 (1952).
7. O. I. Koblentz-Mishke, V. V. Volkovinsky, J. G. Kobanova, in *Scientific Exploration of the South Pacific*, ed. W. Wooster (Washington, D.C.: National Academy of Sciences, in press).
8. J. H. Ryther, in *The Sea*, ed. M. N. Hill (London: Interscience, 1963), pp. 347–380.
9. H. W. Menard and S. M. Smith, *J. Geophys. Res.*, 71, 4305 (1966).
10. J. H. Ryther and D. W. Menzel, *Deep-Sea Res.*, 12, 199 (1965).
11. J. H. Ryther, E. M. Hulburt, C. J. Lorenzen, and N. Corwin, "The Production and Utilization of Organic Matter in the Peru Coastal Current" (College Station: Texas A & M University Press, in press).

12. C. D. McAllister, T. R. Parsons, and J. D. H. Strickland, *J. Cons. Cons. Perma. Int. Explor. Mer*, 25, 240 (1960); G. C. Anderson, *Limnol. Oceanogr.*, 10, 477 (1965).
13. T. R. Parsons and R. J. Le Brasseur, in "Symposium Marine Food Chains, Aarhus (1968)."
14. E. Steemann Nielsen, *J. Cons. Cons. Perma. Int. Explor. Mer*, 23, 178 (1958).
15. J. R. Beers and G. L. Stewart, *J. Fish. Res. Board Can.*, 24, 2053 (1967).
16. M. Anraku and M. Omori, *Limnol. Oceanogr.*, 8, 116 (1963).
17. G. D. Grice and H. D. Hart, *Ecol. Monogr.*, 32, 287 (1962).
18. M. R. Reeve, in "Symposium Marine Food Chains, Aarhus (1968)."
19. Personal observation; T. J. Hart and R. I. Currie, *Discovery Rep.*, 31, 123 (1960).
20. Gaarder, K. R., *Report on the Scientific Results of the "Michael Sars" North Atlantic Deep-Sea Expedition 1910*. (Bergen: University of Bergen).
21. T. J. Hart, *Discovery Rep.*, 21, 261 (1942).
22. R. J. E. Sanchez, in *Proceedings of the 18th Annual Session, Gulf and Caribbean Fisheries Institute, University of Miami Institute of Marine Science, 1966*, ed. J. B. Higman (Coral Gables, Fla.: University of Miami Press, 1966), pp. 84–93.
23. R. T. Barber and R. L. Haedrich, *Deep-Sea Res.*, 16, 415 (1952).
24. J. W. S. Marr, *Discovery Rep.*, 32, 34 (1962).
25. S. D. Gerking, *Physiol. Zool.*, 25, 358 (1952).
26. B. J. Dawes, *Mar. Biol. Ass. U.K.*, 17, 102 (1930–31); *ibid.*, p. 877.
27. V. S. Ivlev, *Zool. Zh.*, 18, 303 (1939).
28. W. E. Ricker, *Ecology*, 16, 373 (1946).
29. L. B. Slobodkin, *Growth and Regulation of Animal Populations* (New York: Holt, Rinehart & Winston, 1961), chap. 12.
30. G. E. Fogg, C. Nalewajko, and W. D. Watt, *Proc. Roy. Soc. Ser B Biol. Sci.*, 162, 517 (1965).
31. G. E. Fogg and W. D. Watt, *Mem. Inst. Ital. Idrobiol. Dott. Marco de Marshi Pallanza Italy*, 18, suppl. 165 (1965).
32. S. Z. El-Sayed, in *Biology of the Antarctic Seas III*, ed. G. Llano and W. Schmitt (Washington: American Geophysical Union, 1968), pp. 15–47.
33. Y. Saijo and T. Kawashima, *J. Oceanogr. Soc. Japan*, 19, 190 (1964).
34. P. A. Moiseev, Paper presented at the 2nd Symposium on Antarctic Ecology, Cambridge, England, 1968.
35. T. L. Hopkins, unpublished manuscript.
36. W. S. Wooster and J. L. Reid, Jr, in *The Sea*, ed. M. N. Hill. (London: Interscience, 1963), vol. 2, p. 253.
37. *FAO Yearb. Fish. Statistics*, 25 (1967).
38. R. L. Edwards, *Univ. Wash. Publ. Fish.*, 4, 52 (1968).
39. R. J. E. Sanchez, in *Proceedings, 18th Annual Session, Gulf and Caribbean Fisheries Institute, University of Miami Institute of Marine Science*. (Coral Gables, Fla.: University of Miami Press, 1966), p. 84.
40. The work discussed here was supported by the Atomic Energy Commission, contract No. AT(30–1)–3862, Ref. No. NYO–3862–20. This article is contribution No. 2327 from the Woods Hole Oceanographic Institution.

POPULATION AND PANACEAS
A TECHNOLOGICAL PERSPECTIVE

Paul R. Ehrlich and John P. Holdren

*When we were editing our earlier book (*The Subversive Science: Essays Toward an Ecology of Man. *Boston: Houghton Mifflin Company, 1969) it still seemed important to bring before the reader the most ecologically educated arguments on the impending collision of population and resources. While we ourselves were convinced that crisis was inevitable, that past food shortages only foreshadowed worldwide but locally acute and increasingly frequent famine in the future, the subject was still being treated as controversial in public discussion.*

By 1971, however, the situation had completely changed. Only the most rigid minds were holding doggedly to the illusion that productivity could indefinitely sustain an overnumerous human population. In spite of the occasions when distribution *seemed a more urgent problem; when industrial agriculture seemed to be bringing off a miracle, and when population limitation was used to mask class conflict, national aggrandizement, or genocide, it was apparent that a majority of thoughtful people had finally accepted the population dilemma as real.*

This meant that dialogue could move on to the means of implementing family limitation, communicating information about it to the developing nations, and acknowledging the moral and ethical choices that lie ahead. It meant, too, that a realistic exploration of the technical aspects of food and water production could move into a new, less frenetic, and more realistic phase. A panic scramble to support an additional 70 million people a year could inflict greater potential damage on the planet than that already sustained over 5000 years of (largely bad) agriculture and mining. Thus, to maintain an ecologically healthy earth for the innumerable future generations it may be necessary to moderate emergency programs in the years immediately ahead.

Either the human species a half-dozen generations from now will have bred itself out of existence or it will be living in a reclaimed world. Perhaps for centuries its main task will be restitution of natural processes and cycles. It will be the ultimate post-adversity 'generation' because the planet and most of its species will have taken a terrible beating from the human wave now already rolling. To those "post-future" generations we owe something. Theirs will be a retread earth. Their lives

Paul R. Ehrlich and John P. Holdren, "Population and Panaceas: A Technological Perspective," BioScience, 19 (December, 1969), 1065–1071.

will be shaped not merely by taking a limited and sustainable yield from the earth's life systems but also by rebuilding those systems. Where we live on maximum interest plus increments of capital from a diminishing biosphere, they will take a reduced share of energy in order to detoxify the oceans and air, reestablish forests and grasslands, and rebuild the soil and a livable world.

Today more than one billion human beings are either undernourished or malnourished, and the human population is growing at a rate of 2% per year. The existing and impending crises in human nutrition and living conditions are well-documented but not widely understood. In particular, there is a tendency among the public, nurtured on Sunday-supplement conceptions of technology, to believe that science has the situation well in hand—that farming the sea and the tropics, irrigating the deserts, and generating cheap nuclear power in abundance hold the key to swift and certain solution of the problem. To espouse this belief is to misjudge the present severity of the situation, the disparate time scales on which technological progress and population growth operate, and the vast complexity of the problems beyond mere food production posed by population pressures. Unfortunately, scientists and engineers have themselves often added to the confusion by failing to distinguish between that which is merely theoretically feasible, and that which is economically and logistically practical.

As we will show here, man's present technology is inadequate to the task of maintaining the world's burgeoning billions, even under the most optimistic assumptions. Furthermore, technology is likely to remain inadequate until such time as the population growth rate is drastically reduced. This is not to assert that present efforts to "revolutionize" tropical agriculture, increase yields of fisheries, desalt water for irrigation, exploit new power sources, and implement related projects are not worthwhile. They may be. They could also easily produce the ultimate disaster for mankind if they are not applied with careful attention to their effects on the ecological systems necessary for our survival (Woodwell, 1967; Cole, 1968). And even if such projects are initiated with unprecedented levels of staffing and expenditures, without population control they are doomed to fall far short. No effort to expand the carrying capacity of the Earth can keep pace with unbridled population growth.

To support these contentions, we summarize briefly the present lopsided balance sheet in the population/food accounting. We then examine the logistics, economics, and possible consequences of some technological schemes which have been proposed to help restore the balance, or, more ambitiously, to permit the maintenance of human populations much larger than today's. The most pertinent aspects of the balance are:

1. The world population reached 3.5 billion in mid-1968, with an annual increment of approximately 70 million people (itself increasing) and a doubling time on the order of 35 years (Population Reference Bureau, 1968).

2. Of this number of people, at least one-half billion are undernourished (deficient in calories or, more succinctly, slowly starving), and approximately an additional billion are malnourished (deficient in particular nutrients, mostly protein) (Borgstrom, 1965; Sukhatme, 1966). Estimates of the number actually perishing annually from starvation begin at 4 million and go up (Ehrlich, 1968) and depend in part on official definitions of starvation which

Hungry man in East Pakistan. Photo by E. Ragazzini, from FAO, United Nations.

conceal the true magnitude of hunger's contribution to the death rate (Lelyveld, 1968).

3. Merely to maintain present inadequate nutrition levels, the food requirements of Asia, Africa, and Latin America will, conservatively, increase by 26% in the 10-year period measured from 1965 to 1975 (Paddock and Paddock, 1967). World food production must double in the period 1965–2000 to stay even; it must triple if nutrition is to be brought up to minimum requirements.

Food Production

That there is insufficient additional, good quality agricultural land available in the world to meet these needs is so well documented (Borgstrom, 1965) that we will not belabor the point here. What hope there is must rest with increasing yields on land presently cultivated, bringing marginal land into production, more efficiently exploiting the sea, and bringing less conventional methods of food production to fruition. In all these areas, science and technology play a dominant role. While space does not permit even a cursory look at all the proposals on these topics which have been advanced in recent years, a few representative examples illustrate our points.

Conventional Agriculture

Probably the most widely recommended means of increasing agricultural yields is through the more intensive use of fertilizers. Their production is straightforward, and a good deal is known about their effective application, although, as with many technologies we consider here, the environmental consequences of heavy fertilizer use are ill understood and potentially dangerous [1](Wadleigh, 1968). But even ignoring such problems, we find staggering difficulties barring the implementation of fertilizer technology on the scale required. In this regard the accomplishments of countries such as Japan and the Netherlands are often cited as offering hope to the underdeveloped world. Some perspective on this point is afforded by noting that if India were to apply fertilizer at the per capita level employed by the Netherlands, her fertilizer needs would be nearly half the present world output (United Nations, 1968).

On a more realistic plane, we note that although the goal for nitrogen fertilizer production in 1971 under India's fourth 5-year plan is 2.4 million metric tons (Anonymous, 1968a). Raymond Ewell (who has served as fertilizer production adviser to the Indian government for the past 12 years) suggests that less than 1.1 million metric tons is a more probable figure for that date.[2] Ewell cites poor

[1] Barry Commoner, address to 135th Meeting of the AAAS. Dallas, Texas (28 December 1968).

[2] Raymond Ewell, private communication (1 December 1968).

plant maintenance, raw materials shortages, and power and transportation break-downs as contributing to continued low production by existing Indian plants. Moreover, even when fertilizer is available, increases in productivity do not necessarily follow. In parts of the underdeveloped world lack of farm credit is limiting fertilizer distribution; elsewhere, internal transportation systems are inadequate to the task. Nor can the problem of educating farmers on the advantages and techniques of fertilizer use be ignored. A recent study (Parikh *et al.*, 1968) of the Intensive Agriculture District Program in the Surat district of Gujarat, India (in which scientific fertilizer use was to have been a major ingredient) notes that "on the whole, the performance of adjoining districts which have similar climate but did not enjoy relative preference of input supply was as good as, if not better than, the programme district. . . . A particularly disheartening feature is that the farm production plans, as yet, do not carry any educative value and have largely failed to convince farmers to use improved practices in their proper combinations."

As a second example of a panacea in the realm of conventional agriculture, mention must be given to the development of new high-yield or high-protein strains of food crops. That such strains have the potential of making a major contribution to the food supply of the world is beyond doubt, but this potential is limited in contrast to the potential for population growth, and will be realized too slowly to have anything but a small impact on the immediate crisis. There are major difficulties impeding the widespread use of new high-yield grain varieties. Typically, the new grains require high fertilizer inputs to realize their full potential, and thus are subject to all the difficulties mentioned above. Some other problems were identified in a recent address by Lester R. Brown, administrator of the International Agricultural Development Service: the limited amount of irrigated land suitable for the new varieties, the fact that a farmer's willingness to innovate fluctuates with the market prices (which may be driven down by high-yield crops), and the possibility of tieups at market facilities inadequate for handling increased yields.[3]

Perhaps even more important, the new grain varieties are being rushed into production without adequate field testing, so that we are unsure of how resistant they will be to the attacks of insects and plant diseases. William Paddock has presented a plant pathologist's view of the crash programs to shift to new varieties (Paddock, 1967). He describes India's dramatic program of planting improved Mexican wheat, and continues: "Such a rapid switch to a new variety is clearly understandable in a country that tottered on the brink of famine. Yet with such limited testing, one wonders what unknown pathogens await a climatic change which will give the environmental conditions needed for their growth." Introduction of the new varieties creates enlarged monocultures of plants with essentially unknown levels of resistance to disaster. Clearly, one of the prices that is paid for higher yield is a higher risk of widespread catastrophe. And the risks are

---

[3] Lester R. Brown, address to the Second International Conference on the War on Hunger, Washington, D.C. (February 1968).

far from local: since the new varieties require more "input" of pesticides (with all their deleterious ecological side effects), these crops may ultimately contribute to the defeat of other environment-related panaceas, such as extracting larger amounts of food from the sea.

A final problem must be mentioned in connection with these strains of food crops. In general, the hungriest people in the world are also those with the most conservative food habits. Even rather minor changes, such as that from a rice variety in which the cooked grains stick together to one in which the grains fall apart, may make new foods unacceptable. It seems to be an unhappy fact of human existence that people would rather starve than eat a nutritious substance which they do not recognize as food.[4]

Beyond the economic, ecological, and sociological problems already mentioned in connection with high-yield agriculture, there is the overall problem of time. We need time to breed the desired characteristics of yield and hardiness into a vast array of new strains (a tedious process indeed), time to convince farmers that it is necessary that they change their time-honored ways of cultivation, and time to convince hungry people to change the staples of their diet. The Paddocks give 20 years as the "rule of thumb" for a new technique or plant variety to progress from conception to substantial impact on farming (Paddock and Paddock, 1967). They write: "It is true that a *massive* research attack on the problem could bring some striking results in less than 20 years. But I do not find such an attack remotely contemplated in the thinking of those officials capable of initiating it." Promising as high-yield agriculture may be, the funds, the personnel, the ecological expertise, and the necessary years are unfortunately not at our disposal. Fulfillment of the promise will come too late for many of the world's starving millions, if it comes at all.

Bringing More Land Under Cultivation

The most frequently mentioned means of bringing new land into agricultural production are farming the tropics and irrigating arid and semiarid regions. The former, although widely discussed in optimistic terms, has been tried for years with incredibly poor results, and even recent experiments have not been encouraging. One essential difficulty is the unsuitability of tropical soils for supporting typical foodstuffs instead of jungles (McNeil, 1964: Paddock and Paddock, 1964). Also, "the tropics" are a biologically more diverse area than the temperate zones, so that farming technology developed for one area will all too often prove useless in others. We shall see that irrigating the deserts, while more promising, has serious limitations in terms of scale, cost, and lead time.

The feasible approaches to irrigation of arid lands appear to be limited to large-scale water projects involving dams and transport in canals, and desalination

---

[4] For a more detailed discussion of the psychological problems in persuading people to change their dietary habits, see McKenzie, 1968.

of ocean and brackish water. Supplies of usable ground water are already badly depleted in most areas where they are accessible, and natural recharge is low enough in most arid regions that such supplies do not offer a long-term solution in any case. Some recent statistics will give perspective to the discussion of water projects and desalting which follows. In 1966, the United States was using about 300 billion gal of water per day, of which 135 billion gal were consumed by agriculture and 165 billion gal by municipal and industrial users (Sporn, 1966). The bulk of the agricultural water cost the farmer from 5 to 10 cents/1000 gal; the highest price paid for agricultural water was 15 cents/1000 gal. For small industrial and municipal supplies, prices as high as 50 to 70 cents/1000 gal were prevalent in the U.S. arid regions, and some communities in the Southwest were paying on the order of $1.00/1000 gal for "project" water. The extremely high cost of the latter stems largely from transportation costs, which have been estimated at 5 to 15 cents/1000 gal per 100 miles (International Atomic Energy Agency, 1964).

We now examine briefly the implications of such numbers in considering the irrigation of the deserts. The most ambitious water project yet conceived in this country is the North American Water and Power Alliance, which proposes to distribute water from the great rivers of Canada to thirsty locations all over the United States. Formidable political problems aside (some based on the certainty that in the face of expanding populations, demands for water will eventually arise at the source), this project would involve the expenditure of $100 billion in construction costs over a 20-year completion period. At the end of this time, the yield to the United States would be 69 million acre feet of water annually (Kelly, 1966), or 63 billion gal per day. If past experience with massive water projects is any guide, these figures are overoptimistic; but if we assume they are not, it is instructive to note that this monumental undertaking would provide for an increase of only 21% in the water consumption of the United States, during a period in which the population is expected to increase by between 25 and 43% (U.S. Dept. of Commerce, 1966). To assess the possible contribution to the *world* food situation, we assume that all this water could be devoted to agriculture, although extrapolation of present consumption patterns indicates that only about one-half would be. Then using the rather optimistic figure of 500 gal per day to grow the food to feed one person, we find that this project could feed 126 million additional people. Since this is less than 8% of the projected world population growth during the construction period (say 1970 to 1990), it should be clear that even the most massive water projects can make but a token contribution to the solution of the world food problem in the long term. And in the crucial short term—the years preceding 1980—*no* additional people will be fed by projects still on the drawing board today.

In summary, the cost is staggering, the scale insufficient, and the lead time too long. Nor need we resort to such speculation about the future for proof of the failure of technological "solutions" in the absence of population control. The highly touted and very expensive Aswan Dam project, now nearing completion, will ultimately supply food (at the present miserable diet level) for less than Egypt's population growth during the time of construction (Borgstrom, 1965; Cole, 1968). Furthermore, its effect on the fertility of the Nile Delta may be disastrous, and, as with all water projects of this nature, silting of the reservoir will destroy the gains in the long term (perhaps in 100 years).

Desalting for irrigation suffers somewhat similar limitations. The desalting plants operational in the world today produce water at individual rates of 7.5 million gal/day and less, at a cost of 75 cents/1000 gal and up, the cost increasing as the plant size decreases (Bender, 1969). The most optimistic firm proposal which anyone seems to have made for desalting with present or soon-to-be available technology is a 150 million gal per day nuclear-powered installation studied by the Bechtel Corp. for the Los Angeles Metropolitan Water District. Bechtel's early figures indicated that water from this complex would be available at the site for 27-28 cents/1000 gal (Galstann and Currier, 1967). However, skepticism regarding the economic assumptions leading to these figures (Milliman, 1966) has since proven justified—the project was shelved after spiralling construction cost estimates indicated an actual water cost of 40-50 cents/1000 gal. Use of even the original figures, however, bears out our contention that the *most* optimistic assumptions do not alter the verdict that technology is losing the food/population battle. For 28 cents/1000 gal is still approximately twice the cost which farmers have hitherto been willing or able to pay for irrigation water. If the Bechtel plant had been intended to supply agricultural needs, which it was not, one would have had to add to an already unacceptable price the very substantial cost of transporting the water inland.

Significantly, studies have shown that the economics of scale in the distillation process are essentially exhausted by a 150 million gal per day plant (International Atomic Energy Agency, 1964). Hence, merely increasing desalting capacity further will not substantially lower the cost of the water. On purely economic grounds, then, it is unlikely that desalting will play a major role in food production by conventional agriculture in the short term.[5] Technological "breakthroughs" will presumably improve this outlook with the passage of time, but world population growth will not wait.

Desalting becomes more promising if the high cost of the water can be offset by increased agricultural yields per gallon and, perhaps, use of a single nuclear installation to provide power for both the desalting and profitable on-site industrial processes. This prospect has been investigated in a thorough and well-documented study headed by E. A. Mason (Oak Ridge National Laboratory, 1968). The result is a set of preliminary figures and recommendations regarding nuclear-powered "agro-industrial complexes" for arid and semiarid regions, in which desalted water and fertilizer would be produced for use on an adjacent, highly

[5] An identical conclusion was reached in a recent study (Clawson et al., 1969) in which the foregoing points and numerous other aspects of desalting were treated in far more detail than was possible here.

efficient farm. In underdeveloped countries incapable of using the full excess power output of the reactor, this energy would be consumed in on-site production of industrial materials for sale on the world market. Both near-term (10 years hence) and far-term (20 years hence) technologies are considered, as are various mixes of farm and industrial products. The representative near-term case for which a detailed cost breakdown is given involves a seaside facility with a desalting capacity of 1 billion gal/day, a farm size of 320,000 acres, and an industrial electric power consumption of 1585 Mw. The initial investment for this complex is estimated at $1.8 billion, and annual operating costs at $236 million. If both the food and the industrial materials produced were sold (as opposed to giving the food, at least, to those in need who could not pay),[6] the estimated profit for such a complex, before subtracting financing costs, would be 14.6%.

The authors of the study are commendably cautious in outlining the assumptions and uncertainties upon which these figures rest. The key assumption is that 200 gal/day of water will grow the 2500 calories required to feed one person. Water/calorie ratios of this order or less have been achieved by the top 20% of farmers specializing in such crops as wheat, potatoes, and tomatoes: but more water is required for needed protein-rich crops such as peanuts and soybeans. The authors identify the uncertainty that crops usually raised separately can be grown together in tight rotation on the same piece of land. Problems of water storage between periods of peak irrigation demand, optimal patterns of crop rotation, and seasonal acreage variations are also mentioned. These "ifs" and assumptions, and those associated with the other technologies involved, are unfortunately often omitted when the results of such painstaking studies are summarized for more popular consumption (Anonymous, 1968b, 1968c). The result is the perpetuation of the public's tendency to confuse feasible and available, to see panaceas where scientists in the field concerned see only potential, realizable with massive infusions of time and money.

It is instructive, nevertheless, to examine the impact on the world food problem which the Oak Ridge complexes might have if construction were to begin today, and if all the assumptions about technology 10 years hence were valid *now*. At the industrial-agricultural mix pertinent to the sample case described above, the food produced would be adequate for just under 3 million people. This means that 23 such plants per year, at a cost of $41 billion, would have to be put in operation merely to keep pace with world population growth, to say nothing of improving the substandard diets of between one and two billion members of the present population. (Fertilizer production beyond that required for the on-site farm is of course a contribution in the latter regard, but the substantial additional costs of transporting it to where it is needed must then be accounted for.) Since

---

[6] Confusing statements often are made about the possibility that food supply will outrun food demand in the future. In these statements, "demand" is used in the economic sense, and in this context many millions of starving people may generate no demand whatsoever. Indeed, one concern of those engaged in increasing food production is to find ways of increasing demand.

approximately 5 years from the start of construction would be required to put such a complex into operation, we should commence work on at least 125 units post-haste, and begin at least 25 per year thereafter. If the technology *were* available now, the investment in construction over the next 5 years, prior to operation of the first plants, would be $315 billion, about 20 times the total U.S. foreign aid expenditure during the past 5 years. By the time the technology *is* available the bill will be much higher, if famine has not "solved" the problem for us.

This example again illustrates that scale, time, and cost are all working against technology in the short term. And if population growth is not decelerated, the increasing severity of population-related crises will surely neutralize the technological improvements of the middle and long terms.

Other Food Panaceas

"Food from the sea" is the most prevalent "answer" to the world food shortage in the view of the general public. This is not surprising, since estimates of the theoretical fisheries productivity of the sea run up to some 50–100 times current yields (Schmitt, 1965; Christy and Scott, 1965). Many practical and economic difficulties, however, make it clear that such a figure will never be reached, and that it will not even be approached in the foreseeable future. In 1966, the annual fisheries harvest was some 57 million metric tons (United Nations, 1968). A careful analysis (Meseck, 1961) indicates that this might be increased to a world production of 70 million metric tons by 1980. If this gain were realized, it would represent (assuming no violent change in population growth patterns) a small per capita *loss* in fisheries yield.

Both the short- and long-term outlooks for taking food from the sea are clouded by the problems of overexploitation, pollution (which is generally ignored by those calculating potential yields), and economics. Solving these problems will require more than technological legerdemain; it will also require unprecedented changes in human behavior, especially in the area of international cooperation. The unlikelihood that such cooperation will come about is reflected in the recent news (Anonymous, 1968d) that Norway has dropped out of the whaling industry because overfishing has depleted the stock below the level at which it may economically be harvested. In that industry, international controls were tried—and failed. The sea is, unfortunately, a "commons" (Hardin, 1968), and the resultant management problems exacerbate the biological and technical problems of greatly increasing our "take." One suspects that the return per dollar poured into the sea will be much less than the corresponding return from the land for many years, and the return from the land has already been found wanting.

Synthetic foods, protein culture with petroleum, saline agriculture, and weather modification all may hold promise for the future, but all are at present expensive and available only on an extremely limited scale. The research to improve this situation will also be expensive, and, of course, time-consuming. In the absence of funding, it will not occur at all, a fact which occasionally eludes the public and the Congress.

Domestic and Industrial Water Supplies

The world has water problems, even exclusive of the situation in agriculture. Although total precipitation should in theory be adequate in quantity for several further doublings of population, serious shortages arising from problems of quality, irregularity, and distribution already plague much of the world. Underdeveloped countries will find the water needs of industrialization staggering: 240,000 gal of water are required to produce a ton of newsprint; 650,000 gal, to produce a ton of steel (International Atomic Energy Agency, 1964). Since maximum acceptable water costs for domestic and industrial use are higher than for agriculture, those who can afford it are or soon will be using desalination (40–100 + cents/1000 gal) and used-water renovation (54–57 cents/1000 gal [Ennis, 1967]). Those who cannot afford it are faced with allocating existing supplies between industry and agriculture, and as we have seen, they must choose the latter. In this circumstance, the standard of living remains pitifully low. Technology's only present answer is massive externally-financed complexes of the sort considered above, and we have already suggested there the improbability that we are prepared to pay the bill rung up by present population growth.

The widespread use of desalted water by those who *can* afford it brings up another problem only rarely mentioned to date, the disposal of the salts. The product of the distillation processes in present use is a hot brine with salt concentration several times that of seawater. Both the temperature and the salinity of this effluent will prove fatal to local marine life if it is simply exhausted to the ocean. The most optimistic statement we have seen on this problem is that "*smaller plants* (our emphasis) at seaside locations may return the concentrated brine to the ocean if proper attention is paid to the design of the outfall, and to the effect on the local marine ecology" (McIlhenny, 1966). The same writer identifies the major economic uncertainties connected with extracting the salts for sale (to do so is straightforward, but often not profitable). Nor can one simply evaporate the brine and leave the residue in a pile—the 150 million gal/day plant mentioned above would produce brine bearing 90 million lb. of salts daily (based on figures by Parker, 1966). This amount of salt would cover over 15 acres to a depth of one foot. Thus, every year a plant of the billion gallon per day, agroindustrial complex size would produce a pile of salt over 52 ft. deep and covering a square mile. The high winds typical of coastal deserts would seriously aggravate the associated soil contamination problem.

Energy

Man's problems with energy supply are more subtle than those with food and water: we are not yet running out of energy, but we are being forced to use it faster than is probably healthy. The rapacious depletion of our fossil fuels is already forcing us to consider more expensive mining techniques to gain access to lower-grade deposits, such as the oil shales, and even the status of our high-grade uranium ore reserves is not clearcut (Anonymous, 1968e).

A widely held misconception in this connection is that nuclear power is "dirt cheap," and as such represents a panacea for developed and underdeveloped nations alike. To the contrary, the largest nuclear-generating stations now in operation are just competitive with or marginally superior to modern coal-fired plants of comparable size (where coal is not scarce); at best, both produce power for on the order of 4–5 mills (tenths of a cent) per kilowatt-hour. Smaller nuclear units remain less economical than their fossil-fueled counterparts. Underdeveloped countries can rarely use the power of the larger plants. Simply speaking, there are not enough industries, appliances, and light bulbs to absorb the output, and the cost of industrialization and modernization exceeds the cost of the power required to sustain it by orders of magnitude, regardless of the source of the power. (For example, one study noted that the capital requirement to consume the output of a 70,000 kilowatt plant—about $1.2 million worth of electricity per year at 40% utilization and 5 mills/kwh—is $111 million per year if the power is consumed by metals industries, $270 million per year for petroleum product industries [E. S. Mason, 1957].) Hence, at least at present, only those underdeveloped countries which are short of fossil fuels or inexpensive means to transport them are in particular need of nuclear power.

Prospects for major reductions in the cost of nuclear power in the future hinge on the long-awaited breeder reactor and the still further distant thermonuclear reactor. In neither case is the time scale or the ultimate cost of energy a matter of any certainty. The breeder reactor, which converts more nonfissile uranium (^{238}U) or thorium to fissionable material than it consumes as fuel for itself, effectively extends our nuclear fuel supply by a factor of approximately 400 (Cloud, 1968). It is not expected to become competitive economically with conventional reactors until the 1980's (Bump, 1967). Reductions in the unit energy cost beyond this date are not guaranteed, due both to the probable continued high capital cost of breeder reactors and to increasing costs for the ore which the breeders will convert to fuel. In the latter regard, we mention that although crushing granite for its few parts per million of uranium and thorium is possible in theory, the problems and cost of doing so are far from resolved.[7] It is too soon to predict the costs associated with a fusion reactor (few who work in the field will predict whether such a device will work at all within the next 15-20 years). One guess puts the unit energy cost at something over half that for a coal or fission

---

[7] A general discussion of extracting metals from common rock is given by Cloud, 1968.

power station of comparable size (Mills, 1967), but this is pure speculation. Quite possibly the major benefit of controlled fusion will again be to extend the energy supply rather than to cheapen it.

A second misconception about nuclear power is that it can reduce our dependence on fossil fuels to zero as soon as that becomes necessary or desirable. In fact, nuclear power plants contribute only to the electrical portion of the energy budget; and in 1960 in the United States, for example, electrical energy comprised only 19% of the total energy consumed (Sporn, 1963). The degree to which nuclear fuels can postpone the exhaustion of our coal and oil depends on the extent to which that 19% is enlarged. The task is far from a trivial one, and will involve transitions to electric or fuel-cell powered transportation, electric heating, and electrically powered industries. It will be extremely expensive.

Nuclear energy, then, is a panacea neither for us nor for the underdeveloped world. It relieves, but does not remove, the pressure on fossil fuel supplies; it provides reasonably-priced power where these fuels are not abundant; it has substantial (but expensive) potential in intelligent applications such as that suggested in the Oak Ridge study discussed above; and it shares the propensity of fast-growing technology to unpleasant side effects (Novick, 1969). We mention in the last connection that, while nuclear power stations do not produce conventional air pollutants, their radioactive waste problems may in the long run prove a poor trade. Although the AEC seems to have made a good case for solidification and storage in salt mines of the bulk of the radioactive fission products (Blanko et al., 1967), a number of radioactive isotopes are released to the environment, and in some areas such isotopes have already turned up in potentially harmful concentrations (Curtis and Hogan, 1969). Projected order of magnitude increases in nuclear power generation will seriously aggravate this situation. Although it has frequently been stated that the eventual advent of fusion reactors will free us from such difficulties, at least one authority, F. L. Parker, takes a more cautious view. He contends that the large inventory of radioactive tritium in early fusion reactors will require new precautions to minimize emissions (Parker, 1968).

A more easily evaluated problem is the tremendous quantity of waste heat generated at nuclear installations (to say nothing of the usable power output, which, as with power from whatever source, must also ultimately be dissipated as heat). Both have potentially disastrous effects on the local and world ecological and climatological balance. There is no simple solution to this problem, for, in general, "cooling" only moves heat; it does not *remove* it from the environment viewed as a whole. Moreover, the Second Law of Thermodynamics puts a ceiling on the efficiency with which we can do even this much, i.e., concentrate and transport heat. In effect, the Second Law condemns us to aggravate the total problem by generating still *more* heat in any machinery we devise for local cooling (consider, for example, refrigerators and air conditioners).

The only heat which actually leaves the whole system, the Earth, is that which can be radiated back into space. This amount steadily is being diminished as combustion of hydrocarbon fuels increases the atmospheric percentage of CO_2 which has strong absorption bands in the infrared spectrum of the outbound heat energy. (Hubbert, 1962, puts the increase in the CO_2 content of the atmosphere at 10% since 1900.) There is, of course, a competing effect in the Earth's energy balance, which is the increased reflectivity of the upper atmosphere to incoming sunlight due to other forms of air pollution. It has been estimated, ignoring both these effects, that man risks drastic (and perhaps catastrophic) climatological change if the amount of heat he dissipates in the environment on a global scale reaches 1% of the solar energy absorbed and reradiated at the Earth's surface (Rose and Clark, 1961). At the present 5% rate of increase in world energy consumption,[8] this level will be reached in less than a century, and in the immediate future the direct contribution of man's power consumption will create serious local problems. If we may safely rule out circumvention of the Second Law or the divorce of energy requirements from population size, this suggests that, whatever science and technology may accomplish, population growth must be stopped.

Transportation

We would be remiss in our offer of a technological perspective on population problems without some mention of the difficulties associated with transporting large quantities of food, material, or people across the face of the Earth. While our grain exports have not begun to satisfy the hunger of the underdeveloped world, they already have taxed our ability to transport food in bulk over large distances. The total amount of goods of *all* kinds loaded at U.S. ports for external trade was 158 million metric tons in 1965 (United Nations, 1968). This is coincidentally the approximate amount of grain which would have been required to make up the dietary shortages of the underdeveloped world in the same year (Sukhatme, 1966). Thus, if the United States *had* such an amount of grain to ship, it could be handled only by displacing the entirety of our export trade. In a similar vein, the gross weight of the fertilizer, in excess of present consumption, required in the underdeveloped world to feed the additional population there in 1980 will amount to approximately the same figure—150 million metric tons (Sukhatme, 1966). Assuming that a substantial fraction of this fertilizer, should it be available at all, will have to be shipped about, we had best start building freighters! These problems, and the even more discouraging one of internal transportation in the hungry countries, coupled with the complexities of international finance and marketing which have hobbled even present aid programs, complete a dismal picture of the prospects for "external" solutions to

[8] The rate of growth of world energy consumption fluctuates strongly about some mean on a time scale of only a few years, and the figures are not known with great accuracy in any case. A discussion of predicting the mean and a defense of the figure of 5% are given in Guéron et al. 1957.

ballooning food requirements in much of the world.

Those who envision migration as a solution to problems of food, land, and water distribution not only ignore the fact that the world has no promising place to put more people, they simply have not looked at the numbers of the transportation game. Neglecting the fact that migration and relocation costs would probably amount to a minimum of several thousand dollars per person, we find, for example, that the entire long-range jet transport fleet of the United States (about 600 planes [Molloy, 1968] with an average capacity of 150), averaging two round trips per week, could transport only about 9 million people per year from India to the United States. This amounts to about 75% of that country's annual population *growth* (Population Reference Bureau, 1968). Ocean liners and transports, while larger, are less numerous and much slower, and over long distances could not do as well. Does anyone believe, then, that we are going to compensate for the world's population growth by sending the excess to the planets? If there were a place to go on Earth, financially and logistically we could not send our surplus there.

Conclusion

We have not attempted to be comprehensive in our treatment of population pressures and the prospects of coping with them technologically; rather, we hope simply to have given enough illustrations to make plausible our contention that technology, without population control, cannot meet the challenge. It may be argued that we have shown only that any one technological scheme taken individually is insufficient to the task at hand, whereas *all* such schemes applied in parallel might well be enough. We would reply that neither the commitment nor the resources to implement them all exists, and indeed that many may prove mutually exclusive (e.g., harvesting algae may diminish fish production).

Certainly, an optimum combination of efforts exists in theory, but we assert that no organized attempt to find it is being made, and that our examination of its probable eventual constituents permits little hope that even the optimum will suffice. Indeed, after a far more thorough survey of the prospects than we have attempted here, the President's Science Advisory Committee Panel on the world food supply concluded (PSAC, 1967): "The solution of the problem that will exist after about 1985 *demands* that programs of population control be initiated now." We most emphatically agree, noting that "now" was 2 years ago!

Of the problems arising out of population growth in the short, middle, and long terms, we have emphasized the first group. For mankind must pass the first hurdles—food and water for the next 20 years—to be granted the privilege of confronting such dilemmas as the exhaustion of mineral resources and physical space later.[9] Furthermore, we have not conveyed the extent of our concern for the environmental deterioration which has accompanied the population explosion, and for the catastrophic ecological consequences which would attend many of the proposed technological "solutions" to the population/food crisis. Nor have we treated the point that "development" of the rest of the world to the standards of the West probably would be lethal ecologically (Ehrlich and Ehrlich, 1970). For even if such grim prospects are ignored, it is abundantly clear that in terms of cost, lead time, and implementation on the scale required, technology without population control will be too little and too late.

What hope there is lies not, of course, in abandoning attempts at technological solutions; on the contrary, they must be pursued at unprecedented levels, with unprecedented judgment, and above all with unprecedented attention to their ecological consequences. We need dramatic programs now to find ways of ameliorating the food crisis—to buy time for humanity until the inevitable delay accompanying population control efforts has passed. But it cannot be emphasized enough that if the population control measures are *not* initiated immediately and effectively, all the technology man can bring to bear will not fend off the misery to come.[10] Therefore, confronted as we are with limited resources of time and money, we must consider carefully what fraction of our effort should be applied to the cure of the disease itself instead of to the temporary relief of the symptoms. We should ask, for example, how many vasectomies could be performed by a program funded with the 1.8 billion dollars required to build a single nuclear agro-industrial complex, and what the relative impact on the problem would be in both the short and long terms.

The decision for population control will be opposed by growth-minded economists and businessmen, by nationalistic statesmen, by zealous religious leaders, and by the myopic and well-fed of every description. It is therefore incumbent on all who sense the limitations of technology and the fragility of the environmental balance to make themselves heard above the hollow, optimistic chorus—to convince society and its leaders that there is no alternative but the cessation of our irresponsible, all-demanding, and all-consuming population growth.

Acknowledgments

We thank the following individuals for reading and commenting on the manuscript: J. H. Brownell (Stanford University); P. A. Cantor (Aerojet General Corp.);

[9] Since the first draft of this article was written, the authors have seen the manuscript of a timely and pertinent forthcoming book, *Resources and Man*, written under the auspices of the National Academy of Sciences and edited by Preston E. Cloud. The book reinforces many of our own conclusions in such areas as agriculture and fisheries and, in addition, treats both short- and long-term prospects in such areas as mineral resources and fossil fuels in great detail.

[10] This conclusion has also been reached within the specific context of aid to underdeveloped countries in a Ph.D. thesis by Douglas Daetz: "Energy Utilization and Aid Effectiveness in Nonmechanized Agriculture: A Computer Simulation of a Socioeconomic System" (University of California, Berkeley, May 1968).

P. E. Cloud (University of California, Santa Barbara); D. J. Eckstrom (Stanford University); R. Ewell (State University of New York at Buffalo); J. L. Fisher (Resources for the Future, Inc.); J. A. Hendrickson, Jr. (Stanford University); J. H. Hessel (Stanford University); R. W. Holm (Stanford University); S. C. McIntosh, Jr., (Stanford University); K. E. F. Watt (University of California, Davis). This work was supported in part by a grant from the Ford Foundation.

REFERENCES

Anonymous. "India Aims to Remedy Fertilizer Shortage," *Chem. Eng. News*, 46, 29 (November 25, 1968a).

——————. "Scientists Studying Nuclear-Powered Agro-Industrial Complexes to Give Food and Jobs to Millions," *New York Times* (March 10, 1968b), 74.

——————. "Food from the Atom," *Technol. Rev.* (January, 1968c), 55.

——————. "Norway–The End of the Big Blubber," *Time* (November 29, 1968d), 98.

——————. "Nuclear Fuel Cycle," *Nucl. News* (January, 1968c), 30.

Bender, R. J. "Why Water Desalting Will Expand," *Power*, 113, 171 (August, 1969).

Blanko, R. E., J. O. Blomeke, and J. T. Roberts. "Solving the Waste Disposal Problem," *Nucleonics*, 25, 58 (1967).

Borgstrom, Georg. *The Hungry Planet*. New York: Collier-Macmillan, 1965.

Bump, T. R. "A Third Generation of Breeder Reactors," *Sci. Amer.* (May, 1967), 25.

Christy, F. C., Jr., and A. Scott. *The Commonwealth in Ocean Fisheries*. Baltimore: Johns Hopkins Press, 1965.

Clawson, M., H. H. Landsberg, and L. T. Alexander. "Desalted Seawater for Agriculture: Is It Economic?" *Science*, 164, 1141 (1969).

Cloud, P. R. "Realities of Mineral Distribution," *Texas Quart.* (Summer, 1968), p. 103.

Cole, LaMont C. "Can the World be Saved?" *BioScience*, 18, 679 (1968).

Curtis, R., and E. Hogan. *Perils of the Peaceful Atom*. New York: Doubleday, 1969, pp. 135, 150–152.

Ennis, C. E. "Desalted Water as a Competitive Commodity," *Chem. Eng. Progr.*, 63: (1): 64 (1967).

Ehrlich, P. R. *The Population Bomb*. New York: Sierra Club/Ballantine, 1968.

Ehrlich, P. R., and Anne H. Ehrlich. *Population, Resources, and Environment*. San Francisco: W. H. Freeman, in press.

Galstann, L. S., and E. L. Currier. "The Metropolitan Water District Desalting Project," *Chem. Eng. Progr.*, 63, (1): 64 (1967).

Güeron, J., J. A. Lane, I. R. Maxwell, and J. R. Menke. *The Economics of Nuclear Power. Progress in Nuclear Energy*. New York: McGraw-Hill Book Co., series VIII, 1957, p. 23.

Hardin, G. "The Tragedy of the Commons," *Science*, 162, 1243 (1968).

Hubbert, M. K. "Energy Resources, A Report to the Committee on Natural Resources," National Research Council Report 1000-D, National Academy of Sciences, 1962.

International Atomic Energy Agency. "Desalination of Water Using Conventional and Nuclear Energy," Technical Report 24, Vienna, 1964.

Kelly, R. P. "North American Water and Power Alliance," in *Water Production Using Nuclear Energy*. ed. R. G. Post and R. L. Seale. Tucson: University of Arizona Press, 1966, p. 29.

Lelyveld, D. "Can India Survive Calcutta?" *New York Times Magazine* (October 13, 1968), 58.

Mason, E. S. "Economic Growth and Energy Consumption," in *The Economics of Nuclear Power. Progress in Nuclear Energy*, Series VIII, ed. J. Güeron *et al.* New York: McGraw-Hill Book Co., 1957, p. 56.

McIlhenny, W. F. "Problems and Potentials of Concentrated Brines," in *Water Production Using Nuclear Energy*, ed. R. G. Post and R. L. Seale. Tucson: University of Arizona Press, 1966, p. 187.

McKenzie, John. "Nutrition and the Soft Sell," *New Sci.*, 40, 423 (1968).

McNeil, Mary. "Lateritic Soils," *Sci. Amer.* (November, 1964), 99.

Meseck, G. "Importance of Fish Production and Utilization in the Food Economy," Paper R11.3, presented at FAO Conference on Fish in Nutrition, Rome, 1961.

Milliman, J. W. "Economics of Water Production Using Nuclear Energy," in *Water Production Using Nuclear Energy*, ed. R. G. Post and R. L. Seale. Tucson: University of Arizona Press, 1966, p. 49.

Mills, R. G. "Some Engineering Problems of Thermonuclear Fusion," *Nucl. Fusion*, 7, 223 (1967).

Molloy, J. F., Jr. "The $12-Billion Financing Problem of U.S. Airlines," *Astronautics and Aeronautics* (October, 1968), p. 76.

Novick, S. *The Careless Atom*. Boston: Houghton Mifflin Company, 1969.

Oak Ridge National Laboratory. "Nuclear Energy Centers, Industrial and Agro-industrial Complexes," Summary Report, ORNL–4291, July, 1968.

Paddock, William. "Phytopathology and a Hungry World," *Ann. Rev. Phytopathol.*, 5, 375 (1967).

Paddock, William, and Paul Paddock. *Hungry Nations*. Boston: Little, Brown & Co., 1964.
_____ . *Famine 1975!* Boston: Little, Brown & Co., 1967.

Parikh, G., S. Saxena, and M. Maharaja. "Agricultural Extension and IADP, a Study of Surat," *Econ. Polit. Weekly* (August 24, 1968), 1307.

Parker, F. L. "Radioactive Wastes from Fusion Reactors," *Science*, 159, 83 (1968).

Parker, F. L., and D. J. Rose, *Science*, 159, 1376.

Parker, H. M. "Environmental Factors relating to Large Water Plants," in *Water Production Using Nuclear Energy*, ed. R. G. Post and R. L. Seale. Tucson: University of Arizona Press, 1966, p. 209.

Population Reference Bureau. "Population Reference Bureau Data Sheet." Washington: Pop. Ref. Bureau, 1968.

PSAC. *The World Food Problem*. Report of the President's Science Advisory Committee, vols. 1–3. Washington: U.S. Government Printing Office, 1967.

Rose, D. J., and M. Clark, Jr. *Plasma and Controlled Fusion*. Cambridge, Mass.: M.I.T. Press, 1961, p. 3.

Schmitt, W. R. "The Planetary Food Potential," *Ann. N.Y. Acad. Sci.*, 118, 645 (1965).

Sporn, Philip. *Energy for Man*. New York: Macmillan, 1963.
_____ . *Fresh Water from Saline Waters*. New York: Pergamon Press, 1966.

Sukhatme, P. V. "The World's Food Supplies," *Roy. Stat. Soc. J.*, 129A, 222 (1966).

United Nations. *United Nations Statistical Yearbook for 1967*. New York: Statistical Office of the U.N., 1968.

U.S. Dept. of Commerce. *Statistical Abstract of the U.S.* Washington: U.S. Government Printing Office, 1966.

Wadleigh, C. H. "Wastes in Relation to Agriculture and Industry," USDA Miscellaneous Publication No. 1065 (March, 1968).

Woodwell, George M. "Toxic Substances and Ecological Cycles," *Sci. Amer.* (March, 1967), 24.

THE INADVERTENT MODIFICATION
OF THE ATMOSPHERE BY
AIR POLLUTION

Vincent J. Schaefer

---

*It is widely recognized among experts in air pollution that a large fraction of
pollutants are simply unknown. The effluvia of the chemical and manufacturing
industries and of construction and processing plants, and the exhausts from
engines and the burning of wastes, are almost infinitely varied. Many are further
modified through the photochemical action of sunlight in combination with atmospheric moisture.*

*Medically, our knowledge of pollutants is nearly as poor; we know almost
nothing, for example, of the effects on human health of asbestos fragments, the
molecular particles of automobile tires in the air, the aerial quantities of DDT, or
lead from the combustion of gasoline. Yet all are potentially dangerous and increasing in volume.*

*The elusiveness of ecological dangers is only beginning to be fully apparent.
Thus, the fallout from bombs has been regulated, but the radioactivity from
peaceful uses of nuclear energy has taken its place. When that radioactivity begins to look containable, we discover thermal pollution. If we find a way to deal
with the latter, the capacity of Earth to shift heat into space may be limited,
whatever the source of the energy. Exhaustion of nitrogen fertilizer engenders
fear of nitrogen poisoning of lakes and wells. Fear of the depletion of fossil fuels
is displaced by the bigger threat of oxygen depletion or of being overwhelmed in
some way by carbon dioxide, a constituent of the air which nobody thought to
consider a pollutant a few years ago.*

*Oddly enough, in the long run some of the most dangerous pollutants are
familiar substances normally found in the air even without man's interference,
such as dust, carbon dioxide, and ash. Our modification of heat and light relationships or alteration of large-scale hydrologic balances transform these in-
nocuous materials into greater threats to the planet's future than noxious chemical
wastes.*

*Certainly we must reduce such exhaust and chemical waste pollutants as sul-
phur oxides as much as possible. We must not, however, be deluded into a false
sense of success, nor allow industrial public relations, which tends to focus on
specific areas of improvement, to convince us to accept a fiction. For it is neces-*

Vincent J. Schaefer, "The Inadvertent Modification of the Atmosphere by Air Pollution,"
Bulletin of the American Meteorological Society, *50 (April, 1969), 199–206.*

sary to realize that demands for action can be met incompletely at best when we know so little about the subject.

Perhaps the real reason we cannot afford to have 50 billion people is that urban centers would explode from the violence generated. Similarly, we may not have time to engage in conscious weather modification if air experts are occupied with undoing the effects of our unintentional weather modification.

Abstract

There has been a very noticeable increase in air pollution during the past ten years over and downwind of the several large metropolitan areas of the United States such as the Northwest—Vancouver-Seattle-Tacoma-Portland; the West Coast from San Francisco-Sacramento-Fresno-Los Angeles; the Front Range of the Rockies from Boulder-Denver-Colorado Springs-Pueblo; the Midwest—Omaha-Kansas City-St. Louis-Memphis; the Great Lakes area of Chicago-Detroit-Cleveland-Buffalo; and the Northeast—Washington-Philadelphia-New York-Boston. The worst accumulation of particulate matter occurs at the top of the inversion which commonly intensifies at night at levels ranging from 1000 to 4000 ft or so above the ground. This dense concentration of air-suspended particles is most apparent to air travelers. Thus, it has not as yet disturbed the general public except during periods of stagnant weather systems when the concentration of heavily polluted air extends downward and engulfs them on the highways, at their homes, and in their working areas.

Recent Modification of Our Air Environment

Until recently there is little question that except in very exceptional cases, natural processes dominated the mesoscale weather systems by initiating the precipitation mechanism. The effluent from the larger cities was quickly diluted by the surrounding "country air" so that at a distance a few miles downwind of a city, little evidence of air pollution could be detected.

The recent spread of urban developments due to better roads and the massive proliferation of people and automobiles has led to a nationwide network of county, state, and interstate highways. This interconnection of thousands of smaller towns with large cities and the phenomenal increase in auto, truck, and air traffic has caused a massive reduction in the regions which have "country" type air. This increase in massive air contamination is of fairly recent origin. It is not easy to document this fact in the detail I would prefer since we have not had reliable automatic recording equipment for measuring Aitken, cloud, and ice nuclei until the last few years. However, using simpler devices with which we made measurements at a number of scattered locations during the past ten years, we have in the past year used the same techniques to make comparative observations. The measurements indicate an increase in airborne particulates at these sites of at least an order of magnitude during this ten-year period. At Yellowstone Park in the winter-time, which has the cleanest air we have found in the continental United States, the background levels of Aitken nuclei have increased from less than 100 to the 800–1000 ml^{-1} range within a five-year span. At Flagstaff, Ariz., where in 1962 the background levels ranged from 100–300 the concentration now lies between 800–3000. At Schenectady, N. Y., the average concentration of these nuclei has risen from less than 1000 to more than 5000 with values occasionally exceeding 50,000 ml^{-1}.

While it is difficult to ascribe these increases to any one cause, it is obvious that the increased demand for electric power, the large increase in garbage and trash incineration and the automobile, are likely to represent the major sources of increased pollution, especially since many industrial plants have been forced to reduce their pollution due to more rigorous regulations.

Just as it is not easy to place the blame for increased air pollution specifically on the power plants, incinerators and automobiles, it is equally difficult to demonstrate clean cut or unequivocal atmospheric modification to these sources. I am confident that in time there will be ample proof of these effects which are now inadvertently modifying the atmosphere.

The presence of high concentrations of visible as well as invisible particulates above and downwind of our cities produces a heat island effect as real as a sun-drenched Arizona desert or a semitropical island in the Caribbean.

Those cities like Boston, New York, and Philadelphia which are not affected by geographic barriers as is Los Angeles, Salt Lake City, or Denver are able to get rid of much of their effluent whenever the wind blows. Their plumes of airborne dirt extend as visible streamers for many miles downwind of the source areas. In the case of the metropolitan New York City–northeastern New Jersey complex, these plumes will be found in the upper Hudson Valley, in southeastern New England, or over the Atlantic Ocean.

Commercial airline pilots flying the Atlantic are often able to pick up these pollution plumes hundreds of miles at sea. Hogan recently obtained data which provides a quantitative measurement of the New York effluents near the surface of the Atlantic between the United States and Europe. This same paper [1] amply demonstrates a similar zone of air pollutants being exuded over the seas surrounding Europe, the British Isles, and the east and west coast of the United States.

Properties of Maritime and "Country" Air

We have known for twenty years that maritime air is characterized by low levels of both cloud droplet and Aitken nuclei. Vonnegut [2] showed by a very simple experimental device that about 50 effective nuclei at low water saturation droplet formation existed on the upwind coast of Puerto Rico where the trade wind clouds are seen. We were all much surprised when we established the nature of

trade wind clouds during our research flights near Puerto Rico in 1948 [3].
Following these activities, I pointed out [4] the large difference noticeable even
then between the "raininess" of the clouds upwind of the island and those which
formed over the land after entraining the polluted air from San Juan, the sugar
fields and refineries, the cement mills, and the myriads of charcoal pits which
dotted the island, each sending out its plume of bluish smoke. In our studies in
the vicinity of Puerto Rico we observed that in many instances trade wind clouds
would start raining by the time the clouds had a vertical thickness of not more
than a mile while those over or immediately downwind of the island often reached
three times that thickness without raining.

During a continent-wide flight over a large area of Africa, I found [5] an even
more spectacular effect of inadvertent cloud seeding. As a result of the massive
bush and forest burning initiated by the inhabitants preceding the onset of the
rainy season, huge cumulus clouds, some of them reaching a height of more than
35,000 ft (vertical thickness 4–5 miles) were observed which were not producing
any rain. Instead the clouds grew so high that very extensive ice crystal plumes
hundreds of miles long extended downwind of the convective clouds. No evidence of glaciation was observed in the side turrets of the clouds indicating a
deficiency of ice nuclei at temperatures warmer than the homogeneous nucleation temperature of –40C. Thus it appeared that the precipitation process was
being controlled almost entirely by coalescence and that so many cloud droplet
nuclei were being entrained into the clouds from the fires below, that the coalescence process was impaired so that no rain developed. If ice nuclei were
present, they were probably deactivated by the high concentration of smoke
particles and gases flowing into the base of the clouds. Similar effects have been
observed on a smaller scale in the Hawaiian Islands. During the trade wind cloud
regime, clouds which form over sugar cane fields when they are burned prior to
harvest are actually larger than the surrounding clouds but they have never been
observed to rain even though smaller ones nearby produce showers. Warner more
recently has documented such observations [6].

A further observation of secular change in the microphysics of clouds has
been observed in the vicinity of large cities during airplane flights through convective clouds. The observations I have noted in particular were made in commercial twin engine planes over the past ten years. Of recent years it has been
noticed that such clouds often have so many cloud droplets in them that visibility
is restricted so much that the engine is hardly visible. In my earlier observations
I can never recall being in clouds so opaque that the wing tips could not be seen.
Several of my colleagues have reported similar experiences.

Perhaps the most impressive field evidence of inadvertent weather modification is the overseeding of supercooled clouds which is readily observed over and
downwind of our northern cities in the wintertime.

Ice Crystals From Polluted Air

Although I have been observing such phenomena for more than ten years, the effect was brought to my attention in a vivid way during a flight from Albany to Buffalo on 20 December 1965. After flying above a fairly thin deck of super-cooled stratus clouds downwind of the Adirondack Mountains, I noted a massive area of ice crystals above and downwind of Rochester, N. Y. The crystals were so dense that the reflection from the undersun[1] was dazzling. Since that time I have observed similar high concentrations of crystals at low level above and downwind of most of the large northeastern cities such as New York, Albany, Utica, Syracuse, and Buffalo as well as Detroit, Chicago, Sacramento, and Los Angeles. In all instances the ice crystals were observed at low level (below 5000 ft above the ground in most instances), and extending for at least 50 miles downwind of the city sources and without cirrus clouds above the areas affected. In a few instances when the plane passed through the crystal area, I observed the particles to be like snow dust, though in a number of instances after landing I observed very symmetrical though tiny hexagonal crystals drifting down from the sky.

Misty Rain and Dust-like Snow

For the past several years I have also been observing a number of strange snow and rain storms in the Capital District area in the east central part of New York State. These storms consist of extremely small precipitation particles. When in the form of snow, the particles are like dust having cross sections ranging from 0.02 cm (200 μ) to 0.06 cm (600 μ). When in the form of droplets, they often are even smaller in diameter, at times being so tiny that they drift rather than fall toward the Earth. When collected on clean plastic sheets, the precipitation is found to consist of badly polluted water. It is a well-known fact that precipitation "cleanses the air." In the past much of this cleansing action has been ascribed to the sweeping up of suspended aerosols by rain and snow. Little attention has been given to the possibility that submicroscopic particulates from man-made pollution may in fact be initiating and controlling precipitation in a *primary manner* rather than being involved in the secondary process wherein precipitation elements coming from "natural" mechanisms serve to remove the particles by diffusion, collision, and similar scavenging processes.

---

[1] Note: The undersun is an optical phenomenon caused by the specular reflection of the sun from the surfaces of myriads of hexagonal plate ice crystals. In order to produce an under-sun, it is necessary for the crystals to consist of smooth-surfaced plates which float with their long axes horizontal to the ground. They thus act as many tiny mirrors. If the crystals were not hexagonal plates but rather prisms, the optical effects would include under parhelia and other reflections which are well known and have been related to crystal types during our winter studies at Yellowstone Park.

My first evidence that there might be substances in urban air which would react with other chemicals was encountered while studying ice nucleation effects at the General Electric Research Laboratory in 1946 [7]. At that time I found that laboratory air contained aerosols which would react with iodine vapor to form very effective ice nuclei but that when the air was free of particulate matter, no further ice particles would form.

Potential Ice Nuclei From Auto Exhaust

In 1966 I published a paper [8] which suggested that air pollution in the form of automobile exhaust could account for the high concentration of ice crystals which I have observed downwind of the larger cities in the United States and in any area where a considerable number of automobiles are used. My laboratory studies have shown that submicroscopic particles of lead compounds produced from the combustion of leaded gasoline can be found at concentrations exceeding 1000 cm^{-3} in auto exhaust. These were measured by exposing auto exhaust samples to a trace of iodine vapor before or after putting the samples into a cold chamber operating at -20C. Presumably this reaction with iodine formed lead iodide which is an effective sublimation nucleus for ice crystal formation. Evidence that the active ingredient in auto exhaust consists of submicroscopic particles of lead was determined by comparing its temperature ice nucleation activity pattern with that of lead oxide smoke produced by electrically sparking lead electrodes which was also reacted with a trace of iodine vapor. One of the problems related to the evidence that leaded gasoline is responsible for the ice crystals observed in laboratory and field experiments concerned with auto exhaust is the source of the iodine needed to produce the lead iodide reaction. All evidence thus far encountered shows that only a few hundred molecules of iodine are required to produce a nucleating zone for ice crystal formation. The amount of iodine reported in oceanic [9] air (the order of 0.5 U G. m^{-3}) is orders of magnitude greater than would be required to activate such particles.

I have recently completed further studies in Arizona, New York, and France [10, 11] and have found that wood smoke and other organic sources add iodine to the air which could react with the auto exhaust submicroscopic lead compounds which are always present in urban pollution. Hogan has recently showed [12] that similar reactions will proceed from the vapor phase.

Admittedly we are dealing with chemical reactions in the realm of surface and even "point" chemistry as Langmuir termed such molecule by molecule reactions. This is an area of particulate research for which there is very little experimental data or practical experience. The size of the primary lead particles from auto exhaust which are 0.008-0.010 diameter are far too small for analysis by any currently available chemical reaction techniques. All of my laboratory experiments indicate that the submicroscopic particles in auto exhaust which react with iodine vapor act only as nuclei for ice formation from the vapor phase. No evidence has been found that they act as freezing nuclei.

The Effect of Large Concentrations of Ice Crystals

The presence of high concentrations of tiny ice crystals in air colder than 0C. over thousands of cubic miles raises interesting aspects of the dynamics of weather systems. Such crystals continually modify small supercooled clouds soon after they form. The net result is a reduction in the number of local rain or snow showers and the production of extensive sheets of "false" cirrus. Bryson has pointed out [13] that cirrus sheets and even the presence on a large scale of airborne dust exerts a measurable decrease of insolation. If a much larger supply of moist air moves into such a region, the entrainment of high concentrations of crystals by more vigorous supercooled clouds may trigger the formation of a massive storm through the release of the latent heat of sublimation. Langmuir described [14] such a storm system which he believed was initiated and then intensified when dry ice in successive seeding operations was put into the lower level of a rapidly developing storm.

Findings of Project Air Sample

In order to determine whether or not polluted air above cities contained particles which would react with free iodine molecules, eight transcontinental flights have been made by Atmospherics, Inc., under our auspices during the Fall of 1966 and 1967 and the Spring and Fall of 1968. A Piper Aztec aircraft was fitted with instruments which could measure in a semiquantitative manner the concentration of atmospheric particulates which would become ice nuclei by the reaction with iodine, and which would also measure natural nuclei for ice crystal formation. The iodine reactions were conducted in a cold chamber at -20C. The determination of naturally occurring nuclei was done at -22C. In addition, measurements were also made of Aitken nuclei (a measure of polluted air) and cloud nuclei. This last measurement which is made at very low water saturation is also a measure of the degree of air pollution since values above about 50 cloud nuclei and 500 Aitken nuclei per cubic centimeter is indicative of some degree of air pollution. The flight samples were made mostly just below the top of the haze layer which ranged from 1500 to 5000 ft above the ground throughout the flights. Of the 266 measurements in November 1966, 31 were made on the ground. All of these showed excessive pollution levels. Great care was exercised in making these observations to avoid contamination from the engine exhaust of the aircraft being used for the measurements.

At several locations observations were made above as well as within the upper part of the haze layer. In every instance the air above the visible top of the haze layer was low in lead particles while that just below the top or farther down showed very high concentrations.

All other locations where counts of the ice nuclei were low involved regions free of pollution sources. Of the 266 observations 108 or 40% of the measurements were in areas such as upwind of cities (*9*); above large lakes (*8*); above haze layers (*22*); and above woods and farms (*33*). The 60% remaining had values of potential ice nuclei of 100 per liter or more. Some 115, all of them above or downwind of cities had values in excess of 200 per liter which I consider would lead to definite overseeding of the atmosphere with ice particles if suitable moisture was available. Values of 1000 per liter or more occurred at 101 of the stations. If concentrations of ice crystals that high occurred, the cloud would resemble a stable ice fog such as occurs at Fairbanks, Alaska, or the Old Faithful area of Yellowstone Park [*15*] when the temperatures are colder than –40C. With crystal concentrations of this magnitude, the particles grow very slowly if at all and thus remain floating in the air for extended periods. This then reduces the incoming solar radiation to a noticeable degree. If such areas are extensive, they cannot help but cause changes in the weather patterns of the affected areas.

Similar findings characterized our second, third, and fourth round-trip transcontinental flights covering more than 25,000 additional miles and consisting of over 1500 more observations. In practically every instance where polluted air was present, high values in potential ice nuclei (using the iodine reaction) were found. The only exceptions were instances where the plumes of steel mills, forest fires, and other highly concentrated effluents were measured in areas where auto exhausts could contribute very little if anything to the sampled air.

Flight Observations of Inadvertent Seeding

It is quite feasible to detect and observe the massive systems of ice crystal nuclei which produce inadvertent effects on cloud and weather systems due to man's activities. This is accomplished most easily by riding on the sunny side of a jet aircraft.

I observed and photographed three such systems in 1967 during a flight from Buffalo, N. Y., to Denver, Colo., by way of Chicago, returning directly from Denver to New York City.

Ice Crystals Related to Polluted Air

On Wednesday, 6 November 1967, I left Buffalo at 1035 by Boeing 727 landing at Detroit and Chicago. Upon take-off I noted a heavy pollution pall over Buffalo extending westward to the horizon. Just west of Buffalo we climbed above stratiform clouds estimated to be at 15,000 ft or lower which consisted of very high concentrations of ice crystals as established by an undersun. This extensive zone of ice crystals was observed all the way to Detroit and was associated with visibly polluted air. We flew at 20,000 ft where the temperature was –20C. Enroute from Detroit to Chicago I found the same condition to exist from the 1108 take-off until 1132 at which time only supercooled clouds were visible. At the same time all evidence of polluted air disappeared, visibility between cloud decks was unlimited and no further trace of ice crystals could be seen as we landed at Chicago.

The air pollution from Chicago was being carried to the southeast over Indiana about 30 miles south of our jet route.

Ice Crystals Produced by Dust from Plowed Land

Upon take-off at Chicago in a Boeing 707 at 1320 CST, the air was clear, several decks of stratiform clouds were visible with no evidence of ice crystals. Heading west I saw no ice crystals until 1424. Just previous to that time a peculiar zone of dusty air could be seen ahead of us extending toward the southwest. Within a few minutes a brilliant undersun could be seen which persisted for the next half hour. When we finally emerged from the affected zone over northeastern Colorado it was quite obvious that the 300 miles long zone of ice crystals was due to very extensive dust storms caused by 50–100 mph katabatic ground winds pouring down out of the Front Range of the Rockies and blowing top soil from the extensive wheat fields extending from northeastern Colorado to the region about 50 miles east of Pikes Peak. The low level dust was rising only from tilled land; the grassy areas such as the Pawnee Grass Lands were unaffected.

A similar massive dust storm which produced very extensive cloud seeding was observed by me on the afternoon of 12 April 1967, between Amarillo, Tex., and Denver, Colo. This affected region was so extensive and had such a profound effect on the Great Plains and midwest weather systems that I was able to identify it and see its effects over western Illinois two days later.

On the return flight from Denver on 8 December, a third source of inadvertent weather modification was observed. Take-off in a DC9 occurred at 1206 MST on a non-stop jet flight to New York City. Very fine snow was falling at the ground upon take-off. Four minutes afterward we climbed above an extensive area of ice crystals. A bright undersun became visible and was seen continuously all the way from the Denver area to the Atlantic Ocean east of New Jersey. Jet contrails appeared to be the source of these crystals throughout the entire flight which was conducted at 37,000 ft. More than a dozen different planes were seen coming from the east within the flight corridor we were using, most of them several thousand feet below us. From time to time we were close to contrails being made by planes at our level but ahead of us.

The most striking effect observed was the sharp line of demarkation between the area affected by contrail seeding along our flight corridor and an extensive area of high altocumulus cloud (or cirrocumulus) which paralleled our zone at its southern extremity. This region of non-modified clouds was estimated to be about 10 to 20 miles away and extended over large regions of the country. I expect that an effect such as was observed could be seen on satellite cloud photographs.

Perhaps the most disturbing feature about inadvertent weather modification is that in a subtle manner it seems to be changing the nature of clouds over increasingly large areas of the globe. Much of our current consideration of cloud seeding assumes the ubiquity of supercooled clouds and the effectiveness of a seeding material for triggering the instability of such systems.

If pollution sources lead to increased dustiness from ill-used land, more cloud nuclei from burning trash and many more ice nuclei from the lead-permeated exhaust of internal combustion engines, not only will we lose the possible advantage we now have of extracting some additional water from our sky rivers, but we might even be confronted with a drastic change in our climatological patterns.

Interesting climatological evidence of inadvertent weather modification has been found by Changnon [16] to exist in the area downwind of the Chicago, Illinois-Gary, Indiana, complex of extensive urban, highway, and steel mill concentrations.

A very noticeable increase in precipitation and storminess is evident in the records of the past three decades. The LaPorte, Indiana, region whose record is cited as evidence of this effect is downwind of the heavy pollution source mentioned above as well as the close proximity to a very moist air source in the form of Lake Michigan. It is a common observation to see a lake effect street of cumulus clouds extending in the convergence zone south and southeast of Lake Michigan. The combination of very moist air and an abundance of ice nuclei are apparently in very favorable juxtaposition for an optimum reaction to occur. The LaPorte anomaly was first observed by a local weather observer which was then evaluated by Changnon. He found that there has been a notable increase in precipitation starting about 1925 with definite increases since that time also of the number of rainy days, thunderstorms, and hail storms. There has been a 31% increase in precipitation, 38% of thunderstorms, and 240% increase of hail incidences. The increases show a marked correlation with the production of steel.

Since this data was obtained entirely from an evaluation of the climatological records, it is of great importance that careful "on-the-spot" field observations should be made in the LaPorte area to establish the atmospheric dynamics which are responsible for the apparent change in the precipitation pattern of that area. It is particularly important that the concentration of particulate matter be correlated with storm patterns. The weather systems at the mesoscale level should especially be studied to determine whether the area receiving increased precipitation is in the center or edge of the city-industrial plume effluent and the properties of the moist air moving in from Lake Michigan.

Experimental Production of Large Areas of Ice Crystals

During the past ten winters field operations have been developed by our Yellowstone Expeditions in which we have established certain relationships of ice crystal concentrations in the free atmosphere. The early morning inversions of the Old Faithful Geyser Basin in the wintertime often have liquid water contents ranging from 0.5 to 1 gm m^{-3}. This rich supply of moisture is contained within a strong ground-based inversion having a vertical thickness of about 100 m. At a distance of 2000 m from a point source of seeding, ice crystal concentrations up to 10,000 per liter have been measured. Such crystals at -12C are hexagonal plates with cross sections of from ten to a thousand microns, the size depending on concentration and moisture supply. Those of 200 μ occur typically at a concentration of 200 per liter with a fall velocity of 10 cm sec^{-1}. The brilliance of the undersun and related optical phenomena indicates that the number of crystals observed in areas caused by air pollution, jet contrails, or dust storms often have concentrations as high or higher than observed in our experiments. Thus at Yellowstone we have an ideal outdoor laboratory to study some of the factors which must be better understood if we are to work out the physical interactions resulting from the inadvertent modification of the atmosphere.

The Need and Opportunity to Study These Phenomena

The effects cited are but a few examples of many which I have observed and photographed during the past few years. It is the rule rather than the exception that such massive zones of ice crystals can be observed over large areas of the country which can be related to man-caused modification.

Such occurrences must be exercising a detectable effect on the weather systems of the Northern Hemisphere. I feel that nowhere near enough effort has been directed toward the establishment of an organized and continuing study to determine the effect of such inadvertent seeding mechanisms on the synoptic weather patterns of our country. Such studies should have a major place in the World Weather Watch and the Global Atmospheric Research Project. I strongly recommend that the part played by atmospheric particulates should become an important research feature of this program.

There is a critical need for knowledgeable field scientists having an extremely broad scientific background who can work effectively in the real atmosphere under all types of conditions and extract quantitative and meaningful data from such systems.

Our universities must place far more emphasis on this type of training than is being done at present. The eventual understanding of these complex interrelationships do depend on computers, electron microscopes, mass spectrometers, and other costly instruments and equipment. However, the real atmosphere is the thing that must be understood and it is not enough to rely on data obtained by automatic instruments and uninformed field men as is too often the case. It is not easy to conduct efficient field operations. We must approach nature to an ever increasing degree but this confrontation must involve "intelligent eyes," an understanding of the physics, chemistry, and electricity of the reactions which can occur and a zeal to understand the things which combine to produce atmospheric phenomena.

REFERENCES

1. A. Hogan, "Experiments with Aitken Counters in Maritime Atmospheres," *J. de Recherches Atmospheriques*, 3, 53(1968).
2. B. Vonnegut, "Continuous Recording Condensation Nuclei Meter," *Proc. First Natl. Air Pollution Symposium*, Pasadena, Calif., 1, 36(1950).
3. V. J. Schaefer, *Final Report Project Cirrus*, Part 1. Laboratory, Field and Flight Experiments Report No. RL-785. (Schenectady, New York: General Electric Research Laboratory, March 1953).
4. _____, "Artificially Induced Precipitation and Its Potentialities," *Man's Role in Changing the Face of the Earth*, ed. W. L. Thomas (Chicago: University of Chicago Press, 1956).
5. _____, "Cloud Explorations over Africa," *Trans. N. Y. Acad. Sciences*, 20, 535(1958).
6. J. Warner, "A Reduction in Rainfall Associated with Smoke from Sugar Cane Fires–an Inadvertent Weather Modification," *J. Appl. Meteor.*, 7(1968), 247–251.
7. V. J. Schaefer, "The Production of Clouds Containing Supercooled Water Droplets or Ice Crystals under Laboratory Conditions," *Bull. Amer. Meteor. Soc.*, 29, 175(1948).
8. _____, "Ice Nuclei from Automobile Exhaust and Iodine Vapor," *Science*, 154, 1555(1966).
9. C. E. Junge, *Air Chemistry and Radioactivity* (New York: Academic Press, 1963).
10. V. J. Schaefer, "Ice Nuclei from Auto Exhaust and Organic Vapors," *J. Appl. Meteor.*, 7, 113(1968).
11. _____, "The Effect of a Trace of Iodine on Ice Nucleation Measurements," *J. de Recherches Atmospheriques*, 3, 181(1968).
12. A. Hogan, "Ice Nuclei from Direct Reaction of Iodine Vapor with Vapors from Leaded Gasoline," *Science*, 158, 800 (1967).
13. R. A. Bryson, "Is Man Changing the Climate of the Earth?" *Saturday Review* (April 1, 1967), p. 52.
14. I. Langmuir, "Results of the Seeding of Cumulus Clouds in New Mexico," *The Collected Works of Irving Langmuir*, vol. II (New York: Pergamon Press, 1962), pp. 145–162.
15. V. J. Schaefer, "Condensed Water in the Free Atmosphere in Air Colder than −40°C," *J. Appl. Meteor.*, 1, 481(1962).
16. Stanley A. Changnon, "LaPorte Weather Anomaly, Fact or Fiction," *Bull. Amer. Meteor. Soc.*, 49, 4(1968).

BIOGRAPHICAL NOTES

J. Ralph Audy is Director of the William Hooper Foundation and Professor of Tropical Medicine and Human Ecology at the University of California School of Medicine in San Francisco. He received his M.D. and Ph.D. from the University of London. He is the author of Red Mites and Typhus *(1968), and is currently working on a book to be titled* Manmade Maladies.

John B. Calhoun is a psychologist with the National Institutes of Mental Health. A student of vertebrate ecology and social behavior, he has worked on the effects of overcrowding, including possible implications for man. He is the author of many papers, the best known of which is The Ecology and Sociology of the Norway Rat *(1963).*

F. Fraser Darling has furthered popular understanding of the Scottish Highlands with such classics as A Herd of Red Deer *(1937),* Bird Flocks and the Breeding Cycle *(1938),* Natural History of the Highlands and Islands *(1947), and* A Naturalist on Rona *(1939). His* West Highland Survey *(1955), the record of a survey that he conceived and directed, is an outstanding study of human ecology. He has been Vice President of the Conservation Foundation since 1959 and gave the BBC's Reith Lecture in 1969.*

Wayne H. Davis, a zoologist and mammalogist, is Professor of Zoology at the University of Kentucky. He specializes in the taxonomy of mammals and plant evolution.

Paul R. Ehrlich is Professor of Biology at Stanford University, where he has taught since 1959. His present research includes work on density effects in human populations. He is the author of books on butterflies, evolution, and general biology, and of The Population Bomb *(1968) and is past president of Zero Population Growth, Inc.*

John P. Holdren is a physicist with the Sherwood Division of the Lawrence Radiation Laboratory and has been associated with the Institute for Plasma Research and the Department of Aeronautics and Astronautics at Stanford University.

Mort and Eleanor Karp are practicing members of the American Institute of Architects. He is an Assistant Professor of Architecture at the University of Arkansas. They share interests in architectural and environmental theory and in ecological determinism.

Paul Leyhausen is head of a study group in animal behavior at the Max-Planck-Institut für Verhaltensphysiologie at Wuppertal and a lecturer in Comparative Psychology at the University of Bonn. He specializes in the ethology and sociology of mammals, with particular emphasis on cats.

Charles Augustus Lindbergh, noted flyer and authority on aviation, is President of the World Wildlife Fund.

Betty J. Meggers holds a doctorate in anthropology and is a Research Associate of the Smithsonian Institution. She has collaborated on archaeological investigations with her husband, Clifford Evans, and maintains research interests in cultural evolution and ecology and in the reconstruction of cultural development in northern South America. She is author of Ecuador *(1966) and joint editor of* Aboriginal Cultural Development in Latin America *(1963). Her* Amazonia: Man and Culture in a Counterfeit Paradise *will be published in 1971.*

Stanley Milgram is Professor of Psychology at the Graduate Center of The City University of New York. He has taught at Yale and Harvard. In 1964 the American Association for the Advancement of Science awarded him its socio-psychological prize for his research on obedience to authority.

Sibyl Moholy-Nagy is Professor of Architecture at Columbia University and author of Matrix of Man: An Illustrated History of Urban Environment *(1968).*

John R. Napier is Director of the Unit of Primate Biology at Queen Elizabeth College of the University of London. He is joint author of the definitive Handbook of Living Primates *(1967), and is an authority on primate and human functional evolution. His most recent book is* The Roots of Mankind *(1970).*

Eugene P. Odum is Professor of Zoology and Director of the Institute of Ecology at the University of Georgia. He is the author of several influential books on ecology and radiation ecology, the most important of which is Fundamentals of Ecology *(1959).*

Walter J. Ong, S.J., is Professor of English at Saint Louis University in St. Louis, Missouri. A scholar in the fields of Renaissance and contemporary culture, he has twice received Guggenheim grants. His books include The Presence of the Word *(1967),* In the Human Grain *(1967),* The Barbarian Within *(1962), and* Knowledge and the Future of Man *(1968).*

Scott Paradise graduated from the Episcopal Theological School in Cambridge, Massachusetts, in 1953. After work with the Sheffield (England) and Detroit Industrial Missions, he became Executive Director of the newly-formed Boston Industrial Mission in 1965. In addition to shorter publications, he is author of The Detroit Industrial Mission *(1968).*

John H. Ryther is a marine biologist at the Woods Hole Oceanographic Institution in Woods Hole, Massachusetts. He was director of the U. S. program in biology on the International Indian Ocean Expedition from 1960 to 1965, and served on the President's Science Advisory Commission in 1965–66.

Carl O. Sauer is Professor Emeritus in the Department of Geography at the University of California, Berkeley. The dean of contemporary historical geographers, he is the author of many works on Latin American history and geography and of such classics as The Geography of the Ozark Highland of Missouri *(1920),* Agricultural Origins and Dispersals *(1952), and* Land and Life *(1963).*

Vincent J. Schaefer is Director of the Atmospheric Sciences Research Center and a Professor in the Department of Atmospheric Sciences at the State University of New York at Albany.

Harold F. Searles, M.D., was a staff psychiatrist at Chestnut Lodge Sanitarium in Rockville, Maryland, from 1949 to 1964. He now serves as a consultant in psychotherapy at the Sheppard and Enoch Pratt Hospital in Towson, Maryland, and as president of the Washington Psychoanalytic Society, and teaches psychiatry at various institutions. He has published The Nonhuman Environment in Normal Development and in Schizophrenia *(1960) and* Collected Papers on Schizophrenia and Related Subjects *(1966).*

Paul Shepard is a writer and teacher on the cultural aspects of ecology, particularly environmental perception. For ten years he was director of Green Oaks, the Knox College field station in Illinois. More recently he has taught at Smith and Pitzer Colleges. His books include Man in the Landscape, a Historic View of the Esthetics of Nature *(1967) and* The Subversive Science, Essays Toward an Ecology of Man, *with Daniel McKinley (1969).*

ADDITIONAL READINGS

There can be no such thing as a complete bibliography of the fields touched on in this book. Thus, the emphasis in the following lists of readings is on modernity and usefulness. Very few of the items duplicate listings in The Subversive Science, and interested readers are referred to that book for extensive and sometimes related lists.

This reading list is divided into four parts, corresponding to the divisions within the book, and items are listed only once. Paperback editions are noted where possible, for the benefit of students who wish to buy their own copies and teachers who wish to arrange relatively cheap supplementary readings for students.

Part One. Genesis and Perception

The readings recommended to supplement Part One deal with the capacities of the environment and the human organism to interact, with both ameliorative and devastative effects. In probably no other facet of the ecology of man have more revealing advances in understanding been made in recent years. This new understanding involves a synthesis of two discrete attitudes toward the natural world. The world may be, as Thoreau said, more beautiful than useful, but both views of it are incomplete; we can lose ourselves in the former, and lose the world through the latter. If viewed exclusively as so much inert clay, the world appears dull and uninteresting. Analytical science need not do so, and many of the readings cited below prove how unnecessary it is for scientific writing to be dry.

The primeval simplicities of hunting and gathering, and the sophisticated responses of human cultures, may be grasped by reading Lee and DeVore's Man the Hunter *and Grahame Clark's* The Stone Age Hunters, *and the increasingly intricate symbioses among men, plants, and animals are admirably summarized in Ucko and Dimbleby's book. Some recent books in human evolution and on ecological principles are listed as well, whether or not they achieve a synthesis of the two fields of knowledge.*

Aiton, Arthur S. "The Impact of the Flora and Fauna of the New World upon the Old World during the Sixteenth Century," Chronica Botanica, 12 (1948–49), 121–125.

Anderson, Edgar. Plants, Man and Life. *Berkeley: University of California Press, 1967. Paper.*

Aschoff, Jürgen. "Circadian Rhythms in Man," Science, *148 (1965), 1427–1432.*

Baker, Herbert G. Plants and Civilization. *Belmont, Calif.: Wadsworth, 1965.*

Barker, Roger G. Ecological Psychology. *Stanford: Stanford University Press, 1968.*

Bates, Marston. "The Human Ecosystem," pp. 21–30 in Resources and Man, *National Academy of Sciences–National Research Council. San Francisco: W. H. Freeman, 1969.*

——————. *"The Role of Weather in Human Behavior," pp. 393–407 in* Human Dimensions of Weather Modification, *ed. W. R. Derrick Sewell. Chicago: University of Chicago Department of Geography, 1966.*

Bigelow, Robert. The Dawn Warriors. *Boston: Atlantic Monthly Press, 1969.*

Binford, Lewis R., and Sally R. Binford. "The Predatory Revolution: a Consideration of the Evidence for a New Subsistence Level," American Anthropologist, *68 (1966), 508–512.*

Binford, Sally R., and L. R. Binford. "Stone Tools and Human Behavior," Scientific American, *220 (April, 1969), 70–84.*

Bonifazi, Conrad. A Theology of Things. *Philadelphia: Lippincott, 1967.*

Brace, C. Loring. "The Origin of Man," Natural History, *79 (Jan., 1970), 46–49.*

Brain, C. K. "Who Killed the Swartkrans Ape-man?" South African Museum Association Bulletin, *9 (1968), 127–139.*

Brereton, John Le Gay. "Evolved Regulatory Mechanisms of Population Control," pp. 81–93 in The Evolution of Living Things, *Royal Society of Victoria. Victoria: Melbourne University Press, 1962.*

Burton, Ian. "The Quality of the Environment, a Review," Geographical Review, *58 (1968), 472–481.*

Calder, Nigel. Eden Was No Garden. *New York: Holt, Rinehart & Winston, 1967.*

Campbell, Joseph. The Masks of God, *vols. I–IV. New York: Viking, 1959–1968.*

Case, Humphrey. "Neolithic Explanations," Antiquity, *43 (1969), 176–186.*

Caspari, Ernst. "Selective Forces in the Evolution of Man," American Naturalist, *97 (1963), 5–14.*

Chang, Jen-Hu. Climate and Agriculture. An Ecological Survey. *Chicago: Aldine, 1968.*

Clark, J. G. D. Prehistoric Europe: The Economic Basis. *London: Methuen, 1952.*

Clark, Grahame. The Stone Age Hunters. *New York: McGraw-Hill, 1967. Paper.*

Comfort, Alex. The Nature of Human Nature. *New York: Harper and Row, 1967. Pelican paperback A-1032.*

Craik, Kenneth H. "The Comprehension of the Everyday Physical Environment," American Institute of Planners Journal, *35 (January, 1968), 29–37.*

Crile, George, Jr. A Naturalistic View of Man. *Cleveland: World, 1969.*

Crist, R. E. "Tropical Subsistence Agriculture in Latin America: Some Neglected Aspects and Implications," pp. 503–519 in Smithsonian Annual Report 1963. *Washington: the Institution, 1964.*

Crook, John H. *"Co-operation in Primates,"* Eugenics Review, *58 (1966), 63-70.*
—————— . *"Monogamy, Polygamy and Food Supply,"* Discovery, *(January, 1963), 35-41.*
Crook, John H., and P. Aldrich-Blake. *"Ecological and Behavioural Contrasts between Sympatric Ground Dwelling Primates in Ethiopia,"* Folia Primatologica, *8 (1968), 192-227.*
Darlington, C. D. *"The Silent Millennia in the Origin of Agriculture," pp. 67-72 in* The Domestication and Exploitation of Plants and Animals, *ed. P. J. Ucko and G. W. Dimbleby. Chicago: Aldine, 1969.*
—————— . *"Psychology, Genetics and the Process of History,"* British Journal of Psychology, *54 (1963), 293-298.*
DeLaszlo, Henry, and P. S. Henshaw. *"Plant Materials used by Primitive Peoples to Affect Fertility,"* Science, *119 (1954), 626-631.*
Denbeck, H. Animals and Men. *Garden City, N. Y.: Doubleday, 1965.*
Diamond, Jared M. *"Zoological Classification System of a Primitive People,"* Science, *151 (1966), 1102-1104.*
Driver, Harold E. Indians of North America. *Chicago: University of Chicago Press, 1961.*
Driver, Peter M. *"An Ethological Approach to the Problem of Mind," in* The Mind, *ed. W. C. Corning and M. Balaban. New York: Interscience, 1968.*
DuBrul, E. Lloyd. *"Pattern of Genetic Control of Structure in the Evolution of Behavior,"* Perspectives in Biology and Medicine, *10 (1967), 524-539.*
Efron, Daniel H., et al., eds. Ethnopharmacologic Search for Psychoactive Drugs. *(U.S. Public Health Service, National Institute of Mental Health, Workshop Series of Pharmacology Section, no. 2.) Washington: U. S. Government Printing Office, 1967.*
Ehrlich, Paul R. *"The Biological Revolution,"* The Center Magazine, *2,6 (1969), 28-31.*
Emiliani, Cesare. *"The Pleistocene Epoch and the Evolution of Man,"* Current Anthropology, *9 (1968), 27-47.*
Fabun, Don. The Dynamics of Change. *Englewood Cliffs, N. J.: Prentice-Hall, 1970. Paper.*
Farnsworth, Norman R. *"Hallucinogenic Plants,"* Science, *162 (1968), 1086-1092.*
Ferwerda, F. P., and F. Wit, eds. Outlines of Perennial Crop Breeding in the Tropics. *Wageningen, The Netherlands: Veenman and Zonen, 1969.*
Flannery, Kent V. *"Origins and Ecological Effects of Early Domestication in Iran and the Near East," pp. 73-100 in* The Domestication and Exploitation of Plants and Animals, *ed. P. J. Ucko and G. W. Dimbleby. Chicago: Aldine, 1969.*
Freeman, Derek. *"Thunder, Blood and the Nicknaming of God's Creatures,"* The Psychoanalytic Quarterly, *38 (1968), 353-399.*
Gallup, George H., Jr. *"The U.S. Public Looks at its Environment,"* International Union for the Conservation of Nature Bulletin, *2 (1969), 99-100.*

Garnsey, Morris E., and J. R. Hibbs, eds. Social Sciences and the Environment. *Boulder: University of Colorado Press, 1967.*

Glacken, Clarence J. Traces on the Rhodian Shore. *Berkeley: University of California Press, 1967.*

Glass, David C. Biology and Behavior: Environmental Influences. *New York: Rockefeller University Press and Russell Sage Foundation, 1968.*

Goldman, Marshall, ed. Controlling Pollution: The Economics of a Cleaner America. *Englewood Cliffs, N. J.: Prentice-Hall, 1967.*

Graves, Robert. The White Goddess, *rev. ed. New York: Farrar, Straus & Giroux, 1966.*

Hall, Edward T. "Proxemics," Current Anthropology, *9 (1968), 83–108.*

——————. The Hidden Dimension. *Garden City, N. Y.: Doubleday, 1966.*

Halprin, Lawrence. The RSVP Cycles: Creative Processes in the Human Environment. *New York: George Braziller, 1970.*

Hardin, Garrett. "The Economics of Wilderness," Natural History, *78 (June–July, 1969), 20–27.*

Hare, F. Kenneth. "How Should We Treat Environment?" Science, *167 (1970), 352–355.*

Harris, David R. "Agricultural Systems, Ecosystems and the Origins of Agriculture," pp. 3–15 in The Domestication and Exploitation of Plants and Animals, *ed. P. J. Ucko and G. W. Dimbleby. Chicago: Aldine, 1969.*

——————. "New Light on Plant Domestication and the Origin of Agriculture: a Review," Geographical Review, *57 (1967), 90–107.*

Henderson, Leon J. The Fitness of the Environment. *Boston: Beacon Press, 1958. Paper.*

Heyman, Mark. "Space and Behavior," Landscape, *13 (Spring, 1964), 4–10.*

Higgs, E. S., and M. R. Jarman. "The Origins of Agriculture: a Reconsideration," Antiquity, *43 (1969), 31–41.*

Holdridge, L. R. "The Tropics, a Misunderstood Ecosystem," Bulletin of the Association for Tropical Biology, *5 (1965), 21–30.*

Hole, Frank. "Investigating the Origins of Mesopotamian Civilization," Science, *153 (1966), 605–611.*

Hupp, David. "Annotated Bibliography," Whole Earth Catalog, *(January, 1970), 31–33.*

Huth, Hans. Nature and the American. *Berkeley: University of California Press, 1967.*

Iltis, Hugh H. "The Optimum Human Environment and its Relation to Modern Agricultural Preoccupations," The Biologist, *50 (1968), 114–125.*

Iltis, Hugh H., O. L. Loucks, and P. Andrews. "Criteria for an Optimum Human Environment," Bulletin of the Atomic Scientists, *26 (January, 1970), 2–6.*

Iversen, Johannes. "Forest Clearance in the Stone Age," Scientific American, *194 (March, 1956), 36–41.*

Kahler, Erich. "Culture and Evolution," Centennial Review, *5 (1961); reprinted in* Culture, *ed. M. F. A. Montagu. New York: Oxford University Press, 1968, pp. 3–19.*

Kates, Robert W. "The Perception of Storm Hazard on the Shores of Megalopolis," University of Chicago Department of Geography Research Papers, *109 (1967), 60–74.*

Klein, Richard G., "Mousterian Cultures in European Russia," Science, *165 (1969), 257–265.*

Kolars, John. "Locational Aspects of Cultural Ecology: the Case of the Goat in Non-Western Agriculture," Geographical Review, *56 (1966), 577–584.*

Kormondy, Edward J. Concepts of Ecology. *Englewood Cliffs, N. J.: Prentice-Hall, 1969.*

Kroeber, A. L. Cultural and Natural Areas of Native North America. *(University of California Publications in American Archeology and Ethnology, 38), 1939. Reprinted, Berkeley: University of California Press, 1963.*

Lathrap, Donald W. "The 'Hunting' Economies of the Tropical Forest Zone of South America: an Attempt at Historical Perspective," pp. 23–29 in Man the Hunter, *ed. R. B. Lee and I. De Vore. Chicago: Aldine, 1968.*

Leach, E. R. "Ritualization in Man," Philosophical Transactions of the Royal Society of London, B, Biological Sciences, *251 (1966), 403–408.*

Leakey, Louis S. B. "Development of Aggression as a Factor in Early Human and Pre-human Evolution," UCLA Forum in Medical Sciences, *7 (1967), 1–34. Reprinted in* Aggression and Defense, *ed. C. D. Clemente and D. B. Lindsley. Berkeley: University of California Press, 1967.*

Lee, Richard B. "What Hunters Do for a Living, or, How to Make Out on Scarce Resources," pp. 30–48 in Man the Hunter, *ed. R. B. Lee and I. De Vore. Chicago: Aldine, 1968.*

Lee, Richard B., and Irven De Vore, eds. Man the Hunter. *Chicago: Aldine, 1968.*

Leeds, Anthony, and A. P. Vayda, eds. Man, Culture, and Animals: The Role of Animals in Human Ecological Adjustments. *(Publication 78.) Washington: American Association for the Advancement of Science, 1965.*

Leone, Mark P. "Neolithic Economic Autonomy and Social Distance," Science, *162 (1968), 1150–1151.*

Lévi-Strauss, Claude. The Savage Mind. *Chicago: University of Chicago Press, 1966.*

Levy, G. Rachel. Religious Conceptions of the Stone Age and Their Influence upon European Thought. *New York: Harper, 1963. Paper.*

Lewthwaite, Gordon R. "Environmentalism and Determinism: A Search for Clarification," Annals of the Association of American Geographers, *56 (1966), 1–23.*

Logan, James C. "The Secularization of Nature," pp. 101–127 in Christians and the Good Earth, *ed. Alfred Stefferud (F/M/N Papers No. 1.) Alexandria, Va.: Faith-Man-Nature Group, 1969.*

Lorenz, Konrad. "Evolution of Ritualization in the Biological and Cultural Spheres," Philosophical Transactions of the Royal Society of London, B, Biological Sciences, *251 (1966), 273–284.*

Lovejoy, Arthur O. The Great Chain of Being. *New York: Harper, 1960. Paper.*

Lowenthal, David, ed. "Environmental Perception and Behavior," University of Chicago Department of Geography Research Papers, *109 (1967).*

Lynch, Kevin. "The City as Environment," Scientific American, *213 (September, 1965), 209–219.*

MacNeil, Mary. "Laterite Soils," Scientific American, *211 (November, 1964), 96–102.*

MacNeish, R. S. "The Origins of American Agriculture," Antiquity, *39 (1965), 87–94.*

McKinley, Daniel. "Ethics, Technics, and Biology," The Yale Review, *58 (1969), 617–620.*

Malde, Harold E. "Environment and Man in Arid America," Science, *145 (1964), 123–129.*

Margalef, Ramon. Perspectives in Ecological Theory. *Chicago: University of Chicago Press, 1968.*

Martin, P. S., and H. E. Wright, Jr., eds. Pleistocene Extinctions. The Search for a Cause. *New Haven: Yale University Press, 1967.*

Meggers, Betty J. Amazonia: Man and Culture in a Counterfeit Paradise. *Chicago: Aldine, 1971.*

Mellaart, J. Çatal Hüyük: A Neolithic Town in Anatolia. *London: Thames, 1967.*
——————— . *"A Neolithic City in Turkey,"* Scientific American, *210 (April, 1964), 94–104.*

Merrens, H. Roy. "The Physical Environment of Early America: Images and Image Makers in Colonial South Carolina," Geographical Review, *59 (1969), 530–556.*

Merton, Thomas. "The Wild Places," The Center Magazine, *1 (July, 1968), 40–44.*

Moran, William E., Jr. "A Sourcebook on Population," Population Bulletin, *25,5 (1969), 1–51.*

Northrop, F. S. C. "Man's Relation to the Earth in its Bearing on His Aesthetic, Ethical, and Legal Values," pp. 1052–1067 in Man's Role in Changing the Face of the Earth, *ed. W. L. Thomas, Jr. Chicago: University of Chicago Press, 1956.*

Odum, H. T., and R. C. Pinkerton. "Time's Speed Regulator, the Optimum Efficiency for Maximum Output in Physical and Biological Systems," American Scientist, *43 (1955), 331–343.*

Owings, Nathaniel Alexander. The American Esthetic. *New York: Harper and Row, 1969.*

Peckham, Morse. Man's Rage for Chaos. *New York: Schocken Books, 1967.*
——————— . *"Toward a Theory of Romanticism,"* PMLA, *66 (1951), 5–23.*

Piggott, Stuart. Ancient Europe from the Beginnings of Agriculture to Classical Antiquity. *Chicago: Aldine, 1968.*

Pilbeam, David. The Evolution of Man. *New York: Funk & Wagnalls, 1970.*

Platt, John R., ed. New Views of the Nature of Man. *Chicago: University of Chicago Press, 1965.*

Randolph, Theron G. Human Ecology and Susceptibility to the Chemical Environment. *Springfield, Ill.: Charles C. Thomas, 1962.*

Rapoport, Amos. House Form and Culture. *Englewood Cliffs, N. J.: Prentice-Hall, 1969.*

Reed, Charles A. "The Pattern of Animal Domestication in the Prehistoric Near East," pp. 361–380 in The Domestication and Exploitation of Plants and Animals, *ed. P. J. Ucko and G. W. Dimbleby. Chicago: Aldine, 1969.*

Reid, Kenneth. Nature's Network: The Story of Ecology. *Garden City, N.Y.: Natural History Press, 1970.*

Reynolds, Vernon. The Apes. *New York: Dutton, 1967.*

Rodda, M. Noise and Society. *Edinburgh: Oliver and Boyd, and New York: Benjamin, 1967. Paper.*

Roslansky, John D., ed. Genetics and the Future of Man. *New York: Appleton-Century-Crofts, 1966.*

Rule, Colter. "A Theory of Human Behavior Based on Studies of Non-Human Primates," *Perspectives in Biology and Medicine, 10 (1967), 153–176.*

Russell, W. M. S. "The Slash-and-Burn Technique," *Natural History, 77 (March, 1968), 58–65.*

Schaffer, William M. "Character Displacement and the Evolution of the Hominidae," *American Naturalist, 102 (1968), 559–571.*

Schreider, E. "Possible Selective Mechanisms of Social Differentiation in Biological Traits," *Human Biology, 39 (1967), 14–20.*

Schultes, Richard Evans. "Hallucinogens of Plant Origin," *Science, 163 (1969), 245–254.*

Sebeok, Thomas A., and Alexandra Ramsay, eds. Approaches to Animal Communication. *The Hague: Mouton, 1969.*

Sewell, W. R. Derrick, R. W. Kates, and L. E. Phillips. "Human Response to Weather and Climate: Geographical Contributions," *Geographical Review, 68 (1968), 262–280.*

Shafer, Elwood L., J. F. Hamilton, Jr., and E. A. Schmidt. "Natural Landscape Preferences: a Predictive Model," *Journal of Leisure Research, 1 (1969), 1–19.*

Shepard, Paul. Man in the Landscape: A Historic View of the Esthetics of Nature. *New York: Alfred A. Knopf, 1967.*

Shepard, Paul, and Daniel McKinley, eds. The Subversive Science: Essays Toward an Ecology of Man. *Boston: Houghton Mifflin, 1969.*

Snyder, Richard C. "Adaptive Values of Bipedalism," *American Journal of Physical Anthropology, 26 (1967), 131–134.*

Sommer, Robert. Personal Space, The Behavioral Basis of Design. *Englewood Cliffs, N. J.: Prentice-Hall, 1969.*

Southwick, Charles H. "My Thanks to Hanuman," *Ohio State University Review, Contributions in the Humanities, 4 (1962), 19–34.*

Spurway, Helen. "The Causes of Domestication," *Journal of Genetics, 53 (1955), 325–362.*

Thoday, J. M., and A. S. Parkes, eds. Genetic and Environmental Influences on Behaviour, A Symposium. *(Eugenics Society Symposia no. 4.) New York: Plenum, 1969.*

Thompson, Laura. "The Relations of Men, Animals, and Plants in an Island Community (Fiji)," American Anthropologist, *51 (1949), 253–267.*

Tiger, Lionel, and Robin Fox. "The Zoological Perspective in Social Science," Man, *1 (1966), 75–81.*

Tuan, Yi-Fu. "Attitudes Toward Environment: Themes and Approaches," University of Chicago Department of Geography Research Papers, *109 (1967), 4–17.*

Turček, F. J. "The Zoological Significance of Ecological and Geographical Borderlands," Acta Zoologica Academiae Scientiarum Hungaricae, *12 (1966), 193–201.*

Ucko, Peter J., and G. W. Dimbleby, eds. The Domestication and Exploitation of Plants and Animals. *London: Duckworth, and Chicago: Aldine, 1969.*

Ugent, Donald. "The Potato in Mexico: Geography and Primitive Culture," Economic Botany, *22 (1968), 108–123.*

von Foerster, Heinz, et al., eds. Purposive Systems. *New York: Books, Inc., 1968.*

Washburn, Sherwood L. "Behaviour and the Origin of Man," Proceedings of the Royal Anthropological Institute of Great Britain and Ireland, *(1967), 21–27.*

Waterbolk, H. T. "Food Production in Prehistoric Europe," Science, *162 (1968), 1093–1102.*

Watson, R. R., and P. J. Watson. Man and Nature, An Anthropological Essay in Human Ecology. *New York: Harcourt, Brace & World, 1969. Paper.*

Weisz, Paul B., ed. The Contemporary Scene. Readings on Human Nature, Race, Behavior, Society, and Environment. *New York: McGraw-Hill, 1970.*

Wheeler, Reuben. Man, Nature and Art. *London: Pergamon Press, 1968.*

Wharton, Clifton R., Jr., ed. Subsistence Agriculture and Economic Development. *Chicago: Aldine, 1969.*

Wickler, Wolfgang. "Socio-Sexual Signals and their Intra-Specific Imitation among Primates," pp. 69–147 in Primate Ethology, *ed. Desmond Morris. Chicago: Aldine, 1967.*

Wissler, Clark. The Relation of Nature to Man in Aboriginal America. *New York: Oxford University Press, 1926.*

Wittfogel, Karl. Oriental Despotism: A Comparative Study of Total Power. *New Haven: Yale University Press, 1957. Paper.*

Wolf, Eric R. Peasants. *Englewood Cliffs, N. J.: Prentice-Hall, 1966. Paper.*

Woodwell, George M. "The Energy Cycle of the Biosphere," Scientific American, *223 (September, 1970), 64–74.*

Woodwell, George M., and H. H. Smith, eds. Diversity and Stability in Ecological Systems. *(Brookhaven Symposia in Biology no. 22.) Upton, N. Y.: Brookhaven National Laboratory, 1969.*

Wright, H. E., Jr., "Natural Environment of Early Food Production North of Mesopotamia," Science, *161 (1968), 334–339.*

Zohary, Daniel. *"The Progenitors of Wheat and Barley in Relation to Domestication and Agricultural Dispersal in the Old World," pp. 47–66 in* The Domestication and Exploitation of Plants and Animals, *ed. P. J. Ucko and G. W. Dimbleby. Chicago: Aldine, 1969.*

Part Two. Society and its Creations

Man is a remarkably social animal, and his behavior as an individual offers only partial explanation of his mass behavior. Our understanding of ourselves is undermined by ignorance of the nature of man as a crowd animal. The complexity of a series of nested environments, each interacting with the others but somewhat independent in its functions and evolution, is patently obvious. The difficulties of dealing in a restorative way with the pathologies of any of these environments is equally evident. Because the behavior of mass man in the world and his success as a biological species are so intimately involved, sheer human numbers have taken on overwhelming importance. References to populations and population control are listed below.

Ajax (pseudonym). *"Lepidoptera; or, The Changing World of Walter Curtis,"* Landscape, *2 (Spring, 1953), 29–30.*

Ambrose, J. Anthony. *"The Study of Human Social Organization: a Review of Current Concepts and Approaches,"* Symposium Zoological Society of London, *14 (1965), 301–314.*

Ardrey, Robert. The Social Contract. *New York: Atheneum, 1970.*

Attinger, Ernst O. *"Performance Control of Biological and Societal Systems,"* Perspectives in Biology and Medicine, *12 (1968), 103–123.*

Bronfenbrenner, Urie. Two Worlds of Childhood: U.S. and U.S.S.R. *New York: Russell Sage Foundation, 1970.*

Calhoun, John B. *"Ecological Factors in the Development of Behavioral Anomalies," pp. 1–51 in* Comparative Psychopathology, *ed. J. Zubin and H. F. Hunt. New York: Grune & Stratton, 1967.*

Carter, Luther J. *"Development in the Poor Nations: How to Avoid Fouling the Nest,"* Science, *163 (1969), 1046–1048.*

Ciriacy-Wantrup, S. V., and J. J. Parsons, eds. Natural Resources, Quality and Quantity. *Berkeley: University of California Press, 1967.*

Comfort, Alex. Authority and Delinquency in the Modern State. *London: Routledge & Kegan Paul, 1950.*

Commoner, Barry. *"The Social Significance of Environmental Pollution,"* The Explorer, *11 (Winter, 1969), 17–20.*

Cook, Robert C., and Jane Lecht. People! An Introduction to the Study of Population. *Washington: Columbia Books, 1968.*

Craik, Kenneth H. *"Transportation and the Person,"* High Speed Ground Transportation Journal, *3 (1969), 86–91.*

Crowe, Beryl L. "The Tragedy of the Commons Revisited," Science, *166 (1969),*
    1103–1107.
Crowe, Sylvia. Forestry in the Landscape. *(H. M. Forestry Commission Booklet*
    no. 18.) London: Her Majesty's Stationery Office, 1966.
Dansereau, Pierre. Challenge for Survival: Land, Air and Water for Man in Mega-
    lopolis. *New York: Columbia University Press, 1970.*
Darlington, C. D. The Evolution of Man and Society. *New York: Simon &*
    Schuster, 1970.
Dasmann, Raymond F. A Different Kind of Country. *New York: Macmillan,*
    1968.
——————— . An Environment Fit for People. *(Public Affairs Pamphlet no.*
    421.) New York: Public Affairs Committee, 1968.
Day, Lincoln, and Alice Day. Too Many Americans. *New York: Dell, 1965.*
    Paper.
De Reuck, A. V. S., and J. Knight, eds. Conflict in Society. *(A Ciba Foundation*
    General Symposium.) London: Churchill, 1966.
Deutsch, Morris. Ground-Water Contamination and Legal Controls in Michigan.
    (U.S. Geological Survey Water-Supply Papers 1691.) 1964.
Doxiadis, C. A. "Man's Movement and His City," Science, *162 (1968), 326–334.*
Driver, Peter M. "Toward an Ethology of Human Conflict," Journal of Conflict
    Resolution, *11 (1967), 361–374.*
DuBois, Arthur B., et al. Effects of Chronic Exposure to Low Levels of Carbon
    Monoxide on Human Health, Behavior, and Performance. *Washington: U.S.*
    National Academy of Sciences/National Academy of Engineering, 1969.
Dubos, René. Man Adapting. *New Haven: Yale University Press, 1965. Paper.*
Ehrlich, Paul R., and John P. Holdren. "Hidden Effects of Overpopulation,"
    Saturday Review *(August 1, 1970), 52–53.*
——————— . "The People Problem," Saturday Review *(July 4, 1970), 42–43.*
Eichenwald, H. F., and P. C. Fry. "Nutrition and Learning," Science, *163 (1969),*
    644–648.
Enke, Stephen. "The Economics of Having Children," Policy Sciences, *1 (1970),*
    15–30.
——————— . Zero U.S. Population Growth — When, How, and Why. *Santa*
    Barbara: General Electric–TEMPO, 1970.
Etkin, William. "Behavioral Factors Stabilizing Social Organization in Animals,"
    pp. 63–75 in Comparative Psychopathology, *ed. J. Zubin and H. F. Hunt.*
    New York: Grune & Stratton, 1967.
Feibleman, James K. "The Ambivalence of Aggression and the Moralization of
    Man," Perspectives in Biology and Medicine, *9 (1966), 537–548.*
Finger, F. G., and R. M. McInturff. "Meteorology and the Supersonic Transport,"
    Science, *167 (1970), 16–25.*
Fletcher, Ronald. "The Inflamed Society," Twentieth Century, *177–178, 1039–40*
    (1969), 19–26.

Forbes, R. J. The Conquest of Nature. Technology and Its Consequences. *New York: Praeger, 1968.*

Ford, Amasa B. "Casualties of Our Time," Science, *167 (1970), 256–263.*

Frankel, Lillian B. This Crowded World. *Washington: Columbia Books and Population Reference Bureau, 1970.*

Frederiksen, Harald. "Feedbacks in Economic and Demographic Transition," Science, *166 (1969), 837–847.*

Fried, Morton, Marvin Harris and Robert Murphy, eds. War. The Anthropology of Armed Conflict and Aggression. *Garden City: Natural History Press, 1968.*

Givoni, B. Man, Climate and Architecture. *New York: Elsevier, 1969.*

Glesinger, Egon. "The Mediterranean Project," Scientific American, *203 (July, 1960), 86–103.*

Gruening, Ernest, Chairman. Population Crisis, *14 vols. (U.S. Senate Committee on Government Operations, Subcommittee on Foreign Aid Expenditures.) Washington: U.S. Government Printing Office, 1965–1968.*

Gulick, Addison. "A Biological Prologue for Human Values," BioScience, *18 (1968), 1109–1112.*

Halprin, Lawrence. Freeways. *New York: Reinhold, 1966.*

———————— . Cities. *New York: Reinhold, 1963.*

Hardin, Garrett, ed. Population, Evolution and Birth Control, *2nd ed. San Francisco: W. H. Freeman, 1969.*

Hoagland, Hudson. "Technology, Adaptation, and Evolution," Biological Psychiatry, *1 (1969), 73–80.*

Hubbert, M. King. "Earth Scientists Look at Environmental Limits in Human Ecology," National Academy of Sciences–National Research Council News Report, *14 (July–August, 1964), 58–60.*

Illich, Ivan. The Church, Change and Development: Essays on the Church in Technological and Revolutionary Society. *Chicago: The Urban Training Center Press, 1970.*

———————— . *"Outwitting the 'Developed' Countries,"* New York Review of Books, *13 (November 6, 1969), 20–24.*

Jackson, J. B. "An Engineered Environment," Landscape, *16 (Autumn, 1966), 16–20.*

Jarrett, Henry, ed. Environmental Quality in a Growing Economy. *Baltimore: John Hopkins Press for Resources for the Future, 1966.*

Jordan, P. A. "Ecology, Conservation, and Human Behavior," BioScience, *18 (1968), 1023–1029.*

Juenger, Friedrich G. The Failure of Technology. *Chicago: Henry Regnery, 1956.*

Kryter, Karl D. "Sonic Booms from Supersonic Transport," Science, *163 (1969), 359–367.*

Kuttner, R. "Cultural Selection of Human Psychological Types," Genus, *16 (1960), 3–6; reprinted as pp. 286–289 in* Culture, *ed. M. F. A. Montagu. New York: Oxford University Press, 1968.*

Kyllonen, R. L. "Crime Rate vs. Population Density in United States Cities: a Model," General Systems, *12 (1967), 137–145.*

Lasker, G. W. "Human Biological Adaptability," Science, *166 (1969), 1480–1486.*

Laughlin, William S. "Adaptability and Human Genetics," Proceedings National Academy of Sciences, *60 (1968), 12–21.*

Leighton, Philip A. "Geographical Aspects of Air Pollution," Geographical Review, *56 (1966), 151–174.*

Leinwand, Gerald, gen. ed. Problems of American Society: The City as a Community; The Slums; The Traffic Jam; Air and Water Pollution; Crime and Juvenile Delinquency; The Draft; The Negro in the City; The Consumer; Poverty and the Poor; Civil Rights and Civil Liberties, *10 vols. New York: Washington Square Press, 1970. Paper.*

Linton, Ron M. Terracide: America's Destruction of Her Living Environment. *Boston: Little, Brown, 1970.*

Livingstone, Frank B. "Genetics, Ecology and the Origin of Incest and Exogamy," Current Anthropology, *10 (1969), 45–61.*

Means, Richard L. "Ecology and the Contemporary Religious Conscience," The Christian Century, *(December 3, 1969), 1546–1549.*

Meyer, Jon K. Bibliography on the Urban Crisis. The Behavioral, Psychological, and Sociological Aspects of the Urban Crisis. *(Publication no. 1948.) Washington: U.S. Public Health Service, 1969.*

Michelson, W. Man and His Urban Environment: A Sociological Approach. *Reading, Mass.: Addison-Wesley, 1970. Paper.*

Mill, John Stuart. "Of the Stationary State," pp. 752–757 in Principles of Political Economy, vol. 2, ed. J. M. Robson. *Toronto: University of Toronto Press, 1965.*

Miller, R. S., G. M. Woodwell, W. R. Burch, P. A. Jordan, and R. L. Means. Man and His Environment: The Ecological Limits of Optimism. *(Yale University School of Forestry Bulletin No. 76.) New Haven: Yale University Press, 1970.*

Morris, Desmond. The Human Zoo. *New York: McGraw-Hill, 1969.*

Moholy-Nagy, Sibyl. Matrix of Man: An Illustrated History of Urban Environment. *New York: Praeger, 1968.*

Mumford, Lewis. The City in History. *New York: Harcourt, Brace & World, 1969. Paper.*

——————— . The Urban Prospect. *New York: Harcourt, Brace & World, 1968.*

Myers, K. "The Effects of Density on Sociality and Health in Mammals," Proceedings of the Ecological Society of Australia, *1 (1966), 40–64.*

Noise—Sound Without Value. *Washington: Committee on Environmental Quality, U.S. Council for Science and Technology, 1968.*

Northrop, F. S. C. "The Neurological and Behavioristic Psychological Basis of the Ordering of Society by Means of Ideas," Science, *107 (1948), 411–417.*

Odhiambo, T. R. "East Africa: Science for Development," Science, *158 (1967), 876–881.*

Odum, Howard T. Environment, Power and Society. *New York: Wiley-Interscience, 1970.*

Perloff, Harvey S., ed. The Quality of the Urban Environment: Essays on "New Resources" in an Urban Age. *Baltimore: Johns Hopkins Press for Resources for the Future, 1969.*

Petterson, Max. "Increase of Settlement Size and Population Since the Inception of Agriculture," Nature, *186 (1960), 870–872.*

Ramo, Simon. Cure for Chaos. Fresh Solutions to Social Problems Through the Systems Approach. *New York: David McKay, 1969.*

Rickover, Hyman G. "A Humanistic Technology," Nature, *208 (1965), 721–726.*

Rudofsky, Bernard. Architecture Without Architects. A Short Introduction to Non-Pedigreed Architecture. *Garden City, N. Y.: Doubleday, 1964.*

Russell, W. M. S. Man, Nature and History: Controlling the Environment. *Garden City, N. Y.: Natural History Press, 1970.*

Salzman, P. C. "Political Organization among Nomadic Peoples," Proceedings American Philosophical Society, *111 (1967), 115–131.*

Sayre, J. Woodrow. Paperbound Books in Economics, An Annotated Bibliography 1970. *Albany: New York State Council on Economic Education/Center for Economic Education, State University of New York at Albany, 1970.*

Sears, Paul B. "The Validity of Ecological Models," Proceedings 16th International Congress of Zoology, *7 (1964), 35–42.*

Sewell, W. R. Derrick, ed. "Human Dimensions of Weather Modification," University of Chicago Department of Geography Research Papers, *105 (1966).*

Spengler, Joseph J. "Population Problem: in Search of a Solution," Science, *166 (1969), 1234–1238.*

——————. *"The Economist and the Population Question,"* American Economic Review, *56 (1966), 1–24.*

Stokes, Allen W., and Lois M. Cox. "Aggressive Man and Aggressive Beast," Bio-Science, *20 (1970), 1092–1095.*

Systems Approaches to the City: A Challenge to the University. *Washington: U.S. National Academy of Engineering, 1970.*

Tinbergen, N. "On War and Peace in Animals and Man," Science, *160 (1968), 1411–1418.*

Von Bertalanffy, Ludwig. Robots, Men and Minds: Psychology in the Modern World. *New York: Braziller, 1967.*

Waddington, C. H. "Biology and Human Environment," Ekistics, *21 (February, 1966), 90–94.*

Washburn, S. L., and D. A. Hamburg. "Aggressive Behavior in Old World Monkeys and Apes," pp. 458–478 in Primates: Studies in Adaptation and Variability, *ed. P. C. Jay.* New York: Holt, Rinehart & Winston, 1968.

Watt, Kenneth E. F., et al. A Model of Society. *Davis: Environmental Systems Group, Institute of Ecology, University of California at Davis, 1969.*

Weyl, Nathaniel. "Some Possible Genetic Implications of Carthaginian Child Sacrifice," Perspectives in Biology and Medicine, *12 (1968), 69–78.*

Winkelstein, W., et al., *"The Relationship of Air Pollution and Economic Status to Total Mortality and Selected Respiratory System Mortality in Man,"* Archives of Environmental Health, *14 (January, 1967), 162-171.*

Zimbardo, Philip G. "The Human Choice: Individuation, Reason, and Order Versus Deindividuation, Impulse, and Chaos," pp. 237-307 in Nebraska Symposium on Motivation. *Lincoln: University of Nebraska Press, 1970.*

Part Three. Positions

The nature of the readings listed here is obvious. They draw attention to the walls against which we have repeatedly been butting our heads in recent years. In nearly all there is a leavening of hope, suggestions of things that might be done to alleviate the impact of pollution and of actions and attitudes which might help us avoid a collision course or even lead to a resolution of conflict.

Altschul, Aaron M. "Food Proteins: New Sources from Seeds," Science, *158 (1967), 221-226.*

Bates, Marston. The Forest and the Sea. *New York: New American Library, 1961. Paper.*

Boulding, Kenneth. "The Economics of the Coming Spaceship Earth," pp. 3-14 in Environmental Quality in a Growing Economy, *ed. Henry Jarrett. Baltimore: Johns Hopkins Press, 1966.*

Commoner, Barry. Science and Survival. *New York: Viking, 1966. Paper.*

Commoner, Barry, et al. *"The Integrity of Science,"* American Scientist, *53 (1965), 174-198.*

Darling, F. Fraser. Wilderness and Plenty. *Boston: Houghton Mifflin, 1970.*

Darling, F. Fraser, and John P. Milton, eds. Future Environments of North America. *New York: Natural History Press, 1966.*

Dasmann, Raymond F. Environmental Conservation, *2nd ed. New York: Wiley, 1968.*

DeBell, Garrett, ed. The Environmental Handbook. *New York: Simon & Schuster, 1970. Paper.*

Douglas, William O. A Wilderness Bill of Rights. *Boston: Little, Brown, 1965.*

Dubos, René. Man, Medicine, and Environment. *New York: Praeger, 1968.*

Ehrenfeld, David W. Biological Conservation. *New York: Holt, Rinehart & Winston, 1970. Paper.*

Ferkiss, Victor C. Technological Man: The Myth and the Reality. *New York: George Braziller, 1969.*

Fuller, Buckminster. Utopia or Oblivion. *New York: Bantam Books, 1969. Paper.*

Fuller, Buckminster, and John McHale. World Design Science Decade, *6 vols. Carbondale, Ill.: World Resources Inventory Office, 1963-1967.*

Hardin, Garrett. "Not Peace, But Ecology," pp. 151-161 in Diversity and Stability in Ecological Systems, *ed. G. M. Woodwell and H. H. Smith. (Brookhaven Symposia in Biology no. 22.) Upton, N.Y.: Brookhaven National Laboratory, 1969.*

——————. *"Semantic Aspects of Abortion,"* ETC.; A Review of General Semantics, *24 (1967), 263–281.*

——————. *"The History and Future of Birth Control,"* Perspectives in Biology and Medicine, *10 (1966), 1–18.*

Hay, John. In Defense of Nature. *Boston: Little, Brown, 1969.*

Holling, Crawford S. "Stability in Ecological and Social Systems," pp. 128–141 in Diversity and Stability in Ecological Systems, *ed. G. M. Woodwell and H. H. Smith. (Brookhaven Symposia in Biology no. 22.) Upton, N. Y.: Brookhaven National Laboratory, 1969.*

Huxley, Aldous. The Politics of Ecology: The Question of Survival. *(Occasional Paper on the Free Society.) Santa Barbara: Center for the Study of Democratic Institutions, 1963.*

Joffe, Joyce. Conservation: Maintaining the Natural Balance. *Garden City, N. Y.: Natural Science Press, 1970.*

Joranson, Philip N. "A Focus in the Humanities for Resource Management Education," Environmental Education, *2 (Autumn, 1970), 20–23.*

Kuenen, D. J. "Man, Food and Insects as an Ecological Problem," Proceedings 16th International Congress of Zoology, *16, 7 (1964), 5–13.*

Kuhns, William. Environmental Man. *New York: Harper and Row, 1969.*

Leopold, Aldo. A Sand County Almanac. *New York: Oxford University Press, 1966 and 1968. Paper.*

Lotspeich, Frederick B. "Water Pollution in Alaska: Present and Future," Science, *166 (1969), 1239–1245.*

McHale, John. The Future of the Future. *New York: George Braziller, 1969.*

McHarg, Ian L. Design with Nature. *Garden City, N. Y.: Natural History Press, 1969.*

MacKaye, Benton. From Geography to Geotechnics. *Urbana: University of Illinois Press, 1969.*

McKinley, Daniel. "Human Ecology: Some Thoughts on Brash Pioneering in an Orderly World," Atlantic Naturalist, *19 (1964), 165–174.*

Macinko, George. "Saturation: A Problem Evaded in Planning Land Use," Science, *149 (1965), 516–521.*

Mayer, Jean. "Toward a Non-Malthusian Population Policy," Columbia Forum, *12 (Summer, 1969), 5–13.*

——————. *"Starvation as a Weapon: Herbicides in Vietnam, I,"* Scientist and Citizen, *9 (1967), 115–121.*

Means, Richard L. "The New Conservation," Natural History, *78 (August-September, 1969), 16–25.*

Moore, John A., compiler. Science for Society: A Bibliography. *Washington: Commission on Science Education, American Association for the Advancement of Science, 1970.*

Nicholson, Max. The Environmental Revolution. *New York: McGraw-Hill, 1970.*

Odum, Howard T., and W. C. Allee. "A Note on the Stable Point of Populations Showing Both Intraspecific Cooperation and Disoperation," Ecology, 35 (1954), 95–97.

Piper, Arthur M. Disposal of Liquid Wastes by Injection Underground—Neither Myth nor Millennium. (Circular no. 631.) Washington: U.S. Geological Survey, 1969.

Platt, John R. "What We Must Do," Science, 166 (1969), 1115–1121.
————————. The Step to Man. New York: John Wiley & Sons, 1966.

Price, Don K. "Purists and Politicians," Science, 163 (1969), 25–31.

Price, Edward T. "Values and Concepts in Conservation," Annals of the Association of American Geographers, 45 (1955), 64–84.

Sartorius, I. P., and H. Henle. Forestry and Economic Development. New York: Frederick A. Praeger, 1968.

Shepard, Paul. "Whatever Happened to Human Ecology?" BioScience, 17 (1967), 891–894, 911.
————————. "The Wilderness as Nature," Atlantic Naturalist, 20 (1965), 9–14.

Stefferud, Alfred, ed. Christians and the Good Earth. (F/M/N Papers No. 1.) Alexandria, Va.: Faith-Man-Nature Group, 1969.

Tuan, Yi-Fu. The Hydrologic Cycle and the Wisdom of God: A Theme in Geoteleology. Toronto: University of Toronto Press, 1968.

Van Dyne, George M., ed. The Ecosystem Concept in Natural Resource Management. New York: Academic Press, 1969.

Wagar, J. Alan. "Growth Versus the Quality of Life," Science, 168 (1970), 1179–1184.

Wallace, A. F. C., "On Being Just Complicated Enough," Proceedings of the National Academy of Sciences, 47 (1961), 456–464.

Watt, Kenneth E. F. Ecology and Resource Management: A Quantitative Approach. New York: McGraw-Hill, 1968.

Webber, Harold H. "Mariculture," BioScience, 18 (1968), 940–945.

Wheeler, William Morton. Essays in Philosophical Biology. Cambridge, Mass.: Harvard University Press, 1939.

White, Lynn, Jr. Machina ex Deo: Essays in the Dynamics of Western Culture. Cambridge, Mass.: M.I.T. Press, 1969.

Whittaker, Robert H. "Evolution of Diversity in Plant Communities," pp. 178–196 in Diversity and Stability in Ecological Systems, ed. G. M. Woodwell and H. H. Smith. (Brookhaven Symposia in Biology no. 22.) Upton, N. Y.: Brookhaven National Laboratory, 1969.

Whittlesey, Derwent. "The Horizon of Geography," Annals of the Association of American Geographers, 35 (1945), 1–36.

Whyte, William H. The Last Landscape. Garden City, N. Y.: Doubleday, 1968.

Wright, F. F. "Rape of Alaska Can Be Rational," Science, 166 (1969), 1220–1222.

Part Four. The Crunch

It might be argued that one of the things we need most is a global view: it is not enough to suppose that we have merely applied the wrong techniques to the solution of our problems. It may be that we need to look more closely at the nature of man and the immensity of the task. Any answers we propose surely must take the realities of both man and nonhuman nature into account.

It has proved impossible to segregate diagnoses of what is wrong and prescriptions for what to do about it. In a sense, this whole book has been devoted to orchestrating these two themes. But some things are more deeply wrong than others, and certain prescriptions for survival ring more convincingly than others. A fair sampling of works in these areas is listed below.

Air Conservation. *(Publication no. 80.) Washington: American Association for the Advancement of Science, 1965.*

Bardach, John E. Harvest of the Sea. *New York: Harper and Row, 1968.*

Barrons, Keith C. *"Some Ecological Benefits of Woody Plant Control with Herbicides,"* Science, *165 (1969), 465–468.*

Berelson, Bernard. *"Beyond Family Planning,"* Science, *163 (1969), 533–543.*

Boffey, Philip M. *"Japan: a Crowded Nation Wants to Boost Its Birthrate,"* Science, *167 (1970), 960–962.*

——————. *"Radioactive Pollution: Minnesota Finds AEC Standards Too Lax,"* Science, *163 (1969), 1043–1046.*

——————. *"Smog: Los Angeles, Running Hard, Standing Still,"* Science, *161 (1968), 990–992.*

Borgstrom, Georg. The Dual Challenge of Health and Hunger—a Global Crisis. *(Selection no. 31.) Washington: Population Reference Bureau, 1970.*

——————. Too Many: A Study of Earth's Biological Limitations. *New York: Macmillan, 1969.*

Brady, N. C., ed. Agriculture and the Quality of Our Environment. *(Publication no. 85.) Washington: American Association for the Advancement of Science, 1967.*

Broecker, Wallace S. *"Man's Oxygen Reserves,"* Science, *168 (1970), 1537–1538.*

Brown, Lester R. *"A New Era in World Agriculture."* First Annual Senator Frank Carlson Symposium on World Population and Food Supply, December 3, 1968.

——————. *"The Agricultural Revolution in Asia,"* Foreign Affairs, *(July, 1968), 688–698.*

——————. *"The World Outlook for Conventional Agriculture,"* Science, *158 (1967), 604–611.*

Bryson, Reid A., and David A. Baerreis. *"Possibilities of Major Climatic Modification and Their Implications: Northwest India, a Case for Study,"* Bulletin American Meteorological Society, *48 (1967), 136–142.*

Burns, William. Noise and Man. *Philadelphia: Lippincott, 1969.*

Carefoot, G. L., and E. R. Sprott. Famine on the Wind. *Chicago: Rand McNally, 1967.*

Carson, Rachel. Silent Spring. *Boston: Houghton Mifflin, 1962.*

Carter, Luther J. *"Conservation Law, II: Scientists Play a Key Role in Court Suits,"* Science, *166 (1969), 1601–1606.*

—————— . *"DDT: The Critics Attempt to Ban Its Use in Wisconsin,"* Science, *163 (1969), 548–551.*

Chemical and Bacteriological (Biological) Weapons and the Effects of Their Possible Use. *(A United Nations Report.) New York: Simon & Schuster, 1970.*

Clark, J. R. *"Thermal Pollution and Aquatic Life,"* Scientific American, *220 (March, 1969), 18–27.*

Clawson, Marion, H. H. Landsberg, and L. T. Alexander. *"Desalted Seawater for Agriculture: Is It Economic?"* Science, *164 (1970), 1141–1148.*

Cole, LaMont C. *"Man's Effect on Nature,"* The Explorer, *11 (Fall, 1969), 10–16.*

Cowan, Ian McTaggart. *"Ecology and Northern Development,"* Arctic, *22 (1969), 3–12.*

Committee on Solid Waste Management, National Research Council. Policies for Solid Waste Management. *(Publication 2018.) Washington: U.S. Public Health Service, 1970.*

Commoner, Barry. *"Nature Unbalanced: How Man Interferes With the Nitrogen Cycle,"* Scientist and Citizen, *10 (Jan.–Feb., 1968), 9–12, 14–19.*

—————— . *"Threats to the Integrity of the Nitrogen Cycle: Nitrogen Compounds in Soil, Water, Atmosphere and Precipitation." Global Effects of Environmental Pollution Symposium, American Association for the Advancement of Science, 1968 (for future publication).*

Conway, William G. *"The Consumption of Wildlife by Man,"* Animal Kingdom, *73 (June, 1968), 18–23.*

Currie, Lauchlin. *"Economics and Population,"* Population Bulletin, *23, 2 (1967), 25–38.*

Curtis, Richard, and Elizabeth Hogan. Perils of the Peaceful Atom. *Garden City, N. Y.: Natural History Press, 1969. Ballantine paperback, 1970.*

Daniels, Farrington. Direct Use of the Sun's Energy. *New Haven: Yale University Press, 1964.*

Dasmann, Raymond F. The Destruction of California. *New York: Macmillan, 1965.*

Davis, Kingsley. *"Colin Clark and the Benefits of an Increase in Population,"* Scientific American, *218 (April, 1968), 133–138.*

Djerassi, Carl. *"Prognosis for the Development of New Chemical Birth-Control Agents,"* Science, *166 (1969), 468–473.*

Edberg, Rolf. On the Shred of a Cloud. *University, Ala.: University of Alabama Press, 1969.*

Edmisten, Joe A. *"Hard and Soft Detergents, Their Effect on Aquatic Life,"* Scientist and Citizen, *8 (1966), 4–12.*

Ehrlich, Paul. *"Eco-Catastrophe!"* Ramparts, *7 (September, 1969).*

Eipper, Alfred W. *"Pollution Problems, Resource Policy, and the Scientist,"* Science, *169 (1970), 11–15.*

Egler, Frank E. *"Pesticides in Our Ecosystem,"* Ecology, *47 (1966), 1077–1084.*

Elton, Charles S. The Ecology of Invasions by Animals and Plants. *London: Methuen, 1958.*

Enke, Stephen, and R. A. Zind. *"Effect of Fewer Births on Average Income,"* Journal of Biosocial Science, *1 (1969), 41–55.*

Enke, Stephen. *"Birth Control for Economic Development,"* Science, *164 (1969), 798–802.*

Etter, Alfred G. *"Why Nothing Gets Done about Pesticides, a Case History,"* Atlantic Naturalist, *19 (1964), 28–36.*

——————. *"Mathematics, Ecology and a Piece of Land,"* Landscape, *12 (Spring, 1963), 28–31.*

——————. *"Dying in the Smog,"* The Land, *9 (Summer, 1950), 185–191.*

Ewald, William R., Jr. Environment and Change. The Next Fifty Years. *Bloomington: Indiana University Press, 1968. Paper.*

Fenlon, Mark V., et al., Thermal Discharge Bibliography. (Publication no. 61.) *Albany: Atmospheric Sciences Research Center, State University of New York at Albany, 1968, pp. 53–68.*

Fisher, James, Noel Simon, and Jack Vincent. Wildlife in Danger. *New York: Viking, 1969.*

Galston, A. W. *"Changing the Environment: Herbicides in Vietnam, II."* Scientist and Citizen, *9 (1967), 122–129. See also letter to the editor of* Science, *164 (1969), 373.*

Glaser, Peter E. *"Power From the Sun: Its Future,"* Science, *162 (1968), 857–861.*

Graham, Frank, Jr. Since Silent Spring. *Boston: Houghton Mifflin, 1970.*

Gruchow, Nancy. *"Detergents: Side Effects of the Washday Miracles,"* Science, *167 (1970), 151.*

Hardin, Garrett. *"Finding Lemonade in Santa Barbara's Oil,"* Saturday Review, *(May 10, 1969), 18–21.*

——————. *"Pop Research & the Seismic Market,"* Per/Se, *(Fall, 1967), 19–24.*

——————. *"The Semantics of Space,"* ETC., A Review of General Semantics, *23 (1966), 167–171.*

Hendricks, Sterling B. *"Food From the Land,"* pp. 65–85 in Resources and Man, *National Academy of Sciences—National Research Council. San Francisco: W. H. Freeman, 1969.*

Hibbard, Walter R., Jr. *"Mineral Resources: Challenge or Threat?"* Science, *160 (1968), 143–149.*

Hickey, R. J., et al. *"Relationship Between Air Pollution and Certain Chronic Disease Death Rates,"* Archives of Environmental Health, *15 (December, 1967), 728–738.*

Holcomb, Robert W. *"Insect Control: Alternatives to the Use of Conventional Pesticides,"* Science, *168 (1970), 456–458.*

——————. *"Power Generation: The Next 30 Years,"* Science, *167 (1970), 159–160.*

Howard, Walter E. *"The Population Crisis Is Here Now,"* BioScience, *19 (1969), 779–784.*

Hubbert, M. King. "Energy Resources," pp. 157–242 in Resources and Man. *San Francisco: W. H. Freeman, 1969.*

Jamison, Andrew. The Steam-Powered Automobile: An Answer to Air Pollution. *Bloomington: Indiana University Press, 1970.*

Johnson, Huey D., ed. No Deposit—No Return; Man and His Environment: A View Toward Survival. *Reading, Mass.: Addison-Wesley, 1970. Paper.*

Kesteven, G. L. "A Policy for Conservationists," Science, 160 (1968), 857–860.

Ketchel, Melvin M. "Fertility Control Agents as a Possible Solution to the World Population Problem," Perspectives in Biology and Medicine, 11 (1968), 687–703.

Keyfitz, Nathan. "United States and World Populations," pp. 43–64 in Resources and Man, National Academy of Sciences-National Research Council. San Francisco: W. H. Freeman, 1969.

Kline, J. R., and C. F. Jordan. "Tritium Movement in Soil of Tropical Rain Forest," Science, 160 (1968), 550–551.

Kraybill, Herman F., ed. "Biological Effects of Pesticides in Mammalian Systems," Annals of the New York Academy of Sciences, 160 (1969), 1–422.

Lauwerys, J. A. Man's Impact on Nature: Technology and Living Things. *Garden City, N. Y.: Natural History Press, 1970.*

McCaull, Julian. "The Black Tide," Environment, 11 (November, 1969), 2–16.

MacInnis, Joseph B., and Jon M. Lindbergh. "Underwater Man: His Evolution and Explorations," Smithsonian Institution, Edwin A. Link Lecture Series, 1969.

McKinley, Daniel. "Thoughts on the Survival Game," Snowy Egret, 32 (Spring, 1969), 11–22.

——————. "Oil Barrels and Muk-Tuk: An Arctic Year," The Yale Review, 52 (1962), 72–89.

Maxwell, Kenneth E., ed. Chemicals and Life. *Belmont, Calif.: Dickenson, 1970. Paper.*

Middleton, John T., "The Air We Breathe," Population Bulletin, 24 (1968), 114–123.

Miller, Morton W., and George G. Berg, eds. Chemical Fallout. *Springfield, Ill.: Charles C. Thomas, 1969.*

Moore, N. W. "A Synopsis of the Pesticide Problem," Advances in Ecological Research, 4 (1967), 75–129.

Morgan, George B., G. Ozolins, and E. C. Tabor. "Air Pollution Surveillance Systems," Science, 170 (1970), 289–296.

Mueller, Marti. "DDT: Criticism, Curbs Are on the Upswing," Science, 164 (1969), 936–937.

National Academy of Sciences-National Research Council. Resources and Man. *San Francisco: W. H. Freeman, 1969.*

The Nation's Water Resources. The First National Assessment of the Water Resources Council. *Washington: Water Resources Council, 1968.*

Niering, William A. "The Effects of Pesticides," BioScience, 18 (1968), 869–875.

Novick, Sheldon. *"Earthquake at Giza,"* Environment, *12 (January–February, 1970), 2–13.*

——————. *"A Mile from Times Square,"* Environment, *11,1 (1969), 10–15, 39.*

——————. The Careless Atom. *Boston: Houghton Mifflin, 1968.*

——————. *"'Breeding' Nuclear Power,"* Scientist and Citizen, *9 (June–July, 1967), 97–105, 113.*

"On the Use of Herbicides in Vietnam," Science, *161 (1968), 253–256.*

Parker, Frank L. *"Radioactive Wastes from Fusion Reactors,"* Science, *159 (1968), 83–84; also, 159 (1968), 1376.*

Peterson, Eugene K. *"Carbon Dioxide Affects Global Ecology,"* Environmental Science and Engineering, *3 (1969), 1162–1169.*

Peterson, Malcolm. *"Krypton 85, Nuclear Air Pollutant,"* Scientist and Citizen, *9, 3 (1967), 54–55.*

Piper, A. M. *"Has the United States Enough Water?"* (Water–Supply Papers no. *1797.) Washington: U.S. Geological Survey, 1966.*

"Poisoning the Wells," Environment, *11 (January, 1969), 16–23.*

Powers, Charles F., and A. Robertson. *"The Aging Great Lakes,"* Scientific American, *215 (November, 1966), 95–104.*

Quinn, Frank. *"Water Transfers: Must the American West Be Won Again?"* Geographical Review, *58 (1968), 108–132.*

Rantz, S. E. *"Urban Sprawl and Flooding in Southern California,"* U. S. Geological Survey Circular 601-B (1970), 1–11.*

Regier, Henry A. *"Ecological Aspects of Overcoming World Hunger,"* Canadian Audubon, *32 (January, 1970), 12–16.*

Report of the Secretary's Commission on Pesticides and Their Relationship to Environmental Health, *Parts I and II. Washington: U.S. Department of Health, Education and Welfare, 1969.*

Ricker, William E. *"Food from the Sea,"* pp. 87–108 in Resources and Man, *National Academy of Sciences-National Research Council. San Francisco: W. H. Freeman, 1969.*

Risebrough, Robert, and Virginia Brodine. *"More Letters in the Wind"* (on polychlorinated biphenyls, or PCBs), Environment, *12 (January–February, 1970), 16–27.*

Rudd, Robert L. Pesticides and the Living Landscape. *Madison: University of Wisconsin Press, 1964.*

Sargent, Frederick, II. *"Taming the Weather, a Dangerous Game,"* Scientist and Citizen, *9 (May, 1967), 81–88, 96.*

Schweighauser, Charles A. *"The Garbage Explosion,"* The Nation, *(September 22, 1969), 282–284.*

——————. Solid Waste Practices in Berkshire County. *Williamstown, Mass.: Center for Environmental Studies, Williams College, 1969.*

Shurcliff, William A. S/S/T and Sonic Boom Handbook. *New York: Ballantine Books, 1970. Paper.*

Snow, Joel A. *"Radioactive Waste from Reactors,"* Scientist and Citizen, *9 (May, 1967), 89–96.*

Snow, Joel A. "Radioactivity From 'Clean' Nuclear Power," Scientist and Citizen, *10 (May, 1968), 97–101.*

Stewart, Ronald, and H. H. Howard. Water Pollution by Outboard Motors. *(Publication no. 61.) Albany: Atmospheric Sciences Research Center, State University of New York at Albany, 1968, pp. 49–52.*

Stickel, Lucille F. Organochlorine Pesticides in the Environment. *(Special Scientific Report—Wildlife no. 119.) Washington: U.S. Fish & Wildlife Service, Bureau of Sport Fisheries and Wildlife, 1968.*

Stockholm International Peace Research Institute. SIPI Yearbook of World Armaments and Disarmament 1968/69. *New York: Humanities Press, 1969.*

Storer, John H. The Web of Life. *New York: New American Library, 1956. Paper.*

Swain, Harry. "The Great Stinking Sea" (a review of Pollution, Property & Prices *by J. H. Dales, University of Toronto Press, 1968),* The Canadian Forum, *(December, 1968), 197–199.*

Swenson, H. A., and H. L. Baldwin. A Primer on Water Quality. *Washington: U.S. Geological Survey, 1965, 1969.*

Teal, John, and Mildred Teal. Life and Death of the Salt Marsh. *Boston: Little, Brown, 1969.*

Tribus, Myron. "Physical View of Cloud Seeding," Science, *168 (1970), 201–211.*

van den Bosch, Robert. "Pesticides: Prescribing for the Ecosystem," Environment, *12 (April, 1970), 20–25.*

Walsh, John. "Environment: Focus on DDT, the 'Uninvited Additive,'" Science, *166 (1969), 975–977.*

Watt, Kenneth E. F., ed. Systems Analysis in Ecology. *New York: Academic Press, 1966.*

Weather and Climate Modification: Problems and Prospects. Final Report of the Panel on Weather and Climate Modification to the Committee on Atmospheric Sciences, *2 vols. (Publication no. 1350.) Washington: National Academy of Sciences—National Research Council, 1966.*

Weisberg, Barry. "The Ecology of Oil; Raping Alaska," Ramparts, *8 (January, 1970), 25–33.*

Whiteside, Thomas. Defoliation: What Are Our Herbicides Doing to Us? *New York: Ballantine, 1970. Paper.*

Wiley, John P., Jr. "Space: a Barrier to the Species," Natural History, *79 (January, 1970), 70–73.*

Wilson, Billy Ray, ed. Environmental Problems: Pesticides, Thermal Pollution and Environmental Synergisms. *Philadelphia: Lippincott, 1968.*

Woodwell, Beorge M. "Effects of Pollution on the Structure and Physiology of Ecosystems," Science, *168 (1970), 429–433.*

——————. *"Science and the Gross National Pollution,"* Ramparts, *(May, 1970), 51–54.*

——————. *"Toxic Substances and Ecological Cycles,"* Scientific American, *216 (March, 1967), 24–31.*

Wurster, Charles F., Jr. "DDT Reduces Photosynthesis by Marine Phytoplankton," Science, *159 (1968), 1474–1475.*

Wurster, Charles. "Chlorinated Hydrocarbon Insecticides and the World Ecosystem," Biological Conservation, *1 (1969), 123–129.*

——————— . *"DDT Goes to Trial in Madison,"* BioScience, *19 (1969), 809–813.*

——————— . *DDT in Human Milk. Berkeley: Ecology Center, 1969.*

Young, Gale. "Dry Lands and Desalted Water," Science, *167 (1970), 339–344.*

Zelinsky, Wilbur. "Beyond the Exponentials; the Role of Geography in the Great Transition," Economic Geography, *46 (1970), 498–535.*

DATE DUE

OCT 3 0 1974			
GAYLORD			PRINTED IN U.S.A.

esters, *1906*
hia Museum of
ollection.
vatt, staff

Office of